Sex and the Family i

In the early years of the British empire, cohabitation between Indian women and British men was commonplace and to some degree tolerated. However, as Durba Ghosh argues in a challenge to the existing historiography, anxieties about social status, appropriate sexuality, and the question of who could be counted as "British" or "Indian" were constant concerns of the colonial government even at this time. By following the stories of a number of mixed-race families, at all levels of the social scale, from high-ranking officials and noblewomen to rank-and-file soldiers and camp followers, and also the activities of indigenous female concubines, mistresses, and wives, the author offers a fascinating account of how gender, class, and race affected the cultural, social, and even political mores of the period. The book makes an original and signal contribution to scholarship on colonialism, gender, and sexuality.

DURBA GHOSH is Assistant Professor in History at Cornell University. She has co-edited, with Dane Kennedy, *Decentering Empire: Britain, India and the Transcolonial World* (2006).

Cambridge Studies in Indian History and Society 13

Cambridge Studies in Indian History and Society publishes monographs on the history and anthropology of modern India. In addition to its primary scholarly focus, the series also includes work of an interdisciplinary nature which contributes to contemporary social and cultural debates about Indian history and society. In this way, the series furthers the general development of historical and anthropological knowledge to attract a wider readership than that concerned with India alone.

A list of titles which have been published in the series can be found at the end of the book.

Sex and the Family in Colonial India

The Making of Empire

Durba Ghosh

Cornell University

CAMBRIDGE
UNIVERSITY PRESS

CAMBRIDGE UNIVERSITY PRESS
Cambridge, New York, Melbourne, Madrid, Cape Town, Singapore, São Paulo

Cambridge University Press
The Edinburgh Building, Cambridge CB2 8RU, UK

Published in the United States of America by Cambridge University Press, New York

www.cambridge.org
Information on this title: www.cambridge.org/9780521857048

First published 2006
This digitally printed version 2008

A catalogue record for this publication is available from the British Library

Library of Congress Cataloguing in Publication data

Ghosh, Durba, 1967–
    Sex and the family in colonial India: the making of empire / Durba Ghosh.
        p. cm. – (Cambridge studies in Indian history and society ; 13)
    Includes bibliographical references and index.
    ISBN-13   978-0-521-85704-8 (hardcover)
    ISBN-10   0-521-85704-X (hardcover)
    1.   Interracial marriage–India–History–18th century. 2.   Interracial
marriage–India–History–19th century. 3.
Concubinage–India–History–18th century. 4.
Concubinage–India–History–19th century. 5.
Family–India–History–18th century. 6.   Family–India–History–19th
century. 7.   India–Race relations–History–18th century. 8.
India–Race relations–History–19th century. I. Title. II. Series.

    HQ669.G48 2006
    306.850954′09033–dc22   2006025599

ISBN 978-0-521-85704-8 hardback
ISBN 978-0-521-67379-2 paperback

Contents

Paintings credits

1.1: Auriol and Dashwood families, 1733–1787 (oil on canvas), family conversation piece with two families drinking tea, Johann Zoffany (1783–1810), by permission of R. H. Dashwood, Esq.

1.2: Sir Elijah and Lady Impey and Their Three Children, 1783–1784 (oil on canvas), Johann Zoffany (1733–1810), Private Collection, © Christie's Images; Bridgeman Art Library.

1.3: Dancing-girl, Faizabad 1772 (oil on canvas), Tilly Kettle (1735–1786), Yale Center for British Art, Paul Mellon Collection.

1.4: Portrait of a Mogul Lady, 1787 (oil on canvas), Francesco Renaldi (1756–c.1799), Private Collection, © Christie's Images; Bridgeman Art Library.

1.5: Muslim Lady reclining, smoking a hookah, 1789 (oil on canvas), Francesco Renaldi (1756–c.1799), Yale Center for British Art, Paul Mellon Collection.

2.1: Colonel Mordaunt's Cock Match, c. 1784–1786 (oil on canvas), Johann Zoffany (1733–1810); Tate Gallery, London/Art Resource, NY.

2.2: The Palmer Family, 1786 (oil on canvas), Johann Zoffany (1733–1810), Oriental and India Office Collection, British Library.

6.1: Lord Clive receiving from Najm-ud-daula, nawab of Murshidabad, a legacy for the East India Company's Military Fund, London 1772 (oil on canvas), by Edward Penny, Oriental and India Office Collection, British Library.

Acknowledgments

Writing a book can be a solitary affair, and I am pleased to say that writing this has been anything but. It has been a pleasure and a privilege to have the support and friendship of the following friends and colleagues.

At Berkeley, I benefited enormously from the firm and opinionated guidance of Tom Metcalf whose imprint is felt throughout this book. Members of the larger community of historians and South Asianists, including Gene Irschick, Raka Ray, Barbara Metcalf, and Tabitha Kanogo have nurtured me in various ways, provoking difficult questions at important junctures of this project. Participants of the Empire Studies group provided social and intellectual companionship that has sustained me over the years. Friends and colleagues in the Five College area, particularly those at Amherst and Mount Holyoke colleges have been involved in ongoing conversations: Siraj Ahmed, Lisa Armstrong, Allan Babb, Amrita Basu, Vivek Bhandari, Brodwyn Fischer, Holly Hanson, Margaret Hunt, Nasser Hussain, Amy Martin, Lynda Morgan. Special thanks to Amrita Basu and Margaret Hunt, whose interventions have proved critical. Colleagues at Wellesley College, among them Margery Sabin, Rosanna Hertz, Geeta Patel, Elena Creef, Susan Reverby, Anjali Prabhu, Alejandra Osorio, Lidwien Kapteijns, and Sally Merry, made it an especially productive and enriching place to write, learn, and teach. Further afield, the support of Antoinette Burton has been indispensable, as has the ongoing encouragement of Susan Pedersen, Mrinalini Sinha, Philippa Levine, and Kathleen Wilson.

Colleagues who read parts or all of the manuscript and offered suggestions that expanded and improved the arguments herein: Swapna Banerjee, Indrani Chatterjee, and Rochona Majumdar. Special thanks to Michael Fisher and Peter Marshall who read early drafts and suggested many much-needed improvements and corrections. Clare Anderson, Natasha Eaton, Manu Goswami, Maya Jasanoff, Vijay Pinch, Anupama Rao, and Sudipta Sen were extremely generous and forthcoming with advice and critical insights. Needless to say, any flaws or oversights are entirely my own.

Friends at Berkeley, among them, Carina Johnson, Anne Keary, Rachel Sturman, Andrea Zemgulys, David Engerman, Ethan Pollock, and Doug Shoemaker have watched this project develop from its inception and have offered support as only lifelong friends can. My intellectual debts to my "knitting circle," Michelle Tusan and Deb Cohler, are larger than I can ever repay. Thanks to them, this is a readable work (I hope).

Several of the chapters are revised versions of the following articles: parts of the Introduction and Chapter 4 appeared in "Decoding the Nameless: Gender, Subjectivity, and Historical Methodologies in Reading the Archives of Colonial India," in *A New Imperial History: Culture, Identity, Modernity, 1600–1840*, edited by Kathleen Wilson (Cambridge: Cambridge University Press, 2004); chapter 5 is a revised version of "Household Crimes and Domestic Order: Keeping the Peace in Colonial Calcutta, c.1770–c.1840," *Modern Asian Studies* 38, 3 (July 2004): 598–624; and chapter 6 appeared in an earlier form as "Making and Un-making Loyal Subjects: Pensioning Widows and Educating Orphans in Early Colonial India," *Journal of Imperial and Commonwealth History* 31 (January 2003): 1–28. Grateful acknowledgment is made to publishers for allowing me to build on this earlier work.

Many institutions and libraries in India and in Britain have made this project possible: a junior research grant from the American Institute of Indian Studies, a summer grant from the Mellon foundation, and a grant from the history department at Berkeley enabled the research, while a grant from the American Association of University Women and a Five College Fellowship at Amherst College enabled the writing. Faculty research grants from Wellesley College, Mount Holyoke College, and Cornell University provided financial support in making this into a book. I have benefited from the generous assistance of librarians and archivists at the Oriental and India Office Collections in London, National Archives in New Delhi, National Library, West Bengal State Archives, the libraries at the High Court and at the Asiatic Society in Kolkata, the Uttarpara Library, and the Baptists missionary library in Serampore.

It also takes a large extended family to make such a book possible: in Calcutta, in New Delhi, and in London, I have cherished the generosity and hospitality of too many to name here. Particular thanks to Maya Tarafdar, Ganga and Sudamoy Mitra, Arup, Joya, Rue and Rupan Roy, Atreyee Dakshy, Ana Knight, Atanu, Tamal, Alakananda, and Anamika Ghosh.

It takes a small village to support an academic life and I am pleased to acknowledge the women that make such a life possible: Mabel Lee, Jane Stahlhut, Rhea Cabin, Margaret Centamore, Holly Sharac, Judy Burkhard, Barb Donnell, Maggie Edwards, and Katie Kristof.

Finally, it has been my good fortune to land in a lovely family. There is no adequate way to thank my parents and sister, without whom this book would not have emerged as it did. My sister's support has been generous and unconditional. My sister-in-law, Olivia, has provided us with a lovely home away from home during our London summers. In a book about family and intimacy, I would be remiss if I did not end by acknowledging the miracle of my new family, who have been a constant joy. The book is dedicated to them, Robert, Ravi, and Lila.

Introduction

The image of a European man and a native woman living in familial harmony has long been an enduring vision of colonial societies. In early colonial British India, creolization, conjugality, and cooperation between men and women of different cultural backgrounds created the image of a golden age in which racial hierarchies and boundaries were unimportant. By many accounts, the ideal eighteenth-century East India Company man was one who learned local languages, participated in native customs, such as hooka-smoking, and lived intimately and had a family with a local woman. A collaborative Raj was phased out by a coercive Raj, and native female companions were replaced by the influx of white women from Europe. By 1857, when Indian soldiers rose up against their British masters and gave Britons cause to establish more rigid racial hierarchies, an age of many kinds of partnership between Britons and those they ruled on the Indian subcontinent came to an abrupt end.

Sex and the Family in Colonial India goes beyond this conventional narrative about the progressive racializing of British colonialism on the Indian subcontinent to closely examine the familial dynamics of interracial sexual contact for native women and European men who participated in these relationships. Comprised of European fathers, indigenous mothers, and their mixed-race children, such colonial families formed a constitutive part of Anglo-Indian colonial society in its formative years, endangering the whiteness of British rule, and potentially undermining its political authority. Multi-ethnic and interracial, these families were crucial grounds on which racial and gender hierarchies were built and consolidated, giving rise to the hierarchies of colonial settlements. The growing social and sexual distance between Britons and Indians has often been explained as part of a growing empire's demand to become morally conscious, recognizing the demands put on colonizing groups to uphold their racial, national, and religious superiority. This book argues that the process of "making empire respectable," was never a straightforward or sequential process, but rather a process that was rife with ambivalence.[1]

This history of intimate relations between Britons and Indians was based on a complex process by which the early colonial state's interests intersected with and supported the anxieties of the members of colonial societies who feared they had become too intimate with those they ruled. At various times, European men and native women expressed unease about their social and racial status. These anxieties merged with the concerns over social propriety of early colonial settlements and their governments. By examining what sorts of social, racial, and class borders native women and European men crossed when they became involved with one another, and what kinds of racial, class, and gender hierarchies structured their experiences, this study argues that interracial sexual relationships were a crucial and constitutive part of early colonial state formation and governance in British India, laying the foundations for the colonial social order.

During these early years of British colonialism, from 1760 to 1840, the English East India Company expanded its dominions and consolidated its authority on the Indian subcontinent through military conquest and by subsidiary alliances with local leaders. By relying on local trading and banking networks for much of the eighteenth century, the British succeeded by insinuating themselves as another actor in the fragmented political situation of India. The transition from the East India Company as a commercial enterprise to a government charged with collecting revenues and managing judicial systems of the Indian subcontinent produced growing anxieties about how to regulate expansion. Interactions between British officials and local traders, merchants and informers became suspect to charges of corruption. Simultaneously, the domestic and private living arrangements of East India Company servants and their local female companions were linked with the rise of British political authority in India. Accusation of various types of corruption – moral, social and political – gave rise to disciplinary regimes that regulated the proximity between Britons and indigenous subjects.

The expansion of the Company's territorial frontiers corresponded closely with growing anxieties about social frontiers and the ways in which they ought to be managed, particularly in defining whose bodies

---

[1] Ann Stoler, "Making Empire Respectable: the politics of race and sexual morality in 20th-century colonial cultures," *American Ethnologist* 16 (1989): 634–60.

were contained within them.[2] Although conjugal relationships between European men and native women were commonplace in many colonial settlements on the Indian subcontinent, cohabiting with or marrying a native woman was often regarded as a socially and sexually transgressive act, one that gave rise to multiple types of regulation. In spite of the image that men who participated in interracial sex were socially enlightened and cosmopolitan, European men often kept these relationships secret, revealing them only in final wills and testaments. By expressing some embarrassment about their native mistresses and anxiety about the future status of their descendants, men who had "gone native" articulated the dangers of assimilation. At the level of colonial governance, institutions such as judicial courts and charitable funds, which regulated and supported the East India Company's activities, were drawn into disputes about the legal status of interracial families and the various religious, racial and national identities of the individual members of these families. In establishing whose rights might be attended to by the institutions of the East India Company state, courts and charities came to define what constituted a "family," and in a larger sense, who was a British subject and who was putatively "Indian" before a formal conception of India existed.

Distinctions about race and gender articulated from within the household and the colonial state merged with a common purpose of hierarchizing the rights and privileges of different members of the "colonial family," in its broadest sense. In India, as in other British colonies, the gender order of the family, with a father as a patriarch who was both legally and financially responsible for the females, servants, and children of the household, was an ideal that was mapped onto early colonial institutions of governance in India and the ways in which these institutions were conceived and managed.[3] Unlike other colonies, however, colonial families in British India were often not "legitimate," in the sense that the parental conjugal unit were frequently unmarried and some men kept several women in a harem-like arrangement. In the process of structuring and limiting their fiscal responsibilities, colonial fathers and officials showed the ways in which patriarchal authority

[2] Kathleen M. Brown, "The Anglo-Algonquin Gender Frontier," in Nancy Shoemaker, ed., *Negotiators of Change: Historical Perspectives on Native American Women* (New York: Routledge, 1995); Ann Stoler, *Carnal Knowledge and Imperial Power: race and the intimate in colonial rule* (Berkeley: University of California Press, 2002), ch. 4.

[3] Kathleen Brown, *Good Wives, Nasty Wenches, and Anxious Patriarchs: Gender, Race and Power in Colonial Virginia* (Chapel Hill: University of North Carolina Press, 1996); Anne McClintock, *Imperial Leather: Race, Gender and Sexuality in the Colonial Contest* (New York: Routledge, 1995), pp. 42–56.

within the family was a process that was reinforced by institutions of governance, such as courts, the military, and the church. For many men, taking responsibility for familial obligations was repaid by greater political and legal legitimacy.

In this model colonial household/state, indigenous women who were often without full names, were assumed to be voiceless, denied rights or exercising any agency. In spite of archival efforts to render them invisible, native women were represented in various ways by themselves and by others in hundreds of archival documents, such as final testaments, court records, church registers, and family papers. More important, in spite of the ways in which the state and its archives attempted to suppress the subjecthood and agency of these nameless women, many women were able to avail themselves of the limited benefits that participating in interracial conjugal relationships offered. At relatively elite levels, women inherited property, managed large households, and showed that they were literate and politically savvy. At less elite levels, women who provided sexual and domestic labor to rank-and-file soldiers and lower-ranking Europeans were drawn into negotiations with colonial institutions by seeking financial restitution for their work. Present in the various contact zones of the Anglo-Indian colonial encounter – European households, judicial courts, military cantonments, local palaces, churches, orphanages – native women were key figures of early colonial society. By enabling indigenous women to become visible, this study demonstrates how intimately involved the Company and its various employees and institutions were in the lives of these marginal subjects of early Anglo-Indian colonial settlements and the ways in which these subjects were drawn into the workings of the nascent colonial state on the Indian subcontinent.

I

From 1600, when the East India Company was first founded until about 1760, the Company was primarily a trading company chartered by the English monarch to conduct trade in India. Between 1600 and 1707, the Company worked within the ruling structures of the Mughal empire and in competition with other European trading companies, such as the Dutch VOC and the French Compagnie des Indes l'est.[4] By the end of the eighteenth century, the East India Company had become an ad hoc colonial power on the Indian subcontinent, edging out its European competitors.

[4] Om Prakash, *European Commercial Enterprise in Pre-colonial India* (Cambridge: Cambridge University Press, 1998).

Between 1707 and 1750, the Mughal empire was in continual crisis.[5] Because the authority of the Mughal empire was unstable, European trading companies began to negotiate directly with provincial service elites in Bengal, Awadh, Arcot, and Hyderabad for access to trade, merchants, and banking.[6] By the 1750s, political affairs on the Indian subcontinent responded to both global and local tensions.[7] Succession battles within the provinces drew in British and French trading company officials who sought to stabilize local political matters for the sake of profitable commerce.[8] British military and diplomatic victories in global conflicts such as the Seven Years' War (1756—1763) resulted in British-led military forces effectively eliminating the French as a possible European rival on the subcontinent.

Along with deterring the expansion of French influence in south India, in the north, successive British military victories over native rulers, such as the nawab of Bengal, the nawabs of Awadh, and the Mughal emperor, enabled the East India Company to incorporate more territories under their influence. In 1757, Robert Clive led royal troops and the Company's forces into battle against Siraj-ud-daulah at the Battle of Plassey and defeated the nawab of Bengal's forces.[9] The British accession to diwani conferred the right to collect revenues in the Bengal province and marked the beginning of British rule in Bengal.[10] Subsequently, the Bengal Presidency was established as the seat of the East India Company's administration and by 1840 extended from Calcutta beyond Delhi, the Mughal capital.

In this period of expansion, the East India Company established its government in India in piecemeal fashion. Many of its military and political activities were conducted by Englishmen who took up an

[5] Muzaffar Alam, *The Crisis of Empire in Mughal North India: Awadh and the Punjab, 1707–1748* (Delhi: Oxford University Press, 1986); Richard Barnett, *North India Between Two Empires* (Berkeley: University of California Press, 1980), chs. 1–2; Michael Fisher, *A Clash of Cultures: Awadh, the British and the Mughals* (Delhi: Manohar, 1987); Stewart Gordon, *The Marathas, 1600–1818* (Cambridge: Cambridge University Press, 1993), chs. 5–6; Andre Wink, *Land and Sovereignty in India: Agrarian Society and Politics Under the Eighteenth-century Maratha Svarajya* (Cambridge: Cambridge University Press, 1986).

[6] C. A. Bayly, *Rulers, Townsmen and Bazaars: North Indian Society in the Age of British Expansion, 1770–1870* (Cambridge: Cambridge University Press, 1983).

[7] For a broad overview of this process, see C. A. Bayly, *Imperial Meridian: the British Empire and the World, 1780–1830* (New York: Longman, 1989).

[8] See Sarojini Regani, *Nizam-British Relations, 1724–1857* (Hyderabad: Booklovers, 1963) for conflicts over local control in Hyderabad. See P. J. Marshall, *Bengal: The British Bridgehead, Eastern India 1740–1828* (Cambridge: Cambridge University Press, 1987), chs. 2–3 on succession battles in Bengal.

[9] Marshall, *Bengal*, pp. 81–90.

[10] *Ibid.*, ch. 4.

orientalized lifestyle with great appreciation and admiration for local customs and traditions; this lifestyle enabled many British officials to establish the social bonds necessary for successful diplomacy. Early British officials participated in such local customs as smoking the hookah, enjoying the nautch and living in the style of a "nabob," marked with oriental luxury and excess.[11] Some scholars have reclaimed a more positive definition of "orientalism," arguing that British officials of the period before Cornwallis were genuinely interested and respectful of local customs and traditions of scholarship, and that the late eighteenth century was marked by Anglo-Indian friendship – an amicability that later enabled the British conquest of Bengal.[12] And as other scholars have pointed out, scholarly knowledge about India often coincided with "carnal knowledge" about native women.[13]

Throughout the 1750s and 1760s, as the East India Company's dominions expanded in India, military and bureaucratic costs mounted while the Company's profits declined. Although individual members of the Company's service made huge profits from their activities in India, the Company itself was unable to effectively transfer enough revenue to Parliament to pay for its administration.[14] In spite of the accession to diwani and the promise of Bengal's revenues to fund the Company's expenses, the windfall was never realized. A famine in 1769–1770, which wiped out an estimated one-fifth of the population of Bengal, further exacerbated popular and parliamentary allegations that Company officials were mismanaging British affairs in India. By the 1770s, various factions in England clamored for a close examination into the Company's activities.[15]

A Regulating Act in 1773 attempted to reform the Company's affairs by bringing the Company's activities under the surveillance of parliament. The following year, Warren Hastings, governor of Bengal, was named governor-general of all of India and he was expected to form policy in consultation with the Supreme Council, a group of civil servants charged with protecting parliamentary and Company interests

---

[11] T. C. P. Spear, *The Nabobs: English Social Life in 18th century India* (New York: Penguin, 1963), pp. 135–6.

[12] Thomas Trautmann, *Aryans and British India* (Berkeley: University of California Press, 1997).

[13] Rosanne Rocher, "British Orientalism in the Eighteenth Century: the dialectics of knowledge and government," in Carol A. Breckinridge and Peter van der Veer, eds., *Orientalism and the Postcolonial Predicament* (Philadelphia: University of Pennsylvania Press, 1993), p. 217n. "Carnal knowledge," is a paraphrase of Ann Stoler's title.

[14] C. A. Bayly, *Indian Society and the Making of the British Empire* (Cambridge: Cambridge University Press, 1988), pp. 51, 65.

[15] Huw Bowen, *Revenue and Reform: The Indian Problem in British Politics, 1757–1773* (Cambridge: Cambridge University Press, 1991).

in India. A High Court in Calcutta was established to adjudicate and preside over civil and criminal suits over British subjects in the Company's extensive domains. Domestic violence cases, such as the type discussed in chapter 5, were an unanticipated feature of the court's deliberations, drawing colonial judges into policing intimate violence in the households of British men in the Company's territories. As well, members of the court, such as William Jones, took on the task of codifying India's legal practices in order to rationalize Anglo-Indian law.[16] The commercial operations of the East India Company were increasingly being reinforced by an administrative and legal component overseen by Parliament.

Despite these reforms, charges continued to circulate back to England that Company rule in India was corrupt and despotic. A second regulating act, Pitt's India Act of 1784, expanded parliamentary supervision over the Company and separated the civil service and military administration of the Company's presidencies from the commercial operations, hoping to resolve the tension between the Company's role as merchant and sovereign in India.

As Edmund Burke argued repeatedly in Parliament in the impeachment hearings against Warren Hastings, the first governor-general of India, British affairs in India had taken a dangerous turn and threatened not only the British constitution but British ideals about morality, justice, and sovereignty.[17] Hastings, who had learned local languages, studied Indian literature, and adopted political practices was assumed to be infected by such oriental "vices" as greed, luxury, and despotism; he was replaced because he was accused of allowing corrupt local practices to permeate all levels of the East India Company's activities. In the context of this galvanizing public debate, Hastings's conduct in India was read as a political felony in Britain.[18]

Under Governor-General Lord Cornwallis (1786–1793), various social and political reforms were instituted to prevent British officials

---

[16] Bernard Cohn, "Law and the Colonial State in India," in *Colonialism and Its Forms of Knowledge* (Delhi: Oxford University Press, 1997); Nasser Hussain, *The Jurisprudence of Emergency: Sovereignty and the Rule of Law in British India* (Ann Arbor: University of Michigan, 2003), ch. 2.

[17] George Bearce, *British Attitudes Toward India, 1784–1858* (London: Oxford University Press, 1963), pp. 1–33. The trial went from 1786 until 1795 when Hastings was eventually acquitted.

[18] Peter Marshall, *The Impeachment of Warren Hastings* (Oxford: Clarendon Press, 1965); Marshall, *The Launching of the Hastings Impeachment 1786–1788: The Writings and Speeches of Edmund Burke* (Oxford: Oxford University Press, 1991). See also Kate Teltscher, *India Inscribed: European and British Writing on India, 1600–1800* (Delhi: Oxford University Press, 1995), ch. 4; Sara Suleri, *The Rhetoric of English India* (Chicago: University of Chicago Press, 1992), ch. 3.

from being corrupted by local political and trading practices. Salaries were raised so that no official would be vulnerable to bribery and civil servants were prohibited from engaging in private trade. The civil apparatus of the Company was cordoned off from the commercial establishment so that civil servants, charged with collecting taxes, adjudicating disputes, and managing local administrative tasks, would not be affected by commercial transactions.[19] Credited with elaborating the first systematic imperial ideologies of conquest and colonial rule in India, when Lord Wellesley arrived in India in 1798, he instituted policies that further bureaucratized the Company's establishment and expanded its dominions.[20]

For the period between 1786 and 1800, standard historical narratives have argued that the prohibitions instituted by Cornwallis and later affirmed by Wellesley brought anxieties about interracial sexual relationships into the forefront of colonial policies.[21] After the mid-1780s, the East India Company attempted to become a much more insular operation that was less reliant on local personnel than it had previously been. The Cornwallis prohibitions on admitting mixed-race subjects to the civil service and to the military was seen to be a sign of the times. Instead of depending on a mixed-race elite to manage colonial affairs, the expulsion of these elites from the Company civil service served as a reminder that people of mixed races were seen as colonial subjects whose loyalty was compromised.[22] The influence of *dubashes, banias,* and other local intermediaries was severely limited and a British service elite was expanded to replace the labor of indigenous elites who had previously served to link local populations with the British company state.[23] High-level officials were discouraged from keeping Indian companions and lower-level soldiers and employees of the company were

---

[19] Ronald Hyam, *Empire and Sexuality: The British Experience* (Manchester: Manchester University Press, 1991), ch. 1; Kenneth Ballhatchet, *Race, Sex and Class Under the Raj: Imperial Attitudes and Policies, 1793–1905* (New York: St. Martin's Press, 1980), Introduction; Suresh Chandra Ghosh, *The Social Condition of the British Community in Bengal, 1757–1800* (Leiden: E. J. Brill, 1970, reprint 1988), ch. 1.

[20] Bayly, *Indian Society,* pp. 81–9.

[21] *Ibid.,* pp. 71, 78, 83.

[22] The text of this directive is partially reprinted and critically analyzed in Gayatri C. Spivak, *A Critique of Postcolonial Reason: Toward a History of the Vanishing Present* (Cambridge: Harvard University Press, 1999), pp. 164–8; C. J. Hawes, *Poor Relations: the Making of a Eurasian Community in British India, 1773–1833* (London: Curzon, 1996), ch. 4; S. C. Ghosh, *Social Condition of the British Community,* ch. 4.

[23] See Bayly, *Indian Society;* Rosanne Rocher, "British Orientalism," and David Ludden, "Orientalist Empiricism: transformations of colonial knowledge," in Carol A. Breckenridge and Peter van der veer, eds., *Orientalism and the Post-colonial Predicament* (Philadelphia: University of Pennsylvania Press, 1993).

allowed and enabled to turn to prostitutes to satisfy their heterosexual impulses.[24] These kinds of measures contributed to a growing sense that the proximity between Britons and Indians required careful regulation if / the British were to retain political authority on the Indian subcontinent.[25]

These changes in policy have widely been assumed to be a definitive break in the everyday interactions between Europeans and natives, but the reach and the success of the Cornwallis reforms were initially limited. Interracial relationships continued in the post-Cornwallis era, with families and their European patriarchs relying on different strategies to manage the "problem" of their native companions and mixed-race children. What the Cornwallis reforms did was to crystallize existing anxieties about interracial sex that had existed in Anglo-Indian colonial society throughout the late eighteenth century and to create legislation to formalize an end of all forms of Anglo-Indian social intimacy.

While the Cornwallis and Wellesley reforms of the late eighteenth century were an administrative injunction against interracial relationships and mixed-race children, other developments are often attributed to the decline in Anglo-Indian intimacies. Echoing Kipling's image of the racist, narrow-minded memsahib, many scholars have argued that racial concerns and sexual jealousies expressed by growing numbers of Englishwomen in India ended a period of mutual understanding between the British and Indians and the practice of interracial cohabitation.[26] The 1857 mutiny is thus often described as a more decisive and widespread break in the history of Anglo-Indian cordiality, particularly given the rise in anxieties about sexual attacks against Englishwomen.[27]

This study complicates this progressive narrative of the British empire in India, long considered at its height in the late nineteenth century, and argues that the building blocks of colonial ideologies about racial

[24] Ballhatchet, *Race, Sex, and Class*, ch. 1.

[25] P. J. Marshall, "British Society in India under the East India Company," *Modern Asian Studies* 31 (February 1997): 101. See also David Arnold, "European orphans and vagrants in India in the nineteenth century," *Journal of Imperial and Commonwealth History* 7 (1978): 104–27.

[26] Spear, *Nabobs*, p. 143. See foreword by James Lunt, pp. xvii–xviii, in Dennis Kincaid, *British Social Life in India, 1608–1937* (London: Routledge and Kegan Paul, 1938); Sumanta Bannerjee, *Under the Raj: Prostitution in Colonial Bengal* (New York: Monthly Review Press, 1998), pp. 48–50; Elizabeth M. Collingham, *Imperial Bodies: the Physical Experience of the Raj, c. 1800–1947* (London: Polity Press, 2001), pp. 74–5.

[27] Jenny Sharpe, *Allegories of Empire* (Minneapolis: University of Minneapolis Press, 1993); Nancy Paxton, *Writing under the Raj: Gender, Race and Rape in the British Colonial Imagination, 1830–1947* (New Brunswick: Rutgers University Press, 1999).

superiority and moral probity were in formation from the middle of the eighteenth century onward, prior to the development of scientific racism and biological claims about the genetic differences between Caucasians and others.[28] Building on the work of Kathleen Wilson, Sudipta Sen, and others,[29] this book demonstrates that national affiliations and imperial priorities were being actively worked out from the earliest moments of the Anglo-Indian encounter, particularly on the bodies of native women, who represented a clear and present danger to maintaining Britishness within the frontiers of the household and the empire in India. As Chris Bayly has noted, "For all the talk of the high point of imperialism in the later nineteenth century, the basic system of British imperial dominance was put in place between 1760 and 1860."[30]

In this early phase of British rule, the social lives of Englishmen were linked as much to their rising status as members of privileged class groups in India as it was to their social status in Britain. Although these men exhibited eighteenth-century Company masculine ideals – they learned local languages, they wore local dress and they bedded local women – they were always intimately aware of clarifying their class and racial status to their white peers within the colonial settlement and to their families in Britain. For instance, William Fraser, resident in Delhi (1833–1835), was reportedly "half-Asiatic in his habits, but in other respects a Scotch Highlander."[31] Fraser, renowned in Delhi as a Persian-speaking poet, kept the news of his newly adopted practices from his family in Scotland. Likewise, the wills and letters of more ordinary British men show the ways in which they were determined to maintain respectability among other Europeans, in spite of their sexual and cultural practices across racial lines.

Social connections, in Britain and on the subcontinent, sustained the networks of patronage that supplied suitable recruits for desirable

---

[28] Nancy Stepan, *The Idea of Race in Science: Great Britain, 1800–1960* (Hamden, CT: Archon Books, 1982); Robert Young, *Colonial Desires: Hybridity in Theory, Culture and Race* (London: Routledge, 1995).

[29] Sudipta Sen, *Distant Sovereignty: National Imperialism and the Origins of British India* (New York: Routledge, 2002); Kathleen Wilson, *The Island Race: Englishness, Empire and Gender in the Eighteenth Century* (London: Routledge, 2003).

[30] C. A. Bayly, "The British and Indigenous Peoples, 1760–1860: power, perception and identity," in Martin Daunton and Rick Halpern, eds., *Europe and Its Others: British Encounters with Indigenous Peoples, 1600–1850* (Philadelphia: University of Pennsylvania Press, 1999), p. 22.

[31] According to Victor Jacquemont, a French traveler who visited Fraser, Mildred Archer, "Artists and Patrons in Residency Delhi, 1803–1858," in R. E. Frykenberg, eds., *Delhi Through the Ages* (Delhi: Oxford University Press, 1986), pp. 161–2; Mildred Archer, *India Revealed: The Art and Adventures of James and William Fraser, 1801–1835* (London: Cassell, 1989).

positions as covenanted servants and cadets within the East India Company's establishment.[32] Family connections were especially crucial to incorporating mixed-race children into European society, particularly when they were prohibited from working in the company forces by the Cornwallis prohibitions.[33] When it came to their children, men who had "gone native" by bedding a local woman demonstrated that they were deeply anxious about the moral upbringing, education, and social status of their offspring. Many men asked that their children be brought up with appropriate forms of morality, expressing an anxiety over what Ann Stoler has called "cultural competence," and the ways in which racial background was performed in social practice.[34] High-ranking, wealthy men who sired children with a native female companion often relied on relatives in England, Scotland, and Wales to bring their children up as socially "white," erasing any sign of their maternal lineage. Although sending children to Britain was a way of severing the ties of the child from his or her native mother, such traffic in children created ties between families in Britain to families on the Indian subcontinent, putting children borne of different mothers under the same patrilineal roof. Such was the case of William Makepeace Thackeray who was raised in the same household as Amelia, the illegitimate daughter of his father, Richmond, who had been a district collector in Sylhet, and an unnamed native woman.

Various definitions of "family" were critical to understanding how different subjects were treated by various institutions of the East India Company state.[35] In comparison with definitions of family in Britain, colonial families in India were often temporary and not bound by a marital contract, making them "illegitimate" in legal and religious terms. In the process of negotiating between legal codes established by common law in Britain and local practices brought about by colonial contact, British judges and military officials repeatedly demonstrated that at the heart of debates about the company's intervention in family matters lay the problem of family relationships that were outside conventional definitions of "family," such as concubinage, household

---

[32] S. C. Ghosh, *Social Condition of the British Community.*
[33] Hawes, *Poor Relations.*
[34] Stoler, *Carnal Knowledge,* chs. 4 and 5.
[35] Ground-breaking studies on the family include Lawrence Stone, *The Family, Sex and Marriage in England, 1500–1800* (New York: Harper and Row, 1977); also by Stone, *Broken Lives: Separation and Divorce in England, 1660–1857* (New York: Oxford University Press, 1993); John Gillis, *For Better, For Worse: British Marriages, 1600 to the Present* (New York: Oxford University Press, 1985); Catherine Hall and Leonore Davidoff, *Family Fortunes: Men and Women of the English Middle Class, 1780–1850* (London: Hutchinson, 1987).

slavery, and polygamy. In dealing with family disorder, paternal authority was often carefully guarded and European and Indian men were allowed to maintain control over what transpired in their households, for instance, in judicial cases involving domestic violence and marital disturbance.[36] Even in families that were considered illegitimate, the assumption of male authority over the members of his household was always closely supported by institutions of colonial governance, such as the courts and the church.

Although the East India Company was before 1813, strictly speaking, a commercial operation and not a state, various bureaucratic institutions that operated within the Company's dominions, such as the military, the courts, and the church enacted the forms of governmentality that were the nucleus of the colonial state.[37] The Company's statehood was complicated by its contested relationship to other sovereign political entities such as the Mughal empire,[38] but it was especially complicated when it came to identifying which political authorities were sovereign over the subject bodies of native women living in the households of European men. The question of how families were defined was closely connected to who was considered subject to the legal and social protection of being counted as "British"; if British men were not allowed to speak for their families, however informal and "illegitimate," the company state might be seen as ineffectively securing him his paternal rights. This conundrum, over who was counted a British subject, was constantly being considered by various institutions within the East India Company as it evolved from a trading company to a colonial government on behalf of the Crown.[39]

In India, as in Britain, definitions of family included persons who resided in the household, such as servants and apprentices, as well as blood or legal kin, such as children, spouse, and in-laws.[40] In Britain and its colonies, men held civil obligations and reaped certain civil benefits as heads of households in terms that were recognized by various

---

[36] Radhika Singha, "Making the Domestic More Domestic: Criminal Law and the 'head of the household,' 1772–1843," *Indian Economic and Social History Review* **33** (July–Sept. 1996): 309–44.

[37] Michel Foucault, "Governmentality," in James D. Faubion, ed., *Essential Works of Foucault, 1954–1984*, vol. 3 (New York: The New Press, 2000).

[38] Huw Bowen, "British India, 1765–1813: the metropolitan context," *Oxford History of the British Empire*, vol. II (Oxford: Oxford University Press, 1998).

[39] Lauren Benton, *Law and Colonial Cultures: Legal Regimes in World History, 1400–1900* (Cambridge: Cambridge University Press, 2002), pp. 2–3, 9, 29, 131–40.

[40] Naomi Tadmor, "The concept of the household-family in eighteenth-century England," *Past & Present*, 151 (May 1996): 111–30.

institutions of the state.[41] In maintaining the relationship between the state and its subjects, the family unit was central: men as patriarchs were assumed to have civic authority over the bodies that were constitutive of their households and families.[42] Thus being a subject of the empire was a gendered process that affected men and women differently. In British India, this sexual social contract was also a highly racialized one that constructed white men as having familial and political authority over native women.[43] Even though many of these relationships lacked a marital contract or legal justification for the state to uphold the right of the father and husband, criminal and civil courts treated these conjugal relationships as if a legal marriage had occurred. As chapter 5 shows, legal judgments in criminal trials of domestic violence between unmarried partners showed that British judges often felt that men may have been justified in beating or robbing their companions. In chapter 6, mixed-race orphans, many of them born of unmarried parents, were absorbed into various jobs within the military establishment, in the hope of making them productive and loyal members of the colonial settlement although they were "illegitimate." In return for defining "family" in a broad way, through its governing institutions, the company state was able to extend and legitimize its political authority over some of the most marginal members of colonial society – native women and mixed-race children – by protecting the interests of European men within their families and households.

As Ann Stoler has forcefully argued, the domestic space of colonial family life was crucial for working out anxieties about race and class that existed between colonizer and colonized;[44] these family-based anxieties

---

[41] Susan Dwyer Amussen, *An Ordered Society: Gender and Class in Early Modern England* (Oxford: Blackwell, 1988), pp. 38–41, 68; Ann Twinam, *Public Lives, Private Secrets: Gender, Honor, Sexuality, and Illegitimacy in Colonial Spanish America* (Stanford: Stanford University Press, 1999), p. 28; K. Brown, *Good Wives, Anxious Patriarchs*.

[42] For Europe, see Carole Pateman, *The Sexual Contract* (Stanford: Stanford University Press, 1988); Amussen (1988), ch 2; Susan Dwyer Amussen, "Being stirred to much unquietness: violence and domestic violence in early modern England," *Journal of Women's History* 6 (1994), pp. 72–3. For colonial India, see Lata Mani, *Contentious Traditions: the Debate on Sati in Colonial India* (Berkeley: University of California Press, 1998). For Latin America and the Middle East, respectively, see Sarah Chambers, *From Subjects to Citizens: Honor, Gender, and Politics in Arequipa, Peru, 1780–1854* (State Park: Pennsylvania State Press, 1999); Elizabeth Thompson, *Colonial Citizens: Republican Rights, Paternal Privilege and Gender in French Syria and Lebanon* (New York: Columbia University Press, 2000).

[43] S. Sen, *Distant Sovereignty*, pp. 88–92.

[44] Ann Stoler, *Race and the Education of Desire* (Durham: Duke University Press, 1995); Julia Clancy-Smith and Frances Gouda, eds., *Domesticating the Empire* (Charlottesville: University of Virginia Press, 1998).

were transposed to a broader discourse about how rights were granted to different subjects of the state making this process resonant with contradictions inherent to citizenship and colonialism.[45] While imperial ideologies and governmental policies partially set the stage for the enforcement of various anxieties about race and sexuality, the ways in which British men disciplined themselves and ordered their families gave rise to and crystallized widespread and deeply felt anxieties about the loss of class status, fears of racial degeneracy, and concerns about social acceptability.

A crucial element in discussing anxieties about race, sexuality, and family is the question of hybridity, both cultural and racial, that destabilized the homogeneities of the colonial social order. While hybridity produced anxieties about the loss of various types of "purity," embracing hybridity informed one's cosmopolitanism because it signaled tolerance and even appreciation of various types of heterogeneity.[46] To Britons, India was exotic and different, and as the eighteenth century progressed, India was also increasingly in need of rescue or restoration to its former glory.[47] These conflicting demands fueled the making of racial, social, and gender classification and hierarchies, particularly as the expansion of British dominance continued.

Although I have used "race" loosely, I draw a distinction between the eighteenth-century understanding of "race" and the nineteenth-century sense of scientific polygenesis.[48] In the eighteenth century, "race" represented a much more diffuse sense of difference. Many eighteenth-century observers referred to those they encountered in alien lands as

---

[45] Lora Wildenthal, "Race, gender and citizenship in the German empire," in Frederick Cooper and Ann L. Stoler, eds., *Tensions of Empire: Colonial Cultures in a Bourgeois World* (Berkeley: University of California Press, 1997); Alice L. Conklin, "Redefining 'Frenchness': citizenship, race regeneration, and imperial motherhood in France and West Africa, 1914–40," and Jean Elisabeth Pedersen, "Special Customs: paternity suits and citizenship in France and the colonies, 1870–1912," in *Domesticating the Empire*.

[46] In making this distinction between cultural and racial hybridity, I have relied largely on the works of Young, *Colonial Desires* and Homi Bhabha, *The Location of Culture* (London: Routledge, 1992), esp. pp. 102–22; see also Roxann Wheeler, *The Complexion of Race: Categories of Difference in Eighteenth-century British Culture* (Philadelphia: University of Pennsylvania Press, 2000), pp. 145–6; 173; McClintock, *Imperial Leather*, pp. 61–71.

[47] Jyotsna Singh, *Colonial Narratives/Cultural Dialogues* (London: Routledge, 1996), chs. 1–2; Teltscher, *India Inscribed*, chs. 4–7.

[48] Saul Dubow, *Scientific Racism in Modern South Africa* (Cambridge: Cambridge University Press, 1995); Paul Rich, *Race and Empire in British Politics* (Cambridge: Cambridge University Press, 1986); Nancy Stepan, *The Idea of Race in Science: Great Britain, 1800–1960* (Hamden, CT: Archon Books, 1982); George Stocking, *Colonial Situations: Essays on the Contextualization of Ethnographic Knowledge* (Madison: University of Wisconsin Press, 1991); Stoler (1995), ch. 3.

the "race" of Indians, Persians, Portuguese, and so on; it is fairly clear
that "race" in this context was a way of marking out otherness in the
ways that other groups had different manners, languages, habits,
politics, and religious practices.[49] The word "race" was bound up
with a larger set of discourses having to do with culture, geography,
religion, and daily practice;[50] it is with this broad, historically specific
sense that "race" has been used in this study. Nonetheless, these fairly
loose definitions of race in the eighteenth century laid the foundations
for the more radical measures that emerged from the middle of the
nineteenth century onward. Mixed-race subjects were commonly called
"country-born," "East Indian," "half-cast," and "Eurasian," in this
period, as the East India Company state made numerous distinctions
based on racial differences which were further elaborated as the
Company state matured into the British Raj.[51]

The shift that occurred between 1760 and 1840 happened gradually
and unevenly. Although the East India Company's state responded
in specific ways at particular moments during this period, these
responses were by no means uniform, monolithic, or coherent. As
several of the chapters demonstrate, officials at various levels of the
Company's administrative bureaucracy grappled with the problems
posed by Indian companions and mixed-race children, responding to the
demands made by their constituents. By juxtaposing the ways in which
European men expressed anxieties about their families and the ways in
which bureaucratic institutions dealt with the putative members of these
families, this project shows how indigenous household members became
objects of the colonial state's concern.

II

A crucial part of this study are the ways in which indigenous women
were made into subjects by the colonial social and legal order and made
themselves into subjects. Native women engaged with institutions of
colonial governance as a way of negotiating financial provisions, gaining
legal privileges, and expressing their cultural and religious affiliations,

---

[49] Wheeler, *Complexion of Race*, especially ch. 1; see also Kim F. Hall, *Things of Darkness: Economies of Race and Gender in Early Modern England* (Ithaca: Cornell University Press, 1995).
[50] On the shift from the orientalism of the late 18th century to the Anglicist position of the early 19th century, see Javed Majeed, *Ungoverned Imaginings: James Mill's The History of India and Orientalism* (Oxford: Clarendon Press, 1992) and Trautmann, *Aryans*.
[51] For a more complete account of this shift, see Thomas R. Metcalf, *Ideologies of the Raj* (Cambridge: Cambridge University Press, 1994).

thereby making themselves into subjects. These native women were able to maximize various opportunities made possible through their household relationships with European men. This should not lead us to the facile conclusion that colonialism or the intimate activities it gave rise to benefited native women. Rather, the activities of the East India Company opened up limited social, material, and legal opportunities for native women, allowing them some mobility within positions of relative powerlessness.

In theorizing a more complex notion of agency for these subjects, this study does more than restore hidden voices to history; it addresses the ways in which native women were drawn into maintaining and reproducing colonial regimes that were effective at maintaining race, gender, and class hierarchies. In Janaki Nair's words, "The responsibility of feminist historiography is to contextualize the question of female agency in a way that does not conceal how consent for broader patriarchal structures has been historically obtained."[52] Although native women remained marginal to colonial society, their marginality was a key site from which colonial authority was articulated and consolidated. By locating female colonial companions as historical subjects in the history of early British rule in India, we start to see the ways that marginal figures were drawn into and helped to constitute the politics of the nascent colonial state.

The historiography of women's and gender history in South Asia has thus far made few claims about native women's subjectivity and agency in eighteenth-century India. This oversight suggests that the lives of local women are historically unimportant unless they were spectacular figures such as satis or nationalist heroines. One category in South Asian feminist historiography, inaugurated by Lata Mani's article on sati and Partha Chatterjee's essay on how nationalists resolved the women question, has emphasized the ways in which women have served as important signifiers within the British and the Bengali middle-class notion of Indian society.[53] In these accounts, women are represented as absent of historical agency, subjectivity, or claims to be seen as

---

[52] Janaki Nair, "On the question of agency in Indian feminist historiography," *Gender & History* 6 (1994), p. 95.

[53] Lata Mani, "Contentious Traditions: debates about Sati in colonial India," and Partha Chatterjee, "The nationalist resolution on the women question," in Kumkum Sangari and Sudesh Vaid, eds., *Recasting Women* (New Brunswick: Rutgers University Press, 1988).

individuals of historical consequence both historically and by the √ scholars who have written these important essays.[54]

Another strand of scholarship on South Asian women's history has expanded historical understandings of the activities that women undertook, often within the nationalist struggle. These works have focused on elite or middle-class women, many of whom were educated and aware (in some measure) of their own historical importance.[55] The scholarship on these women has been tremendously useful for bringing women back into the history of India yet has largely overlooked the place of lower-class women. Although there are signs that histories of lower-class, uneducated women are being reconstructed in various ways, much of the work is based in the late nineteenth and twentieth centuries.[56]

A key reason for these absences in the fields of imperial history and South Asian women's history may be the problem of sources and the ways in which scholars use these sources. As several scholars have noted, recovering female subjects, indeed subaltern voices, from the archives of √ colonial history is difficult if not problematic.[57]

Colonial archives have been very successful at keeping the voices of native women out. Native women were often not identified by complete names, but recorded incompletely by first name or a nickname given by the men who kept them. While naming practices ordinarily make

[54] Nair, "On agency," p. 86. See also Kamala Visweswaran, "Small speeches, subaltern gender: nationalist ideology and its historiography," *Subaltern Studies IX* (Delhi: Oxford University Press, 1996), p. 89.

[55] Most recently, Geraldine Forbes, *Women in Modern India*, see also J. Krishnamurty, ed., *Women in Colonial India: Essays on Survival, Work and the State* (Delhi: Oxford University Press, 1989); Bharati Ray, ed., *From the Seams of History: Essays on Indian Women* (Delhi: Oxford University Press, 1995); Radha Kumar, *History of Doing*; Malavika Karlekar, *Voices from Within* (Delhi: Oxford University Press, 1991); Meredith Borthwick, *The Changing Role of Women in Bengal* (Princeton: Princeton University Press, 1984).

[56] See *We Were Making History!* (New Delhi: Kali for Women, 1988); Ritu Menon and Kamla Bhasin, *Borders and Boundaries* (New Delhi: Kali for Women, 1999); Samita Sen, *Women and Labour in Late Colonial India: the Bengal Jute Industry* (Cambridge: Cambridge University Press, 1999); Indrani Chatterjee, *Gender, Slavery and Law in Colonial India* (Delhi: Oxford University Press, 1999).

[57] Indrani Chatterjee, "Testing the local against the colonial archive," *History Workshop Journal* 44 (1997), p. 215; Frederick Cooper and Ann Stoler, eds., *Tensions of Empire: Colonial Cultures in a Bourgeois World* (Berkeley: University of California Press, 1997), p. 18; Betty Joseph, *Reading the East India Company, 1720–1840: Colonial Currencies of Gender* (Chicago: University of Chicago, 2004), pp. 1–10; Madhavi Kale, *Fragments of Empire: Capital, Slavery and Indentured Labor Migration in the British Caribbean* (Philadelphia: University of Pennsylvania Press, 1998), pp. 8–9; Gayatri C. Spivak, "Deconstructing historiography," in Ranajit Guha and Spivak, eds., *Selected Subaltern Studies* (Delhi: Oxford University Press, 1988); Spivak, "Can the subaltern speak?"; Carolyn Steedman, *Dust: The Archive and Cultural History* (New Brunswick, NJ: Rutgers University Press, 2002), p. 77.

subjects "legible" to the state for the purposes of governance,[58] the large-scale absence of named native women in colonial archives might suggest that native conjugal companions were historically unimportant. Church records, for instance, recorded the names of mixed-race children and their entry into a community of Christians while many entries recorded "native woman" in the column for the mother's name. The erasure of native women's names in baptism registers juxtaposed alongside the names of their mixed-race children suggests that native women were imagined to be outside this social order, even though their anonymity was acknowledged as the bodies from which these children were born. Reading archives "along the grain," as Ann Stoler has encouraged enables us to better understand the logic of the archive and the governmentality it represents. In early British India, the absence of native women's names in colonial archives correlated with the state's interests to suppress the visibility of subjects who threatened the whiteness of colonial society.[59]

In Anglican church records, baptismal and marriage registers listed native women, when they were identified, either by their Christian names or by their married last names thereby obscuring their natal forms of identification.[60] In court records, such as wills and court cases, women were often marked out by the descriptives given them. For example, in baptismal records, "Anna" listed in quotation marks was followed by "a native woman," or "a Hindoo girl." When "Anna" married, she became Anna Fitzpatrick, thereby erasing archival evidence of her identity as an indigenous woman. In wills, women were referred to by nicknames such as "Bunnoo," "Golaub," and so on. In a court case in which two native female companions of Europeans were indicted for murder, the defendants were listed by the names "Betty" and "Peggy," obscuring their ethnic pasts.

In contrast to most historical research where looking for names and places in indexes is a starting point, in this project, the lack of a name signaled the presence of a native woman. Namelessness showed that a subject's identity did not need to be recorded fully; conversely,

---

[58] James C. Scott, John Tehranian, and Jeremy Mathias, "The Production of Legal Identities Proper to States: the case of the permanent family surname," *Comparative Studies in Society and History* 44 (2002): 4–44.

[59] Durba Ghosh, "Decoding the Nameless: gender, subjectivity, and historical methodologies in reading the archives of colonial India," in Kathleen Wilson, eds., *A New Imperial History: Culture, Identity, Modernity, 1660–1840* (Cambridge: Cambridge University Press, 2004); Ann Stoler, "Colonial Archives and the Arts of Governance: on the content in the form," in Carolyn Hamilton *et al.*, eds., *Refiguring the Archive* (Cape Town: David Philip, 2002).

[60] Joseph, *Reading the East India Company*, pp. 7–10.

namelessness also served as a code, for instance in the baptismal registers, as a way to mark the racial status of the child being baptized. Directories and calendars of the East India Company's servants printed names of British subjects carefully, while the births of children to the company's officers and officials in a way that marked the legitimacy or illegitimacy of the birth.[61] In the cases where the officer was married, commonly to a European or half-European woman, notice of the birth was listed as "Born on the 15th instant, a son to Col. and Mrs. Monson." In cases where a marriage was not evident, the notice read, "Born on the 15th instant, a son to the lady of Col. Monson at Berhampore."[62]

The kinds of conventions used in recording the names of people who were born, who died or who were married within the East India Company's dominions confirms that colonial subjects were recorded in colonial archives only when necessary to mark out racial and social status: the absence of the mother's name marked the legitimacy or illegitimacy of the child in baptismal registers; the bracketing in quotes of a name in marriage registers marked the race of the native woman convert; and the presence of the native woman with a European name suggested that she had been renamed and separated from her natal history. These examples demonstrate how naming practices charted the racial and gendered topographies of this budding Anglo-Indian community. More important, the absence of complete names highlighted the multiple and conflicting ways in which the subjectivities of local women were simultaneously produced and made anonymous by common practices in record keeping.

The making of status and subjectivity through naming practices and conventional record-keeping may seem inconsequential and unintentional. One might imagine that Englishmen renamed their mistresses with European names in order to pronounce their names more easily, but such renaming had the consequence of detaching women from their own communities by erasing a crucial sign of their origins.[63] As is well

---

[61] Gayatri Chakravorty Spivak, "The Rani of Sirmur: an essay in reading the archives," *History and Theory* 38 (1985): 247–72.

[62] In the case of the death of an infant, it was often listed "Died on the 15th instant, the son of Col. and Mrs. Monson," or in the case of the illegitimate child "Died on the 15th instant, the son of Col. Monson." Similarly, in baptismal records, the children of native mothers were often listed by one parent, suggesting that the British company state recognized both parents only when both parents were of European descent. This is comparable to the ways in which Spanish colonies recognized "natural children" or *"hijos naturales."* See Twinam, *Public Lives*, pp. 130–9.

[63] Peter Robb, "Clash of Cultures?: an Englishman in Calcutta in the 1790s," School of Oriental and African Studies, University of London, Inaugural Lecture, March 12, 1998, p. 40

known by scholars of South Asia, surnames often serve to locate people by region, religion, and caste. The absence of a surname, or, in the case of many colonial companions, the absence of a local name made it difficult if not impossible to follow the kinds of communities that these women originated in. Because these subjects were not easily situated in a local context, the many types of boundaries they crossed when they entered into conjugal relationships with European men become difficult to apprehend.

What happens when a native woman is baptized or renamed? Who does she become? Who and what does she represent to herself and others? Because archival sources make it difficult to read many aspects of the women's lives, personhood, and subjectivities, I have tried to remain mindful of the concerns raised by feminist historians. As Rosalind O'Hanlon has argued, the retrieval of subaltern subjects can be highly problematic, enabling scholars to enact a political agenda that forecloses the voice of the subaltern and clothe it in the ideological garb of contemporary historical trends.[64] She argues against writing subaltern subjects as "a classic unitary self-constituting subject-agent of liberal humanism," because such a position assumes that self-awareness or consciousness is always necessary to historical agency. O'Hanlon also notes that the idea of identity is highly problematic in a colonial context because the colonizers' definitions of the colonized are contested, unstable and subject to various manipulations by ruler and ruled alike; in the case of native women, "identity" is a highly vexed question, since the ways in which they were named or categorized into caste, religious, and regional classifications were often beyond their control.[65] In order to avoid uncritically recreating historical subjects who possessed fixed identities, rational consciousness, historical agency, and self-awareness, following Kamala Visweswaran, this study makes an attempt to "consider how identities are multiple, contradictory, partial, and strategic."[66]

Identifying women has been one major obstacle; the other methodological problem has been finding women's voices. Unlike several studies that have considered the ways in which women wrote about themselves

---

[64] R. O'Hanlon, "Recovering the Subject: *Subaltern Studies* and histories of resistance in Colonial South Asia," *Modern Asian Studies* **22** (1988): 189–224, especially pp. 190–6.

[65] *Ibid.*, pp. 196–7, 204, 221.

[66] Kamala Visweswaran, "Betrayal: an analysis in three acts," in Inderpal Grewal and Caren Kaplan, eds., *Scattered Hegemonies: Postmodernity and Transnational Feminist Practices* (Minnesota: University of Minnesota Press, 1994), p. 99. See also Dorinne Kondo, *Crafting Selves: Power, Gender and Discourses of Identity in a Japanese Workplace* (Chicago: University of Chicago Press, 1990), pp. 34, 43.

or spoke for themselves, in this study there are relatively few examples of speech acts enunciated by colonial companions. Thus, this study is a partial restoration and encouragement for further study. As Visweswaran argues, "In interrupting a Western (sometime feminist) project of subject retrieval, recognition of the partially understood is not simply strategy but accountability to my subjects; partial knowledge is not so much choice as necessity."[67] Although there are some women's voices – wills, court testimony, letters – these moments of speech were produced in response to particular claims or demands. These examples should be read not as proof of women's agency in absolute terms, but rather that these speech acts emerged under highly regulated conditions.

Historical, social, and political contexts framed the demands, the positions, and the subjectivities produced by female colonial companions. In this sense, Joan Scott's reminder has been particularly useful. As she noted, "And subjects have agency. They are not unified, autonomous individuals exercising free will, but rather subjects whose agency is created through situations and statuses conferred on them."[68] Nonetheless, the question of historical agency is a complicated one, particularly when used to address the subjects of colonialism, even more so when addressing "third-world" or "non-western" women who are often seen to suffer through multiply oppressive regimes. As Nicholas Dirks has implied, historians of British colonialism who argue that Indians had agency under British rule misunderstand the hegemonic effects that colonialism had on the colonized.[69] Meanwhile, Aihwa Ong, Chandra Mohanty, and others have argued that reifying the "third-world" woman-as-victim reinstates race, gender, and geopolitical hierarchies that a progressive, culturally sensitive transnational feminist practice relies on undoing.[70] What we are presented with are a difficult set of choices: to say that colonial companions did things to advance their interests is to suggest that colonialism was a "good thing" that might have expanded women's choices;[71] and yet to suggest that women were powerless is to reinstate the image that brown women were and are unable to speak for themselves, perpetually subjects of the Freudian fantasy that Spivak crystallized so many years ago when she wrote

---

[67] Visweswaran, "Betrayal," p. 99.

[68] See Joan W. Scott, "The evidence of 'experience,'" *Critical Inquiry* 17 (1991): 34.

[69] Nicholas Dirks, *Castes of Mind: Colonialism and the Making of Modern India* (Princeton: Princeton University Press, 2001), "Coda"; see especially, pp. 307–9.

[70] Aihwa Ong, *Flexible Citizenship: the Cultural Logics of Transnationality* (Durham, NC: Duke University Press, 1999); Chandra Talpade Mohanty, *Feminism without Borders: Decolonizing Theory, Practicing Solidarity* (Durham: Duke University Press, 2003).

[71] Niall Ferguson, *Empire*, p. xx.

"White men are saving brown women from brown men."[72] By allowing women of all stripes and shades to form their own agendas and programs and to inhabit their own histories, we break down and resist, rather than reinstate, some of gender, class, race hierarchies that constituted the structures of colonial societies.

In this study, I have spoken of agency in a very limited sense as action that is registered in the archives, with the full understanding that much of these women's lives and experiences as historical subjects exist beyond the knowledge regime of the archive. Making oneself known to the colonial archive was a partial act of resistance, particularly when we consider the ways in which colonial archives sought to make native women illegible. And yet, subaltern women's agency should not be counted as anticolonial resistance. As Jenny Sharpe has noted, a sensitive reading of female subjectivity and agency "raises the possibility of action without negating the unequal relations of power that restrict the ability to act."[73] Although in many cases the acts taken by various native women consolidated the regime rather than challenged or resisted it, native women were not complicit in colonialism; rather, colonial regimes drew women into various confrontations in ways that ultimately consolidated and reaffirmed colonial authority. In chapters 2 and 4, I examine how the experience of high-ranking women can be located along axes of family and larger court politics, particularly in an environment that both offered women opportunities for social advancement while denying them admission as rightful members of the family. In chapters 5 and 6, I show that when lower-ranking native women appeared in front of magistrates, chaplains, and military commanders to press their claims to the Company state, they became its subjects, inadvertently consolidating the paternalistic aspects of the colonial regime. Time and again, from choosing their names to having control over their children's lives, colonial companions were severely restricted by the options available to them, and yet they did act to defend their interests, particularly when the colonial regime was unsure of its policies.

Dirks's argument about the nature of subaltern agency rehearses an old debate within South Asian historiography: one between the so-called "Cambridge" school historians who suggest that Indian elites inserted themselves into colonial hierarchies and negotiated with their colonial

---

[72] Spivak, "Can the subaltern speak?," p. 296.
[73] Jenny Sharpe, *Ghosts of Slavery: a Literary Archeology of Black Women's Lives* (Minneapolis: University of Minnesota Press, 2003), p. xiv, ch. 2.

masters, making them "collaborators,"[74] against the Subaltern Studies collective, whose position has been too neatly summarized as arguing that colonialism produced a hegemonic order that truncated India's development into nationhood. Neither of these summaries does sufficient justice to the range of positions taken by students of each of these "schools," however, they return us to the conundrum about writing agency into colonial histories, particularly when it comes to the subject positions and voices of native women, who are often assumed to be the lowest rung on the colonial ladder.

Recent histories on native women who became involved in conjugal relationships have reified the Cambridge versus Subaltern School oppositions. In *Subaltern Studies X*, Indrani Chatterjee proposed that the position of native women in European households in the late eighteenth and early nineteenth centuries was a model of "slave-concubinage."[75] Her analysis bringing two major institutions, slavery and family, into a single field of inquiry has shown that household slavery was a way in which colonial officials could avail themselves of the sexual, reproductive, and domestic labor of native women while denying them wages and rights as familial subjects. By Chatterjee's account, an extractive family regime was reinforced by a capitalist regime and a colonial state. Although Chatterjee discusses a case of a woman who was at one point a slave, was transacted from regiment to regiment and came to make a living as a small businesswoman, she shies from exploring what native women's responses were and whether they found a way to strain against the possibilities presented to them.[76] In contrast, William Dalrymple suggests that post-Mughal harem culture in this period gave women many opportunities within the household and politics, particularly in arranging relationships between native noblewomen and British political agents. Dalrymple's example is no doubt an exceptional one: his heroine, Khair-un-nissa, belonged to a powerful family in the court at Hyderabad, very unlike the figures that animate Chatterjee's essay. But reading their works against one another, we see that at the heart of their accounts is a position on the agentic possibilities allowed to women under colonialism. Dalrymple specifies that British colonialism, particularly after 1800, was racist and intolerant, but he insists that there was a moment of openness and cultural curiosity in the eighteenth century that was crystallized through love and sexual intimacy that

---

[74] Partha Chatterjee, *The Nation and Its Fragments*, Introduction and ch. 1.
[75] Indrani Chatterjee, "Colouring Subalternity: slaves, concubines and social orphans in early colonial India,"*Subaltern Studies X* (Delhi: Oxford University Press, 1999).
[76] I. Chatterjee, "Colouring subalternity," pp. 60–1.

allowed native women and European men to come together.[77] This vision of imperial multiculturalism overlooks some of the trauma suffered by the female characters in the story, in particular, the heroine of Dalrymple's work, Khair-un-nissa, who found herself a widow in her twenties and suffered through the removal of her children to England in order that they could be raised Anglican. Chatterjee, on the other hand, suggests that familial sentiments were always structured by financial transactions with no advantages for native women and their children. Her account, which is rigorously argued and nuanced, allows little space for imagining how slave and servant women may have crafted or fashioned their selves under colonialism.

Dalrymple and Chatterjee, through their oversights, make clear the risks in writing the lives of native women as historical subjects in this particular historical period. Women are cast either as slaves or as romantic figures, with less attention to understanding their strategies for survival and their ways of locating and fashioning their selves. Chapter 4 addresses this question in some detail, arguing that conjugal relationships offered some native women room to maneuver strategically, fashioning selves that could be both socially and politically advantageous given their circumstances on the margins of colonial society.

Building on Chatterjee's important article, this book goes into some further depth in two ways. First, it extends the idea of concubinage and household slavery as a gendered process. As Atlantic and Caribbean specialists have shown in the last decade, slave women's bodies were valued for their reproductive and productive capacities. The work of Barbara Bush, Hilary Beckles, Philip Morgan, and others suggest that slave women had opportunities for advancement, however limited, that were not available to slave men.[78] In North America, slave women were able to extract concessions from their owners or masters for increased privileges within the household and sometimes manumission for their

---

[77] William Dalrymple, *White Mughals: Love and Betrayal in Eighteenth-century India* (London: HarperCollins, 2002).

[78] Barbara Bush, *Slave women in Caribbean Society, 1650–1838* (Bloomington, IN: Indiana University Press, 1990), pp. 31–2, 38, 114–15; Hilary Beckles, *Centering Woman: Gender Discourses in Caribbean Slave Society* (Kingston, 1999), pp. 33–5; Philip Morgan, *Slave Counterpoint: Black Culture in the Eighteenth-century Chesapeake and Low Country* (Chapel Hill: University of North Carolina Press, 1998), pp. 408–9. See also Shirley Hartley, "Illegitimacy in Jamaica," in Peter Laslett, Karla Oosterveen, and Richard M. Smith, eds., *Bastardy and Its Comparative History* (Cambridge, MA: Harvard University Press, 1980), p. 381; Raymond Smith, "Hierarchy and the Dual Marriage System in West Indian Society," in Jane F. Collier and Sylvia Yanagisako, eds., *Gender and Kinship: Essays Toward a Unified Analysis* (Stanford: Stanford University Press, 1987), pp. 169, 179.

children in exchange for sex and affection. Likewise, on the Indian subcontinent, native women were able to secure financial support for their children, as well as their siblings, parents, and aunts and uncles through the provisions made by the men with whom they cohabited. In households with multiple women, some women were able to become favorites, improving their status within the household. Although these patterns do not mitigate the coercive aspects of household slavery, they do demonstrate that native men and women negotiated the structures of colonial labor extraction in very different ways.

As household slaves, concubines, and temporary spouses, native women were denied the rights they would have been accorded had they been married. But even the large numbers of native women who married, converted either to Catholicism or the Church of England, were still restricted from claiming the benefits that being a wife provided. Although it is tempting to read this disenfranchisement as expressly colonial,[79] this study, particularly chapter 3, complicates the easy equivalence of familial patterns and networks in British India as "colonial" and suggests that some of familial patterns of sentiment, emotion, and inheritance provisions were resonant to those existing in Britain and in other eighteenth-century colonial settlements when it came to wives and children. By locating the racial and gender hierarchies of mixed-race families in early British India along a continuum of gendered orders in Britain and elsewhere, we can start to see how a global gendered order emerged in the late eighteenth century with British men ruling over numerous territories of women, British and native, as well as ever larger groups of native men.

Studies of colonialism have coined a range of terms to explain cross-cultural contact and exchange, from "contact zones," by Mary Louise Pratt, to Richard White's "middle ground," and Kathleen Brown's "gender frontier."[80] Interracial liaisons were constitutive parts of such cross-cultural interaction, and as Ann Stoler has argued, always problematic. Sexual discipline and moral superiority were as central to maintaining empire as colonial bureaucracies. In the process of "making empire respectable," colonial officials substantiated their legitimacy to rule by phasing out interracial unions, frowning upon miscegenation

[79] I. Chatterjee, "Colouring subalternity," p. 94.
[80] Mary Louise Pratt, *Imperial Eyes; Richard White, The Middle Ground: Indians, Empires, and Republics in the Great Lakes Region, 1650–1815* (Cambridge: Cambridge University Press, 1991), ch. 2; Kathleen Brown, *Good Wives, Nasty Wenches, and Anxious Patriarchs: Gender, Race and Power in Colonial Virginia* (Chapel Hill: University of North Carolina Press, 1996), part I.

and treating racial hybridity as a weakness in the creation of an imperial nation. Sophisticated mechanisms that regulated social boundaries within colonies were indicative of larger European anxieties about race and sex in the nineteenth century. Stoler has argued that these colony-based disciplinary regimes circulated back to the metropole and provided the kind of impetus toward generating the discourses of the body and sexuality in post-Enlightenment Europe that Michel Foucault has famously described in *The History of Sexuality*. Following Stoler's reminders, this book collapses the lines between metropole and colony to examine the ways in which anxieties and negotiations over interracial sex and intimacy were manifested within Europe and its colonies across the globe.[81]

Regulating sexuality and interracial intimacy was a transnational phenomenon during the long centuries of European imperialism.[82] For instance, histories of the Hudson Bay Company in western Canada in the period between 1670 and 1820 have shown that men from the British Isles were highly reliant on the domestic and sexual labor of native American women as the company expanded its fur trade; as the trading company expanded and the colonial settlement became increasingly distant from local native Americans, English wives were increasingly brought to Canada to replace native wives.[83] In the same period, such a shift occurred in British colonies and Dutch colonies in south and southeast Asia.[84] For a later period, Hyam's account has shown how British policies and practices in India, Africa, and Southeast Asia corrected the sexual behavior of British men during Britain's imperial century, from 1815 to 1914.[85]

---

[81] Stoler, *Race*; Stoler, *Carnal Knowledge*; Michel Foucault, *The History of Sexuality*, 2 vols. (New York: Pantheon, 1978).

[82] Pamela Scully, "Race and ethnicity in women's and gender history in global perspective," in Bonnie Smith, ed., *Women's History in Global Perspective*, vol. 1 (Urbana, IL: University of Illinois Press, 2004).

[83] Sylvia van Kirk, *Many Tender Ties: Women in Fur Trade Society, 1670–1870* (Norman: University of Oklahoma Press, 1980); Jennifer S. H. Brown, *Strangers in Blood: Fur Trade Company Families in Indian Country* (Vancouver: University of British Columbia, 1980). I thank Bernard Bailyn for these citations.

[84] Jean Gelman Taylor, *The Social World of Batavia: European and Eurasian in Dutch Asia* (Madison, WI: University of Wisconsin Press, 1983), ch. 3; see also Julia Adams, "Principals and agents, colonialists and company men," *American Sociological Review* 61 (1996): 12–28.

[85] Hyam, *Empire and Sexuality*, see esp. pp. 152–9, 214–15. Hyam concludes by arguing, "There is no reason why sex cannot be an act of racial conciliation ... sexual interaction between the British and non-Europeans probably did more long-term good than harm to race relations." For a response to Hyam, see Mark Berger, "Imperialism and Sexual Exploitation: a response to Ronald Hyam's 'empire and sexual opportunity,'" *Journal of Imperial and Commonwealth History* 17 (1988): 83–9.

Like British colonies on the Indian subcontinent, the Dutch trading company's settlement in Batavia, dating from the early seventeenth century, relied on indigenous and mestizo women to be the domestic partners of Dutch company servants, particularly men of lower status. Comparable to the East India Company's early acceptance of these relationships, Dutch traders were drawn into local kinship networks by forming temporary marriages with local women; by the end of the eighteenth century, as the local economy was disrupted, native women came to rely on exchanging their sexual labor for money, thereby becoming morally suspect and detached from their own kin groups.[86] Similar to baptism registers in India, church records in Batavia recorded the names of mothers only if they were Christian.[87] By erasing native women's names from a putatively European community, Asian women in Batavia and in Calcutta experienced parallel processes of disenfranchisement.

Unlike what transpired in British India, middle-class and upwardly mobile Dutchmen married the mestizo daughters of powerful men in the Batavia settlement to secure their positions.[88] Yet by the middle of the eighteenth century, definitions of Europeanness preoccupied elite Dutch men and their mestizo wives as they tried to define themselves as being more European than *indische* (or hybrid).[89] During the British period in Batavia, from 1811 to 1816, mestizo culture came under assault by British officials who relied on their experiences in Bengal to direct their public activities in Batavia; thereafter, Dutch colonial elites and their Asian and mixed-race companions were expected to behave like Europeans in public although they maintained Asian habits at home. In spite of widespread efforts to Europeanize Dutch colonial society, the culture of many households remained *indische* while the public culture of Dutch ruling elites became more Europeanized throughout the nineteenth century.[90] Like British India, in Dutch Indonesia, the emergence of a public social order in which European comportment dominated over native habits paralleled the consolidation of the colonial state's power over its growing colony.[91]

---

[86] Barbara Watson Andaya, "From Temporary Wife to Prostitute: sexuality and economic change in early modern Southeast Asia," *Journal of Women's History* 9 (Winter 1994): 11–34.

[87] Leonard Blusse, *Strange Company: Chinese Settlers, Mestizo Women and the Dutch in VOC Batavia* (Dordrecht, Holland: Foris Publications, 1986), pp. 166–71.

[88] Taylor, *Social World*, ch. 3

[89] *Ibid.*, ch. 4.

[90] *Ibid.*, chs. 5 and 6.

[91] Frances Gouda, *Dutch Culture Overseas: Colonial Practices in the Netherlands Indies* (Amsterdam: Amsterdam Book Depot, 1995).

Even the Iberian empires, which were widely acknowledged as empires in which European men settled down with local women and created large creole communities, interracial relationships produced much anxiety over social mobility and political authority.[92] Joyce Chaplin has noted for the Atlantic world that "It has long been thought that sexual activity across the 'races' was more characteristic of Iberian and French colonies than of English ones," but her essay suggests that it was not that mixed-race people didn't exist in the British colonies, but rather that official recognition of them was missing in the British empire.[93] Unlike the British or Dutch trading empires which were largely commercial, the Iberian empires in the Americas and in India were initially based on the impulse to expand Catholicism.[94] Yet in spite of the large-scale racial creolization which occurred in Iberian empires, the emergence of mixed-race communities in various colonies produced anxieties about color, class, and race. As several scholars have shown, the occurrence of interracial sex posed a challenge to family honor and was often managed through a range of marital practices.[95] In a range of Spanish colonies, the introduction of church-based marital codes transformed less formal sexual practices and family relationships among indigenous communities in order to align them with practices that were seen to be more respectable.[96] In Brazil, stricter church regulations led to making colonial Brazil endogamous; as a result, Brazilians of different ethnicities, class, and color infrequently married outside of their own social groups. But this did not mean that Brazilians did not have

---

[92] C. R. Boxer, *Race Relations in the Portuguese Colonial Empire, 1415–1825* (Oxford: Clarendon, 1963). Although by the late sixteenth century, many Portuguese were concerned about the erosion of Portuguese identity through these "marriages." See *Primor e Hnra de Vida Soldadesca no Estado da India* (1570); I thank Sanjay Subramanyam for this citation.

[93] Joyce Chaplin, "Race," in David Armitage and Michael Braddick, eds., *The British Atlantic World, 1500–1800* (New York: Palgrave/Macmillan, 2002).

[94] Anthony Pagden, *Lords of All the World: Ideologies of Empire in Spain, Britain and France, c. 1500–c. 1800* (New Haven: Yale University Press, 1995).

[95] Verena Martinez-Alier, *Marriage, Class and Colour in Nineteenth-century Cuba* (Cambridge: Cambridge University Press, 1974); Patricia Seed, *To Love, Honor and Obey in Colonial Mexico: Conflicts over Marriage Choice, 1574–1821* (Stanford: Stanford University Press, 1988); Robert McCaa, "*Calidad, Clase* and marriage in colonial Mexico: the case of Parral, 1788–1790," *Hispanic American Historical Review* 64 (1984): 477–501. For a study comparing different Spanish colonies in this period, see Ann Twinam, *Public Lives.*

[96] Ramon A. Gutierrez, *When Jesus Came, the Corn Mothers Went Away: Marriage, Sexuality, and Power in New Mexico, 1500–1846* (Berkeley: University of California Press, 1991). On colonial New England, see Ann Marie Plane, *Colonial Intimacies: Indian Marriage in Early New England* (Ithaca: Cornell University Press, 2000).

conjugal relationships across class or color lines. Instead, men who had conjugal relationships with women of lower status often did not marry them but cohabited with them as concubines, producing large numbers of illegitimate children and a population of creoles. These domestic arrangements, occurring outside of the church's reach, consolidated the inequalities between the male partner and his female concubine and helped to maintain social hierarchies based on color within Brazil.[97]

Interracial cohabitation or concubinage enabled European men to maximize not only their sexual opportunities but their economic ones as well. By *not* legitimating relationships through legal marital rites, many British officials in India who kept native colonial companions were free to move onto more respectable marriages with European women back home who were able to bring some wealth into the marriage.[98] By practicing concubinage as well as observing endogamous marital practices, European men had split domestic lives in which they were simultaneously part of family networks based in Britain and in India. Using the example of the British colonies in the Caribbean, Raymond Smith has called this the "dual marriage system," in which men married women of equal social, racial and economic status, but maintained relationships with women who were unequal by these terms.[99] In the circulation of English soldiers and merchants between Britain and these distant colonies, we start to see how patterns of family life traveled, particularly with men like William Palmer who had a mestizo female companion in the West Indies and a Muslim one in north India.

Extramarital familial relationships, such as concubinage and illegitimacy, seen to be a common feature of colonial societies also existed in Europe. As Ann Twinam has noted, "For more than twenty years, demographers and historians have designated the eighteenth century as the century of illegitimacy."[100] Rates of illegitimacy spiked dramatically between 1750 and 1850 in Europe.[101] Scholars have suggested that this might be indicative of changing conceptions of courtship, perhaps even

---

[97] Muriel Nazzari, "Concubinage in Colonial Brazil: the inequalities of race, class, and gender," *Journal of Family History* 21 (1996): 107–24; Elizabeth Kuznesof, "Sexual politics, race and bastard-bearing in nineteenth-century Brazil," *Journal of Family History* 16 (1991): 241–60. Gutierrez makes a similar argument for New Mexico, see *When Jesus Came*, Part III.

[98] See S. C. Ghosh, *Social Condition of the British Community*, pp. 73–4; Hawes, *Poor Relations*, pp. 6–7.

[99] Smith, "Hierarchy and dual marriage"; see also Twinam, *Public Lives*, pp. 111–12.

[100] Twinam, *Public Lives*, p. 7.

[101] Belinda Meteyard, "Illegitimacy and marriage in eighteenth-century England," *Journal of Interdisciplinary History* 10 (1980): 479.

an adaptive strategy that was the result of couples waiting to marry until they had enough money as many Company servants did. As Laslett has noted, the era was marked by the emergence of a "bastardy prone sub-society," in which out-of-wedlock births became a common occurrence in particular families and communities.[102] Although it would be very difficult to measure the rate of illegitimacy in early colonial India, the large-scale existence of unmarried, but cohabiting men and women and their offspring suggests that illegitimacy in European and European colonial societies was not an irregular occurrence, either in local or in global terms. Premarital sex and out-of-wedlock pregnancies were familiar to Europeans in Europe and in the colonies.

By keeping indigenous women out of European marital and familial networks, concubinage was not a departure from the normative practice of marriage, but rather a practice that sustained the racial and gendered hierarchies of colonial societies by denying interracial relationships the public or social recognition of marriage entailed. The practice of concubinage enabled colonial societies like British India to pretend that they were uncontaminated by racial or cultural mixing while sustaining multiple hierarchies of racial and social inequality.

Although some European men and native women shared long-lasting, monogamous interracial relationships, the absence of marital legitimacy in terms that were understood by the East India Company's bureaucracies failed to protect the spousal and maternal rights of many native women. Women like Helen Bennett, companion to Benoit de Boigne, found her conjugal rights suspended when her partner abandoned her, having brought her to England, to marry another woman. Women like Khair-un-nissa, once a noblewoman, found herself in a relationship with a second Englishman once her children with James Kirkpatrick were sent away to England. Native companions were frequently not recognized as the rightful recipients of charitable benefits, thereby confirming concubinage as the absence of a legitimate family relationship. Illegitimate children were removed from their mothers' influence and resocialized through education, either in the Military Orphan schools or through education in England. The deliberate removal of mixed-race children from the homes of their indigenous mothers revealed that at the heart of British colonial society in India, in spite of moments of cultural tolerance and compatibility, were

---

[102] Peter Laslett, "The bastardy prone sub-society," in Laslett *et al*. For the West Indies, see Hartley, "Illegitimacy," and Smith, "Hierarchy and dual marriage." For Scotland, see Andrew Blaikie, *Illegitimacy, Sex, and Society: Northeast Scotland, 1750–1900* (Oxford: Clarendon Press, 1993).

deep-seated anxieties about hybridity and corrupting British norms of respectability.

III

The first chapter explores the ways in which cultural representations about native female colonial companions developed in European descriptions about eighteenth-century India. Drawing from a growing scholarship on the culture of orientalism, and the culture of literary and visual arts, overlapping notions of sympathy, friendship, and cooperation were reinforced by the kind of cultural sociability that the British-Indian interracial romances represented in the popular European imagination of India in the eighteenth century. Yet this notion of romance was highly circumscribed and limited by concerns about the moral and political corruption that intimacy between Europeans and natives represented in the political sphere. Native women were made invisible while assumed to be the grounds on which these anxieties about sexual and racial transgression were elaborated. These competing discourses of cross-cultural interaction frame some of the shifts that I track through empirical research in the rest of the study.

The second and third chapters address the ways in which European men negotiated the social consequences of their sexual transgressions across racial categories, proving themselves to be both ambivalent and anxious about having gone native by cohabiting with a native woman. Chapter 2 argues that the political culture of the courts of the residents in late eighteenth-century and early nineteenth-century India enabled relationships with women at the court to provide British political agents with privileged access to local princely society. Yet in spite of its relative acceptability, Englishmen were often called to defend their romances, as in the case of Colonel James Kirkpatrick and General William Palmer in the courts at Hyderabad and Pune. Men often expressed ambivalence about how racial hybridity would affect the future prospects of their children in British or in Indian society, whether the mothers were of aristocratic blood or low-ranking female slaves and maidservants. By negotiating between "going native" and the risks this acculturation posed to their children, men made their selves into good patriarchs, providing for and instructing their descendants, even when their families were highly uncommon.

The fourth chapter turns to wills and other documents produced by native women who had some association with a European man. In examining what are often fragments of women's lives, this chapter raises and explores the question of women's subjectivity and agency.

This chapter explores how women fashioned their subjectivities, often in strategic ways to respond to the larger contexts of their worlds. Constitutive of the cultural and gender frontiers between Indians and Britons, many of these women relied on hybrid forms of identification, for instance, using European names, but writing in native languages; or claiming to be Christian, but asking for Hindu and Muslim death rituals; using both European china and Indian brass in their households; owning and wearing native and European dress.

Chapters 5 and 6 turn to the bureaucratic and institutional practices that the East India Company relied on to deal with the problems produced by interracial households. The process of men making themselves into patriarchs converged with a process by which governmental institutions of the early colonial state became increasingly invested in protecting a man's legal rights over his household. By detailing the ways in which native women's interactions with European men in the bazaar, the cantonment, and in their households, became matters of concern to Company bureaucracies, these chapters argue that everyday practices of interracial intimacy became a matter of importance for constituting the policies and practices of the nascent colonial state.

Chapter 5 examines how the English courts dealt with inheritance disputes and incidents of domestic violence within households that were headed by European men but included native women. Because the criminal and civil disputes occurred in households in which the patriarch was a European, they were adjudicated in front of British judges who had little experience with conjugal couples who did not have a legitimate marital contract but assumed that colonial concubinage was legally akin to legitimate marriage. Chapter 6 focuses on the military of the East India Company and examines its reliance on the domestic and sexual labor of native women living in the barracks with European soldiers. In addition to various policy disputes between various arms of the Company's bureaucracy in accounting for and recognizing the importance of local women in the military operations of British expansion in India, this chapter addresses the establishment of two charitable institutions by the East India Company. Lord Clive's Fund, meant to deal with the widows of European soldiers, and the Military Orphan Society, meant to provide schooling and financial support for the orphans of European soldiers, gave rise to various policies that linked the families of Company employees with the Company's growing state apparatus.

Although Indian women were increasingly kept from receiving charitable benefits as the domestic partners of British men, they continued to appear in the archives to make requests of the East India

Company's establishment. Rather than being silent participants in the colonial encounter, Indian women formed their own expectations vis-à-vis the British Company state and pushed British officials to be specific about who could be considered a deserving beneficiary of the Company's charity. I end with this chapter to demonstrate the ways in which class and racial anxieties emerged from the circumstances of interracial sex and miscegenation and merged with the interests of a developing colonial state. By examining the ways in which Indian women made claims on their own behalf and European men articulated their fears, I draw attention to the dialogic mode of interaction that occurred between ruler and ruled to form the sexual norms and hierarchies of race that became critical to the British colonial regime after the middle of the nineteenth century.

Definitions and terms

I have used terms such as *bibi* and *begum* which had specific meanings within the context of eighteenth-century India. Bibi (also spelled beebee) generally meant wife or lady when used by speakers of Hindi or Urdu. In the context of colonial society, however, bibi was often used to refer to the female companions of Englishmen, whether those women were Indian or not. *Burra Bibi* generally stood for the Englishwoman who was the wife of the commanding officer; this term came to have a pejorative tinge attached to it, particularly after the middle of the nineteenth century. In this study, I have used bibi to signify local women who cohabited with Europeans. Begum ordinarily means women of high rank or status, generally women who were Muslim.[103] Yet, in the eighteenth century, women without noble status were often referred to as begum and occasionally, bibi and begum were used interchangeably.[104] The term "companion" was one that British men most often used in their wills to describe their relationships with local women;

---

[103] The OED makes reference to the Begums of Awadh who featured prominently in the impeachment trial of Warren Hastings. A *begum* is defined in *Hobson-Jobson: A Glossary of Anglo-Indian Colloquial Words and Phrases* (London 1886) as "a princess, a mistress, a lady of rank; applied to Mahommedan [Muslim] ladies." Also spelled begam or beegum.

[104] Cf. IOL, Eur MSS E 25, Diary of Mackrabie, dated 9 March 1776: "Mrs. Clavering was there and the Misses and the General and Bebby Johnson..." Later, in the same diary, dated 12 Sept. 1776, "we must sup with the Begum (a lady so called, Begums are widows of Princes and great men). This lady is a relict of Governor [William] Watts." "Bebby" Johnson and "Begum" Watts are one and the same. See *The Calcutta of Begum Johnson*, by Ivor Edwards-Stuart (London: BACSA, 1990). Bibi Faiz Baksh who later became attached with Major William Palmer was also known as Begum.

I have followed their usage in order to preserve historical sensitivity but by no means subscribe to the belief that these relationships were always based on equal and consensual companionship. Other terms that were often used were "my housekeeper," "my girl," "a woman under my protection." As parallel studies on eighteenth-century colonial societies have noted, "'housekeeper' was often a colonial euphemism for concubine."[105]

Another descriptive that needs some clarification is my use of the term "Indian." Because the period covered in the study pre-dates a nationalist consciousness or sense of India, I have avoided using the term. Although many late eighteenth- and early nineteenth-century British documents call the indigenous peoples of the Indian subcontinent "Indian," these groups differentiated themselves from each other through various caste, ethnic, religious, and regional designations. I have also avoided "South Asian," in large part because it is a contemporary term that describes a region of the world that is defined by postcolonial nations that constitute it. Instead, I have used "native," which was the term that was commonly used at the turn of the nineteenth century. To avoid repetition, I have also used "indigenous" women or "local" women to denote female colonial companions, although I am aware that these terms are often wrongly understood as representing only non-European populations. Similarly, I have used European to describe a population that identified as "white," but were often citizens of different national polities. To avoid repetition, I have used "British" and "English," where appropriate. Because so few of the documents indicate clear identity markers for the colonial companion I have discussed here, I have deliberately *not* used terms such as "Bihari [from Bihar]," "chamar [of the chamar caste]," and so on.

---

[105] On the Dutch mixed-race community in Batavia, see Taylor, *Social World*, p. 147. This term was also used in slave colonies in North America and the Caribbean; see Adele Logan Alexander, *Ambiguous Lives: Free Women of Color in Rural Georgia* (Fayetteville: University of Arkansas Press, 1991), p. 34; Raymond Smith, "Hierarchy and dual marriage," p. 173; Beckles, *Centering Women*, pp. 25–6.

1   Colonial companions

An early nineteenth-century British guidebook for India, or "complete guide to gentlemen intended for the civil, military, or naval service of the Honourable East India Company," listed ways that Englishmen could productively avail themselves of native women who would labor as housekeepers and could also become "bosom friends." Capt. Thomas Williamson, who had spent much of the 1780s and 1790s in India noted that concubinage was a widespread practice because it was much more practical and economical to cohabit with a native companion than it would have been to marry a European woman.[1] Other British descriptions similarly acknowledged that European men commonly cohabited with local women: "It is a very general practise for Englishmen in India to entertain a *cara amica* of the Country," wrote one commentator in 1805.[2]

In spite of the prevalence of interracial conjugal arrangements, many British observers agreed that these domestic arrangements were rarely publicly acknowledged. One wrote that these relationships were, "at the same time so tacitly sanctioned by married families, who scruple not to visit at the house of a bachelor that [sic] retains a native mistress."[3] Even Williamson observed that, "no lady, native of India, even though her father should have been of the highest rank in the King's or Company's service, and though she be married to a person of that description, is ever invited to those assemblies given by the governor

---

[1] *East India Vade Mecum or complete guide to gentlemen intended for the civil, military, or naval service of the Honourable East India Company*, 2 vols., by Capt. Thomas Williamson (London: Black, Parry and Kingsbury, 1810).
[2] "A young civilian in Bengal," *Bengal Past and Present*, vol. XXIX, pt. II (April–June 1925), p. 125. The manuscript is attributed to Henry Roberdeau, a writer in the Bengal Presidency for the East India Company during the years 1801 to 1807, who was based mainly in the district of Mymensingh.
[3] *Sketches of India; or observations descriptive of the Scenery etc. in Bengal*, written in the years 1811, 1812, 1813, 1814 (London: Black, Parbury and Allen, 1816), p. 169.

on public occasions."[4] Williamson's guidebook, *The East India Vade Mecum*, was first published in 1810. When it was reissued only fifteen years later in 1825, with corrections by J. B. Gilchrist, linguist and grammarian, the sections about native companions were completely excised, suggesting that instructions on keeping a *bibi* were no longer appropriate for future servants of the East India Company.[5]

While keeping a native female companion and living like a native was a sign of cosmopolitanism, or broad-mindedness, of a level of sophistication unavailable to those who were at "home," it was also a sign of the kind of cultural and racial hybridity that threatened the social whiteness of colonial societies. As Homi Bhabha has suggested, this type of hybridity gave rise to ambivalence within the colonial order and destabilized the authority of colonial forms of power.[6] In early British India, ambivalence about empire and sexuality took several forms. One persistent theme was that European men cohabited with local women because it was only a reasonable by-product of hetero-sexual necessity (and because there were very few European women). A second theme, marked in accounts as peculiar or strange, was that some men came to be so devoted to their exotic companions that they took up native manners, abandoning appropriate British comportment altogether. A third theme was that these women were quite degraded: many were lower-class and uneducated, superstitious, jealous, and violent – in other words, insufficiently respectable for physical intimacy with the British ruling classes. Anxieties over maintaining sufficient bodily proximity to Indians had as much to do with maintaining a sense of Britishness in an alien environment as about legitimizing and preserving British political authority.[7] These recurring themes were repeatedly reinforced through various accounts, demonstrating the ways in which the practice of interracial sex carried grave social risks.

These early accounts described "India" to the uninformed Briton, showing it to be exotic, erotic, and appealing; they also alerted those on the Indian subcontinent of the bodily threats they faced while they

---

[4] *East India Vade Mecum*, vol. I, p. 452.
[5] The second edition was published in 1825 in London by Wm. H. Allen and Co., edited by J. B. Gilchrist. On Gilchrist, see Bernard Cohn, "The language of command and the command of language," in *Colonialism and Its Forms of Knowledge* (Delhi: Oxford University Press, 1996), pp. 34–46.
[6] Homi Bhabha, *The Location of Culture* (London: Routledge, 1992), pp. 111–13.
[7] Elizabeth M. Collingham, *Imperial Bodies: the Physical Experience of the Raj, c. 1800–1947* (London: Polity Press, 2001), chs. 1–3; Felicity Nussbaum, *Torrid Zones: Maternity, Sexuality and Empire in Eighteenth-Century English Narratives* (Baltimore: Johns Hopkins Press, 1995).

lived there. Frequently published accounts of social life in India were repetitive, almost formulaic, showing the process of constructing Britishness in India. Native women are thus often represented, when they do appear, as threats to Britishness precisely because they disrupted the picture of appropriate social and cultural life in the colonial settlement, which was frequently represented as a "whitened" social space of mansions, grand balls, and horseback riding. Indeed, the "city of palaces" could have easily been called the city of white palaces, since Calcutta's many buildings sparkled with limestone.[8] As a plethora of travelers' accounts suggested, life in Calcutta was a series of parties, social engagements, and parade of fashions.[9] Moreover, the exclusion of native women from these accounts was a discursive way of containing the dangers represented by British men cohabiting with and even willingly participating in native domestic life.

European representations of interracial relationships, in text and in art, mirrored much of the historical evidence on colonial companions: commonly acknowledged but rarely publicly discussed. Accounts of interracial liaisons constructed the female colonial companion as exotic but markedly silent. As Felicity Nussbaum has noted, "Indian women are not granted subjectivity ... instead they are represented by others as victimized or erotic, and as greedy and vain."[10] By examining the ways in which this exclusion occurred in literary and artistic discourses of late eighteenth and early nineteenth centuries in northern India, this chapter argues that cultural expressions gave rise to and supported British imperial ideologies and practices.

Textual accounts that European visitors, civil servants, and military officers in India wrote for the benefit of British reading audiences often covered the same ground repeatedly: they commented on the strange manners and customs of the local inhabitants and on the daily social life of Europeans in Calcutta, which was the center of Company activity on the Indian subcontinent. These accounts were noticeably different from accounts that appeared later, particularly those that were published after the mutiny in 1857: for example, the violence that marked

---

[8] J. P. Losty, *Calcutta: City of Palaces, a Survey of the City in the Days of the East India Company, 1690–1858* (London: British Library, 1990); Swati Chattopadhyay, *Representing Calcutta: Modernity, Nationalism, and the Colonial Uncanny* (London: Routledge, 2005), ch. 2.

[9] Lady Maria Nugent, *A Journal from the year 1811 till the year 1815: a voyage to and residence in India, with a tour to the northwestern parts of the British possessions in that country under the Bengal government* (London, 1839), see for instance, vol. I, pp. 92–9; vol. II, pp. 247 ff.

[10] Nussbaum, *Torrid Zones*, p. 170.

later accounts of racial and sexual anxieties were largely absent.[11] Instead, India and its native women were represented as exotic, alien, and peculiar; the dangers they presented were in terms of how they disrupted an idealized British domesticity that included images of middle-class British women drinking tea, wearing white dresses, with elaborately coiffed hair. Portraits and paintings of Indian women, on the other hand, showed colonial companions in saris, jewels, reclining on the pillows, peeking out of picture frames that were an analog to their harem lives. Shown in exhibits and salons in Europe, these paintings visually appreciated India's exotic charms while carefully containing their sensuality on the canvas.

Specific forms of representation worked in tandem with developing a sense that interracial liaisons, although common, threatened white colonial society by their existence. Indian female companions were noticeably excluded from various textual accounts of colonial social life and when they were represented in art, their appearance was carefully managed so that their relationships with British men did not compromise British rule. These British representations, with a widespread circulation in London and Calcutta, worked to define and defend British territorial expansions and political interests on the Indian subcontinent, while they asserted what constituted Britishness in the colonies.[12]

While historians have commonly asserted that the early period of colonial rule was reasonably free of racial and cultural prejudice, that British officials had an appreciation for India and its heritage, and that it was only after the 1830s that Britain started to see itself as distinctly superior, these visual and textual representations suggest that the process of intercultural amity and friendship was much more uneven and contested.[13] Textual and artistic discourses worked side by side with

[11] For careful readings of sexual/racial anxieties post-1857, Patrick Brantlinger, *Rule of Darkness: British Literature and Imperialism, 1830–1914* (Ithaca: Cornell University Press, 1988), ch. 7; Jenny Sharpe, *Allegories of Empire* (Minneapolis: University of Minnesota Press, 1993); Nancy Paxton, *Writing under the Raj: Gender, Race and Rape in the British Colonial Imagination, 1830–1947* (New Brunswick, NJ: Rutgers University Press, 1999). As Paxton argues, by 1857, Burke's late eighteenth-century rhetoric of British men defiling native women had shifted to a different combination of fears about native men sexually violating the bodies of English women.

[12] Kate Teltscher, *India Inscribed: European and British Writing on India, 1600–1800* (Delhi: Oxford University Press, 1995), pp. 3–5; Kathleen Wilson, *The Island Race: Englishness, Empire and Gender in the Eighteenth Century* (New York: Routledge, 2003).

[13] T. C. P. Spear, *The Nabobs: English Social Life in 18th Century India* (New York: Penguin, 1963); Thomas Trautmann, *Aryans and British India* (Berkeley: University of California Press, 1997); C. A. Bayly, *Rulers, Townsmen and Bazaars: North Indian Society in the Age of British Expansion, 1770–1870* (Cambridge: Cambridge University Press, 1983); *Empire and Information: Intelligence Gathering and Social Communication in India, 1780–1870* (Cambridge: Cambridge University Press, 1996).

the development of institutional racial and cultural distance between Britain and its Indian subjects. Through the production of textual and visual discourse, conjugal relationships with local women were seen as partially acceptable but problematic in the course of proper British life in India. Even before the East India Company attempted to regulate and manage interracial arrangements and mixed-race offspring, commentators frequently remarked that interracial relationships should be viewed as irregular, although they were reasonably common.

I

The history of the English in India started officially in 1600 when Queen Elizabeth granted a charter to the East India Company to explore and begin trade with the Indian subcontinent, although Europeans had been going to India at least since the early 1500s. In these early years, Portuguese traders who established trading posts along the western coast of India were known to have married local women and settled down.[14] Dutch and British traders were less numerous and took up with local women sporadically but rarely married the women with whom they had sexual relationships. The earliest marriage registers for the Church of England appeared in 1713: between 1713 and 1729 only about a half-dozen members of the Company's posts were married every year.

Although the numbers of marriages between British men and native women went up, the number of European men in India far exceeded the numbers of marriages that occurred. Between 1757–1800, 1,581 marriages occurred among Europeans in Bengal leading to the rough estimate that "only one in four writers, and just possibly more, married, only one in ten of the cadets did so, and anything from one in fifteen to one in forty-five of the other ranks, and with a perhaps smaller range of error, one in eight of the non-official Europeans in Bengal."[15]

---

[14] For a more complete description, see C. R. Boxer, *Race Relations in the Portuguese Colonial Empire, 1415–1825* (Oxford: Clarendon, 1963), pp. 57–85.

[15] Suresh Chandra Ghosh, *The Social Condition of the British Community in Bengal, 1757–1800* (Leiden: E. J. Brill, 1970), pp. 60–61. Between 1757 and 1800, 756 writers went to Bengal and 1,870 cadets, or military men. With a total of 2,626 cadets and writers, only 339 of the marriages can be attributed among this group. These numbers do not account for rank-and-file soldiers. In 1757, there were about 1,000 troops in Bengal; by 1767, this number had tripled and by 1784, there were over 4,000. The number steadily increased so that by 1800, there were over 5,000 troops in Bengal alone and 18,000 in the three presidencies. By 1826 there were over 30,000 British soldiers in India. See Home Misc. 85, "General Abstract of the Last Return of His Majesty's and the Company's European Forces in India," Feb. 1790, p. 123; see also O.I.O.C., Home Misc. 492, pp. 485, 489.

These numbers suggest that relatively few Englishmen legitimized their relationships with local women in church, although large numbers of Englishmen cohabited with or maintained some sort of sexual arrangement with local women. In the years between 1780 and 1785, one out of three wills filed in Calcutta included a reference to a native companion or concubine.[16] In the same period, over half of the children baptized in St. John's Church were illegitimate, which was marked in the records when the word "natural" appeared next to their names and their mothers' names were absent or were listed with "native" in the column for mother.[17] These proportional figures suggest that although less than 7 percent of all European men were known to be married while serving in India, substantially more, anywhere from 20 to 50 percent, were known to be involved in some sort of sexual liaison with a local woman.

By the early 1800s, some records suggested a drop in the occurrence of interracial relationships. In the wills from 1805 to 1810, one out of every four wills included a reference to a native woman; in the baptism records, fewer than one-tenth of all the children baptized were known to be born of native mothers.[18] While the records show that fewer men married or cohabited with local women and baptized their mixed-race offspring, it may be that fewer men acknowledged their children or their companions publicly through court and church records. By the early nineteenth century, almost one in three Europeans in the presidency towns was Eurasian or mixed-race, suggesting that although there was little documentary proof of interracial liaisons, the mixed-race population was growing as there were six times as many Eurasians being born in India than "pure" Europeans.[19] As in Britain, illegitimacy among Britons in India was a common feature of lower and lower-middle-class family life that was often compensated for by a church baptism.[20] By 1830, although one out of six wills included a reference to

---

[16] C.J. Hawes, *Poor Relations: the Making of a Eurasian Community in British India, 1773–1833* (London: Curzon, 1996), pp. 3–4.

[17] St. John's Church Records, Calcutta; see also O.I.O.C., N-series; *Bengal Past and Present*, vol. XXVI, pp. 142–68, vol. XXVIII, pp. 193–221.

[18] St. John's Church, Baptism registers, 1805–1810.

[19] Hawes, *Poor Relations*, pp. 4, 17.

[20] Peter Laslett *et al.*, *Bastardy and Its Comparative History* (Cambridge: Harvard University Press, 1980); Andrew Blaikie, *Illegitimacy, Sex and Society: Northeast Scotland, 1750–1900* (Oxford: Clarendon, 1993); John Gillis, "Servants, sexual relations, and the risks of illegitimacy in London, 1801–1900," *Feminist Studies* 5 (1979) 142–73. Laslett has noted that the incidence of baptism suggests that parents sought societal and religious legitimacy for the birth of the child, even if s/he had been conceived outside of marriage.

a native companion and the number of mixed-race children baptized was much less than one-tenth of the total,[21] the number of native women who had inherited from men who wrote wills was growing. What these types of contradictory figures show is that this colonial society was highly effective at recording a decline in interracial cohabitation and out-of-wedlock births, although the people who lived in this community continued to live across racial boundaries.

As the Company changed from being a commercial operation to exercising direct political rule over millions of Indian subjects in the eighteenth century, the types of textual accounts that appeared about India in Europe changed. From the 1600s onward, a range of European writers, travelers, clerics, military men, and diplomats recounted stories of their travels to the Indian subcontinent. As Kate Teltscher has noted, throughout the seventeenth and eighteenth centuries, there was steady publication of travel literature about the orient in Europe. French and Dutch accounts were often translated into English and collections of travelers' accounts appeared in journals and newspapers.[22] After the 1750s, however, much of this literature was in English, largely because by then the English had succeeded in becoming the dominant power in the Indian subcontinent.

These accounts ranged from travelers' accounts to historical narratives, political pamphlets, and biographies. Some of the first accounts in the 1750s were by East India Company men-cum-historians and they narrated the history of India and of the declining Mughal empire. Between 1757, when the British defeated the troops of Siraj-ud-daulah, the nawab of Bengal at Plassey, and 1765, when the British gained the right to collect the revenues of Bengal, no less than

---

[21] Hawes, *Poor Relations*, p. 17.

[22] Teltscher, *India Inscribed*, ch. 1. French travelers such as Francois Bernier, Jean-Baptiste Tavernier, and Jean de Thevenot, Dutch travelers such as John van Linschoten, and Portuguese chroniclers such as Ludovico di Varthema all contributed to creating an appetite for the "marvels" of traveling. As well, the twenty-volume collection of travels edited by Richard Haykluyt and Samuel Purchas, first published in 1625, went through dozens of printings by the early 1900s. See also Janice Bailey Goldschmidt and Martin Kalfatovic, "Sex, Lies and European Hegemony: travel literature and ideology," *Journal of Popular Culture* 26 (Spring 1993): 141–53; Mary Louise Pratt, *Imperial Eyes: Travel Writing and Transculturation* (London: Routledge, 1992); Stephen Greenblatt, ed., "Introduction," *New World Encounters* (Berkeley: University of California Press, 1993).

a half dozen historical narratives were written about India.[23] The pace of publication increased through the 1770s and 1780s, as Parliament, and various political figures debated how best to trade in India without becoming too deeply implicated in the habits of oriental despotism and the political corruption that attended it. As Sara Suleri has noted, these public debates exposed a crucial problematic of colonial rule: the ways in which colonial activities threatened "the imperial psyche" with guilt and anxiety.[24] Company rule in India was, from the start, fraught with tension and uncertainty over how involved to be in Indian affairs, although as Bernard Cohn and others have argued, arguments against intervention enabled the further involvement of the East India Company through the course of the late eighteenth century.[25] While literary analysts such as Suleri and Teltscher have focused on the ways in which the imperial psyche attempted to resolve conflicts over political corruption, anxieties about interracial sexual intimacy and miscegenation were central to concerns about moral corruption from the 1770s onward.[26]

Captain Williamson's guidebook, the *East India Vade Mecum*, is perhaps the best-known description of the practice of keeping a native concubine. Published in 1810, the guide detailed much about what a newcomer to India could expect. It listed how much clothing one should take, how much money one could expect to spend and how to manage a household of servants. The second edition, which was published in 1825, was amended and instead of the sections on how to keep a native woman, there were instructions for Englishwomen and

---

[23] Well-known histories were Robert Orme, *A History of the Military Transactions of the British Nation in Indostan*, 2 vols. (London, 1763); J. Z. Holwell, *Interesting Historical Events, Relative to the Province of Bengal and the Empire of Indostan* (London, 1761); Alexander Dow, *The History of Hindostan*, 2 vols. (London, 1768). Other histories, such as R. O. Cambridge, *An Account of the War in India, between the English and French, on the Coast of Coromandel, from the year 1750 to the year 1760* (London, 1761); Claude Marie Guyon, *A New History of the East-Indies, Ancient and Modern* (London, 1757); *A Complete History of the War in India from 1749 to 1761 between the English and the French ... With an accurate detail of Colonel Clive's military transactions, etc.* (London, 1761).

[24] Sara Suleri, *The Rhetoric of English India* (Chicago: University of Chicago, 1992), p. 26.

[25] Bernard S. Cohn, *An Anthropologist Among the Historians* (Delhi: Oxford University Press, 1987), pp. 208–12; see also C. A. Bayly, *Indian Society and the Making of the British Empire* (Cambridge: Cambridge University Press, 1988), chs. 2 and 3.

[26] Kenneth Ballhatchet, *Race, Sex and Class Under the Raj: Imperial Attitudes and Policies, 1793–1905* (New York: St. Martin's Press, 1980), Introduction and ch. 1. See also Bayly, *Indian Society*, pp. 78, 83.

their journeys to India.[27] His lengthy descriptions of interracial liaisons form an important departure point: not only was his work an instruction manual on how a British man ought to live in India, he also conveyed a sense of ambivalence and anxiety as to whether keeping a native woman was ultimately appropriate, no matter how practical it was under the circumstances.

Williamson conveyed both how common was the practice of cohabitation and argued that under local circumstances, it was socially respectable:

In India, a woman "under the protection" of an European gentleman, is accounted, not only among the natives, but even by his countrymen, to be equally sacred, as though she were married to him; and the woman herself, values her reputation, exactly in proportion as she may have refrained from indulging in variety: some are said to have passed twenty years, or more, without the possibility for scandal to attach to their conduct.[28]

In another passage, he noted that even when they lost caste by living in the home of a European man, local women were somewhat religious, albeit in a peculiar way:

I could adduce instances, wherein native women have conducted themselves invariably in the most decorous manner, and evinced the utmost fidelity, in every particular, to their keepers; some have absolutely sacrificed property to no inconsiderable amount, and given up every pretension to *cast*; that is, to admission among those of the same sect, or faith, braving the most bitter taunts, and the reproaches of their friends and relatives.

Here it may not be out of the way to notice that strange medley of religion, and of interest, some may say of love, which is observable in the conduct of native women, either residing under the protection of Europeans, or coming under the ordinary description of *kusbeen* (i.e., prostitutes). Their rigid adherence to, or, at least, their superficial observance of, whatever relates to the purification of their persons, after contact, is admirable! It is not uncommon, among those professing immense purity, both of body, and of soul, to get up several times during the night, for the purpose of ablution.[29]

---

[27] In addition to the *East India Vade Mecum*, Williamson also published a volume titled *Oriental Field Sports* in London in 1807 and the text to a volume of color drawings by Charles D'Oyley titled *The European in India* (London, 1813).

[28] Williamson, *East India Vade Mecum*, vol. I, p. 451.

[29] *Ibid.*, p. 344.

Indeed, Williamson spoke of the devotion that many men felt for their companions:

The attachment of many European gentlemen to their native mistresses, is not to be described! An infatuation, beyond all comparison, often prevails, causing every confidence, of whatever description, to be reposed in the sable queen of the harem![30]

In describing the relationships of military men, Williamson commented:

... in the early part of their career, young men attach themselves to the woman of this country; and acquire a liking, or taste, for their society and customs, which soon supersedes every other attraction; ... it is not to be wondered at, that a connexion, commenced in a casual manner, should become firm and lasting.[31]

The narrative that an Englishman could become so emotionally attached to a native woman that he refused to return to England was one that recurred, suggesting that a relationship with a native woman was often the road of no return. William Hickey, famed memoirist, told a story about Dr. James Wilson, who "became so miserable at the idea of forever quitting a Hindostanee woman who had lived with him many years and borne him several children that he could not prevail on himself to leave her!"[32] Richard Blechynden, a merchant who left a voluminous set of diaries, shows that although his companion caused him a lot of grief, and they fought constantly, he could not bear the thought of abandoning her.[33]

In spite of how stable these interracial relationships appeared, how scrupulously the women could behave, and the valuable services that these women provided in military cantonments, Williamson explained to his European readers that although European men might have preferred a socially appropriate marriage to an Englishwoman, there were not enough to go around. Throughout the two-volume work, Williamson engaged in a kind of conversation with his reader, answering their imagined responses to his account. First, there was the question of numbers: Williamson estimated that there were 250 Englishwomen

---

[30] *Ibid.*

[31] Williamson, *The European in India*, pp. xix–xx.

[32] *Memoirs of William Hickey*, Alfred Spencer, ed. (London: Hurst & Blackett, Ltd, 1839), vol. IV, pp. 271–2.

[33] Peter Robb, "Clash of Cultures?: An Englishman in Calcutta in the 1790s," School of Oriental and African Studies, University of London, Inaugural Lecture, March 12, 1998.

in Bengal, while there were over 4000 "European male inhabitants of respectability" (which included military officers and civil servants, but not rank-and-file soldiers).[34] Second, it would be completely unreasonable to bring women to Bengal: the climate would not suit the delicate constitution of the women and it would cost a fortune to send a young girl to Bengal.[35] Finally, keeping an English household would cost a fortune for the young civil servant. Whereas a native companion would cost Sicca Rs. 40 monthly or £60 yearly, an Englishwoman would cost almost five times that.[36] Williamson concluded, "that matrimony is not so practicable in India as in Europe," meaning that matrimony to a woman who was racially and socially English was not very practical. To the imagined question of whether European men ought to be marrying native women, Williamson noted that since these women and their offspring would never be granted permission to go to England, marriage was out of the question. In Williamson's mind, interracial cohabitation was a by-product of living in India over a long period of time, akin to chronic dysentery or tanned, leathery skin.

But Williamson made some important distinctions for the readers of his books. He repeatedly claimed that although these habits and manners might appear peculiar and uncivilized to European readers, Hindus and Muslims had various behavioral codes that were intrinsic to their cultures; knowledge and appreciation of these cultural practices, however distasteful, heightened one's cosmopolitanism.[37] Although these female companions were faithful and served their masters well (read: obedient), according to Williamson, they tended to be jealous, violent, overly concerned with luxury and opulence and prone to peculiar habits such as chewing pan and smoking a hookah.[38]

---

[34] Williamson, *East India Vade Mecum*, vol. I, p. 452.

[35] *Ibid.*: "no lady can be landed there, under respectable circumstances throughout, for less than five hundred pounds."

[36] *Ibid.*, pp. 173–5; 414–16. See also S. C. Ghosh, *Social Condition of the British Community*, pp. 66–8, where he notes that in 1793, after Cornwallis reformed the pay structure, junior servants made £500 a year after 3 years service. Previous to that, only men in the Calcutta Council and high-ranking officers could afford to have their European wives join them in India.

[37] See, for instance, Williamson, *East India Vade Mecum*, vol. II, pp. 420–3, where Williamson described dancing girls and their traditional role in local life: he noted that although dancing girls were often slave children, Muslims felt that it was better to rescue a child from deprivation by putting her to work than to let her die. Unlike Europeans, who felt strongly against slavery, Muslims, in Williamson's account, had no prohibitions against adopting a slave child and giving her away to the highest bidder.

[38] Williamson, *East India Vade Mecum*, vol. I, pp. 412–13, 449.

The Portuguese companions tended to be better housekeepers than the Hindus and Muslims, but were more prone to embezzling from the household accounts, drinking too much, and engaging in the excesses of Catholic worship.[39] In the text to a volume illustrated by Charles D'oyley, Williamson noted that dancing girls from Bengal were less renowned than those from Awadh, but that all of these women, particularly those who "rise to very important situations, eventually leave their posterity to rank with the greatest family in the country."[40] Nonetheless, there was no comparison between native companions and their putative Others: Williamson noted that "my fair country-women appear most conspicuously pre-eminent," because they had "agreeable manners, polished language, highly cultivated minds, and pleasing attentions."[41]

Perhaps the most important distinction that Williamson drew had to do with class and its concomitant relationship to the effects of racial mixing. Although he argued that interracial relationships were necessary in the absence of more appropriate heterosexual relationships for civil servants and military officers, he suggested that relationships between local women and rank-and-file European soldiers were considered largely beneficial for them and practical for the Company's establishment. For soldiers, who occasionally married their native companions, these women provided a range of household services: they cooked, cleaned, and secured provisions. In sickness, Williamson noted "their attendance is invaluable."[42] Concubinage was, in Williamson's view, far less dangerous for rank-and-file soldiers than taking up with a common prostitute. Moreover, European wives who traveled with military regiments often died and those that survived "present a rather masculine appearance," thereby losing the special feminine traits that European women were known to possess.[43] (Nonetheless, the offspring of these strong, but faux European women and European men "usually prove remarkably hardy; whereas, the issue of an European father by a native woman, is usually of an effeminate, weakly constitution, and

---

[39] *Ibid.*, p. 413. The women Williamson referred to as "Portuguese" were mixed-race women born of Portuguese traders and local women.

[40] *Costumes and Customs of Modern India*, from a collection of drawings by Charles D'oyley, Esq., Preface and copious descriptions by Captain Thomas Williamson (Calcutta, 1810).

[41] Williamson, *East India Vade Mecum*, vol. I, p. 415.

[42] *Ibid.*, p. 453.

[43] *Ibid.*, p. 455.

of a disposition by no means entitled to commendation."[44]) As the colonizing classes defined themselves against natives and lower-ranking Europeans, racial categories were maintained by careful calibration of who could sleep with whom.[45]

A self-consciously styled guidebook such as Williamson's reaffirmed normative codes of British social behavior that were produced by other texts that detailed Anglo-Indian social life in Calcutta. One, the anonymously written epistolary novel, *Hartly House* (1789) followed a romance between an Englishwoman and a Bengali Brahmin that threatened to disrupt the sexual politics of the colonial imaginary. Another text, the *Original Letters of Eliza Fay* (1817), further illuminated how social life in Calcutta revolved entirely around the highest ranking officials and their European wives, carefully skirting the issue of men who had native companions at home. And a series of pulp novels and stories reinforced British sexual and racial correctness through various narrative outcomes. In these stories, either the female colonial companion died or she proved to be faithless and deceitful, thereby proving interracial intimacy with native women as fated for tragedy.

Although all of these works made some claim to veracity, what these narratives reproduced for the British was often not an actual picture / of social life in British India, but an idealized, imagined vision of social engagements in the respectable spaces of white, upper-class British society where the only women present were Englishwomen. In a vision that purportedly imitated aristocratic living in Britain, there were few lower-class Europeans, even fewer Indians (except for household servants), and no native female companions. In spite of the exotic location, British society in Calcutta during the eighteenth century was highly insular, a modified, and often laughable, replica of aristocratic culture in Britain, with behaviors associated with respectable society in England transplanted to India. As Peter Marshall has noted, "In all essentials Anglo-India gloried in its Britishness ... [although] the Britishness of the British in India could look odd or outdated to sophisticated visitors."[46] Indeed, as numerous advertisements in the weekly *Calcutta Gazette* demonstrated, frequent advertisements of the

---

[44] *Ibid.*, pp. 455–6.
[45] Ann Stoler, *Carnal Knowledge and Imperial Power: Race and the Intimate in Colonial Rule* (Berkeley: University of California Press, 2002), ch. 2.
[46] Peter Marshall, "British Society and the East India Company," *Modern Asian Studies* 31 (1997): 107.

latest European goods supplied Calcutta's most fashionable shoppers.[47] The "consumer revolution" of eighteenth-century England clearly reached as far as the empire.[48]

One of the earliest accounts of British social life in eighteenth-century Calcutta was *Hartly House*, which was published in 1789 in London and Dublin and translated two years later into German.[49] Presented in the form of a series of letters from the heroine, Sophia Goldbourne, to her cousin Arabella, the correspondence detailed a range of observations about her daily life in Calcutta. She was the daughter of a Company civil servant and resided in the home of Mr. and Mrs. Hartly, who emerge from her description as the ideal couple and family: Mr. Hartly was an ideal patriarch, benevolent, successful, wise; Mrs. Hartly was a good hostess, an exceptional mother and a well-bred woman. Their comfortable home in Calcutta was attended by a fleet of servants, visited by the most important men, and the center of social activity. The Hartlys also had a bungalow outside Calcutta in which their two young children (aged five and three) resided with a governess who was the widow of a vicar. In the fresh air of the Calcutta countryside, the children were given an education in good morals and correct manners until they would eventually be sent to England for a proper education.[50]

As a young unmarried woman, she was clearly in great demand: one of the repetitive themes was the attention that all women received from men on the Company's establishment because cultivated European women were so few in number. Indeed, even married women basked

---

[47] For example, one advertisement read: "For the Ladies, a Variety of entire new-fashioned Zones, Shields, Medalions, and Centre clasps of Gold ... being such as universally worn at this time in England..." (March 25, 1784). Another advertisement offered "English and Dutch cheese, fine London porter and cider, musical instruments, elegant mahogany furniture, after the newest fashion in London; English cards, Flemish linen,..." (*Calcutta Gazette*, April 25, 1784 and May 6, 1784).

[48] See Neil McKendrick, John Brewer, and J. H. Plumb, *The Birth of a Consumer Society* (Bloomington: Indiana University Press, 1982); Mildred Archer, *Indian and British Portraiture, 1770–1825* (London: Sotheby Parke Benet, 1979), p. 50.

[49] One edition appeared in 1830, while another in 1888 and another in 1908. Recently, the book was reissued by Pluto Press, Winchester, UK, in 1989. The author is not known although several of *Hartly House*'s editors have speculated that it was the work of a couple given its wide-ranging attention to female domestic social life and history and politics. Felicity Nussbaum claims it is the work of Phebe Gibbs, a woman whose son spent some time in India, see Nussbaum, *Torrid Zones*, p. 173, fn. 16. Its popularity continued throughout the nineteenth century, as several more editions were published.

[50] *Hartly House*, pp. 64–6.

in male attention, while their discreet husbands looked away. Sadly, for Sophia, the attention she received was from much older men because "the young ones either chuse country-born ladies for wealth or having left their hearts behind them, enrich themselves in order to be united to their favorite Dulcineas in their native land."[51] Her daytime life was filled with card games, tea, horse races, and visits with other women. Her evenings were filled with balls, theater, and concerts. A steady diet of "English fare," accompanied her busy activities and she marveled repeatedly of the availability of all sorts of meats, fowl, and vegetables.[52]

A contemporaneous account, in the *Original Letters of Eliza Fay*, confirmed the details of an anglicized social life that *Hartly House* presented.[53] The dinner hour was two and their ordinary meal consisted of "a soup, a roast fowl, curry and rice, mutton pie, a fore quarter of lamb, a rice pudding, tarts, very good cheese, fresh churned butter, fine bread, excellent Madeira."[54] The holiday season was a long medley of public dinners, balls and theater. Christmas and New Year's were a big event on the Company's establishment; as well, the King's birthday was celebrated at the governor's house every year.[55] As in *Hartly House*, Eliza Fay confirmed the importance of mixing in the right sort of Calcutta society: by her account, the Fays' marriage fell apart because Mr. Fay failed to pay obeisance to the men in power.[56] Lady Chambers, the wife of Supreme Court Judge Sir Robert Chambers, featured prominently in Eliza Fay's account as a figure at the heart of British social life; indeed, Lady Chambers's diary was

---

[51] *Ibid.* (Pluto, 1989), p. 22. This was a common formula in "domestic" novels of this era: see Alison Sainsbury, "Married to the Empire: the Anglo-Indian domestic novel," in Bart Moore-Gilbert, ed., *Writing India, 1757–1990: the Literature of British India* (Manchester: Manchester University Press, 1996).

[52] *Ibid.*, pp. 32–7, 72, 96–7, 134–7, 153–6.

[53] Although the *Original Letters of Eliza Fay* were not published until after her death in 1817, the letters themselves were written through the early 1780s and traced her twelve-month journey to India, marked by various mishaps, including being taken prisoner by Hyder Ali, the ruler of Mysore's forces. In 1908, another edition was published in Calcutta with various amendments by Walter Firminger. In 1925, the original, without Firminger's corrections, was published in New York by Harcourt Brace; this edition was edited by E. M. Forster who wrote a lengthy introduction, footnotes, and restored Eliza Fay's words to the original that he had found on a visit to Calcutta.

[54] *Original Letters of Eliza Fay*, E. M. Forster, ed. (New York: Harcourt Brace, 1925), p. 191.

[55] *Eliza Fay*, pp. 202–3.

[56] *Ibid.*, pp. 200, 207–9.

filled with appointments with other upper-class European women of the establishment.[57]

Hartly House began with Sophia's promise not to marry in the east and become a "nabobess," or the wife of a nabob. As she restates this vow throughout, Sophia claimed that she has no intention of marrying a wealthy, old East India hand and forsaking true affection and compatibility for wealth.[58] Her promise was packed with anxiety about the moral and social effects of wealth gained through trading in India. The nabob, in late eighteenth-century Britain, was well-known as a man of the middling, or even lower, classes who had gone to India, made a fortune and returned to England with airs beyond his station; worse still, nabobs were often accused of having oriental tastes. Returning nabobs were thought to be showy, extravagant, gluttonous, and vulgar. Although they were wealthy and bought up country estates, nabobs were thought to lack gentility and modesty and, by their ostentatious behavior, threatened the landed aristocracy in England.[59] The term nabob was though to be a play on the Mughal term for local ruler, *nawab*, which was associated with the despotism of the Orient. Samuel Foote's play, "The Nabob or Asiatic Plunderer," performed in London in 1777, brought out several levels on which nabobs were worthy of satire for their relentless greed for opulence.[60] Other works of this period invoked the figure of the nabob as signs of how time spent in the orient corrupted one's morality and natural British sensibility. The anxiety that the orient, in the guise of the orientalized image of the nabob, was contaminating genteel British society with his inappropriate comportment, was repeatedly expressed in the literature at the turn of the nineteenth century.[61] William Thackeray's

---

[57] O.I.O.C., Mss. Eur. A 172, Lady Chambers's diary for 1784 of her social activities with Mrs. Warren Hastings, Mrs. William Jones, Mrs. John Hyde, Mrs. Nathaniel Halhed, Mrs. John Bristow, and Mrs. Trevor Plowden, who were wives of the Governor-General, the Chief Justice, a Supreme Court Judge, and three high-ranking civil servants, respectively.

[58] *Hartly House*, pp. 6, 157. For a clear articulation about the dangers of European women "Indianizing," see Collingham, *Imperial Bodies*, pp. 36–40.

[59] Spear, *Nabobs*, p. 37. See also Philip Lawson and Jim Philips, "'Our Execrable Banditti': perceptions of nabobs in mid eighteenth-century Britain," *Albion XVI* (1984): 225–41; Michael Edwardes, *The Nabobs at Home* (London: Constable, 1991).

[60] See Jyotsna Singh, *Colonial Narratives/Cultural Dialogues: Discoveries of India in the Language of Colonialism* (London: Routledge, 1996), pp. 52–60; Nandini Bhattacharya, *Reading the Splendid Body: Gender and Consumerism in Eighteenth-Century British Writing on India* (London: Associated University Presses, 1998), ch. 4.

[61] Collingham, *Imperial Bodies*, chs. 1–3; Renu Juneja, "The Native and the Nabob: representations of the Indian experience in eighteenth-century English literature," *Journal of Commonwealth Literature* 27 (1992): 183–98.

Vanity Fair (1837) introduced the laughable figure of Jos Sedley, the effeminate, cowardly district collector of Bogleywallah, who found himself the object of ridicule because of his opulent attire and corpulent body.[62] By disavowing a marriage with a nabob, Sophia in *Hartly House* invoked an element crucial to class anxiety among Britons in India ✓ and in Britain: she refused to marry a wealthy, but corrupt, man.

Although many men paid attention to her, it was the attention of a young Bengali Brahmin, the nephew of her father's *sarkar* (personal banker), that she found most pleasing. In a lengthy passage, she decides that Brahmins are men of the highest order. Pious, celibate, wholly nonviolent, and ethically scrupulous, Sophia claims,

to please a Bramin [sic] I must have perfections of the mental sort, little inferior to the purity and benignity of angels: – in a word, my good dispositions would be cultivated and brought forward by such an acquaintance, and my bad ones corrected; and as celibacy is their engagement, the soul would be the only object of attachment and admiration.[63]

With platonic love feeding her growing infatuation with this young, implicitly effeminate, man, she pursued a friendship with him while he tutored her in the basics of Hinduism. Her romance with him, such as it was, was transformed very shortly into a romance and sympathy with India and its traditions.[64] She confessed to her confidant, Arabella, "Ashamed of the manners of modern Christianity ... I am become a convert to the Gentoo faith, and have my Bramin [sic] to instruct per diem."[65] Sophia's tutoring sessions with the young Brahmin continued simultaneous to a flirtation with a young man named Doyly. Although she found Doyly agreeable, and clearly attracted to her, Sophia deferred the relationship, unsure of how Doyly's affection compared with the high-minded and asexual compatibility she shared with the Brahmin.[66] In a side drama in the plot, Sophia became jealous of her father's romance with a widow, wished it away, fell ill, and came to believe that her jealousy caused the illness. So she approves her father's relationship and has a miraculous recovery. After she recovered, she continued her meetings with the Brahmin. The narrative denouement occurs when the Brahmin died: "my amiable Bramin, Arabella,

---

[62] Brantlinger, *Rule of Darkness*, pp. 76–83, 92–6.
[63] *Hartly House*, p. 89.
[64] *Ibid.*, pp. 124–32.
[65] *Ibid.*, p. 191.
[66] The Brahmin is from his introduction presented as an asexual being: he is celibate, spiritual and perhaps the earliest image of the effeminized Bengali babu.

died last night; and died, I am assured, blessing me."[67] She promised to build a shrine to him, "in her heart," and begs to keep a lock of his hair before he is cremated. As Mary Louise Pratt notes of cross-racial relationships in colonial contact zones, "the lovers are separated, the European is reabsorbed by Europe, and the non-European dies an early death."[68]

Although there was no apparent social or sexual threat from Sophia's relationship with the Brahmin (everyone, including Doyly, the British suitor, knew about Sophia's relationship and her deep and abiding affection for the Brahmin), the death of the Brahmin resulted in Sophia coming to the realization that Doyly was the true object of her affection. But before the finale, one final obstacle is presented: the local nawab, perhaps the nawab of Murshidabad, found Sophia so beautiful that he stared at her as he passed her in a procession. Sophia, the rose of English womanhood, has a beauty that is universal, appealing even to the ugly and grotesque figure of the oriental despot who made his way into political tracts of this age. This lengthy gaze left Sophia trembling with excitement: "who could dream of a mortal female's refusing an enthroned adorer, with the wealth of the Indies at his feet?"[69] In the end, the last two letters of the book find her confessing her true love and becoming Mrs. Doyly, sacrificing herself to a life of British domesticity.[70]

The narrative resolution of marriage to an Englishman within the drama of the book – Sophia's affection for the Brahmin and her growing sympathy with Hinduism – suggests that in spite of the possibility of such a friendship, there were few acceptable outcomes to Sophia's sampling of Brahmin education and the nawab's desire. Sophia's infatuation was cut short by the death of the emasculated Brahmin non-romantic anti-hero, enabling her to realize a more socially appropriate fate.

Similar dramas and romance narratives acted as fables with proposed morals for appropriate behavior. While these works were largely fiction, with claims to "truth" from an "informed" observer, the moral lessons

---

[67] *Hartly House*, p. 235.

[68] Pratt, *Imperial Eyes*, p. 97.

[69] *Hartly House*, pp. 271–2. Sophia's exceptional beauty enacted a common colonial fantasy: An Englishwoman's appeal was universal, thereby explaining how Sophia successfully attracted both a nawab and a Brahmin. Nussbaum, *Torrid Zones*, pp. 173–82, 188–90.

[70] *Ibid.*, pp. 277–81; Nussbaum, *Torrid Zones*, p. 182.

embedded in these narratives dramatized the ways in which inter-racial relationships, although seeming to unite people of different races, did quite the opposite and disrupted the colonial body politic. Many were published both in England and in India thereby replicating normative standards for both audiences.[71]

One volume, billed as "a novel – a sketch – a caricature – letters – dramas," recounted a short story in which a relationship with a native woman ended in tragedy.[72] The story featured Captain Wilmer, of the East India Company's army, who lived with a native woman and corresponded with Sophia, an Englishwoman who lived in England. The native woman proved to be unfaithful and ran off with another man.[73] Wilmer's friend, Aubrey, reported that she was nonetheless violently possessive of Wilmer: "You may imagine the violence of a native woman, and the superior energy of her language, which, you know, is on no occasion limited by the restraints of common decency. She threatens you with all manner of evil and vengeance..." Aubrey also reported that the woman was known to be a longtime regiment follower as she had been attached to a regiment first when she was fourteen. Eventually, after many years of stringing Sophia along, Wilmer arranged to marry Sophia and brought her to India. The native woman found out, and bribed the servant boy to poison some bon-bons. Sophia subsequently ate the sweets, fell ill and died.[74]

Another novel, *The Baboo and Other Tales Descriptive of Society in India*, wove a long and lengthy story of another sort of tragedy: an Englishman, who was previously engaged to an Englishwoman, was believed dead and then found to be living with a Muslim woman.[75] Eva Eldridge, an Englishwoman and orphan was sent to Calcutta to reside under the care of Sir and Lady Wroughton. Eva had previously been engaged to Lt. Col. Henry Forester but he had since reportedly died in India. Through various channels, Lady Wroughton finds out that Forester "had married a Mohummedan [sic] girl – or at least lives with her as if married; and some say he has turned Moosulman [sic] to please her."[76]

---

[71] See Nussbaum, *Torrid Zones*, pp. 169–70; see also Roxann Wheeler, "The Complexion of Desire: racial ideology and mid-eighteenth-century British novels," *Eighteenth Century Studies* 32 (1999): 309–32.

[72] *The East-India Sketch Book, Comprising an Account of the Present State of Society in Calcutta* (London: Richard Bentley, 1832), 2 vols.

[73] *The East-India Sketchbook*, vol. I, pp. 109–10.

[74] Ibid., pp. 100–25.

[75] *The Baboo and Other Tales Descriptive of Society in India*, 2 vols. (London: Smith and Elder, 1834). I thank Katherine Prior for this reference.

[76] *The Baboo*, vol. I, pp. 114–15.

The narrative at this point is interrupted with an account of Dilafroz, the native woman with whom Forester cohabited. She had been abducted and sold to Forester; her family had attempted to reclaim her but she refused to go, saying that Forester had done her a great service, not dishonored her and that she wanted to remain with him. Apparently, the choice of this native woman relayed what was at the heart of a particular colonial fantasy: brown women choosing white men over brown men. But why had Forester chosen to have Dilafroz? The narrator explains that it is impossible for a European man to "describe his attraction to an oriental woman to a virtuous woman of his own country ..."[77]

The Baboo resumes the main romance of the story, Eva and Forester, when Lady Wroughton happens by chance to meet Forester. At this point, Forester reveals that he is still very much in love with Eva. Again, the story takes a turn and we find that Dilafroz is kidnapped and Forester and his army companions pursue her so that no harm comes to her. Dilafroz is found but says that she is abandoning Forester, rendering Forester available to marry Eva.[78] The conclusion of the book finds Forester, "a happy married man, with a competence and the rank of major..."[79] His son, born of Dilafroz, returns to England for his education and Dilafroz accompanies them as the ayah. "She yielded to his being brought up as a sahib, instead of a nuwab [sic]" although "it required all the influence and authority of Forester ... to prevent her indulgence from effectually counteracting the efforts of his [the son's] instructors, and defeating the purpose of his education."[80]

The Baboo, formed in the mold of sentimental novels, with its romance narrative and various digressions presents a narrative resolution that affirmed the socially correct choice of a marriage with an Englishwoman by depicting the native woman as having been faithless in abandoning her relationship. The final scene of the book, in which the native woman is persuaded that her son would be better equipped for life with the manners of a sahib or Englishman than as a nawab, completes the effect of establishing that a British upbringing in the bosom of an English family was the only possible solution to the counteracting the effects of interracial romance. Forester's son is on his way to being trained as an Englishman as Forester is being retrained for a racially

---

[77] *Ibid.*, vol. I, pp. 150–1.
[78] *Ibid.*, vol. II, pp. 270–1.
[79] *Ibid.*, vol. II, p. 271.
[80] *Ibid.*

appropriate relationship.[81] White endogamy, so central to colonial political authority was maintained.

The fear that native women were inadequate mothers to the children of Englishmen, replayed in other accounts. *The East India Sketchbook* noted:

> Native women of the higher class are *never* the mothers of children by Europeans: on the contrary, these women are generally of the very lowest class, frequently menials of the most degraded description, and ... ignorant of the moral obligations of chastity and fidelity ... During the first five or six, and sometimes ten or twelve years of life, their unfortunate children – the children likewise of a European *gentleman* – are left to their companionship, having no additional society but that of bearers and other servants, almost always unacquainted with any other language.[82]

Educating Englishness and inculcating the children of Englishmen with traits such as chastity and fidelity was clearly something not to be left to female native companions; as Felicity Nussbaum demonstrates, maternity was a crucial axis along which gender, race, and class was defined, separating men from women, working women from middle-class women, Englishwomen from native.[83] To counteract the effects of native households on the children of Englishmen, officers of the East India Company's armies had established the Military Orphan Society in 1782 to educate these mixed-race children while removing them from their mothers' care. Subsequently, many more schools to train the children of Englishmen were founded, and by the 1800s, over 30 such schools existed in Calcutta alone.[84]

Women who were Eurasian, or mixed-race, were always sexually suspect, even when they converted and married, making themselves into "legitimate" wives.[85] Another chapter of *The East-India Sketchbook* featured a dialogue between Lieutenant Wartnaby and the narrator in which the lieutenant claimed he would never marry a woman with Indian blood. The narrator warns him, "such a declaration would draw on you the wrath of three-fourths of the female part of

---

[81] A similar type of narrative was played out in Flora Annie Steel's *On the Face of Waters* (London, 1896); see Nancy Paxton, "Mobilizing Chivalry: rape in British novels about the Indian uprising of 1857," *Victorian Studies* 36 (Fall 1992): esp. pp. 22–4 and Paxton (1999), ch. 6.

[82] *The East-India Sketch Book*, vol. I, pp. 78–9.

[83] Nussbaum, *Torrid Zones*, chs. 1 and 2.

[84] For more on the pension fund and the orphan society, see ch. 6.

[85] See Hawes, *Poor Relations*, pp. 10–14; ch. 5.

the cantonment."[86] When the lieutenant is told of an eligible woman on the cantonment, he asks, "Can you kindly add a much more important piece of information, inasmuch as the circumstance may have been influential in the early nurture of the lady — *who was her mother?* [emphasis in original]"[87] Wartnaby explains his objection: "[I] believe that a well-born and well-educated Englishman may be *denaturalized* by an unhappy marriage with an Eurasian [emphasis added]." The fear that marrying a Eurasian or native woman would transform one's cultivated self reinforced the dangers of "going native." In these accounts, sexual and domestic intimacy with a native woman was a crucial step toward the debilitating transformation of denaturing an Englishman, turning he and his family into an orientalized nabob with an unregulated, oversexualized harem.

These narratives repeatedly confirmed the problematic place of interracial relationships Anglo-Indian colonial society at the turn of the nineteenth century. The discursive thrust of works like the *East India Vade Mecum*, *Hartly House*, and other narratives defined and affirmed a picture of what a suitable social and domestic order for the ruling classes in India would look like. Through these accounts, a normative standard was constructed, the boundaries of which were maintained by the repetition and uniformity of narrative resolutions to the problem of interracial romance.

In spite of Williamson's claim that these relationships were fairly common, British accounts, textual and written, reinscribed these interracial relationships so that they threatened the colonial social and cultural order in various ways. Native women, marginally visible in these accounts, were thus seen as the agents of degeneration who threatened appropriately figured English subjects by their mere presence within the family and the home.

III

In addition to travel diaries, novels, and guidebooks, representing India through the visual arts were one of the most crucial ways in which the social and cultural life of India was relayed both to Britons in India and in Britain. While there were many types of paintings, drawings,

---

[86] *The East-India Sketch Book*, vol. I, p. 58.
[87] *Ibid.*, p. 60.

and prints by British painters at the turn of the nineteenth century,[88] family portraits and portraits of Indian women, some of them reputedly *bibis*, were crucial to imagining how European families lived in colonial settlements.

The Auriol and Dashwood families and the *Impey family listening to strolling musicians*, both painted by John Zoffany represent several aspects of European family life in Calcutta in the late eighteenth century. Both are conversation pieces in which the subjects interact with one another as well as engage with the drama of the painting. In the Impey painting, the family is being entertained by a passing musical troop of Indian musicians; in the Auriol and Dashwood painting, the families are enjoying themselves out of doors with their native servants in attendance. Painted in the 1780s, these portraits served as visual reminders of how a British family in India enjoyed its leisure time.

While painted portraits attempted to capture a likeness of its purported subject(s), art historians have noted the ways in which portraiture was a social and cultural practice that contributed to an imagined and idealized vision of how subjects could be situated and represented. Commissioning family portraits in eighteenth-century England enabled upper- and middle-class families to aspire to a practice that had conventionally been seen as aristocratic and limited to the landed gentry and royalty.[89] Choosing a painter was of particular importance since a painter's fame expressed the family's social position. While in Britain having a portrait painted affirmed particular categories and behaviors associated with class and social status, in India, family portraiture conveyed both a sense of the exotic while reaffirming the propriety of British domesticity as it was replicated in the tropics. Numerous families commissioned family portraits as ways to establish their status within colonial society and as a means of demonstrating that their domestic life in India were appropriate to upper-class British

---

[88] There were landscapes (most notably by the Daniells), historical paintings commemorating various events, watercolors, drawings and prints. See Mildred Archer, *Early Views of India: the Picturesque Journeys of Thomas and William Daniell, 1786–1794* (New York: Thames and Hudson, 1980); Archer and Toby Falk, *India Revealed: The Art and Adventures of James and William Fraser, 1801–1835* (London: Cassell, 1989); H. Chakrabarti, *European Artists and India, 1700–1900* (Calcutta: Victoria Memorial, 1987); Pratapaditya Pal and Vidya Dehejia, *From Merchants to Emperors: British Artists and India, 1757–1930* (Ithaca: Cornell University Press, 1986); C. A. Bayly, ed., *The Raj: India and the British, 1600–1947* (London: National Portrait Gallery, 1990).

[89] Marcia Pointon, *Hanging of the Head: Portraiture and Social Formation in Eighteenth-century England* (New Haven: Yale University Press, 1994), pp. 4–6.

Figure 1.1   The Auriol and Dashwood families, 1783–1787 (oil on canvas), Johann Zoffany (1733–1810), by permission of R. H. Dashwood, Esq.

domestic life. Thus, visually, social standing in India was linked with behaviors of status, such as commissioning a portrait or playing the piano, that were understandable in Britain and to Britons abroad.[90]

The Auriol and Dashwood families portrayed three East India Company families who were joined by marriage (see figure 1.1). James Auriol was a civil servant in Bengal from 1770 until the mid 1780s. His two sisters, Sophie and Charlotte, had married John Prinsep and Thomas Dashwood, respectively; the men were both civil servants in different branches of the Company's service. Two other Auriol brothers, John and Charles, were also in service in India. In the painting, all seven members of this extended family, related through blood and marriage

[90] See Archer, p. 57: "Those who were struggling to gain an entry into the fashionable set were only too willing to imitate the aristocratic fashion and commission a portrait to set a seal on their new position ... A portrait could do much to enhance prestige." See also Richard Leppert, "Music, Domestic Life and Cultural Chauvinism: images of British subjects at home in India," in Leppert and Susan McClary, eds., *Music and Society: The Politics of Composition, Performance and Reception* (Cambridge: Cambridge University Press, 1987), pp. 63–104.

enjoy tea under a large jackfruit tree. In the background on the right was a palm tree, on the left was what appears to be a mosque or mausoleum, marking this landscape as a tropical terrain different from the English countryside. The subjects of the painting appear to be engaged in various types of activities. As Charles and John Auriol, and John Prinsep converse on the left, a servant prepares John Prinsep's hookah. In the center, the two sisters, Sophie Prinsep and Charlotte Dashwood look out distractedly while another servant pours tea from a silver teapot. On the right, James Prinsep and Thomas Dashwood are interrupted in their chess match by the presence of the banian holding a stack of papers. In the three groups within the painting, servants perform part of the action of the painting and send a message about the status of this family group. Through their dress, their comportment, their color, and their activity in the painting, the four native servants provide a contrast against the pale beauty of the women, the refined clothes of the men, and the cultured manners of the family.[91]

This type of visual representation reconstructed features associated with elite status in eighteenth-century Britain – wealth, material consumption, high fashion, and refined taste.[92] Like many eighteenth-century family portraits painted in Britain where the colonies were represented in the form of colonial wealth such as tea, china, chocolate, Turkish carpets, and African slaves in the backdrop of a sumptuous parlor, Anglo-Indian portraits often outwardly displayed the wealth of its subjects through imperial commodities.[93] Like their British counterparts, Anglo-Indian portraits often included appropriately dressed servants or ayahs in the background, suggesting that the household's servants were as central to creating the family's class position as the main subjects of the portraits.[94] While in England, colonial commodities in family portraits represented the wealth of the family in being able to afford exotic goods from far away. In India, these representations reinforced the vision of colonial supremacy over Indians.

[91] Kim Hall, *Things of Darkness: Economies of Race and Gender in Early Modern England* (Ithaca: Cornell University Press, 1995), pp. 226–51.

[92] Linda Colley, *Britons: Forging the Nation, 1707–1837* (New Haven: Yale University Press, 1992), ch. 4.

[93] David Dabydeen, *Hogarth's Blacks: Images of Blacks in Eighteenth Century English Art* (Athens: University of Georgia Press, 1987), pp. 87, 90; David Solkin, *Painting For Money* (New Haven: Yale University Press, 1993) pp. 66–7, 72–3; Pointon, *Hanging of the Head,* pp. 146–9.

[94] McKendrick *et al., Birth of a Consumer Society,* p. 58.

Portraits such as that of the Auriol and Dashwood families staged a version of European colonial life that represented the exotic presence of India within the painting and yet contained those elements that might undermine Britishness and colonial authority. By "picturing imperial power," British visual arts throughout the eighteenth century anticipated colonial ideologies.[95] As Beth Tobin has shown, although British subjects occasionally dressed in oriental costumes, or participated in local activities like smoking the hookah, visual representations of this period carefully managed these activities by showing them in a way that Europeanized the practice and stripped it of local meaning, thereby lessening the threat of cultural corruption or hybridity.[96] For instance, the subject in this painting is shown smoking a hookah prepared by a native servant in the background, while dressed wearing the latest European fashions. Hookah-smoking thus became an accessory to the image of the high-ranking European official in India, making him a cosmopolitan subject rather than one who had completely assimilated into Indian practices.

A second family portrait by Zoffany of High Court Judge Elijah Impey and his family visualized how the Impeys lived at home (see figure 1.2). One of about a half a dozen commissioned by Impey, while most portraits commemorated his role as a member of the court, showing him in judicial robes and wig, this one showed him with his hair down. His public persona was well represented through a series of official portraits and his authority as a judge was consolidated by the public display of these paintings in the courthouse and later in the Victoria Memorial.[97] This portrait, of Elijah Impey at home with his family represented how Impey cast himself outside his official duties. However, to address the official portraits as "public" and the family portrait as "private," sidesteps the ways in which portraits dramatized family life for a public stage.[98] The Impey family portrait visualized an upper-class British family in India for a broad set of overlapping audiences such as other members of the Anglo-Indian community, viewers in Britain, and to the Impey descendants.

In the *Impey family listening to strolling musicians*, the scene is set on the veranda. There is a classical column in the background on the left

---

[95] Beth Tobin, *Picturing Imperial Power: Colonial Subjects in Eighteenth-century British Paintings* (Durham: Duke University Press, 1999).

[96] Tobin, *Picturing Imperial Power*, ch. 3.

[97] Archer, *Indian Portraiture*, pp. 89, 135–8.

[98] Michael Flint, "The Family Piece: Oliver Goldsmith and the politics of everyday in eighteenth-century domestic portraiture," *Eighteenth-Century Studies* 29 (1995–96): 127–52.

Figure 1.2   Sir Elijah and Lady Impey and Their Three Children,
1783–1784 (oil on canvas), Johann Zoffany (1733–1810), Private
Collection, © Christie's Images; Bridgeman Art Library.

and a jackfruit tree on the right joining the architecture of the home
with the tropical landscape. A group of musicians play their instruments along the right side of the painting, flanked in the front by the
Impeys' ayahs who sit on the ground, listening to the music. One ayah
holds a fan while the other holds one of the Impey children. On the left
side of the painting is Elijah Impey, clapping to the music and watching
his young daughter prance around wearing what appears to be the
native costume of a dancing girl. Lady Impey is seated on a chair,
with one of her children standing on a footstool next to her. Behind
the Impeys are two more servants: one is holding a baton, the other
is holding a *pan dan* or betel nut server. Chewing pan, which was
a mixture of betel nut and chewing tobacco was, in addition to smoking
the hookah, among the local practices that British visitors to India took
up in the late eighteenth century.

In similar ways to the Auriol and Dashwood painting, the Impey
family portrait emphasized the congeniality of British family life in
India. The family unit, surrounded by its servants, remained intact even

when it was far from home in England. Yet these were not simply portraits for private consumption. In both paintings the men, in their professional capacities, were identifiable as the men who ruled India in the late eighteenth century. Elijah Impey was the Chief Judge of the Supreme Court when British judges first arrived in Calcutta in 1774 to administer criminal and civil law for British subjects in north India. The Auriol brothers and their brothers-in-law were all high-ranking members of the Bengal civil service. James Auriol had become Secretary to the General Department; his brother John was a senior merchant; Charles was a captain in the army; John Prinsep became the superintendent of investments for the Company and also operated an indigo plantation and copper mint outside of Calcutta; and Thomas Dashwood was a senior merchant. By portraying colonial officials *en famille*, family portraits served to consolidate the vision of colonial officials leading socially "white" lives that conformed to domestic life in Britain.

The presence of unnamed and unidentified servants in both paintings followed a European convention dating to the seventeenth century. This compositional strategy worked to highlight the relative wealth, status, and beauty of the named subjects against the anonymous face of the household servant.[99] Beauty in this context was framed as whiteness and the implication of being a leisured subject who did not have to labor. More important, the anonymity and invisibility of the native servants, and of natives generally, was reinforced by these portraits that commemorated only the important members of the colonial establishment. These visual narratives created images in which natives could only be painted as nameless and unidentifiable.

Portraits of native women helped Europeans to visually imagine and represent another type of unnamed native. Eighteenth-century paintings, drawings, and watercolors depicted several types of native women: women in the harem or *zenana*, women at work, and village women.[100] In contrast with the family portraits discussed above, the female subjects of these paintings often stood for Indian womanhood

---

[99] Tobin, *Picturing Imperial Power*, ch. 1; Hall, *Things of Darkness*, ch. 5; Sander Gilman, "Black Bodies, White Bodies: toward an iconography of female sexuality in late nineteenth-century art, medicine and literature," in Henry Louis Gates, Jr., ed., *"Race," Writing and Difference* (Chicago: University of Chicago Press, 1985).

[100] Pran Nevile, "Early European portrayal of Indian women," *India Perspectives* (September 1998): 41–4. See, for instance, "Native Bengal women grinding flour," by Arthur Devis, Bengal, *c.* 1800; "Ablutions of a young woman on the banks of the Ganges," by Mrs. S. C. Belnos, *c.* 1820.

more broadly rather than representing individuals who had any local importance or traceable biography.

Some of the most popular subjects of eighteenth-century portraitists were dancing girls and women from the zenana. The seclusion of women in the harem produced a deep and abiding fascination for Europeans about oriental women, their sexuality and their exoticism.[101] Dancing girls, or *nautch* girls, performed a practice specific to India: these were women who, jeweled and bedecked, entertained Europeans by dancing and singing after dinner. Nautch parties were commented on as early as the sixteenth century by Francois Bernier when he visited the Mughal emperor Akbar. Other travelers' accounts suggested that the dancing was highly sexualized and that the dancers were thought to be sexually available to visiting Europeans.[102]

A painting by Tilly Kettle titled *Dancing Girl* (1772), and one by Francesco Renaldi titled *Muslim Lady seated with a hookah* (1787), showed the figures of native women, dressed in full regalia, wearing jewels, gold-bordered saris and holding a hookah. These portraits of anonymous women reproduced what was imagined to be a glimpse into the secluded and secret life of women in India.

Tilly Kettle's *Dancing Girl* shows a native woman wearing a red sari, adorned with gold and silver ornaments around her neck, arms, wrists and ankles, standing in bare feet on a red flowered carpet, holding a hookah in her left hand (see figure 1.3). As she looks out toward the left side of the canvas, there are two other women in the background, outside the room in conversation but notably disengaged from the main subject of the painting. Framed by a white marble classical column on the right and a side of a scalloped arch on the right, the figure of Kettle's *Dancing Girl* is remarkable for its attention to the details of her jewelry and the richness of its color.

Painted in Faizabad in 1772, the painting was similar to another series of six paintings Kettle had exhibited in England in the same year. For Britons who viewed these works, India was materialized through visual images of women of the harem who wore luxury items such as jewelry and silk saris on their bodies.[103] The woman in this painting wore two silver ankle bracelets, one, a chain and another, a set of bells

---

[101] Rana Kabbani, *Europe's Myths of the Orient* (Bloomington: Indiana University Press, 1986); Mallek Alloula, *The Colonial Harem* (Minneapolis: University of Minnesota Press, 1986); Billie Melman, *Women's Orients: English Women and the Middle East, 1718–1918* (Ann Arbor: University of Michigan Press, 1992).

[102] Teltscher, *India Inscribed*, ch. 2, especially pp. 41–5.

[103] Archer, *Indian Portraiture*, p. 79.

Figure 1.3 Dancing-girl, Faizabad, 1772 (oil on canvas), Tilly Kettle
(1735–1786), Yale Center for British Art, Paul Mellon Collection.

that dancers often used to tap to music. She also wore five sets of gold
bracelets on her wrists and three sets of gold or silver armbands on
her upper arms. Around her neck, she wore several sets of gold necklace chains that were rows of gold beads strung with other rows of
gold beads. This was apparently a common form of necklace called
a *punchlerry* that local women wore frequently at the turn of the
nineteenth century.[104] Across her forehead and along the part of

---

[104] Several wills and inventories of deceased local women show that along with earrings
and rings, these necklaces were items that a woman of property would have
had. See, for instance, O.I.O.C., L/AG/34/27/27, Bengal Inventories, 1802, pt. 2,
nos. 100–1 (property of Mary Carey), nos, 113, 172 (property of Elizabeth, "a native
woman").

her hair, she wore another chain of rubies and pearls. On her ears, she wore dangling earrings of rubies and pearls known as *jhumkus*.[105] A large nose ring dangled from the middle lobe of her nose. Her sari, a red silk sari with gold-threaded border, was wrapped around her body several times eventually covering her head, her legs and most of her upper body. Her bodice, a gold-beaded silk garment served as the background to the layers of gold chains around her neck. In contrast with portraits in which the subjects were clearly identified, the spectacular array of jewelry and the lavishness of the clothing on this figure was associated with the abundant, corrupting opulence of India rather than with a particular (British) family's wealth and prestige.[106] Embodying luxury and wealth, the girl in Kettle's *Dancing Girl* represented one of several excesses of the orient.

Another painting, Francesco Renaldi's *Portrait of a Mogul Lady*, (1787), similarly drew on some of the forms represented by Kettle (see figure 1.4). In this painting, a seated woman looks out from the canvas, holding a hookah pipe in her right hand. The pipe of the hookah curls around behind her and in front of her is a silver *attardan* to hold her perfume. Cushioned by deep red cushions, the subject in this painting wore toe rings on each of her toes and several ankle bracelets around her legs which are folded under her. As one scholar has noted, the abundance of jewelry represented a form of imprisonment, limiting, even more than the harem, the ability of native women to be mobile.[107] Rings on all but three of her fingers and several bracelets on her wrists marked her as a woman of some wealth. She also had a gold chain around her upper arm, several gold necklaces, a large nose ring, large dangling earrings and a pendant dangling over her forehead attached to a chain around her head and forehead. Her clothing included gold stripes on green silk pants with a *kameez* or tunic of white organza.

---

[105] These types of earrings were highly popular in portraits, see for instance, Zoffany's Palmer family portrait which is discussed in the next chapter, James Wales's portrait of *Amber Kaur* (1792), Thomas Hickey's portrait of *Jemdanee* (1787), William Daniell's *Rajpootnee Bride* (1826).

[106] Bhattacharya, *Reading the Splendid Body*, pp. 30–5.

[107] *Ibid.*, p. 34 cites John Ovington, *Voyage to Surat in the Year 1689* (London, 1696), who wrote "Toes are adorn'd with rings, and their legs with shackles of gold, silver, or some other metal..." A similar description is found in Alexander Hamilton, *A New Account of the East Indies* (Edinburgh, 1728) in which he writes about native women: "They wear also rings on their toes, and shekels on their legs... "

Figure 1.4 Portrait of a Mogul Lady, 1787 (oil on canvas),
Francesco Renaldi (1756–*c.* 1799), Private Collection,
© Christie's Images; Bridgeman Art Library.

In comparison with Kettle's painting, Renaldi's portrait is a very close study of his subject. Her features are finely drawn: while her face, her hands, and her feet are the only parts of her that are visible, they are drawn with special attention. Indeed, there is another similar painting of a woman reclining in her zenana (see figure 1.5) titled, *Muslim Lady Reclining* (1789). Given the detail in these Renaldi paintings, Mildred Archer speculates that these unidentified women were likely the companion of an Englishman, and thus permitted to sit for a portrait in close proximity with the painter.[108]

One of the crucial features of these paintings is that the native women were represented alone. In the Kettle painting, although there were two Indian women outside, the main figure of the painting seems to have no relationship with them, not even as attendants. In the Renaldi paintings, the background is a shaded brown hue, suggesting

---

[108] Archer, *Indian Portraiture*, p. 286.

Figure 1.5 Muslim Lady reclining, smoking a hookah, 1789 (oil on canvas), Francesco Renaldi (1756–c. 1799), Yale Center for British Art, Paul Mellon Collection.

that the location of the woman was not nearly as important as her posture and apparel. By isolating native women on the canvas, the seclusion of women of the harem was thus neatly captured in paintings. By framing these women in such a way, these artistic representations suggested to patrons and viewers alike – including in Europe where many of these paintings were displayed – that women of the harem were detached from any community, which in turn affirmed their invisibility in a larger social context.

Unlike the family portraits, these two paintings elide the relationship between the painter and the subject, giving off the impression that the fame of painter barely affected the status of the subject. As Mildred Archer has speculated, the native women represented by Kettle and by Renaldi may have been their companions.[109] Tilly Kettle is known

[109] *Ibid.*, pp. 74, 286.

to have had two "natural" daughters by an unnamed native woman in India. The children, who were baptized in 1773 and 1774, were christened Ann and Elizabeth. The father was listed, but the mother was not, indicating that she was not Christian herself and the couple were not legitimately married.[110] Tilly Kettle married an Englishwoman in England in 1777, had two more children and after several trips back to India, he died in Aleppo in 1786. Reasonably well-known, Tilly Kettle's portraits are among those in the National Portrait Gallery in London.

Renaldi, on the other hand, left little evidence of his private life. His professional life was not as successful as Kettle's or Zoffany's, nor is his surviving work considered among the finer samples of late eighteenth-century art. Renaldi is better known for his well-drawn depictions of native women and his "intriguing" work painting families of Europeans who openly kept zenanas.[111] In addition to the paintings discussed here, Renaldi painted one other in which a European man dressed in turban and *kurta* and *pajama*, posed with his two native companions. Archer argues that Renaldi's expertise in painting mixed-race families and native companions of Englishmen serve as examples of Renaldi's sympathy for these types of relationships, gesturing to the possibility that Renaldi kept a zenana of his own.[112]

Similar to literary representations of the turn of the nineteenth century, visual representations expressed an ambivalent position on the question of interracial intimacy between European men and local women. The visual display of family life in a tropical milieu demonstrated repeatedly that in spite of how commonly Englishmen were rumored to cohabit with native women, a more appropriate and public version of family life was preserved through paintings. In ways that were parallel to textual narratives of this period, visual discourses expressed the deep-seated sense that interracial liaisons needed to be carefully managed and contained in order to not threaten colonial society.

---

[110] "Baptisms in Calcutta, 1767 to 1777," *Bengal Past and Present* XXV (1923): 130–55.
[111] Tobin, *Picturing Imperial Power*, pp. 111–17; Archer, *Indian Portraiture*, pp. 280–97.
[112] Archer, *Indian Portraiture*, p. 286.

2   Residing with begums: William Palmer, James Achilles Kirkpatrick and their "wives"

> Then...dash of brave carriage driving up, and entry of a strangely-
> complexioned young lady, with soft brown eyes and floods of bronze-
> red hair, really a pretty-looking, smiling and amiable, though most
> foreign bit of magnificence and kindly splendour;...her birth,
> as I afterwards found, an Indian *Romance*, mother a sublime *begum*,
> father a ditto English official, mutually adoring, wedding, living
> withdrawn in their own private paradise, Romance famous in the East.
>
> Thomas Carlyle, *Reminiscences* (1823)

Thus noted Carlyle of Catherine Kirkpatrick, the daughter of
James Achilles Kirkpatrick, resident of Hyderabad, and the Begum
Khair-un-nissa, a noblewoman of the court at Hyderabad. As Carlyle
remarked, there was something strangely endearing about the woman
he knew as Kitty: "she was charming in her beautiful *begum* sort." She
was not very clever, not very witty but she was "amiable," affectionate,
sensuous, and loved perfumes. In assessing her character, Carlyle
concluded that she was a "half-begum in short; an interesting specimen
of the Semi-oriental Englishwoman."[1] Carlyle's description evokes a
sense of oriental romance: because Kitty was born of nobility, because
she was the product of a love affair between an Indian noblewoman
and a British official, Kitty was charmed in a way that was sublime.
Through this characterization, Carlyle expressed what others would
note about elite mixed-race men and women who went from India to
Britain: that although they spoke English and lived as Europeans, their
manners and appearance marked them out as being not quite Brit.

For many high-ranking European officials of the late eighteenth
century, keeping a *zenana* (secluded women's quarters within one's
household) and having an Indian female companion was a fundamental
component of constructing a political persona while circulating among
native rulers and their households. Familial alliances were often central

---

[1] T. Carlyle, *Reminiscences* (1823), p. 247.

to forging political alliances, and through their intimate relationships with elite women, British political agents gained access to knowledge about the court's household and local affairs.[2] The lives of two high-ranking officials, William Palmer (1742–1816), resident to the Peshwa in Pune and James Achilles Kirkpatrick (1762–1805), resident to the Nizam of Hyderabad,[3] demonstrate the relative political advantages of these relationships as well as the social disadvantages.

Cohabitive relationships between Company servants and Indian noblewomen within local princely courts paved the way for symbolic incorporation into local politics and enabled diplomatic cooperation. But these interactions were also often fraught with tension. When familial intimacy intersected with political affiliations, the private domain of the household challenged the public profile of British political authority, showing Britons to be commingling with Indians on an equal level rather than standing apart from them. For many European men in colonial settlements, sexual relationships with native women were a type of public secret in which the community at large was aware of these relationships, but native companions and their children were rarely seen, acknowledged or entertained at public events.[4] For many political agents of the East India Company, in spite of the political advantages that interracial familial intimacy provided in negotiating with local rulers, the complex dynamics of mixed-race families provoked social anxieties about status and respectability and threatened to undermine the position of residents as men of authority within the colonial state. As Kathleen Brown has noted, "... colonial domination was a complex process involving sexual intimacy, cultural incorporation and self-scrutiny."[5] This disjuncture is crucial in understanding how interracial relationships were simultaneously central to diplomatic efforts

---

[2] C. A. Bayly, *Empire and Information: Intelligence Gathering and Social Communication in India, 1780–1870* (Cambridge: Cambridge University Press, 1996), pp. 91–4. For a feminist reading of how the exchange of women serves to cement relationships between men, Gayle Rubin, "The Traffic in Women: notes on the political economy of sex," in Rayna R. Reiter, ed., *Towards an Anthropology of Women* (New York: Monthly Review Press, 1975).

[3] Peshwa stands for chief minister under the Maratha chief. In the late eighteenth century, the Peshwa came to stand for the leader of a conglomeration of the different families and communities that comprised the Maratha confederacy. Nizam is the title for the ruling head of household in Hyderabad.

[4] Ann Twinam, *Public Lives, Private Secrets: Gender, Honor, Sexuality, and Illegitimacy in Colonial Spanish America* (Stanford: Stanford University Press, 1999), p. 29.

[5] Kathleen M. Brown, "The Anglo-Algonquin gender frontier," in Nancy Shoemaker, ed., *Negotiators of Change: Historical Perspectives on Native American Women* (New York: Routledge, 1995), p. 36.

and transgressive as the British colonial government became politically dominant.

This chapter traces these overlapping themes by examining the parallel and occasionally connected stories of the Palmer and the Kirkpatrick families. The two men, William Palmer and James Kirkpatrick, became close friends in part because they shared similar positions as residents in court of powerful indigenous rulers of the Indian subcontinent. Their lives have been recently dramatized by William Dalrymple, who has argued that the two men were exemplars of eighteenth-century cosmopolitanism, able to bridge two cultures through their intimate relations and domestic practices.[6] As open-minded as they may have been, this chapter argues that both men voiced anxieties that their sexual activities cast a shadow over the respectability of their families. Their correspondence discussed official matters such as treaties and political negotiations, while the postscripts often contained messages about the various members of their respective families and advice on how to improve the social and racial status of their mixed-race offspring. Both men made concerted efforts to make their children seem British in spite of their mixed parentage. In Kirkpatrick and Palmer's accounts, definitions of "race" were contingent upon other markers of identity such as gender, class, social status, complexion, dress, and comportment.[7] Their correspondence suggest that personal anxieties about race, social status, and cultural behaviors within the household mattered as much as did colonial administrative policies; family-based concerns about the loss of cultural and racial status supported and intersected with the politics of colonial settlements which increasingly demanded a separation between Britons and others.

From the 1760s onward, the East India Company used the residency system to establish political alliances with indigenous princely courts around India. Representatives, known as residents, were sent to the territories beyond the Company-ruled presidencies and became crucial to maintaining the Company's political and commercial connections with local rulers in provinces throughout India. The residency system was adapted from the pre-existing Mughal tradition of sending ambassadors to regional courts as a means of keeping up contact between rulers in the Indian subcontinent. As early as 1615, British residents had been sent to the Mughal court in order to smooth relationships

---

[6] William Dalrymple, *White Mughals: Love and Betrayal in the Eighteenth Century* (New York: HarperCollins, 2003).

[7] See Roxann WheeC, *The Complexion of Race: Categories of Difference in Eighteenth-century British Culture* (Philadelphia: University of Pennsylvania Press, 2000), especially pp. 6–8.

between the Company and the Mughals.[8] Even in the earlier Mughal period (1526–*c.* 1739), family negotiations were often deeply intertwined with imperial affairs, as is shown by the oft-cited example of Akbar marrying a Rajput princess to cement the Mughal empire in the northwest.[9] For the East India Company, installing a resident became a cost-effective way of managing the Company's interests in areas that were not directly controlled by the Company; by forming alliances and making agreements with local princes, the Company was able to extract permission to trade without having to secure the area using its own manpower. Residents acted as the Company's liaison to the courts and provided local information to the Company's officers in Calcutta who forwarded summaries to the Court of Directors in London. In the early years of Company rule, the residents controlled all the political communication in and out of the court and acted as officials who lived as if they were members of the court.

As a part of gaining influence within the court, British agents participated in local practices: they often kept up separate courts of their own as a means of bolstering their situation within the local courts of India. As Michael Fisher has argued, taking part in court rituals, speaking and reading Persian, which was the primary language in which business was transacted, and living as if native were important components of the political culture of the turn of the nineteenth century in northern India.[10] Derived from Mughal political practices that emphasized rituals which incorporated visiting officials into the court, residents exchanged gifts, ate local food, wore Indian clothes, and smoked a hookah.[11] Although several of these political agents were reported to have married their native conjugal companions, there are no documents attesting to this; rather, most were assumed to having been married "in the custom of the country," or by Muslim marital rites. By participating in various indigenous practices, residents communicated with local rulers using a political vocabulary that was available to both parties

[8] Sir Thomas Roe was an English ambassador in the court of Jahangir. His journal was published in Samuel Purchas, *Hakluytas Postumus or Purchas His Pilgrime*, 20 vols. (Glasgow, 1905–1907), vol. iv. See Kate Teltscher, *India Inscribed: European and British Writing on India, 1600–1800* (Delhi: Oxford University Press, 1995), pp. 20–8, 109–11.

[9] John Richards, "Norms of comportment among imperial Mughal officers," in Barbara D. Metcalf, ed., *Moral Conduct and Authority: the Place of Adab in South Asian Islam* (Berkeley: University of California Press, 1984), pp. 262–7.

[10] Michael Fisher, *Indirect Rule in India: Residents and the Residency System, 1764–1858* (Delhi: Oxford University Press, 1991).

[11] Bernard Cohn, "Representing authority in Victorian India," in Eric Hobsbawm and Terence Ranger, eds., *The Invention of Tradition* (Cambridge: Cambridge University Press, 1983), pp. 168–74.

and signaled the Company's approval of the court on indigenous terms. Although, as Bernard Cohn has argued, throughout the eighteenth century, British officials and scholars in Company presidency towns began a concerted effort toward mastering local languages so that they could rule the subcontinent without relying on local informants and translators. British officials on the margins of British rule, such as the residents, continued to rely on their *banians* and *munshis* and the informal teaching they gained from being among the mofussil among native men and women.[12] By using local terms, the Company's representative could present himself as an equal participant in the court rather than a hostile adversary.[13]

A famed Zoffany painting, titled Colonel Mordaunt's Cock Fight, now in the Tate gallery in London, is evidence of the camaraderie enjoyed by European officers, local noblemen, and the Nawab of Awadh (see figure 2.1). The commemoration of this informal familiarity, between Awadhi officials and British political agents, suggests that in the latter part of the eighteenth century, the culture of the Indian ruling courts was more cooperative rather than adversarial. In more formal circumstances, the British resident sat on the ground, an Indian court practice, to negotiate a treaty. A painting of Charles Warre Malet, resident to the court in Pune when he negotiated a treaty between the Peshwa and the Company, represents the political and bodily intimacy of sitting side by side on a carpet among local Indian officials.[14] Malet, like Kirkpatrick and Palmer, also cohabited with a local noblewoman while he was in Pune. In the later phases of Company rule (*c.* 1798 onward), particularly as the Company gained territories, the residents set up separate courts of their own that rivaled those of the local ruler and adapted local practices to their own needs.[15] Indeed, the

---

[12] Cohn, "The command of language and the language of command," *Subaltern Studies IV* (Delhi: Oxford University Press, 1985), pp. 281–95.

[13] Fisher, *Indirect Rule*, pp. 178–86; Elizabeth M. Collingham, *Imperial Bodies: the Physical Experience of the Raj, c. 1800–1947* (London: Polity Press, 2001), pp. 15–18.

[14] C. A. Bayly, ed., *The Raj: India and the British, 1600–1947* (London: National Gallery Publications, 1990), pp. 162–3; see also Mildred Archer, *India and British Portraiture, 1770–1825* (London: Sotheby Parke Bernet, 1979), pp. 145–6; "Warren Hastings meeting Jawan Bakht," by Zoffany (Lucknow, 1784).

[15] Michael Fisher, *Indirect Rule*. Fisher divides the era into several parts. In the early phase (1764–1797) residents were much less interventionist and acted as "the man on the spot," appointed to protect the company's interests. After 1798, from Lord Wellesley's term as governor-general onward, with brief interruptions, the residents became more directly involved in the affairs of each court, and the residencies themselves became more bureaucratized and came under the influence of officials in Calcutta and London. See also Michael Fisher, *A Clash of Cultures: Awadh, the British and the Mughals* (Delhi: Manohar, 1987), ch. 4.

Figure 2.1   Colonel Mordaunt's Cock Match, *c.* 1784–1786 (oil on canvas), Johann Zoffany (1733–1810); Tate Gallery, London/Art Resource, NY.

resident's court often became an alternative site for negotiation within the princely courts, showing the Company's growing influence.

The residencies, as the Company's embassies in Indian princely states, were at the frontiers of the Company's dominions in India in which emerged a distinctive political and social culture that was a blend of Mughal and European traditions.[16] These courtly codes of conduct were available not only to Britons, but to Hindus in Muslim courts and vice versa.[17] The cultural hybridity that emerged in places such as Lucknow, Delhi, and Hyderabad has been treated both as a case of British officials having been corrupted by native influences as well as a cosmopolitan scene of Anglo-Indian familiarity and sympathy.[18] In spite of the anxieties about familiarity

[16] See Fisher, *Clash of Cultures*, pp. 41–9 for his description of the influence of Persian court culture in the practices of the princely courts in northern India. See also John Richards, "Norms of comportment."

[17] Philip Wagoner, "Sultans Among Hindu Kings: dress, titles and the islamicization of Hindu culture at Vijayanagara," *Journal of Asian Studies* 55 (1996): 851–80.

[18] See Cohn, "Representing authority," p. 171; Bayly, *Empire and Information*, pp. 105, 108, 119–21.

with local customs that sprung up in Calcutta, the situation was noticeably different in the residencies. There, the Company's servants continued to participate in local practices, often to productive ends. Contemporary British travelers to India such as Emma Roberts noted that "going native" was a critical aspect of negotiation. In her account, taking up native modes of self representation was inevitable for Englishmen living in local courts, "A gentleman, who succeeded to the appointment of resident at the neighboring court [of the Nawab Nazim at Moorshedabad]...from long domestication with native princes in distant states, had adopted the pomp and circumstance of oriental splendour, so necessary to create and retain the respect due to the governors of the country..."[19]

The harem, or *zenana*, was a crucial local site that provided many opportunities for this type of cultural negotiation. Although in the British imagination of oriental cultures, the harem as a space that secluded women was held up as an example of the backwardness in Islamicate societies, Persian accounts of eighteenth-century politics in northern India indicate that the harem was central to negotiating family and dynastic politics. The women's quarters of the local courts were, as Bayly has noted, important spaces for exchanging information, hearing gossip, and conducting negotiations. The women of the zenana, most often the wives, mothers, and daughters of local rulers often contributed a great deal to the running of the household as well as to the imperial realm.[20] Often women had their own sources of wealth, jewels, cash, and landed holdings from which they collected revenues. In some cases, their family connections and their independent wealth made women of the zenana important political actors within the court and the residency. Their importance was often recognized by the Company's residents: Charles Warre Malet, for instance, maintained

---

[19] Emma Roberts, *Scenes and Characters of Hindustan: with sketches of Anglo Indian Society* (London: Wm. H. Allen and Co., 1835), vol. II, pp. 102-3.

[20] For recent treatments on orientalist notions of the harem, see Kate Teltscher, *India Inscribed*, Lisa Lowe, *Critical Terrains* (Ithaca: Cornell University Press, 1991); Inderpal Grewal, *Home and Harem* (Duke: Duke University Press, 1996); Malek Alloula, *The Colonial Harem* (Minneapolis: University of Minnesota Press, 1986); Rana Kabbani, *Europe's Myths of Orient* (Bloomington: Indiana University Press, 1986). For Persian accounts of the importance of the women's quarters, see Ghulam Hussain, trans. by Nota Manus, *Seir-Mutaqherin*, 4 vols. (Calcutta, 1783); Muhammad Faiz Baksh, trans. William A. Hoey, *Memoirs of Delhi and Faizabad*, 2 vols. (Allahabad, 1888); Indrani Chatterjee, *Gender, Slavery and the Law in Colonial India* (Delhi: Oxford University Press, 1998); see also the Ottoman empire; see Leslie Peirce, *The Imperial Harem* (New York: Oxford University Press, 1993). For Persian documents relating to harem politics, see S. A. I. Tirmizi, *Edicts from the Mughal Harem* (Delhi, 1979).

an account book of the gifts he gave to the women in the Peshwa's zenana while he was resident in Pune.[21] He even celebrated his female companion with a portrait painted by James Wales.

The development of communities of interracial couples with mixed-race children, especially among high-ranking European officials, existed across the Indian subcontinent in towns that were outside the Company's dominions. In the court of Awadh in Lucknow, which was a province of the Mughal empire until 1801 when it was annexed by the British,[22] many residents and civil servants of the Company had Indian mistresses. Covenanted Company officials such as Harry Verelst, Philip Francis, James Rennell, John Shore, Neil Edmonstone, Charles Warre Malet, and John Bristow kept Indian female companions. John Bristow and Nathaniel Middleton, both Company residents between 1775 and 1780, had mixed-race children baptized at St. John's Church in Calcutta before they were legitimately married.[23] These relationships and resulting offspring were not considered a bar to marrying an Englishwoman: Bristow married Emma Wrangham in Chinsurah on May 27, 1782, several years after the baptisms of his four illegitimate children. Indeed, in 1829, when Bristow's companion's will was filed in the Calcutta High Court, Mahondy Khanum asked that her debts be paid from what was due her from Bristow's estate.[24]

---

[21] Oriental and India Office Collections at the British Library (hereafter, O.I.O.C.), Eur. Mss. F 104/87.

[22] Awadh was increasingly drawn into battles and contests with the British and lost several provinces in 1765, after the Nawab was defeated by British forces at Buxar, and then was partially annexed in 1801. For a more complete account, see Muzaffar Alam, *The Crisis of Empire in Mughal North India: Awadh and the Punjab, 1707–1748* (Delhi: Oxford University Press, 1986); Richard Barnett, *North India Between Two Empires* (Berkeley: University of California Press, 1980), chs. 1 and 2; Fisher, *A Clash of Cultures*.

[23] Suresh Chandra Ghosh, *The Social Condition of the British Community in Bengal, 1757–1800* (Leiden: E. J. Brill, 1970), pp. 73–4. "Baptisms in Calcutta, 1767 to 1777," *Bengal Past and Present* (hereafter *BPP*), vol. XXV, pt. 1, ser no. 49 (Jan–March 1923): 130–55; see p. 137 and footnote 56 recording the baptism of Bristow's son, John on May 20, 1774 and the baptism of his daughter, Mary in September, 1777. See *BPP*, vol. XXVI, pt. II, ser. no. 52 (Oct–Dec. 1923): 148 for further baptisms of William (born in Calcutta, July 1778) and of daughter, Charlotte (born in Delhi in March 1776) on April 7, 1780. Bristow married Emma Wrangham in Chinsurah on May 27, 1782, several years after the baptisms of his four children. See *Ibid*, p. 148, footnote 41 for the baptism of Middleton's daughter on October 24, 1780, Eliza, aged 22 months. It was the same day that he married Anne Frances Morse, a sister of Robert Morse who was an advocate at the Supreme Court. For a portrait of Anne (Morse) Middleton, see Archer, *Indian Portraiture*, p. 137, plate 85: "The Morse and Cator Families," by Zoffany (Calcutta, *c.* 1784). Middleton was painted by Tilly Kettle in Calcutta, *c.* 1773; see Archer, *Indian Portraiture*, p. 87, plate 41.

[24] H.C.O.S., 1829–1830, pp. 57–9.

John Shore, a one-time inhabitant of Lucknow and later Governor-General (1793–1798) also had a companion in Lucknow and later married an Englishwoman.[25] Charles Malet, at one time resident in the court of the Peshwa, had three children with a native woman known as Amber Kaur, whose face was immortalized in a painting he commissioned by James Wales in 1792. Several years later, when Wales died, leaving five children, Malet returned to England and married Wales's eldest daughter.[26] Aside from the civil servants, the commander of the Company's troops in service to the nawab from 1771 to 1780, was also the father of several half-Indian children before he married a young Scottish woman.[27]

Lucknow was an especially cosmopolitan place, known as the center for art and literature among Persian and Urdu-speakers.[28] Under the patronage of Nawab Asaf al daulah, the court at Awadh was particularly generous toward European painters. Painters such as Tilly Kettle, John Zoffany, Francesco Renaldi, Ozias Humphrey, Charles Smith, and the Daniells, who were not employed by the East India Company, flocked to Lucknow for patronage. Along with the residents, who were official inhabitants, and freelance soldiers and painters, who were unofficial inhabitants, a significant cross-section of European society in Awadh cohabited with Indian female companions, including Walter Reinhardt, Benoit de Boigne, Claude Martin, Hercules Skinner, and Antoine Polier, showing that Lucknow was a hub for aspiring Europeans.[29]

---

[25] "Baptisms in Calcutta, 1767 to 1777," *BPP*, vol. XXV, pt. 1, ser. no. 49 (Jan–March 1923): 130–55, footnote 91. John Shore married Charlotte Cornish on February 14, 1786.

[26] Archer, *Indian Portraiture*, pp. 347–9.

[27] "Baptisms in Calcutta, 1767 to 1777," *BPP*, vol. XXV, pt. 1, ser. no. 49 (Jan–March 1923): 130, footnote 5. He was knighted in 1779, several years before his death.

[28] Maya Jasanoff, "Collectors of Empire: objects, conquests and imperial self-fashioning," *Past and Present* 184 (2004): 109–35; Dalrymple, *White Mughals*, pp. 269–72.

[29] Walter Reinhardt and Benoit de Boigne are discussed in the next chapter as are their companions, Begum Samru and Helen Bennett, respectively. Claude Martin was a wealthy Frenchman who resided in Lucknow and acted as a go-between for the Nawab of Awadh and the Company; see Rosie Llewellyn-Jones, *A Very Ingenious Man: Claude Martin in Early Colonial India* (Delhi: Oxford University Press, 1992). Hercules Skinner was the father of James Skinner, famed half-Asian leader of Skinner's Horse, a troop of irregular forces who eventually contributed to the founding of St. James's Church in New Delhi. Antoine Polier was a Swiss man in Awadh who is represented in several of Zoffany's paintings. See Archer, *Indian Portraiture*, pp. 84–5 for an eighteenth-century gouache done after a portrait by Tilly Kettle of Col. Antoine Polier, enjoying a nautch with a hookah by his side. See also *BPP*, vol. XXX: 79–107,
contd.

Tilly Kettle, who painted Nathaniel Middleton and Antoine Polier, had an Indian companion who he painted.[30] Likewise, Zoffany, who painted the Palmer family portrait, also had a family with an Indian woman. Zoffany later painted a conversation piece showing several of his friends, also men with native female companions, Polier, Claude Martin, and John Wombwell, the paymaster at Lucknow, sitting around a card table.[31] Wombwell's companion became the subject of a portrait by Charles Smith. Zoffany, who also painted the nawab, resided with Polier and like Polier had several children in India.[32] Likewise, Benoit de Boigne, who cohabited with General Palmer's sister-in-law, also resided with Polier for five months.[33]

While it was well-known that many of these high-ranking men cohabited with native women, the men rarely brought these women to public social and political events such as balls, breakfasts, teas, and dinner parties that performed the Britishness of colonial society.[34] As Mrs. Richard Plowden wrote in her diary in November, 1787, when she arrived in Awadh, she was invited to a dinner with "a party of gentlemen" that included Capt. William Palmer, Col. Antoine Polier, and the painter John Zoffany. There were no other European or Indian women present, although all three of these men had Indian companions in Awadh.[35] Similarly, Lady Nugent dined with a Mr. Brooke, who had

---

footnote 29 contd.

see p. 84 for the baptisms of Polier's two daughters, Wilhelmina and Sophia on Dec. 31, 1787. Polier's Persian correspondence have been recently edited and translated into English by Muzaffar Alam and Seema Alavi, *A European Experience of the Mughal Orient: the I'jaz-i Arsalani (Persian letters 1773–1779) of Antoine-Louis Henri Polier* (New Delhi: Oxford University Press, 2001).

[30] See Archer, *Indian Portraiture*, p. 79, plate 31 ("Dancing Girl," Faizabad, 1772); p. 85, plate 39 ("Col. Polier watching a Nautch," Faizabad, 1772); p. 87, plate 41 ("Nathaniel Middleton," Calcutta, *c.* 1773); p. 95, plate 52 ("N. Middleton with Nawab Asaf-ud-daulah and his ministers," London, *c.* 1784).

[31] See Archer, *Indian Portraiture*, pp. 154–6, color plate VII; Bayly, ed., *The Raj*, pp. 117–18, plate 138.

[32] Archer, *Indian Portraiture*, p. 79.

[33] *BPP*, vol V, July–Sept. 1910: pp. 176–7; De Boigne was a prominent general in the Maratha army. He lived with Bibi Faiz Baksh's sister and had two children with her. De Boigne's bibi is the subject of the next chapter. He was also very close with the Skinner family and gave James Skinner his first commission in the Maratha regiment under his command. See Stark, 1892, pp. 22–31.

[34] Spear, *Nabobs*, pp. 83, 132–3.

[35] O.I.O.C., Eur Mss. F 127/94. Diary of Mrs. Richard Chicheley Plowden (Sophia Elizabeth Prosser) between Jan. 1787–June 1789. See entry for November 22, 1787: Zoffany was apparently so taken with her children that he offered to paint them without charging her a fee.

lived in India for forty-three years and she described him that in spite of this long stint in India, he had a charming demeanor; Mr. Brooke, whose companion was a literate Persian-speaking woman was not to be seen.[36]

The friendships between these men constituted the visible social networks that existed in the Company's establishment in the residencies.[37] As Sara Suleri has noted, colonial contact was largely masculine and homosocial, although homosociality was carefully regulated and monitored so that the "imperial erotic" did not disrupt the semblance of imperial dominance and authority.[38] Roxann Wheeler has taken this further by suggesting that, "The numerous sexual liaisons between European men and other women allow us to see it as constitutive of European masculinity in forging an empire."[39] Friendships among men were widely commemorated: as well as paintings that showed male camaraderie, many men left behind "mourning rings" for their male friends when they died as a tangible symbol of the friendship. These networks between men were the bedrock on which European colonial society was constructed and became the publicly acknowledged face of empire and its social networks.

The less visible network between these men was one that centered around the women with whom they cohabited. Although native women rarely appear in memoirs or portraits as a constitutive part of this larger social fabric, male sociality was cemented by relationships with native women since many men met their partners through the female companions of their friends. Such was the case with Benoit de Boigne who took up with the sister of his friend, William Palmer's companion, Faiz Baksh. Because these intimate relationships with native women often put European men, regardless of their rank, on the territorial and social margins of European society, it cemented the bonds between them. This William Palmer and James Achilles Kirkpatrick found out in their climb up the East India Company's administrative ranks.

---

[36] Lady Maria Nugent, *A Journal from the year 1811 till the year 1815: a voyage to and residence in India, with a tour to the northwestern parts of the British possessions in that country under the Bengal government* (London, 1839), see for instance, vol. I, p. 246.

[37] S. C. Ghosh, *Social Condition of the British Community*, p. 55.

[38] Sara Suleri, *The Rhetoric of English India* (Chicago: University of Chicago Press, 1992).

[39] Wheeler, *Complexion of Race*, p. 138.

Figure 2.2 The Palmer Family, 1786 (oil on canvas), Johann Zoffany
(1733–1810), Oriental and India Office Collection, British Library.

The Palmer family and the firm

The Palmer family portrait is rare because it is one of the few public
commemorations of an interracial, transcultural household and family.
Painted circa 1786 by Zoffany, it is an unfinished portrait of William
Palmer, his companion, Faiz Baksh, her sister (later de Boigne's
companion), three children and several ayahs (see figure 2.2).[40]
William Palmer is seated in the center, looking over his female companion, Bibi Faiz Baksh and their three children, William, Mary, and
Hastings. While William poses in a military-style red waistcoat, his wife
sits on the ground, cradling a baby and wearing a sari with her head

---

[40] See also Archer, *Indian Portraiture* p. 293, pl. 203 ("A European with his family,"
Lucknow, *c.* 1794–1795; by Renaldi) and "George Beechey and his Indian wife," *BPP*
XXIV (Jan–Dec. 1922), pp. 49–52.

covered.[41] Unlike individual portraits in which bibis were represented in isolation from their families, this painting is a bold statement because it situates Faiz Baksh as a mother, a consort to William, and a member of a household and an extended family. In comparison with other family portraits of mixed-race families in which the man dressed in native clothes, this portrait dressed Palmer as a European rather than as someone dressing up in Asian clothes.[42] By pictorially reifying their cultural identities – Palmer seated in a chair, wearing European dress, his companion in sari sitting on the ground – the portrait marks the coexistence of two cultures in the same household.[43] The love story between William Palmer and Faiz Baksh was later reproduced in a fictionalized account by Meadows Taylor's Victorian novel, *Seeta*, about an interracial marriage between an English officer and a Brahmin widow.[44]

William Palmer was born in 1740 in England and went to the West Indies as an ensign in His Majesty's army in 1760.[45] There, he became sexually involved with a creole woman named Sarah in 1761 and fathered three sons, Samuel, William George, and John who all later joined him in India.[46] In 1766, he arrived in India and joined the Bengal Army. He fought in the first Rohilla war in 1774 and then

[41] The portrait has recently been the subject of some controversy: a crucial debate is over whether the painting was done by Francesco Renaldi, a British painter of Italian descent, or by John Zoffany, a German painter who resided in England. Another question mark is whether the woman sitting on the ground to Palmer's left was Palmer's second wife or whether she was Bibi Faiz Baksh's sister, a woman named Halima who later became the companion of the French general, Benoit de Boigne. See Archer, *Indian Portraiture*, pp. 281–6, pl. 196 ("The Palmer Family," Calcutta, 1786); printout by O.I.O.C., prints and drawings division.

[42] See, for instance, "European man with his family," by Renaldi, *c.* 1794–1795 or the portrait of Claud Martin with Boulogne, his companion.

[43] Beth Fowkes Tobin, *Picturing Imperial Power: Colonial Subjects in Eighteenth-century British Painting* (Durham: Duke University Press, 1999), pp. 111–17.

[44] Nancy Paxton, "Mobilizing Chivalry: rape in British novels about the Indian uprising of 1857," *Victorian Studies* 36 (Fall 1992): esp. p. 17, fn. 8; Patrick Brantlinger, *Rule of Darkness: British Literature and Imperialism, 1830–1914* (Ithaca: Cornell University Press, 1988), pp. 212–18; Jyotsna Singh, *Colonial Narratives/Cultural Dialogues* (London: Routledge, 1996), ch. 3.

[45] For a more detailed account, see Dalrymple, *White Mughals*, pp. 273–7.

[46] Maj. V. C. P. Hodson, *List of the Officers of the Bengal Army, 1758–1834* (London: Constable & Co., 1927). See entries for Samuel Palmer (1762–1814) and William George Palmer (1763–1814). Both brothers accompanied their father as military escorts to the residency at the court of Scindhia in 1792 and fought in the Second Maratha Wars (1803–1805). They are both buried in the Park Street cemetery. The third son born after his father's departure for India was John, who became the Palmer of Palmer and Sons in Calcutta. John Palmer (1767–1836) was originally

contd.

became Warren Hastings's aide-de-camp and was Military Secretary in Lucknow from 1776 through 1782. He learned several local languages, becoming known as a proficient Persian speaker and an amateur orientalist scholar.[47] Thereafter, he and Hastings were great friends and Hastings secured commissioned posts for all of Palmer's sons and even served as the godson of his namesake, Hastings Palmer. William Palmer later became the commander of the governor-general's bodyguards from 1778 until some time in 1782. He was posted to Lucknow to be resident in 1782 briefly holding that post during the period when John Bristow and Nathaniel Middleton were alternating the residency of Awadh.[48] In 1786, he was appointed the commander of a battalion of sepoys and remained in Calcutta for the next ten years. After that, in 1797, he was posted to the Scindhia's court in Gwalior; a year later, he was posted to the Peshwa's court in Pune until 1801. In the final years of his life, he was demoted to the command at Monghyr (in the Bengal Presidency) and eventually died in Berhampore in 1816; his fall from a high position was because of his failure to secure a favorable treaty from the Marathas because he was reputed to be sympathetic to the aims of indigenous rule. His public accomplishments aside, Palmer's private life was like many men of his generation: he cohabited with an Indian noblewoman and had several children with her.

In his will, Palmer wrote, "I give and bequeath to Beebee Fyse Buksh Saheba Begum who has been my affectionate friend and companion during a period of more than 35 years, the house which I now inhabit

footnote 46 contd.

in the navy and saw some action on the Coromandel coast in the early 1780s. Then he joined an agency house in Calcutta and eventually founded his own house in 1787. His firm handled many of the accounts of deceased Europeans and managed the funds of many Indian wives and families left behind. (For John Palmer, see entry in Buckland, *Dictionary of Indian Biography* (London: Swan, Sonnenschein and Co., 1906)). One of the Palmer brothers apparently got married in November 19, 1784, according to Lady Frances Chambers's diary for that year. See O.I.O.C., MSS. Eur. A 172: Diary, written in between lines of an almanac for 1784; Lady Chambers was the wife of Sir Robert Chambers (1737–1803), chief justice of Bengal, 1789–1799.

[47] See Rosanne Rocher, "British Orientalism in the Eighteenth Century: the dialectics of knowledge and government," in Carol A. Breckinridge and Peter van der Veer, eds., *Orientalism and the Postcolonial Predicament* (Philadelphia: University of Pennsylvania Press, 1993), p. 217n.

[48] Whether he was officially Resident to the court at Awadh or whether he was appointed something else and titled Military Secretary or Private Agent is unclear. See Archer, *Indian Portraiture*, p. 282; Hodson entry; *BPP*, vol. XXVI, pt. II, ser. no. 52 (Oct–Dec. 1923): 167; *BPP* XXX, "Editor's notebook," pp. 115–16.

near the cantonment of Berhampore..." The remainder of his modest estate was distributed among his children and other relatives according to instructions left with his executors.[49]

Given the date of the will, Palmer probably met the Begum Faiz Baksh in 1781, when he was Hastings's aide-de-camp in the Lucknow court. Their son, William's baptism in March, 1782, confirms this as a likely date.[50] Faiz Baksh was the daughter of a nobleman of the Mughal court in Delhi, although she was temporarily in the nawab's court in Awadh.[51] In spite of their long relationship and its commemoration by the family portrait, whether they were married by Muslim or Anglican rites is unclear. Palmer's self-proclaimed description – she was "a friend and companion" – suggests that they were not formally married. A marriage ceremony was never recorded in the Company's church registers and on the baptismal registers for their children, her name was never listed (indicating that she was not Christian), yet the Palmer children were treated as legitimate children and the begum retained her noble status after her "marriage" with Palmer. In 1796, the Mughal emperor Shah Alam II, presented her with a *sanad* granting her the title of Begum and thereafter, she was titled the Begum Faiz Baksh and given the name Faiz-un-nissa.[52]

Like other Englishmen, Palmer spoke proudly of his children's accomplishments and sent them to England to be educated. In 1802, Palmer corresponded with his old friend Warren Hastings that his children were being schooled in Britain and were well provided for.[53] At about the same time, he wrote to James Kirkpatrick that his wife and children were doing well and were looking forward to seeing the Kirkpatrick family. Indeed, members of the Palmer family were very influential within the colonial establishment: two of the largest agency houses in Calcutta and Hyderabad were managed by Palmer's sons.

While much is known about Palmer and his sons, there is very little historical information about Begum Faiz Baksh. Given her Mughal

---

[49] High Court (Original Side), Calcutta (hereafter abbreviated as H.C.O.S.), Will Register 1815–1816, pp. 238–9. The executors of the will were John Palmer, his son, and Capt. James Arrow, his son-in-law.

[50] *BPP*, vol. XXVI, pt. II, ser. no. 52 (Oct–Dec. 1923): 151.

[51] Meadows Taylor, *The Story of My Life* (London 1878), p. 62. He married a Palmer grandchild and recounts that the Begum was from Delhi.

[52] O.I.O.C., Persian Mss. I. O. 4440, cited in Archer, p. 283. A *sanad* is a Persian word for grant or honor given by the emperor.

[53] Palmer to Hastings, 6 July 1802, BL, Warren Hastings Papers, Add Mss. no. 29178, p. 240 and pp. 254–5, cited in also S. C. Ghosh, *Social Condition of the British Community*, p. 77.

title, her Muslim burial and that she lived in seclusion for most of her life, Begum Faiz Baksh behaved as any Muslim noblewoman might have at the turn of the nineteenth century. In the process of reconstructing the Begum's story, the contrast between her lifestyle as an Indian noblewoman is striking in comparison to the lifestyle of her children and stepchildren who effectively lived as Europeans: they were all baptized, given European names, and several were educated in Britain and served under the Company as civil servants or officers. While she was interred at a mausoleum near the main mosque in Hyderabad, the remainder of her family is buried in the cemetery at Park Street in Calcutta. Like many ordinary women, most of her children, her stepchildren and grandchildren, married Europeans and their offspring in turn became important civil servants for the British in Bengal.[54] The degree to which she chose these forms of self-representation or whether she kept to various local and Islamic practices as a matter of cultural pride is unclear.

Nonetheless, the genealogy of the Palmer family, biologically mixed race and culturally hybrid, illustrates the range of cultural expressions that were possible in one family and more broadly, the range that was possible during this moment in Anglo-Indian relations. The Begum and Palmer lived together for thirty-five years and yet from their choices in how to dress for their portrait to their burials in sacrally separate places, they preserved different cultural identities for themselves. Their descendants lived primarily as Europeans in India although many were Persian speakers, wore Indian dress, and circulated among Indian and British elites.[55]

In addition to his family with Begum Faiz Baksh, Palmer also had children with a creole woman in the West Indies, which was another important colonial arena of the eighteenth-century British empire. The prevalence of interracial concubinage in the West Indies has been well documented by many Caribbean historians, although no scholar has yet traced the links between social life in the British empire in the Americas with the empire on the Indian subcontinent.[56] Of the children

[54] Pradip Sinha, *Calcutta in Urban History* (Calcutta: Firma, 1978), p. 46.
[55] Lady Nugent, *Journal*, vol. I, p. 121. She notes the occasion of a dinner party at the home of the John Palmer family and being charmed when, after dinner, the hookahs were prepared for the ladies and gentlemen at the table.
[56] Kamau Brathwaite, *The Development of Creole Society in Jamaica, 1770–1820* (Oxford: Clarendon Press, 1971); Michael Craton, "Reluctant Creoles: the planters world in the British West Indies," in Bernard Bailyn and Philip D. Morgan, eds., *Strangers within the Realm: Cultural Margins of the First British Empire* (Chapel Hill: University of North Carolina Press, 1991).

of William Palmer's first marriage, Samuel, the eldest son, married a Muslim woman named Khairan, suggesting that marriage across racial, ethnic, and religious boundaries was somewhat acceptable within the Palmer family. Samuel came to India in 1779 when he was seventeen and joined the Company's army as a cadet. He died in 1814 while commanding a battalion at Aligarh.[57]

John Palmer, born in 1767, was also William's son by his first marriage. In contrast to his brothers, he did not join the Company's service but became independently wealthy by founding his own trading firm. Between 1790 and his death in 1836, he became one of the largest financial managers and bankers in Calcutta. His trading firm, in partnership with other agencies, emerged as one of the biggest agency houses in Calcutta and one of the largest holders of the Company's bonds. Known as the "Prince of Merchants," he lived lavishly in the Chowringhee area of Calcutta with his wife, the former Mary Sarah Hampton, daughter of a wealthy army colonel in Calcutta. His eldest son, Francis, went to Eton and finished at Haileybury and then joined the army.[58] His second son, Henry John, joined the Bengal Civil Service. His three daughters all married very well and produced descendants who were employed in India as high-ranking civil servants.[59] Through his business connections, John Palmer knew most of the prominent officials in Calcutta and was frequently appointed executor in managing the estates of men who left behind legitimate and illegitimate families.[60]

The offspring of Palmer's second marriage were similarly well-placed in the British commercial affairs on the Indian subcontinent.

---

[57] William George, Palmer's second son born in St. Kitts, also joined the army and was an officer of the Bengal army. These two brothers died a month apart from one another in Calcutta and were both buried in the Palmer family plot at Park Street cemetery. See entry in Hodson, vol. III, p. 450. *BPP* pt. II, ser. no. 68, (Oct–Dec. 1927): 146–7.

[58] See entry in Hodson for Francis Charles Palmer (1792–1862), their son. He then became a career army official until he was pensioned at the end of 1827. In 1832, he married Miss Anne Elizabeth Burrows. He died in Calcutta in 1862.

[59] One daughter married William Taylor (Bengal Civil Service, 1829 to 1859). Their six children either were also in the civil service or married into it. A second daughter married Sir Charles Parry Hobhouse (B. C. S. 1844 to 1871) and the third daughter also married a Bengal civil servant, Robert Castle Jenkins. The youngest daughter married Capt. Llewellyn Conroy, commander of the Calcutta native infantry. See *BPP* XXXIV, pt. I, ser. no. 67 (July–Sept. 1927): 72–4.

[60] For instance, he was the executor to Claude Martin, the famous and spectacular founder of La Martiniere. See Rosie Llewellyn-Jones, *A Very Ingenious Man: Claude Martin in Early Colonial India* (Delhi: Oxford University Press, 1992).

William Palmer, son of the Begum and of William Palmer the elder, was first an officer in the Deccan and eventually founded Palmer and Co., an agency house in Hyderabad after a brief career as an officer. Palmer, the elder's, daughter Mary married Capt. James Arrow who aided his father-in-law when William was at Berhampore at the end of his career. The remaining Palmer sons, Hastings, Charles, and Robert became members of the firm at Hyderabad after brief careers as entrepreneurs in Calcutta and Delhi.[61]

Although the general trend toward interracial relationships was in decline, the history of various members of the Palmer family demonstrates that during the period from 1760 until 1830, some of the offspring of high-ranking, high-status British officials and Indian women were able to overcome their racial hybridity by relying on their elite social status. The marriages of William Palmer's children and grandchildren to members of the Company's civil and military elites suggests that race, and in this case, mixed race was not a bar to marrying European men or women.

William Palmer, the elder's, connections with the Company were useful to his sons, John and William, who were the heads of agency houses in Calcutta and Hyderabad, respectively, while the begum's connections seem to have helped her son William in his business dealings with the Nizam of Hyderabad. The begum, William the younger's, mother, resided in Hyderabad from the death of her husband in 1816 until her own death in 1828. She maintained some contact with the court at Hyderabad, befriending Kirkpatrick and his family, and aided her son in sustaining the connections that were necessary for the success of the family firm. In the residencies and Indian states that were outside the Company's domains, it appears that these hybrid families were well positioned to capitalize on their Indian connections while using British patronage to the best advantage.[62]

The relationship between the Nizam of Hyderabad and his growing indebtedness to Palmer and Co. developed from the amity between the Nizam and William Palmer (the son) and the cooperation of British officials. As an Eurasian, Palmer was considered an Indian subject and thus not liable to regulations that applied to British subjects of the

---

[61] *BPP*, XXXIV, pt. I, ser. no. 67 (July–Sept. 1927): 72–4. Hastings Palmer owned an indigo plantation near Murshidabad as a young man, where, like his half-uncle John, he was known as a sociable and extravagant man.

[62] See C. J. Hawes, *Poor Relations: The Making of a Eurasian Community in British India, 1773–1833* (London: Curzon Press, 1996), p. 101.

Company.[63] Moreover, because of his dual cultural ancestry, Palmer possessed many important skills. He spoke Persian and was conversant with courtly culture; these abilities enabled him to have a close and intimate tie with the Nizam and the Nizam's chief minister who was an important cog in the money-making schemes of Palmer and Co. In addition, through his mother's relationships with the women of the court, he solidified his special status with the nizam. Col. Meadows Taylor, author of *Confessions of a Thug* and *Seeta*, who married Palmer's daughter Mary, wrote that Palmer was one of the most knowledgeable and well-connected businessmen in Hyderabad and attributed this to Palmer's mixed ancestry.[64]

Through the family's connections with Palmer and Co. in Calcutta, which was an agency house managed by William's half-brother John, the firm enjoyed the support of British officials based in Calcutta, most importantly the Governor-General, the Marquis of Hastings. In Hyderabad, the offices of the firm were for many years located at the British residency. As a joint-stock company that invested the money of its investors, many of whom worked for the East India Company, Palmer and Co. linked the interests of Company employees (Europeans as well as Indian) with the private interests of the agency house and the financial affairs of the nizam. Palmer and Co., from its founding in 1801, until its demise in the 1820s, loaned upwards of sixty lakh rupees to the nizam; in cases where the nizam forfeited, Palmer accepted revenue-producing districts as payment on his loans.[65] Thus, with the knowledge of Company officials, many of whom personally benefited from these transactions, Palmer's agency house issued large loans to the nizam to pay the Company. These loans were often backed by Company bonds so that when the nizam failed to pay back his loans, the already-precarious finances of the Company were endangered while the agency house and its investors profited.[66]

In what became an embarrassing affair for the resident and the governor-general, the East India Company helped to keep the Palmer family's agency house in business much longer than was profitable for

---

[63] See Hawes, *Poor Relations*, pp. 105–6.

[64] Meadows Taylor, pp. 62, 69. They married in Secunderabad in August 1832. He wrote of his future father-in-law, "There was a fascination about him quite irresistible to me, his knowledge so varied – classical, historical and political."

[65] Fisher, *Indirect Rule*, pp. 388–90; Hawes, *Poor Relations*, pp. 103–5. See also Karen Leonard, "Banking firms in nineteenth-century Hyderabad politics," *Modern Asian Studies* 15 (1981): 177–201.

[66] S. B. Singh, *European Agency Houses in Bengal (1783–1833)* (Calcutta: Firma K. L. Mukhopadhyay, 1966), pp. 250–73.

the Company and put the Palmers in conflict with the Company's regulations against using the Company's protection for private gain for its employees. When the matter was finally resolved, Charles Metcalfe, then resident in Delhi commented,

> Here is a native subject of the British empire, half British by his birth, British in language and education, and habits,... [living] within the precincts of the British Residency, owing all his advantages to British power and influence, and pretends he is not legally bound of the order of the British government.[67]

By juxtaposing Palmer's European manners and self-fashioning as an Englishman, against Palmer's disavowal that he should be considered a British subject in legal terms, Metcalfe exposed what was a crucial distinction in the Company's policies: to be considered and held to the standards of being a British subject, one needed to be of European descent on both sides. Although Metcalfe himself had a native companion and several mixed-race children, he expressed the Company's party line about race, which was understood through distinctions balancing ancestry against manners: even though Palmer had European manners, he was not technically British.

Metcalfe noted ironically that had Palmer "and his native associates" remained more distant from British support and patronage, the whole affair would not have been considered illegal; yet, it was the support of British officials that enabled the early successes of Palmer's agency house.[68] Palmer and Co. in Hyderabad went bankrupt in the 1820s and Palmer and Co. followed in Calcutta in 1835, and the fortunes of the Palmers effectively collapsed.[69]

The saga of the Palmer family's rise and fall is critical for understanding how family networks, both British and Indian, were important for negotiating the cultural and racial politics at the residency in Hyderabad and more broadly, across the Indian subcontinent. This family genealogy allowed its members to adopt various positions for strategic advantage. William Palmer, the elder, managed to place all

---

[67] Cited in R. Bingle, O.I.O.C. Mss. Eur. C 256/2, p. 452, *The Marquess of Hastings, 1813–23*; see Hawes, *Poor Relations*, p. 106.

[68] Hawes, *Poor Relations*, p. 106.

[69] For a complete treatment of the affairs of Palmer and Co. in Hyderabad, see Hawes, pp. 101–6; Peter Wood, *A Vassal State in the Shadow of Empire: William Palmer's Bank in Hyderabad, 1810–1824*, Ph.D. Dissertation, University of Wisconsin, 1981; Sunil Chander, *From a Pre-colonial Order to a Princely State: Hyderabad in Transition, c. 1748–1865*, Ph.D. Dissertation, Cambridge University, 1987, see esp. chapter 3. For affairs in Calcutta, see S.B. Singh, *European Agency Houses*, chapters 6–8. See also, O.I.O.C., Home Misc/743, II, "Affairs of William Palmer and Co."

of his sons in good positions in the army and navy, including William (the younger) and Hastings who were legally barred from being officers or joining the Company's covenanted service because they were mixed race. Two of his sons, John and his half-brother William, converted their positions and the contacts they made into lucrative businesses. That the Palmer family was mixed-race was not a deterrent to its successes; indeed, many of their successes were enabled by the contacts they gained through their aristocratic Indian mother and their British father.

Husmat Jung and Khair-un-nissa: James Achilles Kirkpatrick and his begum

Similar to the Palmers, the Kirkpatrick family was another colonial family that had multiple connections to various parts of India. Like the Palmers, the Kirkpatricks came to India in the 1760s from the British empire in the Americas and took their places as military officers in the Company's armies. The two oldest brothers married British daughters of prominent colonial officials, while James, the youngest, married an Indian noblewoman at the nizam's court at Hyderabad. Like William Palmer, James Kirkpatrick was a high-ranking officer in the Company's army who married a woman from the court of a local ruler; unlike Palmer, however, Kirkpatrick's marriage was a source of some controversy. Although the matter was investigated and resolved, the Company's concern over Kirkpatrick's marriage was indicative of a growing concern with eliminating any sources of possible political corruption and social impropriety within the Company's establishment. By 1800, anxieties about interracial marriages, especially at this high level, became much more focused on questions of respectability and the ways in which these conceptions were central to British rule.

The story of the Kirkpatrick family in India begins with Col. James Kirkpatrick, the father of James Achilles. Colonel Kirkpatrick was known within the family as "Handsome" Colonel Kirkpatrick, largely because he was reputed to be a ladies' man.[70] Indeed, his eldest (acknowledged) son was William, borne to him by a Mrs. Booth, who

---

[70] O.I.O.C., Mss. Eur. F 127/478: "Sketch of the Kirkpatrick Family, as collected by Lady (Richard) Strachey." The colonel's father was a Dr. Kilpatrick, a man who owned a plantation in the Carolinas and reputedly cohabited with a creole slave with whom he had two sons, William and then James. Whether the elder James Kirkpatrick was mixed-race is unclear.

was the wife of a friend of his.[71] Colonel Kirkpatrick came to India in the early 1760s and married Katherine Monro in Madras; she was the daughter of a fellow officer and they had two sons together, George and James Achilles.

The three brothers all had illustrious careers in India. The oldest, William (1756–1812), reputed to be illegitimate (having been born before his father's marriage),[72] came to India as a cadet in 1773 at the age of nineteen. From 1777 until 1785, he was the Persian interpreter to Major General Giles Stibbert, who was commander-in-chief of the Bengal Army. In addition to his official duties, he was a prolific writer and managed to publish four major works in his lifetime, including a grammar book for Persian, Arabic, and English.[73] He was appointed to the residency at Gwalior in 1787 and then went to Nepal to negotiate a treaty for the Company between Nepal and China.[74] In 1795, he came to Hyderabad as resident, where he remained for two years, when his brother succeeded him. During this period, he was responsible for overseeing the partitioning of Mysore after the third Mysore war in which Tipu Sultan, the leader of Mysore, was forced to cede land and pay reparations to the British. William Kirkpatrick subsequently translated and published Tipu Sultan's Persian correspondence.[75]

Shortly thereafter, William Kirkpatrick returned to England. He had four legitimate daughters by Maria Pawson, one of whom, Julia, married Edward Strachey, a Bengal Civil Servant from 1793 to 1811.[76] William Kirkpatrick also had at least one illegitimate child, a daughter named Cecilia who was baptized in 1783.[77] Among William Kirkpatrick's many

[71] O.I.O.C., Mss. Eur. F 228/55, "Letter Book of J. A. Kirkpatrick," pp. 14–15. The handsome colonel also had two daughters with another married Englishwoman whom he met on a journey home to England. One daughter died; the other, Georgiana, eventually ended up living with her father as an adult when her own parents had died. From James Achilles's letters to his brother William, it is apparent that Georgiana had applied to them, as her half-brothers, for some financial support.

[72] According to Julia Strachey, his great-granddaughter who compiled genealogical materials on the family in the 1880s. O.I.O.C., Mss. Eur. F 228/96, Kirkpatrick Collection, pp. 34–7, dated April 3, 1886.

[73] Published in London in 1785, Kirkpatrick compiled *A Vocabulary, Persian, Arabic and English* for Company servants wanting to learn conversational "Hindustani."

[74] As a result of these travels, he wrote a book titled, *An Account of the Kingdom of Nepaul*, which was published originally in 1793 and has been reissued six times since.

[75] *Select Letters of Tippoo Sultan to various public functionaries . . . arranged and translated by W. Kirkpatrick. With notes, observations and an appendix containing several original documents never before published* (London, 1811).

[76] They had three sons, all of whom joined the Bengal Civil Service: Sir Edward, Sir Henry, and Sir Richard.

[77] "Baptisms in Calcutta, 1783–1785," *BPP*, XXVIII, pt. II, ser. no. 56 (Oct–Dec. 1924): 196.

civic activities, he was also the founder of the Military Orphan Society, a charitable fund for educating orphans of European soldiers. When he returned to England, he was an important fundraiser, showing his commitment not only to his own offspring but to men in the Company's military service who were financially less secure.[78]

The second Kirkpatrick brother, George, was resident in Bombay and Madras and married Eleanor Metcalfe, daughter of Sir Thomas Theophilus Metcalfe, a member of a prominent civil servant family in the Company's service. George and Eleanor Kirkpatrick had five children, all of whom served the empire either as civil servants or as military officers.

From all accounts, the Kirkpatrick brothers were ideal Company servants of the late eighteenth century: they all read and wrote Persian, they negotiated beneficial treaties with local rulers and they had good relationships with Company officials and local officials alike. In other ways, they were typical of late eighteenth-century Company men: all three cohabited with Indian women and had several illegitimate children. Of the three, however, only James was forced into the position of publicly acknowledging his Indian female companion.

James, the youngest son, followed his older half-brother William to Hyderabad as a Persian translator and succeeded him as resident in Hyderabad in 1798. James was born in 1764 in Madras and was sent to England at a young age to receive an education. He returned in 1779 as a cadet on the Madras Establishment and was involved in several battles in the Carnatic. He was present at Seringapatnam, at the final defeat of Tipu Sultan in 1792; thereafter, he was appointed to be the Persian translator to his brother's detachment that was serving the Nizam of Hyderabad. William Kirkpatrick became the resident in Hyderabad in 1795 and James became his assistant. In 1798, when William left this post, James succeeded him and remained in that post until his death in 1805.

In 1800, while he was the resident in Hyderabad, James met Khair-un-nissa, the granddaughter of a court nobleman, Bauker Ali. He began a relationship with her, in the course of which, she became pregnant. Within a few months, the matter was brought to Governor-General Wellesley's attention. Wellesley deputed Lord Clive, Capt. John Malcolm, and Neil Edmonstone to investigate and the

---

[78] The Military Orphan Society is the subject of Chapter 6 of this study. General Stibbert, who William Kirkpatrick had served, became one of the head managers of the Military Orphan Society.

resulting investigation revealed tensions among the players in the court and the Company. Dissension among noblemen in the court became apparent during the course of the investigation; by cohabiting with Khair-un-nissa, James had favored one faction within the court at Hyderabad over another.[79] The affair challenged Wellesley and his ideas of good governance and effective diplomacy: Wellesley believed that Kirkpatrick had lost the respect of the local populace and no longer had the ability to negotiate with the nizam – indeed, Wellesley saw the matter as a question of "national respectability." The investigation was shaped by these tensions as well as the question of how the relationship came about; in other words, how did a seventeen-year-old woman who was secluded in the nizam's zenana meet the British resident? In the process of examining witnesses, British officials and inhabitants of the nizam's court emphasized repeatedly that the affair between James and Khair-un-nissa was not simply a romance but a matter of state importance. Local gossip, hearsay, and dinner party conversation were all offered as evidence that there were political considerations at stake in the interactions between the resident and women of the nizam's court.

The relationship was first revealed to William by James in a letter that James wrote to his brother on May 23, 1800. In it, he wrote that he had been subject to frequent overtures by the women of the zenana to induce him to fall in love with the young woman. He had been shown a portrait, he had seen her sleeping through a curtain and finally, she was brought to him at night. In his account to William, he cast the story as a romantic one: she had fallen in love with him but due to a prior family obligation was betrothed to an older nobleman. She had threatened to commit suicide if she were forced to forgo her infatuation for the resident for marriage to an old man and thus, her mother and her grandmother had arranged for a meeting with the resident. He described her as young, romantic, very emotional and perhaps slightly imbalanced; nonetheless, she was appealing and it was difficult for James to refuse her attentions. He wrote:

...I did once safely pass the fiery ordeal of a long nocturnal interview with the charming subject of the present letter...I had a full and close survey of her lovely person. It lasted during the greatest part of night and was evidently *contrived* by the grandmother and mother whose very existence hang on hers to indulge her in uncontractable wishes...I contrived to command myself so far as to abstain from the tempting feast I was manifestly invited to...She declared

[79] Dalrymple, *White Mughals*, chs. 2, 4–6.

to me again and again that her affection had been irrevocably fixed on me for a series [sic] of time that her fate was linked to mine and that she should be content to pass her days with me as the humblest of handmaidens.[80]

He asked his brother rhetorically how long it was possible to resist such vulnerability and given her reluctance to marry this old man, how could he have done anything other than take her into his home.[81] James's story, then, paralleled narratives produced in many novels of the romantic era: he maintained that he rescued an emotional young woman from "a hateful marriage," thereby entering into a more companionate conjugal arrangement based on sentiment and affection.[82] By refuting the specter of immorality, James turned around the logic of impropriety by arguing that no Englishman could have behaved otherwise given the threat of a forced marriage between a young girl and an old man. Diminishing his own agency in bringing about the affair, Kirkpatrick claimed the women of the nizam's zenana manipulated the circumstances to arrange the meeting. He hinted that the women, Khair-un-nissa's mother and grandmother, had acted independently of the nizam and of Bauker Ali.

Lord Wellesley saw the matter in different terms; he viewed interracial relationships as a messy by-product of imperial expansion and attempted to suppress public acknowledgment that they existed. The matter of Kirkpatrick's affair was brought to Wellesley's attention by a nobleman in the Nizam's court, Mir Alam. Mir Alam invoked British understandings of the harem as a secluded space that enclosed helpless women: he represented the case as a story about coercion, about the resident using his influence inappropriately to seduce a helpless young woman and through her, gain access to the zenana and thus to Bauker Ali, the woman's grandfather. Mir Alam and Bauker Ali were rivals in the court of the nizam. Bauker Ali represented the affair as one that brought dishonor and outrage to his family and that the whole family was considering "turning Fakir" and shedding their noble clothes and leaving Hyderabad, due to James's unwelcome advances.[83]

---

[80] O.I.O.C., Eur. Mss. F 228/83, Letter to William, from Hyderabad, dated 23 May 1800, p. 2.

[81] O.I.O.C., p. 3.

[82] Jyotsna Singh (1996), *Colonial Narratives*, p. 1; Wheeler, *Complexion of Race*, p. 149.

[83] Bauker Ali had been an ally of the company since the arrival of the Kirkpatricks in Hyderabad. Several years earlier, James had written to his brother, that he had increased Bauker Ali's salary and had approved a loan of Rs. 1,000 for the wedding of his granddaughter. He later wrote about attending the wedding and all the attention he had received from the women of the household. "Private Letters from my Brother James, Kirkpatrick," O.I.O.C., Eur. Mss. F228/11–12, dated Jan. 2, 1799 and April 30, 1800.

When the matter was investigated, Lt. Col. Bowen, who was in command of the nizam's subsidiary force at the time, based his testimony on local gossip. Lord Clive, who was investigating on the behest of the Governor-General, inquired about whether Kirkpatrick had initiated the relationship or whether the idea originated with the women of the harem, and Bowen testified,

...it is said that the lady fell in love with the Resident, and the free access very unusual in Mohammedan families which had been allowed him with the females of that family may appear to confirm the opinion of design on their part...the manners of Bauker's family are known to be unusually free from the prejudices of the sect...it would appear to me that Bauker was not acquainted with the facts, but that the women of the family probably were.[84]

Bowen further stated, based on a vague understanding of local morality and referred to British knowledge about Muslim societies, "Our intercourse with the principal inhabitants of the city were very limited... I cannot therefore state particular facts from immediate communication... our knowledge of the opinions of the Mohammedans regarding women did not dispose us to doubt this impression [that the local inhabitants were discontent with news of the relationship]."[85]

Further testimony followed, again based on local gossip and hearsay. Major Orr, the Persian interpreter to the subsidiary forces, testified that the matter had come to the attention of the previous commander, Dalrymple, when Bauker Ali revealed in confidence that his granddaughter had been betrothed to a man of some status and that the resident had attempted to prevent the marriage from occurring. According to Orr's testimony of what Dalrymple had reported, Bauker Ali had threatened to go to the city's main mosque and reveal the resident's behavior to other notable Muslims in the city, which would "whip up the local Muslims into defending their honor." Dalrymple, according to Orr, then went to the resident and after warning him of the personal and political dangers he was implicated in due to his affair, extracted a promise from Kirkpatrick that he would refrain from his relationship with the young woman. Unfortunately, Dalrymple died soon after this conversation and Kirkpatrick, according to unnamed local sources, took up again with Khair-un-nissa.

As in Bowen's testimony, Orr was asked how the relationship came about. Was it initiated by the resident or by the family or the young woman? Orr testified that in spite of Bauker's complaint to Dalrymple,

---

[84] O.I.O.C., Home Misc. series, H/464, pp. 357–75.
[85] *Ibid.*

he believed that Bauker's indignation had been for show. The day after Bauker Ali had visited the commander, "[Bauker] took his portion of Shiraz at the Resident's table with his usual ease and familiarity." Indeed, Orr continued, "[It was known] by general report that the male branches of the family had so far appeared to be accessory to the connexion as to permit the old Begum, her daughter and granddaughter to remain in the Resident's zenana for days and nights on the avowed pretext of visiting the Resident's concubine."[86] Orr further divulged that he believed that the affair would not have occurred without the cooperation of the women in the several zenanas of the Nizam's household, of Bauker Ali Khan's family, and of the resident's household. In response to the question about local public opinion, Orr restated what Bowen had said: that although he had had no direct contact with any local inhabitants, he believed that people were unhappy with the situation.

The matter was represented as a case of the local outrage against a romantic affair between a young Indian noblewoman and the British resident, although these types of interactions had long been the norm at the courts of princely rulers. The circulation of gossip and its use in the testimony demonstrated the high level of interaction between British officers at the army camp, the Indian noblemen of the court, and the women in the nizam's zenana. That there was a consensus between these three socially and culturally separate groups suggests, as Bayly argues, that the transfer of information and local knowledge was highly effective. Although all parties testified that the affair had come about with the aid of the women in the household, when Wellesley corresponded with Kirkpatrick, he treated the liaison as one that contravened local custom and threatened the Company's alliance with the nizam. What remained unstated in the course of the investigation was that Kirkpatrick already kept a zenana and had several illegitimate children by the concubines in his harem. Indeed, it was through visits between the women of the three households, the nizam's, his chief minister's, and the resident's, that the fateful nighttime meeting had occurred. What also remained unsaid was that the men who were conducting the investigation, Lord Clive and Neil Edmonstone, were known to have Indian companions as well. While Wellesley treated the matter as one that was aberrant and berated Kirkpatrick for not coming forward with the details himself, Kirkpatrick noted that the

---

[86] *Ibid.*

affair was an intimate matter and not significant in the performance of his duties.[87]

The matter was effectively resolved when Dr. Kennedy, the Residency surgeon, interviewed the women of Bauker Ali's household, the Begum Sherriffe ul nissa and her daughter-in-law, and they confirmed that they had known about the young woman's relationship with the Resident. They reported that when Khair-un-nissa became pregnant, the men of the family decided to proceed with the previously arranged marriage. The women of the family, Khair-un-nissa's mother and grandmother decided otherwise and attempted to arrange an abortion.[88] Upon hearing of this, Kirkpatrick intervened and vowed not to desert either the young woman or his heir.[89] In the women's account, they stated that although they had initially been opposed to the relationship, given the circumstances, they were persuaded that an alliance would be appropriate. Khair-un-nissa's mother believed that since "her daughter's character had been ruined in the eyes of the world," she believed it would be wrong to marry her to someone else.[90] In reconciling Bauker Ali's complaints with the account of the women of Bauker Ali's household, Kennedy and Orr concluded that it was a matter of household politics where the women had been sly in manipulating the relationship and subsequent marriage between Khair-un-nissa and Kirkpatrick.

At the end of 1801, the investigation was completed and Wellesley concluded that although Kirkpatrick had acted inappropriately and had "tarnished the National reputation," there would be no public censure. In a private correspondence with James's brother, William, Capt. John Malcolm, Wellesley's assistant, confided that since James had been so effective in negotiating the Treaty of Bassein between the Nizam and the Company and securing the Nizam's cooperation against the Marathas, Wellesley had felt that James was more useful than detrimental and had decided against removing him from his post.[91]

---

[87] O.I.O.C., Mss. Eur. F228/18, Letter of J. A. Kirkpatrick to Capt. John Malcolm, assistant to Lord Wellesley, dated Hyderabad, 4 January 1802.

[88] This strategy is perhaps not so different to that recounted in Ranajit Guha, "Chandra's Death," *Subaltern Studies* V (Delhi: Oxford University Press, 1987) about the death of a young woman that resulted from an abortion arranged by her female relatives to protect her from the dishonor of an illicit affair.

[89] O.I.O.C., Home Misc. series, H/464, pp. 357–75. See Orr's testimony, pp. 368–75.

[90] O.I.O.C., Home Misc. series, H/464, pp. 377–93, Enc. no. 5.

[91] O.I.O.C., Mss. Eur. F228/83, Letter from Capt. John Malcolm, assistant to Lord Wellesley, to Wm. Kirkpatrick, dated Mirzapoor, 2 December 1801.

Indeed, James himself had noted that his private relationships were the subject of investigation because of his public performance: "I have not been so pliably accommodating to his unsurmountable political views as he [Wellesley] perhaps thought he had a right to expect."[92]

The results of the investigation implied that this relationship offended the British as much as it did the local populace that was often spoken of in the course of the investigation. Yet, John Malcolm, Wellesley's assistant, as well as Neil Edmonstone, longtime secretary of the Persian and Political departments, knew well enough that these types of relationships were common, although their correspondence on the matter expressed outrage.[93] Malcolm implied as much when he wrote to William Kirkpatrick that he felt the whole matter was unfair.[94] Nonetheless, later, Malcolm noted in a letter to William Kirkpatrick that it was "imprudent to have an indulgence at a native court with a woman of such rank."[95] Again, in the public censure of Kirkpatrick, what remained unstated was the prevalence of such relationships in other Residencies, for instance, in Pune, where William Palmer was resident to the Peshwa.

Although the eras of governor-generals Cornwallis and Wellesley are credited with clamping down on interracial relationships, some prominent Englishmen living on the frontiers continued to maintain relationships with local women well into the 1830s with little harmful impact on their careers. Charles Theophilus Metcalfe, Wellesley's protégé and subsequently Resident in Delhi, was the father of three sons born to a native woman. His three sons were sent to England to

---

[92] O.I.O.C., Mss. Eur. F228/18, Letter of J. A. Kirkpatrick to his brother William, dated 23 November 1801.

[93] See for instance, O.I.O.C., Mss. Eur. F 228/18, Letter of Capt. John Malcolm to Wm. Kirkpatrick, dated Patna, 7 October, 1801: "It is with the utmost degree of pain and sorrow that I inform you, that intelligence has reached me from various quarters which leaves no doubt... that your Brother, the Resident at Hyderabad, has abused my confidence in the most criminal manner... The effect at Hyderabad is mischievous in the extreme, as might be expected from such an outrage upon the general principles of morality, and upon the most revered prejudices of Mussulmans..." See also, O.I.O.C., Mss. Eur. F 228/83, Neil Edmonstone to J. A. Kirkpatrick, dated 18 May 1802, when he called the whole matter "highly improper" and "wholly demeaning." Edmonstone himself had a longtime Indian female companion with whom he had several children; see Bayly, *Empire and Information*, p. 91.

[94] O.I.O.C., Mss. Eur. F 228/18, Letter of Capt. John Malcolm to Wm. Kirkpatrick, dated 29 October, 1801.

[95] O.I.O.C., Mss. Eur. F 228/18, Letter of Capt. John Malcolm to Wm. Kirkpatrick, dated Chunar, 30 November 1801.

be educated, where they were taken care of by their aunt.[96] Charles Metcalfe maintained a close relationship with Wellesley, writing a heartfelt letter to him in 1834, marking over thirty years' friendship. In it, Metcalfe wrote:

I shall never forget the kindness with which you trusted me, from first to last, during your stay in India...I have a right to attribute all of Good thus has since happened to me, to the countenance most favorable with which you distinguished me as that early period. My public principles were learned in your school, preeminently the School of House, Zeal, Public Spirit & Patriotism; and to my adherence to the principles there required I venture to ascribe all the success that has attended me.[97]

As a result of Metcalfe's service to the empire, he became the Governor of Jamaica (1839–1842) and then Governor-General of Canada (1843–1845). He was given a hereditary peerage in 1845 and died in 1846. Because none of his sons were legitimate heirs, the baronetcy lapsed. Sir David Ochterlony and William Fraser, also Residents in Delhi and officials who served alongside Charles Metcalfe, were also known for being European men living in the native style. A nineteenth-century gouache of Sir David Ochterlony shows him enjoying a nautch and smoking a hookah in his zenana.[98] Through the 1830s, high-ranking men of the Company's service continued to cohabit with native women, even under the supervision and tutelage of disapproving officials like Wellesley. In many ways, the official notions of respectable behavior that maintained an appropriate distance from native lifestyles contrasted sharply with domestic lives based on interracial conjugality, particularly in regions that were far from the Company's trading centers in Calcutta, Bombay, and Madras.

Although high-ranking men rarely addressed their family matters in official documents, Englishmen privately shared anxieties about what they faced in terms of their families and the status of their mixed-race children. William Palmer, the elder, was a strong supporter of Kirkpatrick's while Kirkpatrick's affair with Khair-un-nissa was being investigated. In diplomatic matters, they were in frequent communication over the matter of the alliance between the peshwa, the nizam, and the Company. In personal matters, it was apparent that they were

---

[96] O.I.O.C., Mss. Eur Photo Eur 31, Bayley Family Records, compiled by M. S. T. Clive Bayley, vol. 1, In "Great Grandmother's Days: a family record," compiled by Mary Stuart Theophila Clive Bayley, dated 1925, pp. 24–6.

[97] British Library, Add Mss. 37,311 Wellesley Papers, pp. 198–200.

[98] Bayly, ed., *The Raj*, p. 178.

closely allied over the issue of Kirkpatrick's zenana relationship. In the postscripts of James Kirkpatrick's correspondence with William Palmer, Kirkpatrick revealed that Palmer had been a helpful mentor and model. He also revealed that the two families had become very friendly: Kirkpatrick and Palmer were colleagues, but their wives apparently had a relationship of their own. Soon after the treaty and the investigation were completed, Kirkpatrick wrote to Palmer, "P. S. Pray do not omit presenting my kindest remembrances to Fyze, and her little daughter by adoption, with whom the little Prince Soleyman Jah was so smitten, that he himself begged the females of my family to intercede in his behalf. They all join in kind wishes to Fyze, including her little namesake – Sahiba Begum – who is improving daily."[99] In subsequent letters, Kirkpatrick continued to send regards and reminisce about visits the two families had shared and promised that the women of his family were weaving *dupattas* for the women of Palmer's household and that he would send them along with the next dak.[100] Quite separate from the public realm of the residency, the women in both quarters were well acquainted with one another, particularly in the later years of their lives.[101]

Through these letters, Kirkpatrick shared mundane news such as his children's vaccinations and reported that he had recommended to the nizam and his ministers that they do the same.[102] Likewise, Palmer recounted news of his children's whereabouts and Kirkpatrick promised to do what he could to ensure their success. When Palmer's elder son, John, merged agency houses with Cockrell, Trail, and Palmer in 1802, Kirkpatrick sent congratulations and invested money with John Palmer. When the younger William Palmer was given a commission in the Deccan, Kirkpatrick promised Palmer the elder that he would keep an eye out for him.[103] It was at this time that the younger Palmer first became acquainted with the residency in Hyderabad, in which he later founded his own agency house. As well, the Begum Faiz Baksh, Palmer's widow moved to Hyderabad after her husband's death in 1816 to be closer to her son. According to the account books of the Palmer agency

---

[99] O.I.O.C., Mss. Eur. F 228/57, Letter Books of J. A. Kirkpatrick, dated Hyderabad, 6 May 1802, letter to Col. Wm. Palmer.

[100] O.I.O.C., Mss. Eur. F 228/57, Letter Books of J. A. Kirkpatrick, see, for instance, dated 24 July 1802, 1 Sept. 1802.

[101] Dalrymple, *White Mughals*, pp. 304–7, 463.

[102] O.I.O.C., Mss. Eur. F 228/57, Letter Books of J. A. Kirkpatrick, dated 2 October 1802.

[103] O.I.O.C., Mss. Eur. F 228/57, Letter Books of J. A. Kirkpatrick, dated 2 October 1802 and 10 Dec. 1802.

house, Begum Faiz was in contact with her old friend, Khair-un-nissa; indeed, Khair-un-nissa received a regular allowance from the income of the Palmer agency house.[104] The amity between the two families, and more importantly, the friendship between the women of the two families demonstrate the ways in which the women's quarters of prominent Englishmen were important sites for communication and exchanging information.

In 1803, James Kirkpatrick was granted a sixty-acre plot of land in Hyderabad by the nizam, and he built a magnificent resident's house to represent his own influence and the Company's newly gained power in the Deccan. For his bride, Kirkpatrick built a smaller version of this building and placed it in her garden so that she could envision where he was. Although her enclosed quarters no longer stand, Company records indicate that it was a large open building with galleries and terraces that opened onto a courtyard with fountains, paths, and gardens.[105] In this building, she entertained the wives and concubines of the men who came to meet with her husband in the residency. The style of their home was part-imperial vision, part-Islamicate practice: the grandeur of the residency juxtaposed with the secluded space of the zenana. By building both of these components into his home with Khair-un-nissa, Kirkpatrick drew simultaneously from imperial and Indian styles of architectural representation and assured himself a comparable position with the nizam. By making the women's quarters part of the residency, Kirkpatrick recognized, in architectural language, the importance of the women in the household.

Khair-un-nissa gave birth to a son in 1801, and the next year, gave birth to a daughter. The children were called Sahib Allum and Saheb Begum, respectively, and resided in the women's quarters with their mother. Aside from the investigation into his affair with Khair-un-nissa, Kirkpatrick and his family lived, it seems, harmoniously; his children lived with their maternal family in the women's quarters of the residency while he carried out the business of the residency. Nonetheless, his children's future occupied Kirkpatrick and in various letters to his brother he voiced his concern about raising mixed-race children; in particular, he focused on their education, their level of cultivation, and their complexions. William Kirkpatrick returned to England in 1802 for health reasons but also to spend more time with his four daughters. In a letter written to William before his

---

[104] Wood, p. 166n.
[105] Philip Davies, *Splendours of the Raj* (London: John Murray, 1985), pp. 94–9, 249.

departure, James referred to a natural son he had already sent to England and speculated about the future of his newborn son with Khair-un-nissa:

I entreat you will take an early opportunity of ascertaining after your arrival in England, the bent and extent of my son's inclinations and abilities, and communicate the result to me with your opinion as to the line he is most likely to attain some eminence in. I still retain the opinion I expressed to my father of his future happiness... in the country he is in [England], rather than his native one, and that for the very same reason, that induced me to offer this opinion, the truth of which, will not I imagine be disputed by any one acquainted with the illiberal prejudices entertained against children born of native women, be their colour ever so fair, their conduct ever so correct, or their spirit ever so indisputable.[106]

Then James Kirkpatrick went on to address the question of fair complexions and passing as European:

In point of complexion, my little boy here, has greatly the advantage of his Brother in England, being as fair as it is possible I conceive for the offspring by any European female to be, and yet, he would I have no doubt, be exposed to the same illiberal objections and obloquoy, should he ever (which I trust he will not) be obliged to seek his misfortunes in manhood, in the country which gave him birth.[107]

Kirkpatrick revealed that he felt that his son and daughter would be better treated in England than in India; that prejudices against half-caste children were more entrenched in India than in England.[108] By arguing this, he exposed a crucial fault line in the racial and cultural politics among mixed-race families. Although Kirkpatrick was described as "going native," keeping his fingers dyed with henna,[109] and living with an Indian noblewoman, he envisioned a life for his children that was more British than Indian. Like Palmer, Kirkpatrick's children were baptized in the Church of England. Like Palmer's

---

[106] O.I.O.C., Mss. Eur. F 228/55, Letter Books of J. A. Kirkpatrick, dated 6 September 1801.

[107] Ibid.

[108] O.I.O.C., Mss. Eur. F 228/55, Letter Books of J. A. Kirkpatrick, dated 21 September 1801, "I will certainly endeavour to send my little Hyderabady to England as early as possible: but it will go to my very soul to part with him, to say nothing of the opposition I may expect to meet with on this point in another quarter in spite of any agreements; for you must know, that he is considered by his female connexions as a downright prodigy of loveliness of every kind."

[109] See Davies, Splendours, p. 97: Mounstuart Elphinstone, later Governor of Bombay, described him in his diary, "He wears mustachios; his hair is cropped very short, and his fingers are died with henna."

children, the Kirkpatrick children were raised within the household of their Indian mothers, but spent their later years (after age five) in England. Indeed, when Kirkpatrick offered Palmer advice on the question of sending Palmer's daughter to England, he commended Palmer's decision to send the young girl to England but tried to dissuade Palmer from accompanying her, "I should... [prefer] some snug secure situation in this country where you have passed so large a portion of your life." And in contrast to what was typical of Englishmen in India – complaining about the tropical weather – Kirkpatrick advised Palmer against the harsh British climate: "...you were long ago doubtful, how far you could stand the rigour of an English summer, how then can you think of braving an English winter?"[110] In Kirkpatrick's vision, India had transformed him and Palmer: they would be happier to remain in India rather than to return to England. For their children, however, an English education would be more appropriate.

This type of ambivalence as expressed by Kirkpatrick, particularly in making decisions about sending his children to be educated in England while being committed to remaining in India, is perhaps a permutation of what Homi Bhabha describes as "the terror" experienced by colonized subjects.[111] The levels of ambivalence that were present among a group of men who were commonly considered "colonizers" suggests that the dynamics of colonial contact, especially as it worked itself through family relationships and cultural practices, produced multiple anxieties about which culture to affiliate with in a hybrid environment. The crisis of ambivalence affected subjects on both sides of the colonial divide, as Rosemary George has argued, but particularly those at the crossroads of cultural exchange.[112] In "going native," Kirkpatrick's imitation of Indian cultural practices resulted in a significant dislocation. His anxieties, about "going native" but not wanting his children to do the same, play out the way in which hybridity could be highly destabilizing for colonial families.

These contradictions, exemplified by the lives of the Kirkpatricks and the Palmers, speak to the ways in which notions of cultural and racial hybridity circulated between Britain and India. What emerges from these family biographies were families who were mixed race,

---

[110] O.I.O.C., Mss. Eur. F 228/57, Letter Books of J. A. Kirkpatrick, dated 10 Dec. 1802.
[111] Homi Bhabha, *The Location of Culture* (London: Routledge, 1994), p. 113.
[112] Rosemary Marangoly George, *The Politics of Home: Postcolonial Relocations and Twentieth-century Fiction* (Cambridge: Cambridge University Press, 1996), Introduction.

multi-ethnic, not exclusively Indian or British. And yet, as Carlyle noted about Kitty, these families did not fit into a category that was widely recognized in Britain. They were not creole or mestizo: they were a kind of semi-oriental English. Although Kirkpatrick played native, his children actually *were* native. From his correspondence, it appeared he was ambivalent about the differences between the two. Kirkpatrick's successes as a resident were due in part to his abilities to participate in a Persian court culture. However, he feared that his mixed-race children would not be able to overcome their racial status in India; by sending them to England, he clearly hoped that their opportunities would be improved.

When Kirkpatrick died in Calcutta in 1805, his will illuminated his life and personal commitments. He left a considerable estate, in cash, Company paper, and other investments, valued at Sicca Rs. 400,000 to various friends and extended family both in India and in Britain. For each of his children he asked that Sicca Rs. 100,000 or £12,000 be invested in Company paper until they turned 25; for his father and each of his brothers, he left a mourning ring and £100. To his elder half-brother William's four daughters who were then residing in England, he left Sicca Rs. 25,000 (£1,500) each and then he made smaller bequests to other friends and family members, including his father's illegitimate daughters.[113] He also rewarded his munshi with 10,000 Sicca Rs. and the munshi's brother with Sicca Rs. 2,000. His wide-ranging generosity indicated that James's sense of family and community included not only his immediate family, his brothers and his father, but also his brothers' children, his father's illegitimate children, and his aunts and uncles and *their* children. Kirkpatrick's thoughtful bequest to his munshi of "my Emerald Ring with my Titles from the King of Delhi [the Mughal emperor] engraved in Persian," indicates that Kirkpatrick remembered his native friends as well.

To his wife, he left 10,000 Hyderabad rupees because, as he wrote, "[she is] amply provided for by Jagheers and other possessions both hereditary and acquired, independent of her personal property, and Jewels which cannot amount to less than half a Lack of rupees, [thus] I have not thought it necessary to provide particularly for her."

---

[113] H.C.O.S. (Calcutta), Will Register, 1805–1806, pp. 125–33. James's brother George received an additional Sicca Rs. 50,000 to relieve him of his debts. The two illegitimate daughters sired by James's father were granted £1,000 each, "which with proper management will I trust relieve them from any actual or future distress." Two aunts and an uncle, and their respective children were to receive £100 each in England.

Apparently, in spite of the Wellesley's investigation and the complaints of her grandfather against the immorality of such a union, Khair-un-nissa was not disowned from any family wealth as a result of her marriage to a Briton.

Finally, Kirkpatrick ended his will on this poignant note: he wished his children to be brought to England and accepted into Anglican society, avoiding the exclusions to public life that Catholics and Dissenters were subject to in England.

I nominate and appoint at the same time the Lord High Chancellor of Great Britain for the time being and the Court of Chancery at large Guardians of my said natural children Saheb Allum and Saheba Begum whom it is my wish and intention and most positive and urgent injunction, to have christened as soon as possible after their arrival in England, in order that they may become members of our holy Religion, and partakers of all its benefits, both temporal and eternal.[114]

After Kirkpatrick's death, his children were sent to England to reside with their uncle, William, who was then residing in London. From then on, they were effectively removed from their mother's household in Hyderabad. The children were renamed James George and Catherine Aurora and they boarded a ship in September 1805.[115] Before they left, George Chinnery painted a portrait of the two children in oriental dress. Unlike other visual representations of Europeans cross-dressing in oriental costume, the subjects in this painting could not undress and become Europeans. By drawing on the racial and cultural hybridity of its subjects, this portrait is a reminder of how complicated were the boundaries between native and European. The portrait was displayed for a long time in Khair-un-nissa's zenana and is now part of a private collection in Britain.[116]

The transformation of the Kirkpatrick children, from the children of an aristocratic household in the Deccan, into society children in London was almost complete. From all accounts, they were wealthy, well-educated young children. George died young, leaving a widow and three children. Catherine, according to Carlyle's account two decades later, became a merry young woman who with her cousin, Julia Strachey, hosted grand parties. Catherine eventually married Captain John Phillips (who Carlyle glibly described as "some idle

---

[114] H.C.O.S. (Calcutta), Will Register, 1805–1806, pp. 125–33.

[115] As noted by Captain George Elers, who was on the ship with the two children. "George Chinnery, artist," by J.J. Cotton, *BPP.*, vol. XXVII, pt. II, ser. no. 54 (April–June 1924).

[116] Davies, p. 99; Archer, *Indian Portraiture*, pp. 360–1.

ex-Captain of Sepoys") and had seven children with him in Exeter. She died at Torquay in 1889.

Conclusion

The centrality of quasi-marital alliances between European men and Indian women in the households of local rulers and British political agents of the East India Company shows that family and household interactions were bound up in a larger political culture that joined Company servants and local rulers. In spite of how politically productive such familial intimacy seemed, among Britons, this type of cultural contact produced many anxieties about hybridity and degeneration that threatened to undermine British superiority and the "national character."

The narratives of the relationships and families of William Palmer and James Achilles Kirkpatrick demonstrate the ways in which inter-racial relationships and mixed-race families of high-ranking officials and noblewomen of the local princely courts contributed to intercultural negotiation and exchange but were also constitutive of anxieties and ambivalences that emerged from these encounters. Both public and private, these families and their patriarchs were constantly negotiating their social, political, and racial status in ways that epitomized the unstable and fragile nature of cultural, social, ethnic, and racial boundaries between the British and Indians in the late eighteenth century.

By comparing the Palmer family's genealogy in India against the Kirkpatrick family's history in England, this chapter shows how notions of race were variously configured both in India and in Britain: while complexion mattered, manners, dress, education, and comportment also spoke eloquently about how to locate the mixed-race offspring of upper-class domestic arrangements. Palmer cohabited with a Muslim noblewoman, but his children were all baptized and subsequently married Europeans. Yet while Palmer's descendants resided in India with European airs, Kirkpatrick's children lived in England. The contradictions within each family and the kind of ambivalence expressed by Kirkpatrick about the racial and social status of his children suggests that the simultaneous development of race as a concept in England and in India was complicated by concerns about social opportunities, class status and "cultural competence."[117] While the

---

[117] The term is drawn from Ann Stoler, *Race and the Education of Desire* (Durham: Duke University Press, 1995). See also, Peter Robb, ed., *The Concept of Race in South Asia* (Oxford: Oxford University Press, 1992).

investigations into Kirkpatrick's affair with Khair-un-nissa signaled official changes against tolerance for cultural, racial, and social hybridity, the tenor and anxieties over local practices as they were expressed by men like Kirkpatrick and Palmer were much more textured, demonstrating that even the most cosmopolitan of men had parochial concerns when it came to their families.

3 Good patriarchs, uncommon families

> First I do declare and call God to witness that I am married to Punna Purree, a native of Hindostan who since the said marriage is become Punna Purree Pearse and I do firmly believe that our marriage tho' for many years kept secret was in every respect lawfull, and if it were not so I most assuredly would have gone thro' every possible form to have made it so.[1]
>
> Last will and testament of Col. Thomas Pearse, d. 1789

When Col. Thomas Deane Pearse, a high-ranking officer in the East India Company died in 1789, his lengthy will left numerous instructions about how he wanted his estate managed after his death. His will and its many codicils supplemented his military memoir, serving as an autobiographical account of his familial attachments. Like many other men, from high-ranking military and civil servants to ordinary merchants and rank-and-file soldiers, Pearse's bequests focused on the household and family he had with a native female companion. In making financial arrangements for their families, British men like Pearse acknowledged their paternal obligations, while remaining savvy about protecting their estates and maintaining their social standing. Negotiating between expressions of familial sentiment while carefully calculating the bequest that each family member deserved, British men were able to act as good patriarchs, providing for their families, and enforcing the household hierarchies that put them at the head of the table. "Family," in this colonial context, was broadly defined as men narrated complex domestic lives that included native women, "natural" children and perhaps even a more respectable, racially white family conceived in wedlock.

Ranging from long-term cohabitation to short-term sexual alliances as well as polygamous arrangements, a significant proportion of these relationships emerged as part of the master–servant contract between

---

[1] Oriental and India Office Collections, British Library (hereafter O.I.O.C.), L/AG/34/ 29/6 (1787–1790), pp. 26–45.

many men and their housekeepers, maidservants, and slaves, showing that household labor and sexual labor were closely linked in a colonial settlement where domestic help and the socially appropriate companionship of white women were equally scarce. Unlike the relatively famous conjugal relationships of James Kirkpatrick and William Palmer, many of these "marriages" were kept secret and never formally legitimated, although, as the case of Colonel Pearse suggests, final testaments and bequests were ways in which men made their intimate household relationships public and put family matters into the archives of colonial governance.

In spite of the contractual and coercive aspects of these relationships and the unequal position of their female partners, many men spoke of the affection, companionship, and comfort gained from their relationships. By doing so, they revealed that they were men of feeling, moral, compassionate, benevolent, sympathetic to the vulnerabilities of those less fortunate, in this case, native concubines and their mixed-race offspring who stood outside the social circles of colonial society.[2] Members of the eighteenth-century middle-class elites that historian Paul Langford has called "a polite and commercial people," many of these men had aspirations for success in India, hoping to climb the social and corporate ladders of the East India Company while remaining committed to a sense of personal and political virtue.[3] Like James Achilles Kirkpatrick and William Palmer, many of the men discussed in this chapter were keen to be good patriarchs and influential Company men – men who took seriously their family responsibilities for their native companions and mixed-race children, nonetheless aware that interracial conjugality might be at odds with the Company's aims. Unlike Kirkpatrick and Palmer, however, many of these men were well aware that interracial sex had social and professional costs and strategically kept their relationships under wraps.

British men who cohabited with native women may have been genuinely respectful of other cultures, but they were nonetheless always intimately aware of maintaining certain codes of masculinity, providing for vulnerable family members and rescuing women who were seemingly in distress as a means of sustaining their superior class and racial status among their colleagues in India and to their families in Britain. As the will of Col. Thomas Pearse demonstrates, many men were careful to

---

[2] Markman Ellis, *The Politics of Sensibility* (Cambridge: Cambridge University Press, 1996), Introduction; John Mullan, *Sentiment and Sociability* (New York: Oxford, 1988).

[3] Paul Langford, *A Polite and Commercial People: England, 1727–1783* (Oxford: Oxford University Press, 1989), ch. 3, pp. 463–71.

spell out their intentions so that they could maintain control of their households and their wealth even after they died. A well-regulated household, however irregular, remained crucial to maintaining a man's paternal authority over the inmates of his household and many men showed they were deeply invested in fulfilling familial and social expectations, thus laying the foundations for a colonial polity in which British men ruled over a large mass of native subjects, both in and outside his household.

Unlike other types of colonial archival records, wills are autobiographical texts precipitated by the anticipation of death, helping to construct the ways in which a subject wanted to be seen by others once s/he died, perhaps fulfilling a wish to be remembered better in death than in life. As Susan Dwyer Amussen notes of wills in seventeenth-century England, men often identified themselves as members of higher class groups than they were, giving away more money than they possessed.[4] An important element of self-making and registering oneself in the historical record, wills were also an opportunity for European men to construct their lineage as they wanted it to be recognized after their deaths.[5] These lineages, often comprised of the offspring of multiple sexual relationships, were fairly diverse and wide-ranging. In many cases, European men recognized their bloodlines after they died in ways that they had not while living: aside from female companions and children, many men also recognized various familial obligations, ties to close friends and their male servants.

These documents were filled with affect for loved ones and an appreciation for companionate conjugality, expressing what Lawrence Stone and others have argued were important features of the rise of the modern family in the eighteenth century.[6] Many scholars have argued that while this period may have witnessed a "sentimental revolution," patriarchs gained more legal authority over their descendants, having greater control over their own and their family's material interests.[7]

---

[4] Susan Dwyer Amussen, *An Ordered Society: Gender and Class in Early Modern England* (Oxford: Blackwell, 1988); see pp. 78 ff.

[5] See Trevor Burnard, "Family continuity and female independence in Jamaica, 1665–1734," *Continuity and Change* 7 (1992): 181.

[6] Lawrence Stone, *The Family, Sex and Marriage in England, 1500–1800* (London: Harper and Row, 1977); Edward Shorter, *The Making of the Modern Family* (New York: 1975); Randolph Trumbach, *The Rise of the Egalitarian Family* (New York: Academic Press, 1978).

[7] Susan Moller Okin, "Patriarchy and Married Women's Property in England: questions on some current views," *Eighteenth-century Studies* 17 (1983–84): 121–38; David Lemmings, "Marriage and the Law in the Eighteenth Century: Hardwicke's Marriage Act of 1753," *Historical Journal* 39 (1996): 339–60.

Expressions of familial affection were modified by pragmatism about financial responsibilities that kept wives, sisters, and other women within the family from inheriting too much money.[8] In final testaments, the terms of financial provisions show the ways in which a material economy of bequests and estate distribution was concomitant to an economy of sentiment and family affect, supporting a man's responsibilities as the household patriarch to hand down a sizeable estate to his heirs, but only those who he identified as part of his lineage. In negotiating between a sexual past that was often private and creating a respectable future for their families, European men demonstrated some of the complexity and ambivalence that shaped their sense of self, their privileged locations in a colonial society that prized the gendered and racial aspects of household and community order.

In over 600 wills that mentioned bequests to natural children or native companions between 1770 and 1840, many are repetitive in showing that Englishmen often had sexual relationships with local women.[9] Men used various terms to describe their conjugal domestic arrangements. Terms such as "my companion," "my girl," "my housekeeper," the "mother of my reputed child," "the mother of my natural child," suggested a liaison with a native woman. Among these wills, there were a range of conjugal alliances: some of these were harem-like, polygamous arrangements in which Englishmen cohabited with more than one woman, others practiced serial monogamy in which a man had a series of relationships with local women, and some were long-term monogamous relationships. By and large, few of these relationships were legitimated by marriage but existed as informal contracts between native women and their consorts in which men both controlled the purse strings but honored a sense of financial obligation to their extended households. Although the terms of each relationship had its own variations, in very general terms, there were three major types of relationships encompassed by the definition of "colonial companion." This chapter draws out some of the different material, social and cultural demands that structured different categories of relationships.

One kind of relationship was the female slave or domestic servant relationship with the master. Another type were long-term relationships between local women and European men in which both parties behaved

---

[8] Amy Louise Erickson, *Women and Property in Early Modern England* (London: Routledge, 1993); see also Susan Staves, *Married Women's Separate Property in England, 1660–1833* (Cambridge: Harvard University Press, 1990).

[9] I have collected 626 wills from the period between 1770 and 1840. Of these years, 1771–1774 (inclusive), 1801–1802 (inclusive), 1807, 1808, 1821, 1828, 1837 are incomplete.

as if they were legally married; these were relationships in which both parties observed codes of fidelity, raised their children together, and situations in which the woman was left with some earnings from the estate of the deceased. In these two types of relationships, the financial provisions made for the female companions were often restricted by careful executors and the terms of the will. Because few of these relationships were legitimated through marriage, the power disparity between the English master and the Indian slave, servant, or native woman was often replicated in the bequests stated in the will.

Although it is tempting to see this type of trend as indicative of how colonial practices short-changed native women from their inheritance, this pattern of distribution was increasingly common in upwardly mobile middle-class households in England.[10] Wives were often granted a modest allowance paid from the interest on the deceased's estate while the children were handsomely provided for, often inheriting the principal amount of the estate after the death of their mothers or at the age of majority. This allowed the principal of the estate to pass on to the next generation without being eroded by the widow or any man she might marry in the future. As feminist scholars of Britain have noted, this practice removed financial agency from widows and invested it in the hands of sons, thereby depriving women of control over the family's finances. Marking the shift from early modern patterns of household management in which women were central to household finances to the emergence of Victorian family arrangements in which women were seen to be marginal to household finance, upward social mobility was built on men earning and managing the family's wealth.[11] As Catherine Hall and Leonore Davidoff have noted, entering the middling classes in the late eighteenth and early nineteenth centuries was characterized by women moving out of the domain of paid work in family businesses to unpaid work in the home; ironically, this putatively progressive shift from early modern to modern, from working class to middle class, deprived women of control over the family money.[12] When British men in India observed inheritance practices that were reminiscent of their peers in Britain,

---

[10] Indrani Chatterjee, "Colouring Subalternity: slaves, concubines and social orphans in early colonial India," *Subaltern Studies X* (Delhi: Oxford University Press, 1999), pp. 79–83 for households in India; Erickson, *Women and Property*, pp. 166–9; Margaret Hunt, *The Middling Sort: Commerce, Gender, and the Family in England, 1680–1780* (Berkeley: University of California Press, 1996); Catherine Hall, *White, Male and Middle-class: Explorations in Feminism and History* (New York: Routledge, 1992) for households in Britain.

[11] See especially Hunt, *Middling Sort*, pp. 151–5, 157–62 and fn. 40.

[12] Catherine Hall and Leonore Davidoff, *Family Fortunes: Men and Women of the English Middle Class, 1780–1850* (London: Hutchinson, 1987).

they acted as household patriarchs by protecting the family income and establishing themselves as holding conventional middle-class ideals, in spite of their unlegitimated household relationships.

In honoring their familial responsibilities to native women, children, and servants living within their households, the provisions that British men made in India demonstrated that a marital contract was not necessarily required in recognizing family ties and financial responsibilities. Through wills, dying British men confirmed their understanding of a broad definition of "family," particularly because parts of the family were considered illegitimate in religious, social and legal domains and would have been unable to inherit without specific instruction.[13] Following inheritance patterns in Europe and other colonies where men often took financial responsibility for the inmates of their households, Englishmen in India appear to have taken seriously the notion that they ought to provide bequests for those who relied on them.[14] In addition to provisions made for legitimate and illegitimate family members, some men also recognized the services and loyalty of native servants.

The last type of relationship that is only partially represented in wills left by men forms the large majority of the relationships: those involving lower- and lower middle-class men who had few goods and small estates. In these cases, female companions received the bulk of the estates, indicating that at the end of their lives, these men had few familial ties to honor except to their female companions. Moreover, these wills were written by men who had few middle-class aspirations, as many of them were firmly lower class, rank-and-file soldiers. Like their more monied counterparts, they recognized their commitments to the native women with whom they lived; unlike higher-status men, however, they constructed fewer barriers between their estates and their loved ones.

By examining the ways in which European men wrote about their affective ties, this chapter argues that expressions of familial affection and racial anxieties, however contradictory, were constitutive parts of these men's subjectivities and the ways in which they managed their family affairs. While this might seem paradoxical, men who expressed

---

[13] Erickson, *Women and Property*, pp. 32, 78.

[14] For Spanish America, see Twinam, p. 94. By contrast, for the British West Indies, see Sarah Pearsall, "Gender," in David Armitage and Michael Braddick, eds., *The British Atlantic World, 1500–1800* (New York: Palgrave/Macmillan, 2002) p. 8; Trevor Burnard, "Inheritance and Independence: Women's status in early colonial Jamaica," *William and Mary Quarterly*, 3rd series, 48 (1991): 110. For the mid-Atlantic empire, see Lois Green Carr and Lorena Walsh, "The Planter's Wife: the experience of white women in seventeenth-century Maryland," *William and Mary Quarterly*, 3rd series, 34 (1977): 542–71.

great affection for their mixed-race and multicolored families also expressed anxieties about the social consequences of miscegenation both for themselves and for their offspring. By negotiating between their domestic lives with native women and children and their public lives as traders, merchants, civil servants, and soldiers, British men showed that they were keen to stay within the borders of respectability, "making empire respectable" by making their selves respectable, upholding norms of masculinity that required them to be good patriarchs, even to families that might have been not quite socially acceptable.[15]

I

Robert Grant, an officer in the Company army, was such a man. Concerned with appearances, his will tried to explain a conjugal tie to his female slave. One of a dozen lieutenant colonels in the East India Company's army, Grant had been an aide de camp and translator to the nawab of Awadh, which was one of the provinces that had been drawn into an alliance with the East India Company. Grant purchased a teenage girl named Zeenut in Faizabad and had formed a conjugal attachment with her. Shortly before his death, her relatives came to reclaim her, arguing that they had been tricked into selling her. According to Grant's account, she apparently shunned her family and vowed her loyalty to Grant and he added a codicil and bequeathed her a sufficient pension for life.[16]

Grant's estate was sizable and he left the majority of it to his brother, Charles Grant, a prominent official in the East India Company, and Charles's heirs. Grant also had two sisters in England to whom he granted £1,000 each. In one version of his will, he bequeathed the remainder of his estate to Alexander Grant, his first cousin, because "his blood and mine following almost without any foreign mixture from the same sources."[17] In the second version of the will, the provision for Alexander remained intact although the reference to foreign blood was omitted. Clearly, Grant's first imagining of his lineage was based on bloodline that was somehow pure. These first two wills, both dated 12 March 1777, gave specific instructions that the entire estate be

---

[15] Ann Stoler, *Carnal Knowledge and Intimate Power: Race and the Intimate in Colonial Rule* (Berkeley: University of California Press, 2002), ch. 3.

[16] O.I.O.C., L/AG/34/29/4 (1780–1783).

[17] Although the language of "blood" and miscegenation did not exist until the 1830s, some Europeans experienced racial mixing in very bodily terms. See Sudipta Sen, *Distant Sovereignty: National Imperialism and the Origins of British India* (New York: Routledge, 2002), pp. 137–40.

disbursed to British recipients, indicating that at the time of writing, Grant felt his rightful heirs to be in England. In the final codicil, dated 8 October 1779, Grant expanded on his beneficiaries and added six Indian servants who had been working for him.

In the two years between the first will and the final codicil, Grant made five sets of changes, indicating perhaps that he felt especially unwell. In the first codicil, dated 15 June 1778, Grant wrote:

> I do further will and desire that the sum of seven thousand rupees of my estate be set apart and laid out on good security for the purpose of maintaining my present Girl Zeenut and for the maintenance of the child of whom she is now big and that in case of her demise after delivery then the said sum of seven thousand rupees to become the property of such child as she may bring into the world to be applied for its education at the discretion of the aforesaid executors and the remaining principal to be given to the child if a male at the age of 21 to be by him managed if a female at the age of eighteen . . .

A month later, Grant amended this codicil and wrote, "My Girl Zeenut having miscarried I will that the seven thousand rupees beforementioned for her and the child be placed at interest for her maintenance she enjoying the interest for her life at her death the principal to go to my heirs by the foregoing terms."

Although it was fairly clear that Zeenut and Grant had a conjugal relationship, Grant added a clarification several months later: ". . . considering it as my duty to leave my affairs in as little embarrassment as possible, I likewise make some things mentioned in this will more plain viz. . ." The remaining four pages of the will recounted the story of Zeenut and how she became a member of Grant's family.

By retelling Zeenut's biography in the will, Grant wrote that he wanted to ensure that she had some financial provisions after his death: "I owe her in justice a maintenance." But a more analytic reading of the will suggests that Grant needed to legitimize and make explicit his relationship with Zeenut to his family in England, as well as to his friends in India. To a man who was careful to honor his "bloodline" in the first version of his will, recognizing a sexual relationship with a native slave (and possibly an illegitimate, mixed-race child) might have seemed like an unexpected turn of events that required explanation. His letter was addressed to his brother, Charles, who later became a proponent of introducing missionaries into India.[18]

---

[18] Charles Grant (1746–1823) wrote *Observations on the State of Society Among the Asiatic Subjects of Great Britain,* which encouraged the spread of missionary activity as a way of improving the moral character of natives.

Zeenut recounted a complicated tale that involved both family honor and personal loyalty to Grant. According to Grant, Zeenut had told him that she was the daughter of Sheik Mianulla and granddaughter to Sheik Samir who ran a school in Patna. After her father's death, her mother took her to Buxar where Zeenut became ill. A paternal uncle offered to take her to Gyzapoor for treatment and Zeenut's mother consented. The uncle was apparently an inveterate gambler and after becoming indebted, he sold Zeenut at auction in Fyzabad in 1776 to Grant. Grant wrote, "I could learn nothing of her history, but bought her. In the course of seven or eight months she got well. In the year 1778 I first was told her history by herself." When her mother eventually determined that Zeenut was still alive, she and another daughter and son-in-law went to Fyzabad to find out what had happened to Zeenut. After some investigation, they found out that Zeenut had been sold to a European who went to Lucknow. The mother became sick and died in Fyzabad but asked her other daughter to find Zeenut and give her the bulk of the family jewels. Once the second daughter found Zeenut in Lucknow, Zeenut declined to take the jewels and asked that they be divided between the remaining relatives. Nonetheless, the jewels remained in a bank in Lucknow and Zeenut refused to have them. Although Zeenut cried uncontrollably from the sadness of telling this story to Grant, she told Grant that she could not (for whatever reason) return to her family. Grant wrote that he offered to return her to her relatives but she rejected this idea and noted that "they were not desirous of this."

Grant believed that Zeenut's refusal to return to her family and accept her inheritance was an expression of loyalty to Grant. Grant's will continue in a narration of Zeenut's devotion: "In July 18 [sic], she was attacked with measles and a severe fever ... She miscarried at eight months and suffered exceedingly on my being ordered to Chittagong. I ordered her to stay at Lucknow and not to risk such a passage ... but she would bear me company. I permitted her the length at Patna and then left her in decent lodging but I believe in some ire and indignation at my hard-heartedness."

Grant's will ended with an explanatory note, addressed to his brother who was the executor of the will, "... I have taken resolutions in respect to her which if I live I hope God will enable me to keep ... She is an object of companion and tho' my soul ever allowed the least idea of force or seduction, I have been the particular object of sin to this poor creature." And finally, peculiarly, the last sentence read, "She is not handsome."

Grant's lengthy account of Zeenut's life is suggestive for what was left unsaid. Although Zeenut's mother persisted in finding her and gave her a cache of jewelry, Zeenut's claim that she could not return to her family was perhaps indicative not of loyalty to her master, but dishonor from her natal family. From Grant's retelling of Zeenut's life, it is clear that Zeenut was a young woman with a prominent lineage (her father and grandfather were sheikhs) and some fortune (the jewels are valuable enough to be held in a bank). But why did Zeenut refuse her inheritance, refuse to return to her family, and choose to remain with Grant? Although Grant's explanation seems plausible (Zeenut was loyal), we can only speculate how the situation was understood by Zeenut. One possibility is that her sexual relationship with Grant brought dishonor upon her family and that her refusal to return to her family signaled her understanding that she had transgressed a cultural code, although not perhaps through her own choice. It is not made explicit if she was pregnant when her sister found her but given the timing we can assume that she probably was.[19]

Lieutenant Grant's will is unusual in detailing how his liaison with a female slave came about, particularly for someone who was so concerned about "bloodlines." While a generous explanation for Grant's behavior toward Zeenut might be that he loved her and felt the need to ensure her financial future, another reading might be that within the calculus of sentiment and familial responsibility to which men of this era were subject, Grant had little choice but to account for his sexual activities with a woman who was very unequal to him in status and was moreover, a slave. In explaining his emotional attachment to her, Grant's affection for a young woman "who was not handsome," rationalizes a relationship that was highly unequal, not respectable (in his own eyes), and perhaps not worthy of his stature as a high-ranking soldier. Through his narrative, he is her hero; her attachment draws him into a sexual encounter "... tho my soul [n]ever allowed the least idea of force or seduction ..." By his account, sentiment compensates for the specter of violence between dramatically unequal parties and the master can become a rescuer and a hero, rather than an unfeeling cad who took advantage of a defenseless woman.

The master−slave relationship that Grant had with Zeenut was by no means uncommon, but any hint of sexual coercion on the part of the master was often explained as romantic attachment. A well-known case

---

[19] Grant wrote that he heard the story from Zeenut in 1778, and then she miscarried on July 18, 1778, suggesting that she was pregnant when her sister and brother-in-law found her.

of a master—slave relationship was that between the French military adventurer Claud Martin and his slave girl, Lise, who also fell in love with her master. According to Martin's will, she had come into his household as a slave and he had offered to free her and marry her to a man of her own religion, which was Islam, but she refused and insisted on remaining with Martin. In a narrative that paralleled Grant's account of Zeenut, Lise was also the daughter of a noble family who had sold her when they came upon hard times; like Zeenut, Lise also chose to remain loyal to her master than to return to her natal community.[20] Claud Martin wrote about Lise "since I acquired her which was when she was about 9 years old having brought her up and educated her as my own child with the most strickest [sic] decent and accomplished Eastern Education having learned her to read and write Persian and be strict in her religion .... I have loved her as the most chast [sic] and virtuous wife ..."[21] In affirming her virtue, her education, and her piety, Claud Martin's account rewrote the slave origins of Lise, remaking her into a respectable, educated, and more equal and appropriate partner for him.

These accounts of sentiment, emotional attachment, and affect that European men offered as their evidence of their familial ties to their native female servants and slaves explained and legitimated relationships that were considered illegitimate, vastly unequal, and racially transgressive. In these accounts, romantic love became a kind of currency that transcended social and racial divides, allowing European men to come to the rescue of Indian women and enter into a companionate relationship. There was often little doubt who was the more dominant or powerful figure in the relationship, but dramatically unequal social status undermined rather than supported a man's masculinity, and many men were careful to spell out that their slaves were not really slaves, they were high-born and had fallen on hard times, and they were educated, pious, and loyal in ways befitting a woman of higher social standing. While master—slave sex was constitutive of many colonial settlements in which native female slaves and servants lived in the households of white men, some men went to great lengths to record their feelings for these relatively powerless women and the children that were borne of them. By constructing themselves as worthy patriarchs for families that might have been socially inappropriate, men affirmed their

---

[20] See O.I.O.C, L/AG/34/29/12 (1800), p. 45 ff. In Martin's will, he spoke about Lise, "who have [sic] been most faithfully attached to me and never had the smallest room to complain of her ..." See Rosie Llewellyn-Jones, *A Very Ingenious Man: Claude Martin in Early Colonial India* (Delhi: Oxford University Press, 1992), pp. 72–3. Martin also had three other slave girls with whom he had sexual relationships.

[21] O.I.O.C., L/AG/34/29/12 (1800), p. 45 ff.

emotional ties not so much to express certainty about their familial ties
/ and financial obligations but because they were conflicted about
themselves, their class positions, their sexual activities and they
needed these conflicts to be resolved in some manner after their deaths.

In similar other wills, British men made bequests to their "housekeepers," their "slaves," their "girls," drawing attention to conjugal
relationships with women in their households. In a will written the same
year as Grant's, David Dean, a Company mariner, freed his slave girl
Sophia, bought her a house and left her a principal sum that would
produce a monthly income. The daughter borne of this liaison received
the remainder of the estate and her mother's portion upon her mother's
death.[22] Similarly, Henry Foxcraft, a carpenter, left his natural daughter
his entire estate and granted her mother, a native woman slave called
Kate, freedom.[23] In another will written that year, Capt. William
Campbell stipulated that a principal sum of £200 or Rs. 2,000 be
invested for his "housekeeper named Polly and mother" to his natural
son who was also to receive the remainder of the estate.[24]

Financial provisions made for female companions and the children
born of these unlegitimated relationships suggests that these households
and families were based both on servitude and some level of affection.
Although these women were marked by a vague reference, the financial
terms suggest what native women stood to gain for their sexual and
domestic labor. Most often, the female companion of a European
received a small monthly stipend (anywhere from S. Rs. 12 to S. Rs. 100
monthly), even though she often had little control over the principal or
the management of these resources. On her death, the principal and any
house or property would revert to her child or children or to legitimate
heirs such as relatives or other children in England, therefore securing
the wealth to parts of the family that the testator felt should receive it.
This pattern of estate management funneled money away from native
female companions and wives into the hands of a lineage that the
testator felt was more socially appropriate, making it clear that the native
companion, however beloved, stood outside the circles of family
belonging and was an unlikely recipient of the testator's estates.

According to wills, about a third of interracial conjugal relationships
occurred between British men and their female servants, showing that
these relationships came about through proximity and circumstance,

---

[22] High Court, Original Side, Calcutta High Court (hereafter H.C.O.S.), 1777–1780,
pp. 103–5.
[23] H.C.O.S., 1774–1777, no pages, filed 8 February 1776.
[24] H.C.O.S., 1777–1780, pp. 185–7.

bringing men and women of very unequal positions together for relatively short amounts of time. Slightly less common were longtime relationships between men and native women who officially never married. Known as "faithful concubinage,"[25] in contrast to the master–servant relationships examined above, these relationships occurred with women who were not domestic servants and occasionally appeared to have some personal wealth and autonomy, such as Bibi Faiz Baksh, companion of William Palmer for thirty-five years.

Col. Thomas Deane Pearse (d. 1789), whose will served as the epigraph to this chapter, had a longtime attachment to his companion, Punna Purree. A high-ranking officer in the East India Company army whose contributions were much celebrated, Pearse's public profile did not mention his family life until he died, when he revealed that he had married Punna Purree Pearse and bequeathed her a portion of his estate and a portion to their son, Thomas Mahomet Deane Pearse. Because of the money she inherited, Punna Purree Pearse also left a will.

Pearse, who died in the summer of 1789, was a colonel in the East India Company's army, having worked his way up from the bottom of the military ladder. He arrived in India in 1768, after service in the West Indies, and his major military contribution was that he commanded five regiments against Haider Ali in the wars in the Carnatic during the early 1780s.[26] Although much of his military activities occurred in southern India, he maintained a household in Calcutta and was Governor-General Warren Hastings's close friend. In 1780, Pearse served as the second in Hastings's duel against Philip Francis, Hastings's political rival on the Calcutta Council, and Hastings presented Pearse with a diamond ring set in gold when he left India in 1785, which Pearse later gave to his son.[27] The close relationship with Hastings no doubt enabled Pearse to enlist Hastings's help in educating Pearse's son after he died. After Pearse's return to Calcutta in 1786, he became the deputy manager of the Military Orphan Society, a charitable organization that provided education and vocational training for the children and orphans of soldiers and officers of the Company's armies in India. Pearse promoted a plan to give a plot of land to half-cast sons of officers in the Sunderbans so that they could establish their own colony. The plan was approved but received no support from the Council in Calcutta

---

[25] Kenneth Little, "Some aspects of color, class and culture in Britain," in John Hope Franklin, ed., *Color and Race* (Boston: Beacon Press, 1968), p. 237.

[26] *East India Military Calendar*, vol. II, pp. 247–50.

[27] *Bengal Past and Present*, vol. XXI, pt. II, ser. no. 59 (July–Sept., 1925).

so it fell through.[28] By all accounts, Pearse was a prominent officer in the Company's military establishment who was deeply involved in Calcutta civic affairs and socialized with the highest levels of European society in Calcutta, attending dinners with Philip Francis, member of the Calcutta Council. Like many men who kept a native woman, Pearse's public persona did not reflect his most intimate affairs and he attended these gatherings without his "wife."[29]

After his death, his public accomplishments were celebrated: his memoirs detailed the important military campaigns in the Mysore wars and were excerpted extensively in *Bengal Past and Present* in the 1900s and 1910s. His portrait hung (and still does) in the Royal Academy at Woolwich, no doubt an inspiration to aspiring soldiers-in-training who were headed toward India. In spite of the high volume of biographical information about Pearse, only his will revealed his most intimate attachments.

Pearse's will began with a plea to his relatives to consider his long relationship with Punna Purree as "lawfull," as he intended to protect his estate from greedy relatives in Britain who might want to contest the legitimacy of his bequests.[30] He noted that he had one son, born several years after his marriage, "as is known to Nicholas Grueber, now living to whom I disclosed the secret in 1773." "Even if my marriage with her should be defective or set aside," Pearse asked that his bequest be granted her. In claiming legitimacy for a marriage and for a child that might be beyond legality and the approval of colonial social life, Pearse's will shows his attempts to secure this child's future. In spite of the prevalence of conjugal relationships with local women, high-ranking officers were careful to defend these relationships, both to their families and to the colonial settlement.[31]

By his own account, Pearse's relationship with Punna Purree was at least fifteen years in duration and his declaration of commitment in his will served as further testimony that he saw this as a long-term relationship. Although Pearse considered his relationship "lawfull," whether the relationship was solemnized by the Anglican church establishment in Calcutta or through Muslim rites remains unclear.

---

[28] "The Bengal Military Orphan Society," *Calcutta Review* 44, issue 87 (1867): 173.

[29] O.I.O.C., Mss. Eur. E25, Mackrabie Papers, pp. 103–5; Alexander Mackrabie, counsel to Philip Francis noted in his diary on 12 Sept., 1776 that Colonels Pearse, Don and Pottingham came to dinner with Begum Frances Johnson. Notably, all three men came without their native female companions.

[30] O.I.O.C, L/AG/34/29/6 (1787–1790), pp. 26–45.

[31] Kenneth Ballhatchet, *Race, Sex and Class Under the Raj: Imperial Attitudes and Policies, 1793–1905* (New York: St. Martin's Press, 1980).

After settling his debts with his sister Martha and repaying his "wife" Rs. 9,000 that he owed her, Pearse revealed yet more about his domestic life,

To my female friend Moortee also a native of Hindostan who has lived with me many years in my zenana and bore me two female children, long since dead, I owe Rs. 3,000 ...

Like other well-known British officials of this time, such as Lt. Col. James Kirkpatrick in Hyderabad, and David Ochterlony and Charles Theophilus Metcalfe in Delhi, Pearse also kept a zenana. While his commitment to a secret marriage *and* his admission that he kept a zenana might be difficult to reconcile, at his death he divided his estate for who he viewed as his heirs, Punna Purree Pearse, their son Thomas, and another female friend, Moortee. In dividing up the will, Pearse recognized his favored companion by assigning her a larger portion of his estate. This practice was fairly common. For instance, when Lt. Col. Henry Wray died in 1809, he listed various houses that he owned, including one in "Jaun Bazaar which house is now in occupation of my old Beebee called Nancy." Excepting this house, he asked that all his property be sold to form a trust to pay out the monthly stipends as stipulated. He then listed seven children who had three different mothers and asked that Beebee Nancy, "my old Beebee" be given S. Rs. 35 monthly, Ragiah be given S. Rs. 15 monthly and Gudiah the same amount. He ordered that as long as all three women lived in the house with Beebee Nancy, they would continue to receive their monthly allowances.[32] It was far more common to confirm the household's hierarchy through bequests, although some men did grant equal sums to their sexual companions. Isaac Meyers, a pensioner in the pilot service residing at Fort William, left behind two houses and some property when he died in 1821. He ordered that all of his property be sold and that his two female companions be given the equal sums of S. Rs. 3,000. He asked that the two women, "commonly known as Diana and Betty," share all the household effects equally and raise the eleven children in the household. The children were each given S. Rs. 2,000 to be invested in Company bonds until they turned 21 or got married.[33]

As other wills, the hierarchy of authority within the household was reflected in the amount of each bequest. In Thomas Pearse's original will, dated 13 July 1781, three-tenths of Pearse's estate went to Punna Purree, six-tenths to his son, Thomas, and the remaining

[32] H.C.O.S. (1829), pp. 114–21.
[33] H.C.O.S. (1820–1821), pp. 278–93.

one-tenth to Moortee. A year later in a codicil dated 2 September 1782, he asked that any children born to either of his female companions share in the portion that he had bequeathed his son, indicating that he was sexually active with both women. In a later codicil, dated 20 August 1785, he added a further Rs. 1,700 to the amount that he owed his "wife" and clarified the following:

My wife Punna Purree Pearse or, if not, my lawfull wife, Punna Purree a native of Hindostan has purchased two pieces of ground out of her own Pocket Money one piece lies near my garden and the other near Budge Budge. It is my will that these two pieces of ground be not considered as any part of my estate, but as her independent right and property and entirely at her own disposal.

That Punna Purree owned property and that she had loaned him a substantial amount of money suggests that she was herself a woman of property and wealth. In the penultimate codicil dated 12 May 1789, Pearse asked that Rs. 500 be given monthly to his wife, Rs. 250 a month to his female companion and that his house in Chowringhee be maintained by his estate for his "wife" and son. If in 1782, Pearse was compelled to make equal provision for children born of Punna Purree and of Moortee, by 1789, it was clear that Punna Purree had established herself as the more privileged woman in the household and the only one to claim the bulk of the estate for herself and her son. The shift in the relative status between the two women in the household speak to ways in which native women in these households were in a constant process of negotiating with each other, as well as with the patriarch of the household.

In contrast to the master–servant relationship detailed above, these relationships between Company officials and local women were slightly more balanced, although by no means equal. Although (as was true for Pearse) the man sometimes had several female partners while the women were assumed to be monogamous, relationships that were marriage-like conferred significant financial benefits and independence to the women who were in them. Unlike master–servant relationships, these women often received a large lump sum of money, a house or estate, and a generous monthly stipend often up to S. Rs. 250 a month. The long-lasting nature of these relationships and the generous financial provisions made in the will suggests that Pearse intended to fulfill his familial obligations as he might have if this were a legally sanctioned marriage. Indeed, much like Pearse, some men stated the length of the relationship as a way of claiming legal legitimacy for the relationship. Roderick Fraser, Lieutenant Colonel in the Company army, left sizable bequests of between £1,500 to £2,000 to each of his five children, and S. Rs. 55 monthly to the mother of these children, Jower Buksh. In his will, he wrote, "Be it known that the female friend named Jower Buksh in this will lived with me since the year 1790 in order therefore to prevent litigation (being not acquainted with the shiel form of law) I do hereby declare the aforesaid children to be ... born of the said Jower Buksh ..."[34]

In large numbers, most native women in India received a stipend that was paid from the interest on the principal of the estate, while the estate itself was held for a child or other relative in England. The capital amount was most frequently invested by the executor in the Company's bonds and the income produced was to be paid to the female companion.[35] This allowed the woman to benefit as long as she was living, but have no claim on the estate when she died. After the death of the companion, the capital either devolved to their children or to relatives in England. Although some women did receive lump sum payments, most were less fortunate than Punna Purree Pearse and received amounts ranging from S. Rs. 1,000 to S. Rs. 20,000 (£100 to £2,000).

In a relationship comparable in longevity to the Pearses, John Deane of the East India Company's civil service asked that a trust be established by his executors to pay the following bequests. "To Beebee Mussumaut Matloob Brish who has lived with me nearly twenty years and whose kindness and affection towards me during the whole of that period has continued unadulterated, the sum of S. Rs. 100 per month as long as she lives." For their six illegitimate children, Deane asked that each receive £2,000 when they turned 21 and a yearly allowance that was not to exceed £100 yearly. Of the six children, three were christened and living with relatives and friends in England; of the remaining three, two had yet to be christened and one was in Futty Ghur. While Deane's sister and her two sons received outright bequests of £1,000 and £2,000, respectively, Deane's female companion received a stipend and no access to the capital that produced the stipend.[36]

This pattern of inheritance paralleled practices among the married, middling classes in England, suggesting that English women and native women on the Indian subcontinent experienced comparable financial

---

[34] H.C.O.S. (1818), pp. 419–22.

[35] Many of the large agency houses were central in conducting these transactions, most prominently, Palmer and Co. in its various permutations. Palmer and Co. emerged after 1807; before that, it was Cockrell, Trail, Palmer and Co. See Peter Wood, *A Vassal State in the Shadow of Empire: William Palmer's Bank in Hyderabad, 1810–1824,* Ph.D. Dissertation, University of Wisconsin, 1981.

[36] H.C.O.S. (1818), pp. 80–3.

benefits and constraints from marriage. Yet the crucial difference in the family landscapes of interracial Anglo-India is that most conjugal relationships mentioned in wills were not legalized by a marital contract. While a generous interpretation might suggest that Englishmen were honorable for making financial provisions for native women with whom they had no enforceable contractual commitment, another reading suggests that cohabitation might have been a strategic maneuver for Englishmen wanting to rise in the Company's service, allowing the possibility of marrying an English woman when he had enough money and status.

From the perspective of the Englishmen who recognized their conjugal companions when they were dying but didn't legitimize their "marriages" when they were living, maintaining informal households with native women was a way of maximizing one's domestic comforts without damaging one's public reputation. As in the case of Thomas Pearse, for a high-ranking, public figure on the colonial establishment, keeping a bibi was acceptable so long as it was kept in the background. But for some Englishmen, cohabitation was a temporary relationship rather than a long-term commitment. As Raymond Smith and Sarah Pearsall have noted for the West Indies, Englishmen enjoyed interracial conjugality, deferring formal marriage to someone racially appropriate until they returned to England or until an Englishwoman became available.[37] Men such as Thomas Pearse, William Palmer, and others had spent their youth in the West Indies, but a Caribbean experience was not always a prerequisite to maintaining a double sexual-life. William Kirkpatrick, resident in Hyderabad and Pune, brother to James Achilles, kept a bibi, to whom he returned when his marriage to Maria Pawson failed and she returned to England. Richmond Thackeray, father of the novelist, cohabited with a native woman while in India and later married an Englishwoman. When Richmond Thackeray died in 1815, he asked that his illegitimate child named Amelia accompany his wife and son (William Makepeace Thackeray) to England and his wife be appointed Amelia's guardian. He asked that £100 yearly be granted each to his daughter and son and £500 to his wife, putting them into the ranks of the very wealthy in England.[38] In contrast, Amelia's mother,

---

[37] Raymond Smith, "Hierarchy and the dual marriage system in West Indian society," in Jane F. Collier and Sylvia Yanagisako, eds., *Gender and Kinship: Essays Toward a Unified Analysis* (Stanford: Stanford University Press, 1987); Sarah Pearsall, "Gender"; see also Jennifer S. H. Brown, *Strangers in Blood: Fur Trade Company Families in Indian Country* (Vancouver: University of British Columbia, 1980), p. 52.

[38] Langford, *Polite and Commercial People*, see tables on pp. 62–3, showing that families earning £50 per year were in the top twenty percent of earners.

a local native woman, received S. Rs. 16 (about £1) a month or £12 a year.[39] Although Thackeray granted equal maintenance portions to his children, he stipulated that on the death of his heirs, the principle of the estate was to become his son's, thereby protecting the family's wealth.

The existence of legitimate, purely European children alongside illegitimate, mixed-race children produced requests that "natural" children be adopted by the European wives of these men. The will of Charles Hay Campbell, a major in His Majesty's army, made bequests for eight children, three who were born out of wedlock to a native woman between the years 1820 to 1822 and five who were born to he and his wife, Jane Murray, between 1825 and 1831. His wife was given custody over the three "natural" children, with no instructions provided for the children's native mother.[40] Similarly, John Gordon, a captain in the 20th Regiment, Native Infantry, ended his will with the following request, "I leave my daughter Ann born before wedlock to the care jointly of my beloved wife ... and leave it entirely [to her] to give her [my daughter] an education suitable to her rank and expectations in this life."[41]

In these stipulations for how family members should be compensated when the male head of the household died, children were often granted greater financial security than their mothers, although men in Britain and in India varied as to whether they made financial distinctions between their son and daughters, and between their lawful children and those born out of wedlock to native women.[42] Edward Watson, senior merchant for the Company in Bengal, left a will in which he made separate bequests for five illegitimate children and their mother, Shah Bebee, and subsequent provisions for his wife Margaret and legitimate son and daughter.[43] John Williams, captain in the Company's army acknowledged two daughters and a son who were born of his wife, Mary Ann, and a "natural son," who received half that of his legitimate sons.[44] In contrast, Henry Hantry, Lieutenant Colonel in the Bengal Light Cavalry, asked that his shares in the Bengal Laudable Society, an insurance scheme for soldiers, be divided equally between his natural

---

[39] H.C.O.S. (1814–1815), pp. 485–9. The name Amelia resurfaced in William Makepeace Thackeray's *Vanity Fair* in which Amelia Sedley plays the simple-minded heroine.
[40] H.C.O.S. (1832–1833), pp. 1–7.
[41] H.C.O.S. (1822), pp. 16–17.
[42] Erickson, *Women and Property*, chs. 3 and 5.
[43] H.C.O.S. (1818), pp. 189–95.
[44] H.C.O.S. (1809–1810), no pages, filed 31 March 1810.

daughter and two legitimate sons.[45] Similarly, James Nicolson, captain in the Company army, asked that his estate be divided equally among the ten children he had had, some with various native women and two with his wife.[46] Even relatively low-ranking soldiers, such as John Gabb, private in the Native Infantry, acknowledged that he had two illegitimate sons and a younger legitimate son for whom he made provisions.[47]

In relatively wealthier families, as was true for Thomas Pearse, the children were sent to England for an education. The younger Thomas Pearse entered Harrow, where he was known as Muhammad.[48] The children of George Foulis, Major in the Bengal Infantry, were already in Britain. In Foulis's will, filed in 1805, he bequeathed S. Rs. 3,000 to "Beebee Jawn the mother of my natural children." After all the other property was distributed, the remainder of the estate was to be divided between their three children, Ann, Robert, and Elizabeth who could be found "under the care of my Brother James Foulis, Esq., of Hanover Street, no. 37, New Town, Edinburgh."[49] Thomas Gentil, who was living in Bihar at the time of his death, asked that his natural daughter Mary Jane continue her education at a school in Kensington and receive £150 a year until she turned 21, at which point, she was to receive a lump sum of £2,000. His son, George, was already in an apprenticeship with a bookbinder on Fleet Street and received £1,000. Gentil also made a provision for his female companion, Beebee Doomun, and her daughter, Jabun, to whom he left Rs. 1,500 and a desire that she "be married to a respected native."[50] Removing children to Britain, away from the care of the native mother was hardly exceptional. In the volume of wills filed between 1805 and 1807, eight of the thirty-seven wills that mentioned a native female companion, the testator assigned money to "natural children" who were in Europe under the care of relatives at home.[51] Similarly, in the volume for three months December 1819 to February 1820, two of the six wills either ask that the children be sent to Britain or were already resident there.[52] Of the total sample of over six hundred wills, over 10 percent included instructions to either send a child to Europe or addressed a child already in Europe.

---

[45] H.C.O.S. (1833–1834), pp. 298–9.
[46] H.C.O.S. (1834–1835), pp. 328–39.
[47] H.C.O.S. (1823–1824), pp. 179–82.
[48] Dennis Kincaid, *British Social Life in India, 1608–1937* (London: Routledge and Kegan Paul, 1938), p. 120.
[49] H.C.O.S. (1805–1807), pp. 185–6.
[50] H.C.O.S. (1818), pp. 25–9.
[51] H.C.O.S. (1805–1807).
[52] H.C.O.S. (1819).

Siblings of the deceased were often enlisted in bringing up mixed-race nieces and nephews. Adam Freer, superintending surgeon in the service of the East India Company, asked that his natural children, John and Margaret, who were under the care of Freer's brother in Scotland, inherit his estate in equal shares.[53] John Porter McMillan, Lieutenant in the Native Infantry, asked that his three children (one who was still unborn at the time he wrote the will) receive the bulk of his estate, with the instruction that "Lastly, it is my earnest wish and desire that the children may be sent home to the care of my sisters as soon as is convenient."[54]

Like families in many eighteenth-century British colonies, educating children in Europe was a way in which mixed-race children were re-educated and resocialized to "improve" themselves and undo the perceived effects of miscegenation.[55] Appropriate education was considered one way in which a mixed-race child could be cleansed and disciplined into European comportment and many testators asked that their children be inculcated with Christian principles.[56] Robert Crawford, a Company civil servant, stipulated that his natural daughter Ann Crawford be sent to England to reside with his sister Barbara to be brought up "... in the strictest principles of virtue and morality ..."[57] Similarly, Samuel Bacon, a Company merchant, asked that his sister Mary Anne received S. Rs. 8,000 in order to "superintend the education of my child and see that she is brought up in the fear of God and the principle of the Christian religion."[58]

This type of education had mixed results. A case of libel in 1810 in Britain filed against ten-year-old Jane Cummings and her grandmother focused attention on a mixed-race child who accused her school-mistresses of being lovers. Jane, the daughter of an East India Company

---

[53] H.C.O.S. (1810–1811), pp. 44–5.

[54] H.C.O.S. (1826–1827), pp. 212–13.

[55] For North America, see Philip Morgan, *Slave Counterpoint: Black Culture in the Eighteenth-century Chesapeake and Low Country* (Chapel Hill: University of North Carolina Press, 1998), p. 410; Jennifer Brown, *Strangers in Blood*, pp. 53, 56, 184; van Kirk, p. 87; Richard Godbeer, "Eroticizing the middle ground: Anglo-Indian sexual relations along the eighteenth-century frontier," in Martha Hodes, ed., *Sex, Love, Race: Crossing Boundaries in North American History* (New York: New York University Press, 1999), p. 104.

[56] Ann Stoler, "A Sentimental Education: native servants and the cultivation of European Children in the Netherlands Indies," in Laurie J. Sears, ed., *Fantasizing the Feminine in Indonesia* (Durham: Duke University Press, 1996); Ann Stoler, *Race and the Education of Desire* (Durham: Duke University Press, 1995), ch. 5, esp. pp. 152–3, 155–6, 159, 160–2.

[57] H.C.O.S. (1774–1777), no pages, filed 22 April 1776.

[58] H.C.O.S. (1819–1820), pp. 67–8.

merchant and a native woman from Patna, had been sent to her grandmother in Scotland to be enrolled in a girls' boarding school. While sharing a bed with her schoolmistress, the young Jane discovered that while she was sleeping, the schoolmistress was lying naked with another schoolmistress. Dramatized later by the Lillian Hellman play, *The Children's Hour*, the case was based on testimony that constructed Jane into a monstrous being: hypersexualized, overimaginative, and tainted by her birth in India.[59]

A central proviso in instructions about educating children was that the children be placed in homes other than their mother's. Occasionally, a bequest to the female companion was contingent on her consent to give up the children, as was the case in the family of J. A. Cock, who asked that Eliza, "who is now living with me," be given Rs. 150 a month, "as long as she gives up the children to the executors for their education in England."[60] Similarly, Hugh Adams, a mariner in Calcutta, asked that S. Rs. 2,000 be provided to the native mother of his daughter, "provided she gives up my daughter Catherine to my executors and executrix for the purpose of having her educated in England."[61] One man, in the service of the Maratha armies, was explicit and asked that his three children be educated somewhere that was "... most convenient to keep them [the children] from imbibing any ill quality from their bad mother."[62]

By requesting that the children be relocated after their death, either to Europe or to European guardianship in India, British fathers affirmed that what was at the heart of their anxieties was that native life was inappropriate for their offspring. "Placing" their children in appropriate jobs or marriages became one of the critical aims of men as they narrated what they wanted for their offspring in their wills.[63] Ironically, men who were understood to have "gone native" by cohabiting with native women made arrangements that attempted to undo this acculturation in their children. As Chatterjee argues, because the mothers were considered "illegitimate," children were subordinated to the influence of their fathers.[64]

Although companionate, long-term relationships conferred some financial benefits to the women who became involved in them,

[59] Ardel Marie Thomas, *Victorian Monstrosities: Sexuality, Race and the Construction of the Imperial Self, 1811–1924*, Ph.D. dissertation, Stanford University, 1998.

[60] H.C.O.S., (1838), pp. 474–5.

[61] H.C.O.S. (1814–1815), pp. 55–61.

[62] H.C.O.S. (1819–1820), pp. 282–4.

[63] Jennifer Brown, *Strangers in Blood*, ch. 5.

[64] Chatterjee, "Colouring subalternity," p. 76.

the large majority of women had little control over their finances or the fate of their children. Even when women were literate, high-born and moneyed in their own right, their status within these relationships was far from equal with the men that they became involved. While the example of Pearse and his family arrangement account for about half of all the relationships described in wills, these statistics are skewed. Of the men who left wills, most were financially comfortable and had sizable estates to manage. Many of these wills describe men like Pearse: prominent officials who had resided a lifetime in India and formed conjugal attachments with local women. While these were the men that Percival Spear wrote about in his account of eighteenth-century social life in north India, they do not account for *all* of the relationships that existed between European men and native women in northern India.

In contrast to master–servant relationships or relationships of long duration, which were largely taken up by men of some status, men who were foot soldiers, sailors, and lower-class employees of the East India Company form the third category of the relationships between European men and native women. Low-ranking men often left their entire estates to their female companions; their wills are marked by their simplicity of their bequests. In stark contrast to the wills of socially conscious officers and civil servants, these wills involved very few directions for appropriate schooling for the children or conditions for granting money; moreover, any hierarchical distinction between bequests and status were absent. Many lower-class men, who appeared completely dependent on their female companions, did not differentiate financially or constrain the bequests they made to their bibis. As members of the non-elite British, they were not concerned with upholding their class and cultural status in the same ways as more elite men such as Colonel Pearse. Most noticeably, the female companions were named executors suggesting that not all of these bequests to native women were supervised by British male executors.

One will, written apparently at camp by C. Berry, stated very simply, "I desire that whatever property I possess, or may hereafter possess in India after discharging my lawful debts (which may be found detailed in this book) be given to my female companion Noor Jehan Khanum, for her entire use and benefit..."[65] J. J. Tetley asked that everything go to "the old female friend named Munnoo Jan alias Aleemer Beebee and the two young girls that have been brought up by me commonly called Toonoo and Bunnoo."[66] Andrew Robinson, identified as writer to the

---

[65] H.C.O.S. (1803–1805), p. 246.
[66] H.C.O.S. (1827–1828), pp. 305–6.

Judge and magistrate in the district of Tipperah, wrote, "I give and bequeath the whole of my worldly property unto Beebee Khepee my kept mistress being all the compensation in my power for her faithful attachment to me during the number of years we lived together."[67] Even men who identified themselves as members of the royal armies (who could remit their estates home more easily), left their modest estates to their female companions: Thomas Ballis, private in His Majesty's 76th Regiment of Foot, asked that everything he owned be given to "Mary (a native woman of this country) as the only and last token I can leave her of my approbation of her good conduct and affection toward me during the seven years she cohabited with me."[68] This pastiche of wills was remarkably uniform: these men had no other attachments and left their entire estates in the hands of local women, without elaborating any distinctions through their bequests.

Relationships between lower-class men and their local female companions are not easily counted because so many died without leaving wills. Although several hundred ordinary soldiers and merchants died in India every year, there were, on average, fewer than a dozen wills left by them per year.[69] These men, who were not wealthy nor linked to a larger society of Europeans, often relied entirely on local women as their communities and asked that their bequests be managed and received by the native women with whom they lived.

Wills written by lower-class men and rank-and-file soldiers suggest a relative absence of social anxiety based on racial and gender awareness of their superiority over native women. Men of higher status made distinctions between native women and European relatives speaking to the ways in which anxieties about race were most often articulated by members of particular class groups whose positions as powerful members of the colonial establishment required constant affirmation. As Ballhatchet and Stoler have both noted, the emergence of class-based anxieties about racial and sexual intimacy was a crucial part of the mechanisms that regulated the behavior of upper-class officials in relation to the large numbers of lower-class men and native women.[70] From the point of view of lower-ranking men, native women were often

---

[67] H.C.O.S. (1819), p. 139.

[68] O.I.O.C, L/AG/34/29/11, p. 2.

[69] See P. J. Marshall, "British Society in India under the East India Company," *Modern Asian Studies* 31 (February 1997): 96. He estimated that about 4,500 soldiers went to India during this period and about 7 to 10 percent died annually. With that calculation, anywhere from 317 to 450 died every year, although between 1790 and 1810, there was an average of 100 men whose wills were stored.

[70] See Ballhatchet, *Race, Sex, and Class*, chs. 2 and 3; Stoler, *Carnal Knowledge*, ch. 2.

acknowledged as the only attachments and obligations they had while stationed in India. Because few of these men enjoyed the social privileges of class, few were able to imagine the advantages that being European might offer and did not seem to view interracial liaisons as endangering their future prospects.

In comparing the final testaments of European men from different class and status groups, middle-class and socially mobile men were conflicted about their households of native women and mixed-race children while lower-class men had less reason to worry about the sorts of problems that interracial sex and miscegenation gave rise to in a colonial settlement. In spite of the profusion of sentiments, elite men made financial provisions that balanced their sexual pasts against what they imagined could be the future of their lineage and legacy. For less elite men, who perhaps had a different set of hopes for their legacies, sentiment and financial stipulations were often much more closely aligned.

Conclusion

European men who participated in interracial liaisons with native women experienced ambivalence in negotiating between their intimate lives and their public aspirations. Familial anxieties about class and racial status intersected with concerns that men expressed about their status as good patriarchs to uncommon families. Aspiring to professional success and social mobility, middle- and upper-ranking Company men of the long eighteenth century were constantly anxious about the consequences that interracial sexual liaisons might have on them and their heirs. Among those who expressed affective ties for their native companions, many attempted to shore up the respectable futures of their mixed-race descendants by asking that they be removed from the homes of their native mothers and sent to Britain. Through these seemingly contradictory processes, anxieties about race, sexual transgression, and miscegenation became a constitutive part of many mixed-race households.

The dynamics of colonial inequities were often replicated within interracial families, demonstrating the ways in which gender and race hierarchies in interracial households with the British father as patriarch over a native woman and her children paralleled social order in the colonial settlements of the East India Company. These ordinary family relationships were the empire writ small: the discourses embedded within these wills suggest that ethnic, racial, and cultural differences were articulated and hierarchized in various forms long before these relationships became taboo within the larger British empire. While these interracial relationships have conventionally stood for the cultural compatibility between the British and the local populations, unequal material provisions put forth in these wills enacted and reinforced broader conceptions of racial, cultural, and gendered inequalities. Within each family existed an uneasy balance between an economy of sentiment and familial attachments and an economy of familial wealth. Thus not every child or family member was equal, not every companion was equal, and as Company employees who left these wills demonstrated, the micro-managing of financial resources often translated into material effects that were the terms of social status. Couched in the language of sentiment, these men showed themselves to be caring, men of feeling who celebrated the ties and obligations of familial attachments; their final testaments also showed them to be calculating when it came to the management of their estates. While patriarchal duty to provide for one's family and offspring was an important obligation of British men of this era, it was a reciprocal process that allowed men to have greater authority over the households and the futures of its most vulnerable members.

A letter dated 28 May, 1767, from an "Indian-born" woman to her English in-laws read:

Dear Madam,

Although a stranger to you yet give me leave to address you in a manner suitable to the place I have the honor to hold in your family as the wife of Mr. Jervis, your son. I had that happy title conferred on me on the 5th of last March and *though I am an Indian born I flatter myself my family fortune and education will not be disapproved*... [emphasis added]

Six months later, another letter acknowledging a reply, followed:

To Misses Jervis

Dear Sisters,

I received your obliging letter of the 13th Feb. which gave me infinite satisfaction to find that my marriage with your brother W. Jervis had met with the approbation of your mother & family and hope in a few years by a personal acquaintance to verify your good opinion of me ... give me leave in the meantime to assure you that I think myself happy in the best of men whom I sincerely love and have in return every proof of his affection my heart can wish for. I wrote mother last April of the birth of our dear boy Jack on the 24 Jan...[1]

Signed by Beebee Elizabeth Jervis, these letters acknowledged that the circumstances of her marriage were irregular: she was Mr. Jervis's wife and also "Indian born," suggesting that Beebee Jervis was either mixed-race or of native descent. That she hoped that education and family wealth might overcome her racial background emphasized how central to social anxieties was the question of race from the point of view of a native woman. The second letter, which went on to report the imminent visit to Britain of several of her friends, suggests that Beebee Jervis assumed that their mutual discomfort of this interracial marriage

---

[1] Oriental and India Office Collections (hereafter O.I.O.C.), Mss. Eur F 142/1, Robinson Collection.

was overcome. She appears to have "passed" into their world – perhaps because her social world in India seemed to intersect with their social world in England, or perhaps because she had borne a child who might be considered "British" with the appropriate training. Although there was no further correspondence to confirm what happened next, these two letters are a glimpse into the ways in which one woman located herself in relation to an extended family that was at some distance in racial, spatial, and social terms.

The previous chapter examined the process by which British men represented themselves through wills; this chapter examines the wills and letters of native women, showing the ways in which they understood their situations, their cultural and religious locations, and the ways they fashioned their subjectivities.

Understanding female subjectivity, self-fashioning, and self-representation, is complicated when applied to native women, particularly those who were on the social margins, as someone like Beebee Jervis felt herself to be.[2] Notwithstanding efforts to keep the names of native women out of colonial records, particular archival records, such as wills, letters, and other personal correspondence show that native women found ways to record their multiple selves in the archives of the East India Company.[3] In the process of managing their estates, negotiating with executors and officials, and showing their different community affiliations, relatively elite women demonstrated how they were able to register their demands, using available forms of testament-writing and petitioning to express their interests. Nonetheless, the texts that native women generated are incomplete and represent fragments of their lives, showing that these moments of speech emerged under highly regulated and contained circumstances in archival records. By unearthing the lives of some of these women from Company records, this chapter argues that native women's selves were made by themselves and others, thus framing historical subjectivity as something that was brought into being by the various demands of the early colonial state and society as well as

---

[2] Stephen Greenblatt, *Renaissance Self-Fashioning: From More to Shakespeare* (Chicago: University of Chicago Press, 1980), Introduction; on female subaltern subjectivity, see R. O'Hanlon, "Recovering the Subject: *Subaltern Studies* and Histories of Resistance in Colonial South Asia," *Modern Asian Studies* 22 (1988): 189–224; Regenia Gagnier, *Subjectivities: A History of Self-Representation in Britain, 1832–1920* (New York: Oxford University Press, 1991).

[3] Gayatri Chakravorty Spivak, "The Rani of Sirmur: an essay in reading the archives," *History and Theory* 24 (1985): 247–72; Durba Ghosh, "Decoding the Nameless: gender, subjectivity, and historical methodologies in reading the archives of colonial India," in Kathleen Wilson, ed., *A New Imperial History: Culture, Identity, Modernity, 1660–1840* (Cambridge: Cambridge University Press, 2004).

a woman's desire to record herself in particular ways.[4] By historicizing women's subjectivity and agency in the period between 1760 and 1840, archival documents reveal the ways in which native women's subject positions were multiple, strategic, and even contradictory, structured by the various cultural spaces they inhabited.[5]

One of the crucial sites for the articulation of native women's subjectivities was the practice of naming, whether in the names they used to identify themselves or in the names that were used by others in order to refer to them. Many native women who cohabited with a European man were identified only with a first name, or renamed with a Christian or European name, thus becoming provisionally attached to a putatively European or Christian community. For native women, renaming became a way of unnaming and removing the traces of her past, particularly as her history was recorded in the archives. Ordinarily, names may function as markers of religion, ethnicity, status; on the Indian subcontinent, names marked one's region and caste. Thus when native women were unnamed and then renamed, their regional, caste, and religious origins were obscured. While the reliance on names is a conventional way of following historical subjects through archives, the absence of full names and the proliferation of renamed women leaves the archival trail cold; even if we know what a woman named herself in her final testament, we have little knowledge about her prior names and the psychic, geographic, and social travels that the adoption of various names entailed.

While the archives and the men with whom they cohabited recorded native women as particular types of subjects – conjugal, maternal, married, converted – by naming and renaming them in specific ways,

---

[4] In relying on how subjects are produced by various forms of community disciplining and desire, Michel Foucault, *Discipline and Punish*; "Subjectivity and Truth," in Paul Rabinow, ed., *Essential Works of Foucault, 1954–1984*, vol. 1 (New York: The New Press, 1997); "The subject and power," in Hubert Dreyfus and Paul Rabinow, eds., *Michel Foucault: Beyond Structuralism and Hermeneutics* (Chicago: University of Chicago Press, 1983). See also Louis Althusser, "Ideology and ideological state apparatuses," in *Lenin and Philosophy and Other Essays*, trans. Ben Brewster (New York: Monthly Review Press, 1971); Aihwa Ong, "Cultural Citizenship as Subject-making: immigrants negotiate racial and cultural boundaries in the United States," *Cultural Anthropology* 37 (1996): 738.

[5] My use of "strategic" is drawn from Kamala Visweswaran, "Betrayal: an analysis in three acts," in Inderpal Grewal and Caren Kaplan, eds., *Scattered Hegemonies: Postmodernity and Transnational Feminist Practices* (Minnesota: University of Minnesota Press, 1994) and "Small Speeches, Subaltern Gender: nationalist ideology and its historiography," *Subaltern Studies* IX (Delhi: Oxford University Press, 1996); Gayatri Chakravorty, "Deconstructing historiography," in Ranajit Guha and Spivak, ed., *Selected Subaltern Studies* (Delhi: Oxford University Press, 1988).

the names that native women used to identify themselves are reflective of the multiple ways in which they situated themselves in colonial society. Among relatively well-known women and less famous women, names proved to be an important way of representing their selves to the changing social milieu. In emphasizing the names that women took on, in wills and in political negotiations, taking on a name was a crucial part of self-fashioning, a means by which women resisted and remade the names that archives, institutions, or family and community structures gave them.

Women who left wills showed that their cultural contexts shifted, often accommodating several modes of self-representation simultaneously. Although native women were of Indian descent, many wore European clothes, owned European furniture, and ate European food. Some had converted to Christianity and were devoted enough to their churches to donate large portions of their estates to the poor fund. Many of these women owned European garments and housewares, they also had brass pots and pans, hookah implements, betel-eating accessories and wore saris and shawls. In the households of relatively wealthy female companions and widows to Europeans, European and Indian habits coexisted side by side in interracial homes with women keeping china and brass plates in their cabinets, testament to their multiple forms of cooking and eating. The final words of native female companions show how these women availed themselves of cultural markers and forms that were in circulation and widely recognizable, while at the same time, fashioned their subjectivities in ways that were culturally distinctive.

Wills written by local women who were the companions of British men represent a small fraction of all the wills in the High Court of Calcutta and the India Office libraries. The number of men who mentioned interracial relationships in their wills declined after 1800, which has been interpreted by historians as a decline in the number of interracial relationships overall.[6] Nonetheless, there was a sizable increase in the number of wills by indigenous women who were once attached to a European man appearing in the court records.[7] This pattern suggests two emergent patterns: there was an increase in native women who were wealthy enough to draw up wills and own property and the "decline" was not one as such, but a change in who registered

---

[6] Suresh Chandra Ghosh, *The Social Condition of the British Community in Bengal, 1757–1800* (Leiden: E.J. Brill, 1970).

[7] Of the 627 wills I have collected, 37 were written by women who identified themselves as the companions of European men. Over two-thirds of this number filed their wills after 1800. See also Pradip Sinha, *Calcutta in Urban History* (Calcutta: Firma, 1978), Appendix IX. He excerpts six wills relevant to the Eurasian community.

these relationships in testamentary records preserved in colonial archives.

As in the case of British men's wills, the bibis' wills give a sense of their familial lives and how they situated themselves in relation to their kin and community. In addition to revealing the dynamics of their interracial liaisons, wills by native women provided instructions on how their estates should be distributed, how they should be buried or cremated, and who they relied on to execute their final testaments. These final words, as was the case for men who left wills, were reflective of how native women mapped their communities, maintained their familial ties and reaffirmed their religious and linguistic practices.

One of the earliest wills written by a native woman appeared in 1802. She identified herself as Elizabeth and wrote:

In the Name of God, Amen, I, Elizabeth a Native Woman, formerly companion of the late Conductor Ferrier, now living with Serjeant [sic] F. Fitzpatrick, finding myself weak in Body thro Sickness but sound in mind and memory do make this my last will and testament...[8]

Her first bequest was to her daughter, Isabella Ferrier, to whom she left Sicca Rs. 1,500 and a house and a parcel of land, when she turned 18. Elizabeth asked that the interest on this estate maintain her daughter until she reached majority. Her next bequest was to her son, William Hume, for whom she left Sicca Rs. 500 when he turned 21. Her final request was that her second son, William Butler Fitzpatrick, inherit the remainder of her estate, including all her jewelry, clothes, and household effects. Her executors and the guardians to her children were Charles Christopher Francis and James Murray.

This will, like many, is a telling reproductive biography: by her own account, Elizabeth cohabited with a series of European men and bore them children who took their fathers' last names. A note in the margin indicated that Isabella, her only daughter was born in December 1793 and was about 9 years old. William Butler Fitzpatrick, Elizabeth's son was likely younger since Elizabeth took up with Fitzpatrick after Ferrier died. Since the father of William Hume was never mentioned, we can guess he was another of Elizabeth's partners. The will was witnessed by John Hawkesworth, Andrew Moffat, and John Selby, all soldiers in the Company's army, suggesting that in her intimate and social life, she was involved with men who identified as Europeans. According to her inventory, she was owed almost S. Rs. 1,000 by various Europeans

[8] O.I.O.C., L/AG/34/29/14, pp. 10–11.

and Bengalis, showing Elizabeth to be enterprising – perhaps a money-lender – and wide-ranging in her clients.

Elizabeth's estate was worth about S. Rs. 15,000 and included two houses in Malunga, on the outskirts of Calcutta, household effects that included china, silverware, bedding, linens, and leather trunks. In addition, she owned a large collection of gold and silver jewelry with various precious stones. Her possessions show that her domestic life was structured by a varied mix of native and European practices.[9] Although she identified herself as a "native woman," she had several gold crosses and rosaries among her possessions, marking her as a practicing Catholic. She had a five-stranded gold chain known as a "punchlerry," which was commonly worn among native women, and she also kept jeweled hair pins, shoe buckles, and pearl necklaces, which were more common fashion accessories for European women.[10]

Identified only as "Elizabeth, a native woman," this woman's religious, national, and caste affiliations were elided as the details of her life were frozen in the moments in which she planned for her death. Nonetheless, Elizabeth's will shows that she was involved in a complex circuit of relationships – social, financial, conjugal, and domestic – that structured her life and bound her to European and native communities. Although her will is relatively rare, her experience of multiple relationships and affiliations with both communities parallels that of many other native women, those with property and those without.

Wealthier women, judging by the final testaments they left, had a degree of upward social mobility that was not available to the large majority of native female companions, many of whom were renamed or incompletely named in archival documents. Over 95 percent of mixed-race or native women who possessed enough property to require a will were women who had had social or conjugal arrangements with Europeans. This suggests that some relatively wealthy women benefited from their domestic arrangements with Europeans and were able to profit from the material successes of their male consorts, although the range was quite large: the amounts of these estates ranged from S. Rs. 500 to as high as S. Rs. 30,000. The kind of wealth that native women possessed ranged from movable property, which included household effects, jewelry, and clothes, to very significant assets, such as land and houses.

---

[9] High Court, Original Side, Calcutta High Court (hereafter H.C.O.S.), 1803–1805, pp. 141–3; O.I.O.C. L/AG/34/27/30 (1804), no. 159; O.I.O.C. L/AG/34/27/31 (1805, pt. 1), no. 138.

[10] O.I.O.C., L/AG/34/27/27, pp. 113 and 172.

Some women listed their benefactors in their wills, indicating in the origins of their wealth. For instance, Beebee Mehtaub stated that she was the mother of Mrs. Colonel Maria Ann Doveton by "my late Lord and Master Major General Sir John Arnold Knight, K.C.B.," with whom she had resided for 58 years. She bequeathed the house she inherited from Major General Knight in the cantonment in Barrackpore to her daughter.[11] Lady Maria Nugent, the prolific imperial traveler, met the mixed-race woman, Maria Doveton on her travels through the northwest provinces in the 1810s and noted that Mrs. Doveton and her sister, Mrs. Logie, were the only women – native or European – in the settlement.[12] Another woman, "Beebee Kuddumsand, commonly known as Beebee Kurrem," stated that she owned a half-share of a house that was left to her by the late Col. John deCourcy, as well as a lump sum of S. Rs. 28,000. Her will followed the terms of the estate left by Col. deCourcy; leaving the bulk of the estate to their daughter Elizabeth and the remainder to Elizabeth's son, George John deCourcy Stone.[13] Mahondy Khanum of Patna asked that the money due to her from the estate of the late John Bristow, civil servant of the East India Company, be shared between their two children, who were in England. She also asked that a monthly stipend be given to her brother Mirza Husinabe Beg and her nephew Mirza Museetah, showing how income from a relationship with a European could benefit one's natal relatives.[14] Punna Purree Pearse identified herself as the "widow of Thomas Pearse, late a colonel in the Honorable East India Company's establishment in Bengal."[15]

Although most women appeared to inherit wealth from their relationships only after their "masters" died, one woman was given a lump sum of S. Rs. 10,000 by her "master Stephen Davis Reilly," "in anticipation of his own death" before hers so that she and their two children would be well taken care of. The sum had been invested in Company bonds held by Palmer and Co., a Calcutta agency house. She asked that the money be divided between their two children and that the children receive her clothes and jewelry.[16]

Occasionally, the content of a native woman's will suggested that her fortunes were independent of her relationship with a European man.

[11] H.C.O.S. 1838, pp. 520–1.
[12] Lady Maria Nugent, *A Journal from the year 1811 till the year 1815: including a voyage to and residence in India* (London, 1839) vol. II, pp. 22–3.
[13] H.C.O.S. 1832, pp. 143–7.
[14] H.C.O.S. 1829–1830, pp. 57–9.
[15] H.C.O.S. 1819–1820, pp. 277–9.
[16] H.C.O.S. 1820–1821, pp. 200–203.

Beebee Mutthra of Kanpur stated that she had resided in the house of
Brevet Major and Captain George Bunce of H.M.'s 67th Regiment of
Foot for fifteen years and that with his permission, she had adopted
a small girl who had been born in this home. The girl was bequeathed
the bulk of Beebee Mutthra's estate of S. Rs. 28,000, which was invested
in Company bonds. As she noted, this money was "possessed in my own
right," while a bungalow in the cantonment at Kanpur had been deeded
to her by Major Bunce.[17]

Another very wealthy woman, Bunnoo Beebee, listed possessions that
totaled over S. Rs. 20,000. In addition to two homes that she rented
out to Europeans, and bonds valued at S. Rs. 5,000, she had loaned
S. Rs. 4,000 to a local businessman, showing herself as an enterprising
investor. She asked that her two sons, William Paul Milne and John
Milne each receive one of her houses and that her daughter Primrose
Milne should get all the jewelry and cash, which was valued at
S. Rs. 11,500. The accounts of her estate demonstrate that she was able
to provide schooling for her children, as well as able to maintain several
profitable rental bungalows.[18]

While native women who inherited substantial wealth were relatively
fortunate, they were subject to the whims of executors, who occasionally
withheld bequests. Col. Thomas Pearse's "widow," Punna Purree had
trouble realizing her inheritance. In a letter to Warren Hastings, the
former governor-general, in 1792, after he had returned to England to
face impeachment charges, she wrote that her husband's executor had
decreased her allowance and was keeping other property from her. She
asked him to intervene and wished that all was well with her son, "Mr.
Tommy," who remained under Hastings's care.[19] The letters, written by
Punna Purree in Persian, show a woman who was bereft after the death
of her husband and sought protection from her husband's good friend.
The translated version of one letter read: "You are my protector, and
God keeps you over my head, and I am always praying to God to bring
you here, in which I shall be well ..."[20] Hastings's response was not
found.

In spite of her early difficulties realizing her inheritance, she managed
to increase her assets so that by the time she died, she owned much more
than what had been left to her by Colonel Pearse. When she died in 1820,

[17] H.C.O.S., 1832–1833, pp. 55–7.
[18] O.I.O.C., L/AG/34/27/97, pp. 561–4; H.C.O.S., 1830–1831, pp. 135–6.
[19] British Library, Hastings Correspondence, Add. Mss. 29, 172, vol. XLI (1790) folio
410. Another letter appeared in the same volume, folio 317. I thank William
Dalrymple for this reference.
[20] *Ibid.*

her entire estate of four parcels of land totaling 150 biggahs and nine cottahs and two garden houses[21] was bequeathed to her son, Thomas Deane Mahomed Pearse, Esq., "now in England" and his heirs.[22] The value of her inheritance from Colonel Pearse had increased dramatically: she went from owning the house and a four cottah plot in which she lived in Chowringhee in central Calcutta to becoming a significant landowner in the Twenty-Four Pergunnahs. Her move, from the center of British settlement in 1789 to the outskirts of Calcutta by 1820, was indicative of the ways in which attitudes about interracial arrangements had changed in this colonial society, making it less acceptable for a native widow of a European man to live among Europeans in the center of Calcutta.

Although these wills were presumably written by the women themselves, notes in the margin suggest that there were several contexts of translation. Beebee Mehtaub's will had been transcribed from "spoken Hindustani into written by Goluck Chunder Sircar," and then translated into English. Similarly, in the postscript to another woman's will, identified as Anne Elizabeth Smith, the mother of four children named Catherine Lantour, Lydia Swaine, Thomas Smith, and Charlotte Smith, the translator's note read: "Explained to me by Mrs. Anne Elizabeth Smith in the common Hindustanee language."[23] Another female companion's will was translated from Urdu. In it, without invoking any Christian preamble, this woman wrote,

I, Hinda Husunah Khadejah Begum do constitute my Master Stephen Davis Reilly to be administrator . . .[24]

She asked that her estate be divided between the two children she had with Reilly. Finally, she ended with "Whatever in this will may not be conformable to European manner or custom in like cases must be excused." The will bears her signature in Perso-Arabic script. Likewise, Punna Purree Pearse's will was signed in Persian and witnessed by Thomas Christie, William Bell, and Madam Ghosh, who signed in Bengali.[25] Beebee Lucy of Taultollah, asked that her house and grounds be given to her son, Charles Phillips, and signed her will in Nagiri.[26]

---

[21] According to Justice Hyde, a "cottah" was 27' by 27' or 729 square feet. A "biggah" was 20 cottahs, or 14,580 square feet. Hyde Papers, Reel 6, vol. 8, July 12, 1779.
[22] H.C.O.S., 1819–1820, pp. 277–9: she had 113 biggahs and a garden house in Moochee-collah where she lived, a dwelling house in Rammackpore with 4 biggahs, a parcel of land in Futtapore of 12 biggahs and 2 cottahs, and a parcel at Meerpore of 24 biggahs, 7 cottahs (all in 24 Parganas).
[23] H.C.O.S., 1834–1835, pp. 146–7.
[24] H.C.O.S., 1820–1821, pp. 200–3.
[25] H.C.O.S., 1819–1820, pp. 277–9.
[26] H.C.O.S., 1822, pp. 137–8.

The use of local vernacular languages in writing wills shows a certain degree of literacy. As well, given the range of familial and community affiliations that are recorded by wills, households comprised of native mothers and European fathers were often bilingual and even multilingual. The reliance on (and references to) formulaic patterns of testament-writing shows that these multiply situated subjects had some awareness or even legal advice on how a will ought to be structured in order to be legible in the colonial courts. Thus, wills produced a legal subject by the terms of the East India Company, written in a form that was recognizable to those who were reading them, while enabling will-writers to articulate their subjectivities all the while straining against available modes of expression.

Names and aliases were critical components of simultaneously conforming and creating new selves in the final testaments of native women. For instance, one woman identified herself as "Bebee Munnoo, or Jane Mitchell, native of Hindostan."[27] Another woman wrote, "I, Beebee Nancy commonly called Beebee Willoughby of Calcutta" and left her son, James Willoughby her entire estate.[28] Chand Beebee was also "commonly called Beebee Shore."[29] Changing aliases shows the ways in which the names women used were contingent on whether they situated themselves as native women or as members of European families. One woman, not a bibi but the daughter of one, identified herself as "I, Moosummat Isabella Rawstone, daughter of General Rawstone..." signaling that she was both a Rawstone and of Muslim descent. She left a bequest to her brother Edward Rawstone, and wrote her will in Urdu.[30] Similarly, Bibe Mary, listed only as "single woman," was the daughter of William Gwilt and Bibee Balsah Khanum.[31]

While some native women had Christian names, such name-calling was no sure guarantee of a woman's religious identity.[32] Nor did religious affiliation fix oneself to other forms of identification; indeed, religious identity was often one component of a set of cultural and social affiliations that native women held. As scholars have long noted, religious conversion in South Asia was rarely a decisive event for an individual, but rather a relational and gradual process by which

[27] H.C.O.S., 1838, pp. 416–18. Her heirs included her daughter Sarah Buttress and her three grandchildren.
[28] H.C.O.S., 1829, p. 49.
[29] H.C.O.S., 1835–1836, pp. 275–96.
[30] H.C.O.S., 1819, pp. 223–4.
[31] H.C.O.S., 1838, pp. 575–83.
[32] Peter Robb, "Clash of Cultures?: an Englishman in Calcutta in the 1790s," School of Oriental and African Studies, University of London, Inaugural Lecture, March 12, 1998, p. 40.

individuals accepted one set of religious practices juxtaposed alongside others.[33] For many native women who cohabited with Englishmen, religious identities expressed either through wills or through other documents were partial fragments of who they were and the markers that they used in ways that might exceed more limited definitions used today.

The form of these native women's wills were remarkably uniform in their opening oaths: "In the Name of God, Amen, ..." and yet these invocations were not necessarily signs that they were asking for Christian final rites. As one wealthy bibi, Beebee Kuddumsand, commonly known as Beebee Kurreem, wrote,

I direct that my body be buried with all the ceremonies and usages of the Mohametan [sic] religion as soon as possible after my decease and that nothing be omitted which may be requisite towards the performance of such rites.

In a postscript, she added:

I do further desire that a mullah or priest of the Mahometan religion should be employed for the purpose of reading the Koran over my Grave and also that every ceremonies Fatiahs or other rites necessary to be performed for the dead and in usage in the said Mahometan religion shall be done for this purpose.[34]

The instructions for her burial were fairly clear: although her bequests were to the daughter she had with Col. John De Courcy, Elizabeth De Courcy Stone, and her money was largely invested in a British agency house in Calcutta, she wished to be buried a Muslim.[35] Similarly, Mokuma Khanum, "alias Beebee Tucker at present in Tolltollah in Bengal," asked to be buried according to Muslim rites.[36] The call for particular types of burials and interment suggests that native women, in spite of their familial, cultural, and religious affiliations in life, were very concerned with what happened to their bodies in death.

Roza Hickey, "alias Bebee Rozie," asked to be buried by Catholic rites, assigned her estate to her godchildren and two friends and appointed Anna Woodhouse the executrix. According to the text of the will, she had inherited her money from a European who had long since

[33] Susan Bayly, *Saints, Goddesses and Kings: Muslims and Christians in South Indian Society, 1700–1900* (Cambridge: Cambridge University Press, 1989); see also Gauri Viswanathan, *Outside the Fold, Conversion, Modernity, and Belief* (Princeton: Princeton University Press, 1998), ch. 5 and Richard M. Eaton, *The Rise of Islam and the Bengal Frontier, 1204–1760* (Berkeley: University of California Press, 1993).

[34] H.C.O.S., 1832, pp. 143–7.

[35] Her will is remarkable for her wealth: she had an estate of Sicca Rs. 28,000 in addition to two houses in Chinsurah. One house and half that wealth was inherited from De Courcy when he died in 1824.

[36] H.C.O.S., 1833–1834, pp. 347–8.

returned to England. In the postscript to her will, however, the translator wrote, "read and explained [to the testator] in Bengali."[37] Although she sometimes went by a European name and identified as Catholic, she spoke and communicated in Bengali.

Beyond their connections to a British man, some of these women revealed their communities to be among other *bibis* or relatives and friends who were of local descent. Paralleling a pattern that was common in early modern England, widows were more likely (than men) to make provisions for other women and family members who were otherwise unlikely to inherit.[38] For instance, Mahondy Khanum of Patna, asked that a monthly stipend of S. Rs. 20 and S. Rs. 15 a month be arranged for her brother and his son.[39] Another woman, Beebee Munnah Biggum (alias Beebee Cox), left bequests to her mother, Raj Beebee, and to her son, George Cox, who resided in London.[40] Jugdissery Davy (maybe Devi?), listed as "bibby," left Sicca Rs. 4,000 to her son Edward Sherburne, and then asked that Sicca Rs. 2,000 be spent "For the building of a church or religious house of custom in the Hindoos." Her remaining contributions were to complete some building projects in Krishnagar and her executor was Cossynath Mullick (Kashi Nath), a local Brahmin.[41]

Similarly, when Mohar Bibee, "alias Bibee Furquaharson, living in Calcutta" died, she set aside Sicca Rs. 2,000 for a funeral with Muslim rites and asked that her friends, Bibee Peary Khanum and Bibee Stewart oversee the funeral arrangements. Later in the will, she gave several pieces of gold jewelry to these two women and identified them further: Bibee Stewart was identified as the mother of Mrs. R. F. Crowe; Bibee Peary Khanum was "well known by the name of Bibi Reed," showing their familial ties to British men. Some of Mohar Bibee's other heirs were married to British men or were in England: she left a house and 5 cottahs of land to her daughter, Mary Foley, widow to an Englishman in Kanpur, a bungalow to her granddaughter Mrs. Charles Greenway, another house to her youngest daughter Mrs. Eliza King, and shares of stock to her four grandchildren. To two grandsons who were in England,

---

[37] *Ibid.*, pp. 335–7.
[38] Amy Erickson, *Women and Property in Early Modern England* (London: Routledge, 1993), pp. 19, 221–2 and chs. 11 and 12; see also Susan Dwyer Amussen, *An Ordered Society: Gender and Class in Early Modern England* (Oxford: Blackwell, 1988), pp. 90–1. I thank Margaret Hunt for alerting me to these sources.
[39] H.C.O.S. 1829–1830, pp. 57–9.
[40] H.C.O.S. 1817–1818, pp. 159–60; she is listed as Beebee Cox in her inventory, O.I.O.C., L/AG/34/27/59, 1817, v. 3, p. 1965; see also L/AG/34/27/62, 1818, v. 3, pp. 2057–60.
[41] H.C.O.S. 1818, pp. 77–8.

she bequeathed a house on Lower Circular Road. After dispersing all these belongings, Mohar Bibee asked that a pension be paid to her adopted daughter, Noor Bahar and that she receive some of her gold jewelry, especially her "punchlerry" and her brass and copper utensils.[42] In parceling out who received what, Noor Bahar, the adopted daughter, received property that was significantly less valuable than the other descendants. Yet what she received is crucial to understanding the hybrid types of possessions these women had: Noor Bahar received a punchlerry, which was a five ("punch") stranded gold chain that local women of any property considered one of their prized possessions. She also received copper and brass utensils, commonly used in native households, rather than the imported china and silverware that British households more typically had. Noor Bahar, as the only heir who appeared to have no connection with European society, was likely the appropriate recipient of articles that were valued among Indians but not especially desirable among those who lived among the British.

From these examples that revealed the multiple ways in which these women situated themselves in a larger community, it is apparent that there were no easily defined boundaries between British and Indian, Christian and non-Christian, or English-, Hindi-, or Bengali-speaking. Nor were there any uniform characteristics that applied to any of these categories. These women observed a wide range of cultural practices and created familial and religious ties based on these various traditions; in fashioning their subjectivities, we start to see the ways in which native women exercised agency in calling themselves by all the names and cultural and social categories that were applicable to them.

While wills expressed the intentions of their writers and the ways in which their writers imagined their lives and that of their heirs, inventories recorded the contents of the estate and reveal the cultural complexity of domestic lives of local women and European men who cohabited together. Their inventories show a slice of everyday life that was culturally hybrid, with various ways of cooking, eating, dressing, praying, and so on.

Another Elizabeth (one with a very large estate) began "I, Elizabeth, single woman, also known as Bett Carnegy, . . ." She bequeathed a large range of donations to local churches, ranging from Sicca Rs. 5,000 to S. Rs. 12,000. She arranged generous terms for her servants and asked that all of her godchildren be well provided for. Within the text of the will, she revealed that she had "formerly lived with Alexander Carnegy, Surgeon for the Hon. Company," indicating that in spite of her religious

---

[42] H.C.O.S., 1835–1836, pp. 329–33.

beliefs, and having adopted his last name as hers, she never married Carnegy in a church ceremony.[43]

Her inventory is a diverse collection of textiles, jewelry, kitchen goods and servingware.[44] The inventory itself is some 12 pages long including things like an iron meat hook which was sold for 8 annas to a palanquin carriage and horse that were valued at Sicca Rs. 400. Her clothes included a lengthy list of silk petticoats, shawls, shoe buckles, and stockings. Her kitchen implements included a full set of silver serving dishes, saucepans of various sizes, spoons, forks and knives that were engraved; she even had six silver egg cups and a silver toast rack "with paws." Her jewelry numbered over a hundred items including a necklace with 566 pearls and 28 diamond-cut gold beads and matching set of necklace, bracelets, and earrings made in gold with pearls, rubies, and emeralds. Alongside these items that were not culturally coded one way or another (although silverware was much more commonly used among Europeans), more distinctly native possessions were listed among her household effects. Bett Carnegy owned a whole range of accessories to make *pan* (a tobacco and betel nut snack that is still popular) and serve it; as well, she had a hookah rug, hookah bottoms and several silver and ivory mouthpieces. Among her jewelry, she had several punchlerries, as well as a three-stranded gold chain (called a "chunderhar" in her list; "har" means necklace). She also sold several gold "choorees" or bracelets. Exceptionally wealthy, Bett Carnegy's belongings indicate that she lived in a hybrid cultural milieu in which she both wore traditional indigenous jewelry and ate from china with forks and knives.

Like Bett Carnegy, Bibby Young, of Calcutta, left an estate valued about S. Rs. 6,000 including a wide range of jewelry and household effects to her three sons, Robert, William, and Charles. Her possessions were listed in her inventory by their Hindustani names: "jhoomka" for earrings; "chillumchees" for brass wash basins; "currah"; "pounchees" and other pieces of precious metals. In spite of her seemingly European name, she kept brass pots, as did many local native families, as well as a full complement of china, glassware, and silverware, as might suffice for a well-stocked European family. Her possessions were sold at auction with the proceeds going to the Military Orphan Society so that they might take care of her two younger sons, William and Charles.

---

[43] H.C.O.S., 1818, pp. 230–5; his will was filed in 1806 in which he wrote, "I give and bequeath to my housekeeper, commonly called Bett Carnegy the sum of Sicca Rupees twenty thousand lawful money of Bengal..." H.C.O.S., 1805–1807, pp. 325–7.

[44] O.I.O.C., L/AG/34/27/63, pp. 29–40.

Less wealthy women also left households that included both European and indigenous goods. Beebee Jan Murray (alias Genevieve Murray) left personal effects that included gloves, waistcoats, gowns, and silk stockings as well as "cholies" (a short native blouse), and a "jamdanny" gown made of local muslin.[45] Beebee Cox, also known as Beebee Munnah, left a long list of household items that included china tea cups and bowls, a gravy boat, tablecloth, and a mahogany bookcase. As well, she left brass pots and implements, "chappals" (slippers), several "ooranies" (shawls or scarves) with gold and silver embroidery, "one pair hindoostanee earrings set with pearls and benares diamond," and various accessories for making *pan*.[46]

Although some women lived more indigenous lifestyles than did others, it is difficult to quantify the degree to which this was true, or even to track it beyond the time between which they wrote their wills and died, exposing the contents of their estates to the courts. In some sense these women's final testaments are a snapshot of a specific moment in their lives, obscuring a more complete life narrative about the boundaries native women crossed and negotiated when they cohabited with or married European men. Reading the wills and inventories of colonial companions is a way of seeing a subjectivity that was frozen in time, contained largely by practices of testamentary writing and colonial record-keeping.

The next section turns to the lives of two women about whom much more (relatively speaking) has been written in order to see some of the shifts in the subjectivity of two colonial companions of European men. Through their examples, we start to see the consequences of interracial conjugality for native women who became attached to European men, and a broader context for the limited possibilities available to them.

Lives of contrast: Begum Samru and Begum Bennett

Among the many native women who lived with Europeans, two stand out. Begum Samru was a dancing girl who first became the companion of Walter Reinhardt, an Austrian mercenary soldier, and later the successor to Reinhardt's armies and landholdings in northern India. Her spectacular rise to power poses a stark contrast to the less celebrated story of Halima, also known as Helen Bennett, who became attached to a French mercenary soldier, Benoit de Boigne. While Helen's story is often told as an extension of de Boigne's life narrative, the Begum

[45] H.C.O.S., L/AG/34/27/44, 1811, v. 2, p. 1428.
[46] H.C.O.S., L/AG/34/27/59, 1817, v. 3, p. 1965.

Samru's multiple biographies attest that she was a legendary woman.[47] In both cases, these women changed their names and modified their cultural practices as a way of negotiating greater advantages for themselves and their families. While Begum Samru is well-known for her successes in political and military matters, Helen Bennett was less famous, in part because her biography did not end in triumph.

In 1930, *Bengal Past and Present*, the journal of the Calcutta Historical Society, printed a brief note from Jadunath Sarkar, a well-known historian of India. He quoted from a piece of paper that had slipped out of his copy of a biography of General Benoit de Boigne:

> The first wife of General de Boigne was the daughter of a Persian Colonel, named Helene Bennett-Begum – 1788. If the lady was a pure Persian, and if de Boigne did not give her a new name at the time of her marriage, I suggest that Helene Bennett is the French corruption of Halima Bint, both Arabic words, the first meaning 'patient lady' and the second 'daughter'. Halima would be transliterated by a Frenchman as Heleme, which is easily turned into Helene. Alternatively, and more probably, Bennett is a mis-reading for Banu, written as Bennou.[48]

By tracing the ways that names were translated and became corrupted through usage in several languages, Sarkar's anonymous informant pointed out a way in which a native woman of the late eighteenth century had her identity reconfigured by changing her name. According to this slip of paper, names could slip into slightly different names so that Halima (or Banu) could become Helen Bennett.

The easy changing of names complicates the notion of names as static markers for fixing individuals to particular identities and communities. Both women were Muslims and later converted to Christianity; Helen Bennett and Begum Samru were both baptized into Catholicism and took on Christian names, casting off their indigenous names when they converted. Their religious conversions and renamings emphasize one process by which these women fashioned themselves and were represented in the hybrid and unstable political milieu of north India in the late eighteenth and early nineteenth centuries.

---

[47] See, for example, Herbert Compton, *A Particular Account of the European Military Adventurers of Hindustan, from 1784 to 1803* (Karachi: Oxford University Press, 1976 reprint, 1892 orig.). His account of De Boigne's life omits any mention of his high-level liaison with Halima. Biographies of Begum Samru, however, abound and are clear on such a conjugal relationship: the first was published in 1879 by Father Keegan, *Sardhana and Its Begum* and the most recent by John Lall, *Begum Samru: Fading Portrait in a Gilded Frame* (New Delhi: Roli Books, 1997).

[48] *Bengal Past and Present* (hereafter *BPP*) vol. XLIII, 150. Banu was a common nickname given to north Indian girls.

The story of the Begum Samru (1751?–1836) has been narrated in great detail elsewhere. Her biographies emphasize her exceptional skills and political savvy in transforming herself from a dancing girl to a *jagirdar* (landholder) in northern India. Indeed, the story so captures the imagination that no less than half a dozen novels have been written based on Begum Samru's life. According to some sources, she was born to the second wife of a nobleman in Kutana, a village in Meerut district, near Delhi.[49] Other sources claimed she was of Kashmiri descent.[50] All of these sources date from the period *after* her ascent to the position of landholder of Sardhana and seek to validate her elevation from a dancing girl to a woman of noble stature. She did not leave any autobiographical accounts and aside from her letters to Mughal and British officials in which she attempted to extract political concessions, her life as she might have narrated it is absent from historical scrutiny.

Helen Bennett (1772?–1854), on the other hand, attracted little attention in the course of her life, although her similarities to Begum Samru – she was attached to a mercenary soldier, converted to Christianity – are traits that other Indian female companions shared. Born *c.* 1772 to a Persian army officer in Lucknow and a respectable Muslim woman of Lucknow, she was originally named Halima.[51] In contrast to Begum Samru, Halima started her life as a woman of some status and died in much reduced circumstances in a one-room house in the south of England. Her story has been narrated largely through her association with General Benoit de Boigne, a Frenchman who arrived in Madras in 1778 and quickly rose to prominence as a commander who led Maratha armies to victory in the late eighteenth century. Halima was the sister of Faiz Baksh, the consort of William Palmer, one-time resident in the Peshwa court at Pune. Halima, who was painted by Zoffany in the unfinished Palmer family portrait, was previously (mistakenly) identified as Palmer's second wife;[52] she has recently been identified as Palmer's "sister-in-law."[53] She apparently met

---

[49] Brajendranath Banerji, *Begam Samru* (Calcutta: M. C. Sarkar and Sons, 1925), p. 14n; Thomas Bacon, *First Impression and Studies from Nature in Hindostan* (London, 1837); J. Baillie Fraser, ed., *Military Memoirs of Lt. Col. James Skinner* (London, 1851).

[50] Bussy believed she was Kashmiri, Pondicherry Records, Bussy to Marshal de Castries, 3 March 1784, cited in Banerji, *Begam Samru*, p. 17n.

[51] According to Desmond Young, author of de Boigne's most recent biography, "The identity of the Persian colonel remains a mystery... it can be said with certainty that the mother came from Lucknow and belonged to a Muslim family which was at least respectable and may have been of some distinction." *Fountain of the Elephants* (New York: Harper & Brothers, 1959), pp. 99–100.

[52] Mildred Archer, *Indian and British Portraiture, 1770–1825* (London: Sotherby Parke Benet, 1979), p. 284.

[53] Young, *Fountain of the Elephants*, p. 100.

de Boigne when he resided intermittently in Lucknow between 1783 and 1788 and she was living in the household of William Palmer and Faiz Baksh. Once Halima became attached to de Boigne, she left the Palmer household but visited her sister and the Palmer family frequently. From private letters to de Boigne from Queiros, Claud Martin's Portuguese assistant in Lucknow, Halima was described as a beautiful, fair complexioned, compliant woman of respectable manners and a good education (she could read and write both Persian and English). De Boigne's attachment to a woman of some status set him apart from other Europeans who often formed attachments with local women of the bazaar, female slaves in their service, their housekeepers, or dancing girls.

Begum Samru began her life as Farzana, a Muslim nautch girl who was in a tawaif's kotha in Delhi.[54] In 1765, Farzana was "discovered" by Walter Reinhardt, an Austrian mercenary soldier who was in the service of the Jats of western India. From then until Reinhardt's death thirteen years later, she was, by all accounts, his constant companion.

Reinhardt was a mercenary soldier who arrived in India in 1750. He enlisted in the French army until 1756, when he changed sides and enlisted with a Swiss battalion in the service of the East India Company. At this point, according to some accounts, he reportedly changed his name to Sommers or Summers which was later corrupted into Samru by his Indian underlings. Other accounts suggest that Samru was derived from Sombre, the appellation given by his soldiers to describe a man who was dark in skin as well as personality.[55] Whichever the case, Samru was the Hindustani variant of Reinhardt's alias; when Farzana became his companion, she became Samru ki Begum, or Samru's begum.

While Samru was a name derived from uncertain origins, the term "begum" has a clearer lineage. As described in the *Seir Mutaqherin*, the word was used to describe a woman of noble descent. In local practice, "begum" was often attached to the given name of a woman. So, for instance, the begums of Awadh were Bahu Begum and the Nawab Begum; Munni Begum was the consort of Mir Jafar, nawab of Murshidabad; William Palmer's companion was known as Begum Faiz Baksh; and Colonel Gardiner's companion was Begum Dehlmi. The prefix begum was rarely used as a replacement for Mrs. (as in common English usage) as became the case for Begum Samru. By retaining the

---

[54] *Tawaif* means courtesan; *kotha* is her household.
[55] M. N. Sharma, *The Life and Times of Begam Samru of Sardhana* (Sahibabad, 1985) p. 32n; *European Military Adventurers of Hindustan*, p. 400; and Broome, vol. 1, p. 353; Banerji, *Begam Samru*, p. 5.

name Begum Samru, Farzana did two things simultaneously: one was to affirm herself as a noblewoman, the second was to solidify her ✓ connection to Samru, who was by the late 1760s a formidable officer who commanded four battalions and about 2,000 soldiers.

The ways that Begum Samru and Helen Bennett changed their names and identities parallels the lives and careers of Walter Reinhardt and Benoit de Boigne. Like their female companions, Reinhardt and de Boigne self-fashioned personas in this milieu allowed them to exceed their social positions at home. As successful military commanders of troops in north India, they both attained a level of status that would have been unlikely had they remained in Europe. This transformation became possible because of the ways that they positioned themselves: Walter Reinhardt reinvented himself as a local landholder, de Boigne as an aristocrat when he returned to France.

Through her relationship with Reinhardt, alias Samru, Farzana became known as Begum Samru although the question of whether they were legally married, or even what might have constituted a legal marriage has never been conclusively decided. William Sleeman wrote in 1844, that they were married "by all the forms considered necessary by persons of her persuasion when married to men of another."[56] Another contemporary observer, James Skinner, sidestepped the question and noted, "Whether he [Reinhardt] married her or not is uncertain, but she was regarded as his wife..."[57] Charles Theophilus Metcalfe, resident to the Mughal court at Delhi, reported that Reinhardt and the Begum had never married, although many considered the absence of a church marriage adhering to local custom.[58]

Similarly, it is unclear whether Halima and Benoit de Boigne ever married. According to St. Genis, de Boigne's first biographer, de Boigne and Helene were united "by a union in India in 1788, following the customs of the country, with the daughter of a Persian colonel."[59] They had two children, a daughter born in 1789 and a son in 1792 both of whom came to England with their father and mother in 1797. But Helene Bennett was one of several "wives" de Boigne kept: according to one source, de Boigne was attached to a woman named Moti Begum

---

[56] William Sleeman, *Rambles and Recollections of an Indian Official* (Westminster, 1893), ii, p. 268. Skinner (as edited by Fraser), vol. I, p. 285.

[57] Amherst Papers, stored in Amherst College Library. Lady Amherst's diaries, vol. 6, p. 121.

[58] St. Genis (Poitiers, 1873), cited in *BPP*, vol. XLVI (1933): 91

[59] Captain J. Bullock, *Statesman* (November 13, 1932), cited in *BPP*, vol. XLVI (1933): 91–2. The evidence is based on a Maratha court newsletter in which de Boigne is reportedly married to a dancing girl in the court named Moti Begum in 1790.

who resided in Delhi.[60] De Boigne also apparently paid support to two women he had left behind in India, one in Aligarh and one in Delhi.[61] His relationships in India, however, proved no obstacle to marrying again. In 1797, upon arriving in London, he married Adele d'Osmond, the sixteen-year-old French daughter of the Marquis d'Osmond who was then the French ambassador in the King's court.[62] Once in Europe, de Boigne claimed that his relationships with Indian women were not legally binding.[63] As Adele later noted, she never knew that he was previously married and had children. Soon after their marriage, Adele and de Boigne separated although he continued to support her financially.

The kinds of arrangements that Europeans such as Reinhardt and de Boigne entered into were informal, bound only by customary practice. Although there was no juridical infrastructure for legitimating these alliances, it was customary in these cohabitation arrangements that the men provided financial support for any children and often left provisions for a monthly stipend for their female companions.

In the case of Halima, her unlegitimated marriage left her unprotected from de Boigne's decision to abandon her and marry again upon their arrival in England.[64] In comparison, Begum Samru fared better: in the role she assumed as Reinhardt's wife, she became the inheritor of his wealth and his lands, outmaneuvering Reinhardt's first female companion and stepson. Her relative success in capitalizing on her position as the favored "wife" set the scene for her emergence as a landholder in her own right.

Farzana, a.k.a. her highness, Joanna Zeb-un-nissa, the Begum Samru

The career of Begum Samru dovetailed on the upwardly mobile career of the man to whom she became attached. Walter Reinhardt, who was

[60] M. Maurice Besson (Chambery, 1930), cited in *BPP*, vol. XLVI (1933): 92. Whether there was only one woman in Delhi is unclear; see also Young, *Fountain of the Elephants*, pp. 146–7. Apparently, William Palmer was aware of this relationship when he wrote to de Boigne in 1791, "Make my affectionate *salaams* to my sister, the Begum. How will she bear a rival princess?"

[61] Adele d'Osmond, later the Comtesse de Boigne, wrote her own three volume memoir (New York: Scribners, 1908): see esp. vol. III, pp. 130–6 for accounts of her marriage to de Boigne.

[62] d'Osmond, vol. III, p. 133; Ronciere, p. 12.

[63] Her sister, Faiz Baksh, however, remained William Palmer's companion for 35 years and was the only female partner who was recognized in his will. Although Palmer reputedly had another companion, she received no pension and their children went unprovided for.

[64] Sharma, *Life and Times*, pp. 30–2.

born in central Europe, was attributed as being Swiss, French, or German and came to India in 1750 to work as a mercenary soldier for the European armies that were stationed in India during the eighteenth century.[65] He had an eventful career, changing sides with some frequency.[66]

As a result of shifting his allegiances between armies of different loyalties, Reinhardt had a complicated relationship with local rulers in northern India. After some skirmishes against the Mughal empire, he rejoined the Mughal service and when he had an audience with the emperor in 1774, asked that he be given a *jaidad* (rent-free land) for his meritorious services to the Mughal empire.[67] Two years later, after various political and military intrigues, Samru was granted a jaidad in Sardhana, a tract of land in the Gangetic doab. The jaidad's revenues were an estimated 6 lakhs of rupees every year and secured a stable source of income for Reinhardt and his armies; this land grant also gave Reinhardt the protection he needed against the British. Samru died a year later and the Begum became, in effect, his successor, both to the jaidad and as commander of his army.

The remarkable emergence of Walter Reinhardt – a mercenary soldier of obscure origins and uncertain political allegiances – as a landholder in northern India was the result of long negotiations with various factions in northern India. Reinhardt's language abilities (he apparently spoke Persian and Urdu, as well as French, German, and English) and his skills as a military commander made him flexible enough to appeal to European and Mughal armies. According to Antoine Polier,

---

[65] At the time of the decisive victory at Plassey in 1757 of the British over the forces of the nawab of Bengal, Reinhardt was in the employ of the British company's forces and became restless for more responsibility. By the 1760s, Reinhardt went out of the realm of European armies and formed alliances with local indigenous rulers. He attached himself to the cause of Mir Qasim of Bengal squarely against the British. In 1763, there was a battle outside of Patna, the site of an East India Company factory, which resulted in the forces of Mir Qasim retaliating against the company's agents at the factory. In what became known as the Patna massacre, Reinhardt was credited with leading an assault that resulted in the deaths of 50 Englishmen and 100 others in the employ of the company. Thereafter, he became an enemy of the British and his surrender became a key precondition for the company when negotiating with the nawabs of Bengal, Awadh and other key local rulers of the Bengal Presidency.

[66] *Calendar of Persian Correspondence* (National Archives of Delhi, hereafter N.A.I.), vol. IV, p. 1298, cited in John Lall, *Fading Portrait*, p. 43. A jaidad was a land grant that produced revenue which was given to military officers so that they could maintain troops for the Mughal emperor; a jagir was a land grant that was given for meritorious service but did not require the landholder to provide troops from the revenues of the land. Jagirdars were allowed to keep or use their revenues without, in theory, any military obligation.

[67] *Asiatic Annual Register* (1800): Miscellaneous Characters.

a contemporary who was a French-Swiss colonel in the service of the nawab of Awadh, Reinhardt dressed "in Moghul dress," kept a zenana, and had gone native.[68] Polier was himself a Persian-speaker, living in a palace with several native women, and maintaining the lifestyle of a local prince.[69] The ways in which Reinhardt represented himself – his dress, his language abilities, his household – all contributed to the making of a local landholder in north India who happened to be of European descent. And yet the rise of a German butcher's son to the position of a landholder in India worth 6 lakh rupees annually is not simply explained by Samru's competence as a military and political figure.

According to several sources, Begum Samru had been central in the behind-the-scenes negotiations at the Mughal court in securing the *jaidad* for Samru in Sardhana. The decision to settle in Sardhana, the region in which she was born, was the Begum's choice. Before Samru's death, the Begum had lived among the troops and had formed strong bonds with the officers in Samru's battalions. Thus, when Samru died, she apparently became the popular choice among Samru's officers to be his successor, superseding the claims of Samru's son by another woman.[70] Begum Samru was favored by the Mughal emperor and soon after Samru's death, she was granted the lands that were previously granted to Samru.[71] Thereafter, she became known as Begum Samru of Sardhana and in addition to being a landed magnate, she also became commander of four battalions.

Her influence within Samru's household and her involvement in the political negotiations between Samru and the Mughal court were not unusual for the time in the context of northern India; her elevation from dancing girl to primary spouse was also not uncommon.[72] What was exceptional about this begum was that she became the successor to Samru's lands and armies, rather than being the custodian on behalf of a favored son.[73]

---

[68] Young, *Fountain of the Elephants*, p. 101; Muzaffar Alam and Seema Alavi, translators and eds., *A European Experience of the Mughal Orient: the I'jaz-I Arsalani (Persian Letters, 1773–1779) of Antoine-Louis Henri Polier* (Delhi: Oxford University Press, 2001).

[69] Lall, *Fading Portrait*, pp. 52–3.

[70] Francklin, p. 91; Keegan, pp. 31–2, cited in Sharma, *Life and Times*, p. 68n.

[71] Indrani Chatterjee, *Gender, Slavery and Law in Colonial India* (Delhi: Oxford University Press, 1999), ch. 2 for the relationship between the household polity to the larger polity.

[72] I. Chatterjee, *Gender, Slavery*, pp. 57–73: she notes that acting as custodian for a son who was named the successor was the most likely means for women to be centrally involved in household political machinations.

[73] Sleeman, ii, p. 273, cited in Banerji, *Begam Samru*, p. 18.

In 1781, three years after the death of Reinhardt, Begum Samru was baptized by a Carmelite monk Father Gregorio and christened Joanna.[74] By converting to the Catholic church, like many other Indian women, Begum Samru exchanged her given name for another name. When Farzana became Joanna, her new name represented a newfound spiritual conversion as well as her lineage to a European tradition of naming. In effect, she secured herself as a member of a community of Christians as well as nominally to a community of Europeans.

Changing her name marked a way in which Begum Samru changed the multiple communities with which she was associated, trading Farzana for Joanna, while retaining the moniker Begum. Her religious conversion occasioned her renaming, expressing her identity to a transnational, cross-cultural community of Christians, one that stood beyond other identities such as family, community, ethnicity, and nationality. But in this case, by converting and taking the appellation of Joanna, Begum Samru/Farzana successfully obscured her status as a dancing girl who had risen through the ranks of Reinhardt's zenana. Keeping both names (Joanna and Begum Samru) enabled her to associate with a larger community of Catholics, as well as to remind her political foes of her military prowess. Although Begum Samru's renaming fixed her identity as Christian and of aristocratic status, her conversion to Catholicism did not preclude her future as a landholder in northern India; indeed, as will become apparent, her strategic taking of names allowed her a wider range of options in how she was able to fashion herself. She represented herself alternately a Muslim noblewoman, a Catholic aristocrat, a pious Christian and patron, and benefactor and benevolent ruler to the people of Sardhana.

After the death of Samru, when the Begum became the leader of his battalions in the politically fraught atmosphere of northern India, she emerged as a savvy politician and loyal leader to the Mughal emperor, Shah Alam, who was effectively a puppet ruler backed by powerful nobles. In the period between 1778 and 1788, the Begum's battalions were drawn into several protracted battles in and around Delhi, a result of being based near the Mughal capital. In these years, as Delhi came under increasing threats (at various times) from the Marathas, the Rohillas, the Jats, and the Sikhs, the Mughal emperor relied on the Begum and her armies for protection. In 1787, Begum Samru was given the name, Zeb-un-nissa, by the Mughal emperor, and given ceremonial

---

[74] Banerji, *Begam Samru*, chapter 3, esp. p. 28; Sharma, *Life and Times*, pp. 75–8; Thorn, p. 386, cited in *Life and Times*, p. 77n; Lall, *Fading Portrait*, p. 75.

robes (*khilat*) for her service in the Rohilla attacks against Delhi in that year. The title, given by Mughal decree, brought the Begum into the circle of trusted nobility that the emperor relied on; by entering the community of Mughal nobility, she was referred to as "my daughter," by the Mughal emperor. She also received an additional land grant south of Delhi, which she deputed the commander of her troops, George Thomas, to administer. During this period, the Begum also came to the attention of the British: she helped secure the release of a young British officer who had been taken prisoner by Sikh chiefs. Major William Palmer, then resident in Gwalior, enlisted the Begum's help and her contribution was noted to the Governor-General.[75]

In 1790, a French nobleman, Le Vassoult, came into the service of the Begum. Well-educated, well-mannered, and born of aristocratic blood, he quickly became the object of the Begum's affections and displaced George Thomas as her trusted confidant and as the officer in charge.[76]

Three years later, Le Vassoult and the Begum Samru were married by the same Carmelite monk who had baptized the Begum nearly a decade earlier. Upon marrying the French nobleman, Begum Samru added Nobilis to her name and adopted a seal that proclaimed her as Joanna Nobilis Somer. In a curious twist, while her marriage to Le Vassoult enabled her to add "Nobilis" to her seal, she kept her attachment to Samru. The seal also included an inscription in Persian which affirmed her status as a noble in the Mughal court; as the Persian reads, under the reign of Shah Alam, in the year Hijrah 1200 (*c*. 1793), Zeb-un-nissa. The Begum's choices of what should be included in her seal intersected with how best to represent herself given the multiple codes of political self-representation available to her. She used English to establish herself as a noblewoman of Europe, Persian to affirm herself as a member of the Mughal nobility. By invoking her noble status through these two means, she doubly affirmed her aristocratic standing

---

[75] *BPP*, vol. LII, pt. I, pp. 18–22; *Calendar of Persian Correspondence* 1651, Nov. 15, 1791 and 1721, Dec. 20, 1791 cited in *Life and Times*, p. 87n.

[76] Some scholars have speculated that George Thomas and the Begum were lovers (Lall, *Fading Portrait*, p. 76); others have assumed it was a relationship based on loyalty and service (Compton, *European Military Adventurers of Hindustan*, p. 110; Banerji, *Begam Samru*, pp. 38–9) that was disrupted by the arrival of the Frenchman. Soon after Le Vassoult arrived, George Thomas left the service of the Begum and joined the service of a prominent Maratha chief, Appa Khandi Rao. For a more complete account of George Thomas's life, see his memoirs and also see Compton, *European Military Adventurers of Hindustan*, pp. 109–221.

within India both among Indian nobility and also among the growing influence of the British.[77]

The simultaneous use of Persian alongside English in her seal also reflected the personality of her rulership in Sardhana: while her military officers were European and usually Catholic, her legal advisers or *diwans* were Persian-speaking, Muslim and Hindu elites.[78] She herself used Persian but apparently also spoke some English. The multiple and simultaneous use of these symbols – titles and language – suggests that rather than seeing the Begum as a woman who crossed cultures, we should view her as someone who occupied several cultural spaces ✓ simultaneously as a way of keeping her strategic options open.

After her marriage to Le Vassoult, the Begum's control over Sardhana and her battalions started to slip. Le Vassoult, for all his manners and noble blood, lacked the ability to lead the Begum's 2,000 soldiers and alienated many of the other European officers. Two of her battalions defected and went to Delhi to retrieve Zafar-yab Khan, Walter Reinhardt's son by his first wife, in order to install him as leader of Sardhana and Samru's troops. At this point, in April, 1795, both the Begum and her husband communicated with various British officials in an effort to seek protection.[79]

These communications with the British were the first of many and suggest that the Begum, as the widow and military commander who had fought against the British and the wife of another military officer who was proving incompetent, was in a difficult position. As she herself wrote,

I am desirous of living under the protection of the English government and of residing in some assigned place in Bengal or Bihar. I will act with the strictest conformity to the orders of the Gentlemen of Council and will demean myself as a subject.... Hence I wish to retire and to pass the remainder of my life under the mild protection of the English government and to extend (enjoy) its protection which may be my only prospect of support.[80]

Begum Samru was given permission to proceed to Patna, in Bihar, with her family and attendants. Simultaneously, matters in Sardhana came to a crisis point and the Begum and her husband fled Sardhana in

[77] Although the power of the Mughal emperor was limited in this period, from various sources, both Persian and English, it is clear that the legitimacy of aristocratic status was recognized as such by British Company servants.

[78] Sharma, *Life and Times*, pp. 144–5.

[79] Political Proceedings, May 29, 1795, no. 37, N. A. I.; *Poona Residency Correspondence*, vol. VIII, nos. 14–14A, "From Zeb-un-nissa, widow of Somru to Governor-General, 22 April 1795."

[80] N.A.I., Political Proceedings, May 29, 1793, no. 37.

the middle of the night toward Patna and were foiled; in the course of the encounter, Le Vassoult killed himself believing that the Begum was dead.[81] The Begum returned to Sardhana as a prisoner of her stepson, but was eventually freed. The Begum was restored to her position and confirmed by the Mughal emperor in the position of jagirdar of Sardhana. Thereafter, she became an ally of the Marathas, who were, in all but name, in control of northern and western India.

From 1796 onward, the Begum Samru devoted her attention to securing herself within a new political situation: the growth of Maratha power in northern and western India and the growing influence of the British in eastern India. Between 1796 and 1803, the Begum carefully played both sides by keeping in the good graces of the Marathas and the British governor-general Lord Wellesley. Based on support provided by William Palmer and John Collins, the resident in Delhi, the Begum was offered a deal with the Company to fight against the Marathas. In 1803, the Begum Samru left the service of the Marathas and joined the British. From then on, she engaged in careful negotiations with Wellesley and other British officials, in order that she could keep her jagirs. In 1805, her position was confirmed by the Governor-General and she was granted the land that she had effectively held since 1778 in exchange for aiding the Company's armies when needed. This agreement solidified her position as the sole landholder of Sardhana. As well, she was given life tenure to these lands and, provided she did not contest British interests in the area, she could manage the day to day activities of Sardhana with little interference.[82]

Begum Samru's emergence as the sole landholder of Sardhana was remarkable, in part, because she was able to negotiate herself into an alliance with the British in spite of being a Mughal noble, a Maratha ally, and the widow of an infamous British enemy. More importantly, her succession to this position was unusual because she came to this position on her own terms, rather than as the custodial ruler on behalf of a son. As part of her agreement with the Company, her jagir would revert to the British upon her death although her dependents and subjects would continue to receive allowances after the British gained accession.[83]

---

[81] The matter of Le Vassoult's death is a matter of some speculation: some authors believe that the couple had agreed to commit suicide rather than admit defeat (Banerji, *Begam Samru*, pp. 54–7; Sharma, *Life and Times*, pp. 93–5). George Thomas, then the Begum's enemy, believed that the Begum deceived Le Vassoult into killing himself by appearing to stab herself in the chest.

[82] N.A.I., Foreign Dept. Proceedings, August 2–25, 1807, vol. 306, cons. 23–4.

[83] *Ibid.*

Thereafter, she reverted to the name Begum Samru and in public records kept by the British, she was identified almost exclusively as the widow of Samru.[84] Her marriage to Le Vassoult was, in effect, erased from the historical record.

For the remaining years of her life, Sardhana became the Begum's home and personal kingdom. She kept up six battalions, the equivalent of 3,000 soldiers, which included several hundred Europeans of various nationalities. Through her civic activities and public representations, she became an important figure in northern India and employed various cultural strategies to represent her authority and stature. As a local ruler, she improved living conditions, introduced agricultural reforms, and promoted civic services by building schools and hospitals.

As a result of her efforts and her high profile as a female ally of the British, Sardhana became a stopping point for journeying Europeans who were fascinated by the north Indian noblewoman.[85] In the years between 1780 and 1836, when she died, Begum Samru was visited, and written about, by about a dozen Europeans, including Reginald Heber, William Sleeman, Thomas Bacon, George Thomas, William Palmer, David Ochterlony, William Fraser, James Skinner, Mrs. A. Deane, Lady Maria Nugent, Lady Sarah Amherst, and correspondents for several journals including the *Asiatic Annual Register* and the *Calcutta Gazette*. The Begum, as a spectacular noblewoman who had been a dancing girl, represented many elements of the fantastic, the exotic, and the marvelous for these early colonial travelers. Among them, Thomas Bacon, an artillery man who traveled through northern India in the 1830s, commented that the Begum was a renowned local figure known for her public durbars. He wrote:

I have frequently been present at her *durbars*, and have enjoyed the privilege of conversation with her highness, much to my amusement and edification. She usually receives her visitors in a tent pitched outside her palace (except on grand occasions, when she graces the state audience-hall with her presence), and has little display of magnificence or wealth about her person.[86]

As he described her, she was a small woman who enjoyed peculiar habits: while her wealth was widely known and she hosted lavish parties,

---

[84] See especially, O.I.O.C., Home Misc./491–2, "Affairs of Johanna Begum (widow of Sumroo)."

[85] See also a late-Victorian era traveler's essay, "The Begum of Sardhana," *Calcutta Review* (April 1894): 310–26: "... we embrace the opportunity of paying tribute deservedly due to the spirit, activity, and talents of this noble lady."

[86] Thomas Bacon, *First Impression and Studies from Nature in Hindostan* (London, Wm. H. Allen, 1837), vol. II, p. 45.

she herself dressed unostentatiously, wearing a combination of Mughal and European dress.[87] Bacon wrote:

We find her seated upon a dingy shabby couch, in the cross-legged fashion of a tailor, her little person enveloped in a large yellow cashmere shawl, of exquisite texture, though by no means showy; under this shawl a handsome green cloak, of European fashion ... On her head, she is found wearing a turban, after the fashion of men, whom also she apes in other matters; but this head-dress is sometimes with advantage exchanged for a more becoming Mogul cap of dignity, wrought with gold, and jewelled.[88]

As she represented herself in these situations at her court, the Begum was described as being a combination of opposites.

She was described as performing her gender by cross-dressing: she was a woman who wore mannish costume and a turban.[89] As Lady Nugent noted, "Her dress was more like a man's than a woman's – she wore trousers of cloth of gold, with shawl stockings, and Hindoostanee slippers ... a dark turban, but no hair to be seen; and abundance of shawls wrapped around her in different ways."[90] By unsettling gender and cultural identities, Begum Samru created a sense of cultural confusion for her European guests, while simultaneously affirming that her status as a political ruler of some importance afforded her the privilege of eccentricity.

At her Christmas feasts, after high mass, her guests were invited to enjoy a nautch party where local dancing girls and musicians danced for guests. Although she was Christian, she observed north Indian prohibitions against eating with members of a different caste or community and was noted for not eating at these public feasts. In the company of others, she only drank tea and smoked her hookah, although her table was known for its rich cuisine. According to Bacon's account:

The Begam usually gives a grand fete, which lasts three days, during Christmas, and to which nearly all leading the society of Meerut, Delhi and the surrounding stations are invited. I have by me one of her circulars: "Her highness, the Begam Sumroo requests the honour of ...'s company at Sirdhana on Christmas Eve at

---

[87] Sleeman, vol. II, p. 289n, quotes from George Thomas's memoirs: "[She observes] the most rigid attention to the customs of Hindoostan. She is never seen out of doors or in her public durbar unveiled." Sleeman also notes, "She had uncommon sagacity and a masculine resolution."

[88] Bacon, vol. II, pp. 45–6. The description of her wearing "an odd brown velvet cap or turban," is also mentioned by Lady Sarah Amherst, Amherst Papers, Amherst College Library, vol. 5, pp. 105–6.

[89] Judith Butler, *Gender Trouble: Feminism and the Subversion of Identity* (New York: Routledge, 1990); on cross-dressing, see Marjorie Garber, *Vested Interests: Cross-dressing and Cultural Anxiety* (New York: Routledge, 1992).

[90] Lady Maria Nugent, vol. II, p. 51.

the celebration of High mass and during the two following days, to 'nautch' and a display of fireworks." Tents are prepared in the palace-garden for the accommodation of visitors and every luxury which a profuse outlay can secure is provided for the company. The tables are sumptuously spread, the viands and the wines are alike excellent. Upon these grand occasions, the Begam usually honours the guests by presiding at the table but she does not herself partake of any food in their presence. Not only are the numerous visitors entertained in this magnificent style but the whole host of their followers and train are also feasted and feted, in a manner equally sumptuous in proportion of their condition."[91]

By constructing herself as a public person who hosted state occasions in Sardhana, the Begum carefully manipulated various cultural practices to fashion her public identity. She was wealthy and aristocratic, Christian and Indian all at once. She defied the British representations of the Oriental ruler ("depraved, treacherous, and unprincipled") and behaved as an honorable and liberal ruler over her subjects.[92]

Moreover, as host to various Europeans, the Begum entertained visiting diplomats and their ladies through subversive performances, not only her own performance through eccentric social behavior, but by commissioning comedic theater. On one occasion, Lady Sarah Amherst, wife of the Governor-General, reported that she had gone to dinner at the Begum's house in Sardhana and had watched a series of comic sketches, one in which an English corporal had ridiculed the commander, another which was "a mimickry of our Courts of Justice making it appear that much bribery was going on." Lady Amherst felt that "The whole to me was anything but amusing. On the contrary, I thought it was disgusting and improper."[93] The Begum's patronage of these comic sketches suggest that, in spite of her role as an ally of the British, she could be critical of the corruption that British institutions had brought to India.

Nonetheless, as one contemporary British gazette reported:

Whether we consider the celebrity of Her Highness as a successful leader of an Army... against men of the most determined courage; or remember the highly respectable positions she maintains in society for integrity, for her munificent patronage of objects of public weal, or her benevolence to the unfortunate and indigent, we cannot help yielding to the palm of excellence over all those of her sex who hold a place in the annals of India.[94]

---

[91] Bacon, vol. II, pp. 52–3; this account is supported by Lady Nugent, vol. II, p. 53.

[92] "Towns of India – Sirdhana: Her Highness Begum Sombre," *Delhi Gazette* (1832): 292–4.

[93] Amherst Papers, stored in Amherst College Library. Lady Amherst's diaries, vol. 6, p. 117. The resident at Delhi, Charles Metcalfe had even gone so far as to ban the performance of these sketches in Delhi.

[94] "Towns of India – Sirdhana: Her Highness Begum Sombre," *Delhi Gazette* (1832): 292–4.

In her civic activities, the Begum Samru supervised several large-scale building projects in the region, including a cathedral, a palace, and a school for instructing young men in the priesthood.[95] Before her death, she sent £2,000 to the Pope as a contribution to charity. Her patronage of religious causes was not limited to the Catholic church: she sent money to Calcutta to the bishop at St. John's Church for the poor fund and the archbishop of Canterbury to be used for charity for local Protestants.[96] Her generosity also extended to her Hindu and Muslim subjects in Sardhana. She dispensed pensions to over 100 members of her family and household staff; they were of various religions and nationalities and were often dependent on her for their livelihoods.[97] Although she provided buildings and financial support for the advancement of Catholicism in Sardhana, she supported members of other religions in her community, a liberality which brought her into conflict with local Catholic priests.[98]

Between 1805, when she officially allied with the East India Company state, and 1836, when she died, the Begum Samru strategically protected her holdings against further intrusions by other military forces. Her correspondences with various Residents in Delhi and with British officials in Calcutta suggest, on the whole, that she was a savvy and politic negotiator.[99] These exchanges, written in Persian, translated into English and affixed with the Begum's seal, established Begum Samru as a political player in her own right.

When she died in 1836, her lands came under British control. Her estate, valued at around 5 lakh rupees (or the equivalent of £50,000), was divided up among her descendants, the family of George Thomas, and household members. She asked that the British government continue to provide for her pensioners from the revenues of the district.

[95] She built the cathedral of St. Mary's (1829) which is still partially standing; a palace at Kherwa in 1821; and a school nearby. She also had a home in Delhi, now a bank and movie theater in Chandni Chowk. See Lall, *Fading Portrait*, photo insert.

[96] "A Calcutta Benefactress," *BPP*, vol. I (July–Dec. 1907): 137–47.

[97] N.A.I., Foreign Political Proceedings, 23 May 1836, Cons. No. 75. her listed pensioners included 50 pensioners and invalided soldiers and their widows. The total number was over 800 and monthly amount disbursed was almost Rs. 8,000. Complete list reprinted in Sharma, *Life and Times*, Appendix G.

[98] Dyce-Sombre's Diary, British Library, March 16, 1834 in which Begum Samru's adopted heir noted "I spoke to Padre about H.H.'s [the Begum's] intention of confessing, but he told me something which astonished me greatly, that he was afraid if he gave her [Begum] the Sacrament he would get into a scrape, for H.H. having given money to non-Catholic churches – it was against her religion." I thank Michael Fisher for this reference.

[99] See N.A.I., Foreign Political Proceedings, 13 Jan. 1826, Cons. No. 11; *ibid.*, 29 October 1832, no. 71–2; *ibid.* 6 Feb. 1834, no. 43; O.I.O.C., Home Misc. 492.

The remainder of the estate, including her personal effects and household items and homes, was bequeathed to the Begum's adopted heir, David Ochterlony Dyce Sombre.[100]

Her tomb, a large carved marble edifice, shows a life-sized figure of the Begum, attired in local dress, a salwar kameez-like suit, seated on her throne, holding the Mughal emperor's firman confirming her claim to Sardhana. Surrounding her at the base of her chair are David Dyce Sombre, her adopted son, Father Julius Caesar, the local archbishop, and several of her military and provincial officials. The inscription by her adopted son, written in Latin and in English, read:

Sacred to the memory of Her Highness Joanna Zibalnessa, the Begum Sombre, styled the distinguished of nobles and beloved daughter of the State ...[101]

On one side panel on the pedestal of this monument, the Begum was shown on her way to a durbar, atop a procession of elephants, further securing her historical stature as an important noblewoman. On another panel, the consecration of the church is depicted with the Begum handing a chalice to the archbishop. In death, as in life, Begum Samru evoked multiple cultural images in order to fashion herself as a Mughal noblewoman, a pious Christian, and as a woman of substantial wealth and political power. The renaming of Farzana, the dancing girl in Reinhardt's zenana, to Her Highness Joanna Zeb-un-nissa, the Begum Samru implied much larger transformations than simply changing names.

Helene Bennett, a.k.a. Halima

In contrast to Begum Samru, Halima, de Boigne's favorite female companion, had a very different life. Born to a high-born Persian family in Lucknow who were part of the Mughal service elite, she met de Boigne some time between 1783 and 1788 when she resided with her sister, Faiz Baksh, and her sister's partner, William Palmer. Part of a cosmopolitan and mixed-race community in Lucknow, Halima and de Boigne met on the frontiers of the Company's dominions in a city that brought together many high-profile interracial couples.[102]

Like Walter Reinhardt, Benoit de Boigne was a mercenary soldier who made himself from a man of humble background from France into

---

[100] Banerji, *Begam Samru*, pp. 188–205.
[101] *Calcutta Review* (1894): 314; Lall, *Fading Portrait*, pp. 179–80.
[102] Young, *Fountain of the Elephants*, p. 18.

a man of aristocratic status in India. De Boigne was born in 1751 in Chambery, in the Savoy region of France, to Jean Baptiste Leborgne, a furrier and leather merchant. He arrived in Madras in 1778 and joined the British army as an ensign but aspired to bigger ambitions. De Boigne left his low-status position in the Madras army in order to become a mercenary soldier. At this point, he changed his name to the more aristocratic-sounding, Benoit de Boigne, and actively obscured his family's modest merchant past.[103] He went north to Calcutta where he made the acquaintance of Warren Hastings, then Governor-General of the Bengal Presidency. Armed with Hastings's letter of introduction, de Boigne went further north to Awadh and was befriended by Claude Martin, a Frenchman who had long resided in north India and William Palmer, who was then residing in Lucknow.[104]

De Boigne remained in Lucknow for five months during the winter of 1782–1783 and learned Persian and Urdu; as well, he became more knowledgeable about local military practices. Within a year, he accompanied various British political agents through north India and acted under the personal protection of Warren Hastings.[105] In 1784, de Boigne entered the service of Mahadji Scindhia, the Maratha ruler of western India, and raised two battalions of 850 men each. Through the next five years, de Boigne's battalions followed those of the Maratha forces against the Mughal forces. The turning point, in Agra in 1788, established de Boigne as a gifted commander; with this victory, the Marathas were decisively installed as the ruling power of northern India, although they still nominally pledged their allegiance to the Mughal throne. De Boigne resigned soon after this success and retired to Lucknow as a private citizen to invest his fortune amassed through his years of military service. There, in 1788, he resumed his relationship with Halima, sister-in-law of his good friend William Palmer, and they had two children together.[106] In 1789, Halima gave birth to a daughter, nicknamed Banu. When de Boigne returned to active service under the Marathas the next year, she apparently followed him and three years later, she gave birth to a son, Ali Baksh. Upon the birth of the son,

---

[103] *Ibid.*, ch. 4.

[104] O.I.O.C., H/481, pp. 1307–11, "Papers relative to Gen. de Boigne's affairs"; *Fountain of the Elephants*, ch. 5; Compton, *European Military Adventurers of Hindustan*, pp. 22–30: Hastings had provided financial support from his own resources to de Boigne so that de Boigne could pursue his exploration of a road from India to Russia. Traveling under the protection of Hastings's political agents in northern India, de Boigne moved north and west toward Delhi.

[105] Young, *Fountain of the Elephants*, pp. 100–1.

[106] *Ibid.*, p. 138.

William Palmer sent his family's congratulations, "Give our love to the Begum and kiss the young Baron for me."[107] And Halima, now the young mother of two, returned to Lucknow to be near her elderly mother.

When de Boigne rejoined the Maratha service, he came to greater success both as a military commander and as a landed magnate. He was eventually granted a jaidad worth 16 lakh rupees annually and the responsibility of raising ten battalions of infantry and cavalry, the equivalent of an army of 10,000 men. The result of these campaigns established de Boigne as a great military strategist as well as a very wealthy general.

In spite of her consort's growing affluence, according to Claude Martin's aide, Halima was modest in her demands for a living allowance in Lucknow: she inquired about getting housing for less than Rs. 20 per month so that she would not spend too much of de Boigne's small fortune although at the time de Boigne was earning an estimated Rs. 10,000 every month. The aide reported to de Boigne, "I have told her, however, what was your intention and that she should not be so economical."[108] In spite of several other conjugal alliances that de Boigne had, Halima remained his favorite and as the mother of his only children, she remained an esteemed companion. When de Boigne sailed for England in November 1796, he provided a monthly pension for the two other women and gave them permission to marry; and he brought Halima and their two children on board with him along with nine tons of goods from India. When de Boigne left India in 1796, he took the Begum and his two children. At that time he was worth an estimated £400,000.[109]

Upon their arrival in England in April 1797, de Boigne settled in a modest house on Great Portland Street. Within a year, he met and married Adele d'Osmond, the seventeen-year-old daughter of the Marquis d'Osmond, a French nobleman who had been in the service of Louis XV at Versailles before the French revolution. The family was aristocratic but poor. As Adele explained several years after de Boigne's death:

The only passion in my heart was filial love. My mother was overwhelmed with fear that the feeble resources that supported our existence might fail ... Her

---

[107] Ibid.
[108] O.I.O.C., H/556, pp. 195–235. See also Compton, European Military Adventurers of Hindustan, p. 92.
[109] Adele d'Osmond, Comtesse de Boigne. Memoirs of the Comtesse de Boigne (New York: Scribners, 1907), Memoirs, vol. III, p. 131.

lamentations touched my heart less than my father's silence and his face worn with sleeplessness.[110]

De Boigne offered her a gift of £3,000 and told her that he had an income of £20,000 a year and no dependents. In order to protect her parents, Adele secured a further £500 a year for her parents as a part of her marriage agreement with de Boigne. Adele apparently had no idea that he had a wife and two children: "His previous life was but little known, and he deceived me about his past, his name, his family, and his antecedents. I think that at the time he proposed to preserve the character that he had then assumed."[111]

Indeed, as de Boigne himself wrote to Adele:

... before I did see you I had never entertained a decided wish for a matrimonial state ... If I have paid a kind of attention and I may say assiduities to some of the fair, I may affirm its having been more by way of diversion and as an amusement to the mind than from an inclination of heart which, having remained untouched till now, I offer you free from any engagements whatsoever.[112]

Apparently forgetting Halima and their two children, de Boigne insisted to Adele that his love and his considerable financial resources were exclusively his to share with his future wife. For Halima, de Boigne purchased a house for her in Enfield, a town outside of London. He then gave her a yearly allowance of £300 in addition to paying for the schooling of his children. With the help of friends she had known in Lucknow, including Dr. Blane, the nawab of Awadh's personal physician, Halima settled into life in England. Halima and de Boigne corresponded irregularly as he reported his travels to her. She remained as uncomplaining as ever. By the year 1802, de Boigne found his way back to Chambery, his hometown in the Savoy region, and bought a chateau. At some point before he left England, de Boigne wrote to "my dear Begum,"

They [the children] could never be under a better guardian than you, so I am perfectly easy in regard to it when at home, as also in regard to their health, as you have always been to them a good Mother ... I have seen you a good daughter to your mother, *an affectionate wife to me* and tender mother to your two offspring [emphasis added].[113]

---

[110] d'Osmond, *Memoirs*, vol. III, p. 133.
[111] Young, *Fountain of the Elephants*, pp. 210–12.
[112] *Ibid.*, p. 293.
[113] *Ibid.*, pp. 242–3.

Apparently, between themselves, de Boigne considered himself married in some form to the Begum but he left her in England.

After a few years of marriage, de Boigne and Adele were permanently separated in 1804 and de Boigne sent for his daughter, who was then fifteen years old and in school at Mrs. Barker's in Hammersmith. From correspondence found in his personal papers, it is clear that Banu had been baptized by then and became known as Ann; similarly Halima had also converted and was referred to as Helene Bennett. The two were supposed to travel together to Chambery but for some unknown reason, only Ann embarked for France. Ann fell ill on the journey and died in Paris in her father's pied-a-terre. Subsequently, Helene wrote to de Boigne, mournful and sympathetic but also urging de Boigne to take care of their remaining child, Charles Alexander, who had presumably also been recently baptized:

I don't know what to write upon my misfortune ... I think you ought to give thanks to God for having many relations, friends and acquaintances where poor I had very few of next to none.... I see by your letter that you have provided for Charles and also for me. As to myself, I don't much care, but only for Charles. How easy one may wrong him out of his rights by destroying the papers .... Do what you please, only I sincerely hope you will act like a father towards your son ... you may have many more but you are not sure that they are yours ...[114]

And finally, in a poignant afterthought: "I sincerely wish you will send me all my child's things."[115]

Soon thereafter, Helene moved into a cottage near Horsham, a town to the south of London in Sussex while her son attended St. Edmund's College in Hertfordshire. De Boigne remained in Chambery and became a public figure well known for his philanthropy. Helene and de Boigne's son, Charles Alexander, eventually found his way to France in 1814, and after a fifteen-year separation from his father, Charles was welcomed to Chambery. Several years later when de Boigne was ennobled by King Victor Emmanuel of Italy, the elder de Boigne initiated a complicated adoption process by which he made sure that after his death his title would devolve to his son, Charles. In the process, he filed a petition in which he stated that his marriage to Adele had provided no issue and as they were separated and she was well provided for, he expected no future heirs. He also testified that Halima, "Persian by origin and daughter of a Colonel of Cavalry in the service on the Emperor of the Moguls, Shah Alam," and he had a free association before his marriage through which no one had been affected.

[114] *Ibid.*, p. 243
[115] *Ibid.*, pp. 260–1.

Helene had been baptized as had both their children and de Boigne argued that the facts of their conversions as Catholic subjects, although Charles was illegitimate, should suffice as evidence that Charles should be considered his rightful heir.[116] The petition passed and after his father's death in 1830, Charles became the Count de Boigne.

Helene, a.k.a. Halima, ended her days living in a cottage, Rangers' Lodge, on the edge of St. Leonard's Forest near Horsham. From accounts given by various servants she employed, she seemed peculiar: she was pious and attended mass regularly, gave generously to the local poor yet she often remained in bed in a state of undress. She smoked "long pipes" (a hookah?) and spoke of being an Indian princess, yet no one of substance ever came to visit her. Locally, she was known as "the Black woman."[117]

She lived until 1854 and survived both de Boigne and Charles, their son. When she died, her estate was bequeathed to her grandsons in France. Her tomb was marked by a simple inscription: HELENA BENNETT VIDUA DEFUNCTA, or Helena Bennett, the deceased widow, and it continued: GENERAL BENNETT, COUNT DE BOIGNE. Although she was Catholic, she was buried in the local Anglican graveyard; her tomb is situated north to south, as opposed to east and west, thereby confirming in the minds of many that in her burial, she honored her Islamic origin.[118] Helen's tomb, its placement, its location, and its inscription suggest that in England, as well as in northern India, several cultural practices could be invoked simultaneously in the life of one person.

Helen Bennett and Begum Samru, who converted to Catholicism and went by Christian names, lived among Europeans but observed various Indo-Muslim practices. Helen Bennett was buried in an Anglican burial ground but with her grave facing Mecca; Begum Samru converted but maintained the practice of keeping her head covered in public. Like other native women, such as Helen Bennett's sister Faiz Baksh, companion to William Palmer, these women demonstrated how it was possible to have children and other relatives who fashioned themselves as European and simultaneously maintain indigenous practices. While Begum Samru's life demonstrates how one woman maneuvered from her position on the social and geographical margins of the East India

---

[116] *BPP*, vol. XLVI (1933): 94; on similar petitions of legitimation in colonial Spain in this period, see Ann Twinam, *Public Lives, Private Secrets: Gender, Honor, Sexuality, and Illegitimacy in Colonial Spanish America* (Stanford: Stanford University Press, 1999).

[117] Young, *Fountain of the Elephants*, p. 296; *BPP*, vol. XLVI (1933): 93.

[118] *BPP*, vol. XLVI (1933): 93: According to this source, the position of her grave follows the Islamic custom of having the head to the north, the feet to the south. It is the only one in the cemetery that is placed in this direction.

Company's territories, as a former slave-girl who became a concubine to a European mercenary soldier in Sardhana, Helen Bennett's life delineates the significant constraints that native women faced.

Conclusion

The contrast between Halima's and Begum Samru's life stories suggests that the positions of native women in domestic arrangements with European men were often unstable and contingent on the social context in which they circulated. In Begum Samru's case, she managed the symbols of her position — she took on the title of Begum, she negotiated herself into the role of Reinhardt's successor — and was able to fashion herself as a noblewoman. Halima, on the other hand, appears to have started as a noblewoman who followed de Boigne to Britain; her "fall" from her status serves as a useful corrective to the impression of successful social climbing that the Begum's story represents.

The lives of native women who cohabited with or were married to Europeans took place on a cultural stage in which multiple and overlapping customs and practices were available in representing women's subjectivities. As the wills and inventories of affluent native women demonstrate, elite women experienced everyday life in hybrid ways that defy easy categorization as European or native. How they named themselves, who they identified as their heirs and members of their communities, and the ways in which they strained against the categories of identities available to them show that native women were both strategic and resistant when they recorded their subjectivities in final testaments, letters, and political negotiations. In charting the specific conditions under which native women spoke and registered their demands in historical records, such as wills, letters, and political papers, they became historical subjects of a colonial society that was deeply invested in keeping proof of their existence out of the archives. By addressing the ways in which a partial understanding of native women's subjectivity is possible, we start to see that native women were not wholly absent, nor did they absent themselves from the records of early colonial communities.

5   Household order and colonial justice

While native women expressed their cultural, religious, and racial affiliations in their own writings in various ways, early law courts in Bengal made native women into legal subjects in particular ways, especially when they appeared in courts as defendants, witnesses, and plaintiffs. While the courts' understanding of the legal status of native women seemed to undercut any agency these subjects had in fashioning their legal selves, the cases in this chapter show how active and seemingly knowledgeable litigants, defendants, plaintiffs, and their lawyers were in creating narratives and subjectivities that might result in favorable decisions.[1] This dialogic process, however asymmetrical in its results, shows how marginal figures in colonial communities – native women, children, slaves, and servants – were drawn into the institutional apparatus of the British courts as participants, becoming subjects of the court's jurisdiction.[2] By becoming engaged in colonial judicial processes, native subjects, inadvertently and unintentionally, solidified the colonial judiciary's claims to political authority and its ability to construct a normative gendered and racial order within interracial households.

Through two sets of legal disputes, civil and criminal, this chapter explores how various judicial institutions of the East India Company state managed the diverse populations over which it ruled. The first dispute was a civil suit about inheritance in a family with a Muslim mother and a Christian son. The second set of disputes involved domestic violence crimes committed in and around the households of European men that included native women. In traversing between

---

[1] Ranajit Guha, "Chandra's death," *Subaltern Studies* V (Delhi: Oxford University Press, 1987); Natalie Zemon Davis, *Fiction in the Archives: Pardon Tales and Their Tellers in Sixteenth-Century France* (Stanford: Stanford University Press, 1987); Carolyn Steedman, *Dust: The Archive and Cultural History* (New Brunswick, NJ: Rutgers University Press, 2002), ch. 3.

[2] Eugene Irschick, *Dialogue and History* (Berkeley: University of California Press, 1994), see especially Conclusion.

civil and criminal law, these disputes demonstrate the complex ways in which the rule of law was highly malleable in early colonial India. Although, in theory, the courts represented a just process that offered equal restitution for all subjects, in the end, judicial decisions proved to be highly effective at enforcing class, racial, and gender hierarchies that were constitutive of the early Anglo-Indian colonial social order.

At the crux of these disputes was the question common to many colonial societies of how to rule on cases involving parties of different legal status, particularly given the circumstance of plural legal jurisdictions.[3] One of the central elements was how the legal status of the family was defined when its members were of different religions, races, and ethnicities, and thus, of different legal jurisdictions. Another complicating factor was that most of these cases involved cohabiting, rather than married couples. To resolve and simplify these dimensions, judges repeatedly treated these conjugal units as one, taking the principle of legal coverture from common law in England and subsuming the woman's legal identity into her male partner's, even when there was no marital contract.

Throughout, colonial officials protected the rights of Englishmen while holding them accountable for their crimes, particularly crimes committed on the bodies of the courts' most vulnerable subjects – children, slaves, and domestic servants – showing that the state could be fair. In attempting to protect the rights of such marginal groups, the colonial judiciary legitimated its power not only by enfranchising the powerful, but by intervening in matters involving the powerless. Time and again, civil and criminal trials resulted in judgments that supported a notion of paternal authority and the right of European men to enjoy access to the bodies and estates of native women. Implicit in all of these disputes was the strongly held notion that European men had the responsibility to physically discipline or protect the inmates of their households, much as they had the right to rule over the subjects of this colonial society. Coinciding with the expansion of the Company's territory and political authority on the Indian subcontinent, these incremental legal decisions helped to legitimize the authority that individual Europeans had over Indians within the East India Company's dominions.

The early colonial judiciary was introduced as a check on the political and financial corruption that Parliament feared the Company was

---

[3] Sally Engle Merry, "Legal pluralisms," *Law & Society Review* 22 (1988): 869–96; Sally Engle Merry, "Law and colonialism," *Law & Society Review* 25 (1991): 889–922.

engaged in and intended to act independently of the Company.[4] Established in 1774 by a parliamentary regulating act, the Supreme Court was comprised of four crown-appointed British judges who were empowered to protect the rights of Britons and Indians living within the Company's dominions.[5] The court also had personal jurisdiction over British subjects living outside the Company's territories on the Indian subcontinent. The regulating act also elaborated a plan to establish a separate set of native courts for administering justice to natives in the Company's territories; these courts were called the Company courts and were managed by district collectors who relied on local informants, such a maulvis and pundits, for advice on local judicial precedent.[6] While the Company's courts were intended to protect and adjudicate the legal rights of Indians, the Crown courts dealt with "free-born Englishmen" and dealt with civil suits against the East India Company.

The establishment of separate Crown and Company court systems is perhaps best known for creating a split judiciary for Britons, Hindus, and Muslims and establishing unequal definitions of legal status for Indians under the law; less familiar is that the crown court was created to adjudicate criminal and civil disputes involving Europeans and their employees.[7] Crime and moral corruption among Europeans occupied a significant portion of judicial time. In particular, the number of domestic violence cases brought against European men in the early colonial period shows that the question of enforcing the peace was understood in manifold ways.

The establishment of the rule of law has long been claimed the hallmark of the colonial state's attempts to make India's government modern and rational, although it is perhaps better understood as a colonial legacy that bequeathed a misshapen and truncated set of legal

---

[4] For useful overviews on this process, see Radhika Singha, *A Despotism of Law: Crime and Justice in Early Colonial India* (Delhi: Oxford University Press, 1998); J. Fisch, *Cheap Lives and Dear Limbs: The British Transformation of the Bengal Criminal Law, 1769–1817* (Wiesbaden: Steiner, 1983); B. B. Misra, *The Judicial Administration of the East India Company, 1765–1781* (Patna, 1953).

[5] Initially, the territorial jurisdiction applied only to the cities of Calcutta, Bombay, and Madras; later, this was expanded to include the territory of the three Presidencies, Bengal, Bombay, and Madras. M. P. Jain, *Outlines of Indian Legal History*, Fifth edition (Bombay: N. M. Tripathi, Ltd., 1990), pp. 69 ff.

[6] A second set of judical reforms, instituted by Lord Cornwallis in 1790, attempted to more closely regulate the judicial affairs in the East India Company's courts, or those courts that dealt with criminal and civil matters of Hindus and Muslims living in the Company's territories. See Fisch, *Cheap Lives*, pp. 37–50. Substantial changes to the Supreme Court were not made until after 1813.

[7] Jain, *Outlines*, pp. 50–4, 58, 75–7.

practices to post-colonial India.[8] Reputed to be universal, fair, and blind, under colonial law, all subjects of the state had equal status under the law. The enforcement of this fact was a key pillar of the Supreme Court's authority to intervene in domestic affairs, policing household peace and order, and proving instrumental to the governmentality of the nascent colonial state.

As Lauren Benton has recently noted, during this formative period, the colonial "state" as such was not yet in existence. Jurisdictional politics and debates over how to apply the rule of law enabled the Company and various litigants to extend and consolidate the authority of the English courts, so that "legal jockeying helped to create a space for the colonial state, even before such an entity formally existed."[9] Arguing that the law was an "open-ended process" in which litigants, jurists, and defendants were unsure of the outcome but expected favorable judicial decisions, Benton's comparative study of legal regimes demonstrates the ways in which rule of law, through a complex process of negotiation, merged with the interests of the state and privileged members of colonial society who were seen to be more supportive of the state's interests. In progressing from a putatively irrational idiosyncratic precolonial legal order to a rational colonial legal system, Benton shows the ways in which these transitions were hotly contested and a product of judicial compromises that both challenged and affirmed the authority of the colonial judiciary, enabling the judiciary to become a central component of the state's growing political authority.[10]

The Calcutta Supreme Court, composed of Justices William Jones, John Hyde, Robert Chambers, and Elijah Impey, spent a significant proportion of their initial judicial efforts in determining who would be subject to the recently established laws of the Calcutta Court and how legal precedents based on English Common Law should be articulated for a community of subjects that was racially, ethnically,

---

[8] Lloyd and Susanne Hoeber Rudolph, *The Modernity of Tradition* (Chicago: University of Chicago Press, 1967), p. 253; Benard S. Cohn, *Colonialism and Its Forms of Knowledge* (Delhi: Oxford University Press, 1996); *An Anthropologist Among Historians*; J.D.M. Derrett, *Religion, Law and State in India* (London: Faber and Faber, 1968).

[9] Lauren Benton, *Law and Colonial Cultures: Legal Regimes in World History, 1400–1900* (Cambridge: Cambridge University Press, 2002), pp. 9–15; quote is from p. 29.

[10] Lauren Benton, "Colonial law and cultural difference: jurisdictional politics and the formation of the colonial state," *Comparative Studies in Society and History* 41 (1999): 563–88. See also David Washbrook, "Law, state and agrarian society in colonial India," *Modern Asian Studies* 15, 3 (1981): 649–721.

and religiously diverse.[11] Although the Calcutta court was intended for "British subjects" throughout the Company's dominions and for all subjects living within the boundaries of Calcutta, time and again, the court deliberated whether native-born subjects could be counted within this jurisdiction.[12] Native women were often subject to legal rights not as rights-bearing individuals, but as members of various communities and thus, legal constituencies. In following this strategy, the "rule of law" was gendered and communal, split and applied in various ways to different populations: Christians, Muslims, Hindus, high-caste, low-caste, men and women. Thus the goal of equal legal protection for all subjects was highly elusive. This strategy allowed the colonial government to avoid upsetting local legal norms and practices and provoking rebellion.[13]

As the following cases elaborate, the rule of law and the legal practices that resulted from its colonial introduction to India were crucial means through which the Company state established its authority over its many subjects, even socially marginal subjects such as native women. Although these jurisdictional disputes were seemingly concerned with defining the legal status of individuals and protecting their rights, these disputes defined what constituted a family arrangement, and how the individual members of colonial families fit into the hierarchies of the colonial state and society. Through these judicial contests, sexual and racial boundaries between different communities were managed and reinforced, giving rise to hierarchical relationships that ultimately secured, with the authority of the judiciary, the dominance of European men over the bodies of native women and various marginal others.

I

An early nineteenth-century case in the Calcutta Supreme Court, excerpted in a digest of legal precedents, delineated the ways in which definitions of family, customary practice and the law intersected in a

---

[11] The boundaries of Calcutta in the 1770s were the Hooghly River on the west, the "Mahratta Ditch" or Outer Circular Road on the east and south, and what is now Mahatma Gandhi Road on the north.

[12] A key case was a civil action, Michael de Rozio v. Chutgar Gosain (1789), Hyde Notes, vol. 24. The court ruled that because the plaintiff, De Rozio, had been born before 1757 (marking the battle of Plassey), he could not be considered born on British soil. Hyde Papers and Hyde Reports are stored in the Rare Books room of the National Library, Calcutta, on 18 rolls of microfilm.

[13] Upendra Baxi, "The State's Emissary: the place of law in Subaltern Studies," *Subaltern Studies* VII (Delhi: Oxford University Press, 1992), p. 253.

dispute about inheritance. In the case of the Estate of Bibee Hay alias Bibee Hannah, a young Muslim woman, Jaun Bibee, claimed to be the adopted granddaughter of the deceased and thus heir to the estate. As the court deliberated on the matter, one of the crucial issues was that Bibee Hay, the deceased woman, had a son, James Robinson, by an Englishman. Although Bibee Hay had never married the Englishman, the British executors of the estate argued under British law, the half-English son should be considered the only heir.[14]

In these cases, legal status might be defined by religious and national forms of identification, bringing a gendered aspect to the question of legal subjectivity in families that had European fathers and native mothers. While paternal right dictated that children inherited their father's legal status (that affirmed the dominance of particular racial, national, and religious markers), the reluctance of colonial societies to accept mixed-race offspring and native wives and mothers entailed that the law had to find a way to disenfranchise these members of colonial society from making claims to European citizenship and European estates. In a range of colonial contexts, the question of how to categorize the rights of a child born to a European man and a native woman was crucial to forming the gender and race hierarchies central to colonizing societies.[15]

This particular court case about the estate of a Muslim woman who had given birth to the son of an Englishman demonstrates how questions of inheritance were refracted through judicial concerns about family rights, community privileges, and national and religious identities in the first phase of British rule in India. In the judicial debates that this case produced, the law was as much about putative notions of justice as it was about creating social norms for family life and defining the familial in terms that the bureaucracies of the state could comprehend.

From the inception of the Supreme Court in 1774, the East India Company allowed pandits and maulvis to adjudicate over matters of family inheritance in order to uphold locally based social order. In the process of protecting what Britons thought of as local law, textual laws

---

[14] *Morley's Digest*, 181: Sir Edward Hyde East's Notes.
[15] Lora Wildenthal, "Race, gender and citizenship in the German empire," in Frederick Cooper and Ann L. Stoler, eds., *Tensions of Empire: Colonial Cultures in a Bourgeois World* (Berkeley: University of California Press, 1997); Alice L. Conklin, "Redefining 'Frenchness': citizenship, race regeneration, and imperial motherhood in France and West Africa, 1914–40," and Jean Elisabeth Pedersen, "'Special Customs': paternity suits and citizenship in France and the Colonies, 1870–1912," in Julia Clancy-Smith and Frances Gouda, eds., *Domesticating the Empire: Race, Gender and Family Life in French and Dutch Colonialism* (Charlottesville: University of Virginia Press, 1998).

were privileged over customary practices leading, in the case of Hindu
law, to a marked Sanskritization and Brahmanization of existing
legal practices, particularly when it came to family practices, such as
marriage.[16]

The establishment of legal digests, Hindu and Muslim, in the 1770s
and 1780s affected Britons and their families as much as it did Indians,
particularly in matters of civil law. By conceptualizing a field of individual legal subjects who belonged to family units of similar status,
British judicial authorities assumed that families could only belong to
one ethnic or religious category; those who converted lost the civil status
of their natal families and experienced civil death.[17] Through decisions
on family law, the early colonial courts consolidated the boundaries
between British/Christian and Native/Muslim/Hindu and enforced a
normative standard that the members of a family unit necessarily had
only one ethnic/religious identity and the father's legal status was
inherited by all members of the family. In applying the rule of law,
colonial courts effectively collapsed the multiple identities of the
individual subjects they dealt with and produced families as legal
subjects with a single racial and religious identity.

The terms of this particular civil court case were fairly straightforward. In 1819, a young woman, Jaun Bibee, claimed that she had been
adopted by Bibee Hay and had rights to Bibee Hay's estate. The
executors to the estate argued otherwise: Bibee Hay had a son through a
relationship with an Englishman named Mr. Robinson. The son, James
Robinson, had been baptized and was residing in England. In the
arguments made in favor of Jaun Bibee's rights against the rights of the
son, the court balanced the question of an individual's right to inherit
within a context of family law that was seen to be different for Muslims
than for Christians.

Witnesses on both sides testified to the following "facts": Bibee Hay's
servant of 36 years testified that Bibee Hay had cohabited with an
English gentleman, with whom she had a son who was baptized James.
Several years after the birth of James, Bibee Hay purchased an infant
slave girl, Jaun Bibee. One witness testified that Jaun Bibee was the
daughter of a man that Bibee Hay had adopted, thus further unsettling
the question of her status as a slave, adopted granddaughter, or both.

---

[16] Samita Sen, "Offences against Marriage: negotiating custom in colonial Bengal," in
Janaki Nair and Mary E. John, eds., *A Question of Silence: the Sexual Economies of
Modern India* (New Delhi: Kali for Women, 1998).

[17] Gauri Viswanathan, *Outside the Fold: Conversion, Modernity and Belief* (Princeton:
Princeton University Press, 1998), chs. 3 and 4.

As evidence of the right of James Robinson to inherit his mother's estate, several witnesses testified that Jaun Bibee was given away in a marriage arranged by Bibee Hay; when Jaun Bibee divorced, she asked for a maintenance allowance from Bibee Hay. In response, Bibee Hay reportedly stipulated several times that she could make no financial provisions since she intended to leave her entire estate to her son in England. Moreover, lawyers for the estate claimed that since adoption did not exist under Muslim law, Jaun Bibee, slave and adopted granddaughter could not be considered a member of Bibee Hay's family. This argument, that a slave could not be adopted and be considered a member of the family, was a logic that was increasingly employed by the British in other cases involving inheritance and accession to power in Muslim ruling households.[18]

On the other side, supporters of Jaun Bibee's claim reported that they had heard Bibee Hay say "that she had no relatives except Jaun Bibee and her two children, who would be entitled to all her property." A. G. Spankie, Jaun Bibee's lawyer, argued that in the absence of a written will, Bibee Hay's remarks should be taken as a testamentary document. Moreover, and this was central to Jaun Bibee's case, her lawyers argued that the court had no jurisdiction over the matter since the dispute was over a Muslim's estate. Under the statutory laws of the East India Company, the Supreme Court (in which the case appeared) was allowed to rule only on disputes involving Christians or foreign Europeans living within the East India Company's dominions. According to Jaun Bibee's lawyers, Hindus and Muslims (and Bibee Hay should be counted as a Muslim) were under the jurisdiction of customary law.

In the process of investigating the case and what sorts of legal constraints should be applied to ruling in the case, the court asked the *maulvi*, who was in attendance, whether a Muslim could verbally make a will. He replied, yes, as long as there were two witnesses, which there were. The maulvi also stated that the "natural child" of a Muslim woman was not entitled to inherit her estate if he had been raised as a Christian. In other words, the biological right of the son to inherit mattered much less in Islamic codes if he had not been raised a Muslim. The maulvi's statement implied that blood, at the cornerstone of the case made on behalf of James Robinson, mattered much less than cultural practice.

To counter this claim, the Registrar of Wills argued that since the rights of a Christian, and a British subject were being challenged,

---

[18] Indrani Chatterjee, *Gender, Slavery and the Law in Colonial India* (Delhi: Oxford University Press, 1999).

the court should rule in favor of the son who was biologically the heir to the estate and putatively English. In contrast to the maulvi, the registrar argued that the case be argued under British statute because the heir was, by blood, under British jurisdiction. By privileging the idea that James Robinson should be considered a British subject, thereby inheriting his rights from his father, the registrar selectively affirmed the principle of *jus sanguinis*, which meant that a child born of married parents received the father's citizenship regardless of where the birth occurred. Ordinarily when the parents were unmarried, as they were in this case, the child received the citizenship of the mother, but James Robinson's lawyers overlooked this, assuming that since local custom was cohabitation, remaining unmarried was not an irregular event. *Jus sanguinus* was privileged in this case in opposition to *jus soli*, in which those born in a particular territory or on the soil of a particular sovereign state received the rights granted by that state. Although James Robinson had been born in India of a native mother, the registrar argued that he should be considered an Englishman by birth on his father's side, even more so since Robinson "lived as Christian." In contrast to the later nineteenth-century court cases that Gauri Viswanathan discusses, in this case, James Robinson had his status as a Christian convert and British subject confirmed by the court.[19] Indeed, if James Robinson had not been considered British, this court case would have been referred to a local Islamic court that might have been less sympathetic to the rights of a half-caste man living in England.

The case was eventually referred to the court maulvi who was instructed to establish what Bibee Hay's intentions had been. Although the resolution to the dispute did not appear in the court case record, inventories listed with the Supreme Court several years later indicated that a stipend had been settled upon Jaun Bibee (in these documents, she was listed as Beebee John). She received a monthly allowance of S. Rs. 20 and an additional lump sum to purchase a house for herself and her children. The total estate, worth Rs. 23,000 or roughly £2,400, was invested in a local agency house until Jaun Bibee died, after which the estate would revert to James Robinson.[20]

The solution to this case, granting a stipend to the complainant while retaining the estate for the putatively English son, followed a distributive

---

[19] Viswanathan, *Outside the Fold*, ch. 3; she discusses the cases of Ananda Rao (1844), Huchi (1876) and Abraham v. Abraham (1863).

[20] Oriental and India Office Collections, (hereafter O.I.O.C.), L/AG/34/27/70, Bengal Inventories 1821, v. 2, pp. 1297–1308.

pattern that cut across two communities and for the court's purposes, across two jurisdictions. By the court's logic, the rights of the testator, Bibee Hay who was Muslim, were as well protected as the rights of her natural son, James Robinson, who was Christian and half-English. Jaun Bibee's inheritance, a house and a monthly stipend suggested that she was partially recognized as a legitimate heir to Bibee Hay. Nonetheless, the case's resolution maintained the inheritance of a putatively British subject while denying that same inheritance to an indigenous female Muslim subject. In doing so, this case claimed Bibee Hay's estate for her half-European son who lived in England, although Bibee Hay, the testator, may well have intended otherwise. Moreover, in privileging the principle of *jus sanguinus* over *jus soli*, the court understood James Robinson as a British subject, inheriting his father's status, rather than his mother's indigenous legal status, in order to justify the legal decision to grant him Bibee Hay's entire estate.

As Lora Wildenthal has noted for twentieth-century German colonial practices, questions of legal jurisdiction "...dealt with persons as members of a normatively defined family, with its gender and generational categories; any case of disputed citizenship was necessarily a family story."[21] In this case, Bibee Hay's family confronted laws that could not recognize that members of the same family could have different statuses under the law so it privileged the father's legal status. Consequently, the court concluded by finding a solution that benefited the long-term financial prospects of James Robinson, who was understood by the court as a descendant of his British father's status. In the end, although this was a case about Bibee Hay's final bequests, the legal results made Robinson into an heir who inherited Bibee Hay's money but not her legal status.

II

In criminal law as well as the civil law, early colonial courts continually grappled with questions about jurisdiction. When criminal courts ruled on crimes that had occurred in mixed-race households, they tried to account for who was responsible, who had the right to hit whom, and whose body required the protection of the court. When judges and juries ruled on cases in which native women were accused of inflicting violence or were victims of violence within their households, they enforced domestic peace in mixed-race communities and created a gendered and

---

[21] Wildenthal, "Race, Gender and Citizenship," p. 265.

racial social order that allowed European men to have authority over the inmates of their households.

In the years between the 1770s and the 1840s, the court ruled on at least three dozen household violence cases involving violence between men and women, and between masters and slaves. Although British judges were reluctant to intervene in domestic affairs, they did so when other forms of social and sexual regulation, such as male authority within the household, had broken down.[22] In ruling on crimes in which native women were both victims and perpetrators, judges on the Calcutta Supreme Court became intimately involved with containing household violence and disciplining the social and sexual threats posed by interracial relationships between lower-class European soldiers and merchants and the native women with whom they lived. (While high-ranking, upper-class men may have also physically abused native women with whom they were intimate, these relationships rarely drew the scrutiny of British judges, showing that the enforcement of household order only applied to certain classes of British men.) In cases in which native women were accused of harming another member of the household, judges were careful to ensure that an image of justice had been preserved and the patriarchal order of the household had not been disturbed. In cases of domestic violence in which women were victims of rape, murder, and burglary at the hands of European men they knew, trials lay bare the sexual misdeeds of lower-ranking Europeans for the court's surveillance, while jury acquittals enabled lower-ranking men to escape imprisonment.

At the heart of domestic violence cases was the question of what sorts of judicial and legal standards ought to apply to native women who lived in the homes of Europeans and were harmed by men who were putatively responsible for their "protection." In the judicial and legal process of negotiating these issues, the concerns over the safety of native women were superseded by the court's reluctance to usurp a man's right to the body of a woman with whom he had enjoyed a conjugal relationship. Although many of the trials showed a clear culpability, European

---

[22] Christine Daniels, "Intimate violence, now and then," in Daniels and Michael V. Kennedy, eds., *Over the Threshold: Intimate Violence in Early America* (New York: Routledge, 1999), p. 9, notes that a male's authority and responsibility for the inmates of his household were assumed by the rule of law in the early Anglo-American colonies; it was when patriarchal authority broke down and produced excessive violence or a threat to public order that judges stepped in. See also Elizabeth Pleck, "Wife beating in nineteenth-century America," *Victimology* 4 (1979), 67. For early colonial India, see Singha, *Despotism of Law, passim.*

men were frequently acquitted for their actions. Inadvertently, the search for justice enabled the court to justify violence within interracial households and to secure the sexual access of Englishmen to native women's bodies.[23]

In deciding a putatively just outcome, one of the key issues concerned whose criminal behavior was on trial and the ways that individual agency was understood within the law. Two cases of the cases discussed below involved native women who did violence to others within the household; several others were about native women who were victim to sexual crimes within the household. By addressing the legal question of native women's agency in cases in which women were criminals and victims, this analysis opens up a broader vision of how gender and racial inequalities were articulated and consolidated within the criminal law in early British India.

Two early cases involved household crimes that were committed by Indian female companions in the homes of Englishmen. Both cases, Rex v. Betty and Peggy (1777) and Rex. v. William Orby Hunter (1793), appeared in Justice John Hyde's notes during the first two decades after the establishment of the Calcutta Supreme Court. Rex v. Betty and Peggy (1777) was a case of manslaughter filed against Betty and Peggy, both women who were the companions of Englishmen who resided together in a house in Calcutta. They were accused of scalding a young slave girl, Susannah, with hot oil and killing her. The second case, Rex v. William Orby Hunter and Baugwan Khonwar (1796), involved William Orby Hunter, an indigo planter, and his bibi. In this case, the bibi, Baugwan Khonwar was accused of torturing three slave girls who worked in her household.

The cast of characters who were witness to these crimes reveal that the households of lower-ranking Europeans in the East India Company's establishment were entirely different from the world of high-ranking English society that is familiar to us from travel memoirs, diaries, and novels (which were discussed in greater length in chapter 1). At this level of Anglo-Indian society, there was a greater deal of interaction, both cooperative and conflictual, between local Indians, servants, European soldiers, and tradesmen. Households were often permeated by neighbors, domestic servants, and distant relatives and these men and

---

[23] Carole Pateman, *The Sexual Contract* (Stanford: Stanford University Press, 1988); Prabhu Mohapatra, "'Restoring the Family': wife murders and the making of a sexual contract in Indian Caribbean colonies," *Studies in History* 11, 2 (1995): 227–60; see also Singha, *Despotism of Law* (1998), ch. 4.

women were often the first line of surveillance in witnessing household violence.[24] Neighbors, ayahs, valets, and former lovers – characters that were usually silent in historical records – came forward to state their accounts when household interactions became excessively violent, and became matters for the consideration of British judges.

In the multiple narratives of these crimes, the daily lives of low-ranking Europeans and their domestic partners emerge as a stage for arbitrating various disputes between a nascent colonial state and its putative subjects. The witness narratives, constructed in order to gain a favorable verdict, elaborate the social and cultural context in which interracial cohabitation was a common feature, but one in which native women were seen to be inherently suspect and European men were seen to have a right to their bodies.

In Rex v. Betty and Peggy (1777), two native women were accused of killing Betty's twelve-year-old slave, Susannah. Both women lived in the same house and were "kept by Englishmen."[25] Their names, Betty and Peggy, were the names by which their consorts and the court referred to them and yet, as became clear in a discussion of Betty and Peggy, neither Betty nor Peggy was European-born as their names might indicate. The witnesses listed in the indictment were "Jugger naut" (Jagar Nath, a servant), "James Robertson" (a neighbor), "Noorun" (another woman who lived nearby), "Peggy" (the defendant), and "Jaun Bibee" (another woman who lived nearby). The Englishmen with whom Betty and Peggy resided were never mentioned in the course of the indictment, nor were the Englishmen who kept Noorun and Jaun Bibee.

As the witnesses stated, Jagar Nath had found the burned body of the slave and called Noorun and Jaun Bibee to examine her wounds. Peggy testified that she had earlier scolded the slave and had "punished her," but did not kill her. James Robertson, described as present in the neighborhood, stated that he had not heard anything. As the witness list

---

[24] Neighborhood surveillance was a feature of English society as well, see Roderick Phillips, *Putting Asunder: a History of Divorce in Western Society* (Cambridge: Cambridge University Press, 1988), pp. 337–8; Margaret Hunt, "Wife beating, domesticity, and women's independence in eighteenth-century London," *Gender & History* 4 (1992), pp. 22–3; Susan Dwyer Amussen, "'Being Stirred to Much Unquietness': violence and domestic violence in early modern England," *Journal of Women's History* 6 (1994), 78–82; see also Amussen, *An Ordered Society: Gender and Class in Early Modern England* (Oxford: Blackwell, 1988), esp. p. 98, pp. 129–30. See also the case of the death of a working-class woman in Baltimore's port areas, James D. Rice, "Laying Claim to Elizabeth Shoemaker: family violence on Baltimore's waterfront, 1808–1812," in Daniels and Kennedy, *Over the Threshold*, pp. 192–3.

[25] Hyde Reports, vol. 4; dated 19 December, 1777.

suggests, women who were kept by Europeans often lived side by side; Betty and Peggy, although they were the companions to two different men, lived in the same household and shared domestic duties.

The case against Betty was dismissed because she was in the next room and Jagar Nath testified that there was no door to allow access to the room in which the crime was committed. Peggy was found guilty and sentenced to execution. While the case was fairly straightforward, in the debates that followed during sentencing, gender and ethnic/religious difference became central. Although these two women had European names, neither was European nor a converted Christian. In coming to an appropriate punishment, the court, which had been established to adjudicate crimes and civil cases for British subjects who were assumed to be Christian, sought some procedure to deal with a non-British, non-Christian subject.

After her sentencing, Peggy claimed to be two months pregnant and asked for a reprieve from her death sentence. Hyde recorded the following in his notes, "We had some discourse among us Judges, what sort of women ought to be summoned on the jury to try whether the convict of Peggy was, as she alledged [sic], with child or not." The judges were told by a Portuguese member of the jury "that there were no Christian women here who professed themselves midwives, but the midwives were all either Mahomedan women or Hindoo women, but chiefly the Mahomedans. Midwives being proper to be on the jury, we deliberated whether persons of other religions than Christian might not be sworn on this jury."

In the discussion that followed, two of the judges, Impey and Chambers felt that a jury of Peggy's peers would include non-Christian women, since Peggy was non-Christian herself. Hyde persuaded them otherwise (he doesn't write how and why) and in the instructions given to the Sheriff to round up some Christian women: "they ought to be either wives or widows who had had children...the proper persons would be some of the Portuguese women, and if they could be found, some of the inferior Englishwomen." Drawing upon the common law precedence of convening a Jury of Matrons, Hyde was committed to the idea that Peggy ought to be judged by her "peers," whose representatives in this case were "inferior Englishwomen" and Portuguese women, or women of Portuguese descent.[26]

[26] Kathleen Brown, *Good Wives, Nasty Wenches, and Anxious Patriarchs: Gender, Race and Power in Colonial Virginia* (Chapel Hill: University of North Carolina Press, 1996), pp. 97–9, discusses the use of a jury of matrons and the ways that this practice affirmed the centrality of married women as "indispensable legal links between ... court officials ... and female sexual offenders."

Hyde then recorded at length definitions of the terms Portuguese, Feringees, "collah-Feringees" (black Feringees) and other Christians and non-Christians. In his quasi-ethnological analysis, Hyde defined the differences among the multicultural population of late eighteenth-century Calcutta. He noted, "Black women kept as concubines by Englishmen of which there are many, are most often called Portuguese, especially if they conform to Christian customs..." By "Christian customs," Hyde implied that they "eat all kinds of meat," and engaged in behaviors that Muslims and Hindus did not. Rather than ascribing racial or ethnic labels by physical characteristics, Hyde delineated difference through behavior and the habits one kept, a practice not uncommon in the eighteenth century.[27] Because Hyde intended his notebooks to serve as a resource for the establishment of juridical practice in Bengal, his notes classify a population of subjects of different religions, races, and nationalities in order to prescribe how these subjects of the British should be treated by the court.

When "a very proper jury had been summoned by the Sheriff," the court began its deliberations on whether Peggy was indeed pregnant and if so, whether she should be executed for her crime. Of the jury pool of 22 women, some were "Englishwomen," some were "the Black wives of English men," and some were the "wives of Portuguese." Twelve women were chosen and along with four surgeons and three Muslim midwives, they examined Peggy.[28] Their conclusions were that she was not "quick with child" and that she should be executed.[29] When the jury read her the verdict, it was translated into "Hindoostanee" since she did not speak any English.

---

[27] Roxann Wheeler, *The Complexion of Race: Categories of Difference in Eighteenth-century British Culture* (Philadelphia: University of Pennsylvania Press, 2000).

[28] This page is missing from the notebook although two of the jurors were named: Mrs. Mary Bowers, a Christian midwife who was often consulted by Englishwomen, and Polly Bowers, "as she is commonly called."

[29] There was a lengthy discussion of what "quick with child" meant and whether the just definition of when a pregnant woman can or cannot be executed should be judged by whether she can feel her baby move. Since Peggy was deemed not "quick with child" or not able to feel her baby move, she was sentenced to death. Hyde speculated on the term: "Can you feel the child move?... [it] is to be drawn from natural reason and common humanity and Justice for in sound Philosophy we now know that the life of a foetus commences at least as soon as the conception, whatever notions may have prevailed in former times, or do prevail upon the ignorant at this day. And I hold it to be beyond the right which human authority can, without a crime, exercise over the lives of men.... I mean to apply this rule only to the dispassionate exercise of Justice and Law and not to the state of war between nations, nor to any kind of battle or combat."

The case of Rex v. Betty and Peggy highlighted some of the central questions that animated the court in the first decade of the Calcutta Supreme Court's existence. While the details of the jury selection indicate that Peggy was not British, not Christian, nor "quick with child," her given name was never revealed, nor was it clear whether she was Muslim, Hindu, Portuguese (as Hyde defined it), or where she was from. From the records, her identity was defined as the concubine of an Englishman who tortured a slave girl. Yet, in spite of Peggy's vaguely sketched identity, the deliberations involved in this case suggest that in these early years, the judges were careful to create the image of fair and impartial rule of law for judging domestic disputes. By establishing that the death of a slave was punishable by execution, the judges firmly established that a native woman was a legal subject who could be allowed legal agency and held accountable for her crime.

In comparison, the question of accountability in Rex v. William Orby Hunter and Baugwan Khonwar (1797) was understood on different terms. The defendants were charged with assaulting, wounding, and falsely imprisoning their slave, Mussaumaut Ajanassi.[30] Hunter was accused of ordering his bibi, Baugwan Khonwar, to cut off the tip of the servant's nose and ears and subsequently keeping her locked up in irons and chains. In the process of determining whether Hunter was subject to the court's jurisdiction, the judges argued that because Hunter was a British subject, he was liable to be prosecuted by the Calcutta Supreme Court. Because Baugwan Khonwar was in Hunter's employ, she was considered a subject of the court although Chambers "denies that concubinage is employment under the charter [granted to the Company by Parliament]." As various witnesses came forth to describe the relationship between Hunter and Baugwan Khonwar, it became apparent that although Baugwan Khonwar inflicted the assaults on the slaves, Hunter as an Englishman and master of the household was to be held accountable by the court. In comparison to the case of Peggy twenty years earlier where Peggy's European keeper was never identified, the deliberations in this case focused on Hunter's culpability because he, as the head of the household, was the presumed patriarch in the family.

In the testimony provided by the prosecution's witnesses in this case, Hunter and his bibi's relationship was revealed as a financial arrangement as well as a conjugal one. Thus, the court held that Hunter could be held responsible for the crime, both because he was the

---

[30] Hyde Reports, vol. 53, 23 December 1796 to 12 January 1797.

employer and master of the household. The victim, Mussaumaut Ajanassi, testified to the torture she had suffered and stated that it was Hunter's bibi who had instructed another slave, Taje Bibi, to inflict the wounds. As to the nature of the relationship between Hunter and Baugwan Khonwar, the servant said, "Baugwan Khonwar lived with Mr. Hunter as his concubine for seven years, and left him about four months ago ... [she] received Rs. 250 a month from Mr. Hunter as wages, I have seen Mr. Hunter pay her ... I never saw Baugwan Khonwar take any care of Mr. Hunter's cloaths, nor give him his hookah, nor give him a cup of tea or bread and butter; but I have seen him bring tea and bread and butter to her ..." In other words, although he paid her, she never appeared to work.

The next witness, Taje Bibi, stated that she was a slave from Delhi and worked for Baugwan Khonwar. She was responsible for torturing Ajanassi but she did so upon being instructed by Baugwan Khonwar. She confirmed the previous testimony: "The house was Mr. Hunter's house and Baugwan Khonwar used to sleep and lie with him. That was her business. Mr. H. paid her wages." Then Taje Bibi recounted, "I know that Ajanassi had carnal connection with Mr. Hunter, and that Punnah [the cook] had likewise." Apparently Ajanassi had previously belonged to Baugwan Khonwar's mother, who lived nearby, and when Ajanassi first came to the house, she would sleep in Mr. Hunter's room. But she snored and was cast out. When asked if Baugwan Khonwar had been jealous, Taje Bibi commented "Baugwan Khonwar was bibi to Mr. Hunter, she was never employed in any household service, she used to live, eat, and drink in the house as a *bibi*. She told me herself when she hired me that she was Mr. Hunter's bibi. She can best tell you what she meant by the word." When Baugwan Khonwar had left four months earlier, Taje Bibi testified that Mr. Hunter had given her Rs. 900 for back wages.

Next, the cook, Punnah testified. Because she was not a slave and was an avowed Muslim, her testimony was sworn on the Koran. She had been employed by other bibis of Europeans and said that she had been in this household for two years. She had been present when Taje Bibi had mutilated Ajanassi and stated that Taje Bibi had followed the orders of the mistress of the household, Baugwan Khonwar.

When it came time for the defense to argue its case, Mr. Hunter's lawyer shifted the blame from his client and questioned the applicability of British law to this case. He argued that since Muslim criminal law predominated in Bihar, where this crime was committed, British codes of conduct should not be applied. He reasoned that since Muslim law allows a slave to be punished and put in iron fetters, this case should not be considered a crime.[31] He further argued that because Baugwan Khonwar was Hunter's bibi, not his employee, nor his legal companion, Mr. Hunter could not be held responsible for Baugwan Khonwar's misdeeds.

As a series of witnesses, mainly Mr. Hunter's personal servants, came forth and gave statements, the arguments presented for Mr. Hunter's innocence all hinged on proving that Baugwan Khonwar was the wrongdoer in this situation and that she had a history of abusing domestic servants. Mr. Hunter's bearer, Ranjit, stated that there had been another bibi before this one and she had been very amiable and had never caused any trouble.

Baugwan Khonwar's attorney, Mr. Lewison, took a different tack and argued that because she had no legal relationship to Mr. Hunter, there was no reason for her to be part of the court's proceedings. Since the only service she provided was that of a concubine and she did not perform household services, she could not be considered an employee and thus not a subject of the British court. After this argument was presented, Hyde reports that there was "much discourse" on whether a man, subject to British legal codes, could be held responsible for crimes committed by his concubine as he might be for his wife or other dependent family members residing in his household.[32] In opening this subject for inquiry, members of the Supreme Court reasoned that British men in India ought be held accountable for their native concubines as for their wives because men ought to be held responsible for their household units, no matter what the legal bonds between members of the household were. In speculating over how to define household, judges drew on customary practices in England by which households including not just kin relations, but apprentices, servants, and other non-blood related inmates.[33] By framing the inquiry in this manner, the Supreme Court assumed the logic that European men were legal subjects to be held accountable for concubines in the same manner as if they had been wives, bound by a marital contract. In other words, if a concubine failed to understand and uphold humane treatment toward her slaves, her European male consort should certainly be held accountable for her failure.

In the end, both Hunter and his bibi, Baugwan Khonwar were convicted and Hunter was sentenced to pay a fine while Baugwan Khonwar

---

[31] The source for this argument was not cited.
[32] Roderick Phillips, *Putting Asunder*, pp. 323–4.
[33] Naomi Tadmor, "The concept of the household-family in eighteenth-century England," *Past & Present* 151 (May 1996): 111–30.

got six months in jail. In determining the verdict, the court relied on the local magistrate's ruling: "The Magistrate [Mr. Arbuthnot] in reporting his proceeding in this case intimated a suspicion that the Bibbee was greatly culpable but added with reference to Mr. Hunter 'as these horrid cruelties happened under his roof I cannot but think that he must have been acquainted with them, and he was therefore highly to blame in not applying to the civil power, in case he did not himself possess sufficient authority over his girl to prevent her committing such enormities.'"[34] Although he was not directly guilty of committing any crimes, Mr. Hunter ought to be held responsible for the cruelties taking place in his household. His lack of authority within his household required the court's intervention, which restored him to his position as head of the household by disciplining his failure to control his bibi.

In the ways in which the Calcutta Supreme Court adjudicated Rex v. Betty and Peggy and Rex v. William Orby Hunter and Bhaugwan Khonwar, the court understood the question of individual agency and accountability as fundamentally different. Peggy was held singularly accountable for her crime, although she lived in the household of an Englishman. Baugwan Khonwar, on the other hand, was convicted, as was her English partner because he did nothing to stop her. That individual agency was allowable for a native woman in one case and disallowed for another in comparable cases two decades later reflects the ways in which the Supreme Court's understanding of the households of British men and their native female companions developed, transforming colonial families into unitary legal units, rather than as units comprised of individuals each with his or her own legal subjectivity.

In 1777, newly arrived in Calcutta, the judges may have even felt that a non-marital cohabitive relationship made Peggy a legal subject in her own right. The lengthy efforts involved in finding a jury of Peggy's peers to judge her speak to the assumption that women, even the concubines of British men, should and could be held accountable to the same laws as everyone else in the court's jurisdiction. Indeed, the absence of any mention of the man who kept Peggy, suggests that the judges did not see her as part of a conjugal unit that had any legal meaning. Nearly twenty years later, however, Baugwan Khonwar was understood to have a legal subjectivity that attached and identified her as a member of an Englishman's household in Patna.[35] Although Hunter and Khonwar

---

[34] O.I.O.C., O/5/25, Crimes committed by Europeans in the Company's dominions.
[35] The judges involved in these two cases were as follows: Chambers, Impey and Hyde judged Rex v. Betty and Peggy; Chambers, Dunkin and Hyde sat for Rex v. William Orby Hunter and Baugwan Khonwar.

were unmarried, her legal status was sutured to his. The law of coverture did not ordinarily apply to unmarried couples, but in the colonial case, where cohabitation was much more common, native women and European men were increasingly seen as a single legal entity and encompassed by the logic of coverture.

These court records are evocative for the details of intimate life that they reveal. Court documents demonstrate the ways in which marginal subjects were brought under the surveillance of the state, showing that these women were not invisible to the bureaucracies of the East India Company. Moreover, these records show the relationships and hierarchies between women living in the households of European men: Betty and Peggy resided together and shared domestic work. Two other women who testified, Noorun and Jaun Bibee, were also the companions of British men. The presence of an Englishman, James Robertson, described as a neighbor, demonstrates that these communities of European men and their native concubines were racially and ethnically mixed as well as highly interdependent.[36]

Charting household hierarchies were crucial to how the courts judged crimes of intimate violence. Hunter's household included several sexual arrangements: while Baugwan Khonwar was the stated favorite in the household, Hunter had other sexual partners. This was by no means unusual as several Englishmen documented their conjugal attachments to a number of native women.[37] While Hunter's bibi's position within the household may have been recognizable to the English judges as analogous to English households where a "wife" had some influence in how the household and its servants were managed and the "husband's" legal persona was constituted by his authority over the various members of his household, the testimony of both slaves and the cook demonstrated that Hunter's conjugal activities with the various members of this household complicated that particular analogy. Baugwan Khonwar's

---

[36] See, for example, the will of John Sardel, Cornet in the Company's service, died 1769 and ordered that S. Rs. 500 be given to his girl Rossee, and the same amount to the Sergeant Major's girl and that they be given a horse and hackery to share because they lived in the same house. O.I.O.C., P/154/53 (1769).

[37] See, similarly, the will of Matthew Leslie of Calcutta, died 1804, who bequeathed significant inheritances and homes to all three of his female companions. H.C.O.S., 1803–1805, pp. 62–71. See also Col. Richard Lucas, who died the same year, who left sums of money to three women, all described as female servants who had bore him children. In his will, he wrote, "Should the two females Semia and Tyzan agree to live together the Bullock carriage with the large bullocks are to be delivered to them as joint property." H.C.O.S., 1803–1805, pp. 122–4. According to Hodson's directory Lucas died unmarried and left about 3 lakh rupees.

relative status over the other domestic servants and slaves suggests that she had quite a bit of authority within the household. In the case against Peggy, her authority over Susannah, the slave, was presumed; when she exceeded her authority by scalding the young girl the court stepped in. In reading these cases and mapping their criminality, European judges showed that they intervened in domestic affairs when other forms of social and sexual regulation had broken down, particularly the authority of the European male head of household who was held responsible for the social order within the home.

Coinciding with the territorial expansion of the Company and a growing civil service and governmental bureaucracy, these two cases, two decades apart, show a shift in the kinds of legal subjectivities that were allowed native women living in European, male-headed households. Increasingly, judicial decisions eroded a legal reading of native women's agency while legitimizing and amplifying the rights of European men over native women both within the household and in broader terms. In 1777, the court was relatively new, attempting to provide judicial rulings that were fair to all. Thus, Hyde's concern about who should be represented on the jury suggest a sensitivity to the range of social, racial, ethnic, and religious identifications possible in Calcutta; his notes also show a concern for standardizing such forms of identification so that cases might be adjudicated in a rational manner. By 1797, several legal translations of loosely defined Hindu and Muslim legal codes had been published and the range of identifications had narrowed to British, Muslims, and Hindus, particularly when it came to ruling on domestic disputes. While rape and adultery were considered "private" offenses and not worthy of the colonial state's intervention, slavery and the abuse of household servants were considered offenses against the state, in part because the rights of slaves needed to be protected against the putatively cruel and despotic behavior of Muslim men against their slaves; equally important, the laboring productivity of the household needed to be secured to the sovereignty of the colonial state.[38] Thus, in cases of violence between household intimates, justice was decided along an axis of religious, racial, and legal identities and priority over which cases were to be judged as criminal balanced the moral and political imperatives of the colonial state. Indeed, as the sentence to Mr. Hunter demonstrated, his failure was that he

---

[38] See Radhika Singha, "Making the Domestic More Domestic: criminal law and the 'head of the household,' 1772–1843," *Indian Economic and Social History Review* 33 (July–Sept., 1996): 309–44; Singha, *Despotism of Law*, pp. 314–18.

had managed his household affairs in a manner that undermined British rule.

III

Domestic violence cases in which native women were assaulted, robbed, or murdered by European men posed a special challenge to the court because they required the judiciary to keep household peace while upholding the privileges of the male head of household. In several cases, narratives of native women "belonging" to the defendant formed a crucial part of the defense narrative; in verdicts, judges and juries understood cohabitive relationships as equal to a legal marital contract, in which a man had the limited right to physically discipline his wife. By allowing men to rob or beat their presumed "wives," the court consolidated the legal rights of men over the bodies of native women.

While the court's intervention into domestic disputes further extended the Company state's surveillance over ordinary women, servants, and slaves, court cases also allowed these subjects to form expectations that the state would punish crimes against their person. An important arena for native women and girls, courts enabled them to negotiate for the protection of the state, particularly in crimes such as rape and assault. As the following cases demonstrate, witnesses for the prosecution, often the neighbors and family members of the victim, narrated their accounts in ways that were intended to persuade the court. But because native women had no legal status independent of the men with whom they formed conjugal relationships, their rights to be protected from domestic violence were often abrogated by the court.

Rex. vs. Henry Pyne involved the prosecution of a Company merchant for robbing the home of a native woman with whom he had been sexually involved.[39] He was accused of breaking in and stealing about 200 pieces of silver worth £20, and several pieces of gold jewelry. According to some witnesses, he had allegedly broken down the door of Peerun bibi's house and rummaged around until he found her jewelry box. He was confronted by a male neighbor, Farr Mahomed, who said, "it is unbecoming you to come into a black man's house and rob it in this manner." This statement was confirmed by several other witnesses who testified that the "house" – a straw hut worth about Rs. 125 – was not built by Henry Pyne. Peerun bibi, who was sleeping in the house, was able to flee, but her brother and sister who both lived nearby were

---

[39] Hyde Papers, reel 11, vol. 27, 15 Dec. 1789.

witness to the crime that followed. Upon being confronted by witnesses, Henry Pyne swung a sword at the onlookers (of which there were several) and fled.

The case presented by the defense focused on two issues: first, Peerun bibi was "a bad woman," who had enticed Henry Pyne into her bed, and second, the house in which Peerun bibi resided was built by Pyne. According to Pyne's *hurkarah*, or messenger, Pyne was in bed with Peerun bibi at the time of the alleged crime; he was still in his nightclothes and was unarmed when he was confronted by the group of people who had claimed to witness this crime. They threw bricks at Pyne and he fled.

One defense witness, Badrinath Sircar, testified that he saw Farr Mahomed at the courthouse and Farr Mahomed confessed that he was being forced to testify against Pyne by Peerun's brother. Other defense witnesses stated that Peerun was "an infamous woman," while Pyne came from a good family and was industrious and hard-working. Several of the defense witnesses told the court that Pyne had paid for Peerun's house and that it was built by the brother of one of the defense witnesses.

Both sides agreed that Henry Pyne and Peerun bibi had had a conjugal relationship, and all the witnesses testified that they knew both the parties involved. In what appeared to be a case of theft among acquaintances, the court's deliberations centered on the question whether Pyne, if he was to be considered guilty of any crime, was effectively robbing himself. If he had built the house, then he could not be convicted of robbing it. If the jewelry which had allegedly been stolen were originally gifts from Pyne to Peerun bibi, he could not be convicted of theft.

To address the question of who owned and owed what, Peerun bibi's sister, Ramzany, had testified that "Peerun never received a cowrie from the prisoner," adding that Peerun had accompanied Henry Pyne to Dinajpore, Furruckabad, and Chittagong and had not been paid for her services. When she petitioned the magistrate to claim her payment, Henry Pyne had come and robbed her. As to the source of the jewelry, Peerun bibi's sister stated that they had been given to Peerun bibi from Mr. Jeffrey and Mr. Creighton who had been her sister's previous "keepers." Ramzany told the court, "She had all of these ornaments before she went to live with the prisoner with whom she lived about six months."

While the "facts" put into evidence were disputed, the narratives presented to the court are crucial for understanding how the logic of justice worked when the rights of native women were being considered.

Both sides provided testimonies that were structured by a keen consideration of what sort of narrative might appeal to the social coordinates that made sense to British judges and juries. The prosecution's case, which was presented first, was that Henry Pyne had robbed a native woman of her hard-earned property. As several of the witnesses stated, he had burgled another man's house, although no witness revealed to the court which man's house it was. In this eighteenth-century version of he said/she said the prosecution presented a narrative in which an abject native woman, putatively protected under the roof of another man's house, was robbed of personal property while she was sleeping. Peerun was not present in court to testify because she had since moved to Islamabad and could not afford to leave her home, thereby leaving others to speak on her behalf.

Although the prosecution skirted the issue, earnings from Peerun's sex work, as the companion to a series of European men, sustained her brother and sister, who lived in nearby huts. The brother and sister both testified that the theft had left the family destitute and they were now pawning other jewelry in order to survive. Peerun was clearly the primary wage-earner in this family; when Pyne refused to pay her for her services, Peerun's family's income was diminished. It is plausible that Peerun's family resorted to this story as a way of punishing Pyne; it is also possible that they sought some restitution for the domestic and sexual services that Peerun had already provided but not been paid for. If they had fabricated the story, they turned to a narrative that minimized Peerun's autonomy (as a woman living alone) and emphasized Peerun's hard work; this might have been calculated to make the jury sympathetic to Peerun. Peerun's sister testified that Peerun was owed money by the defendant for her services, thus trying to counter the claim that Peerun was a sexual predator, as the defense claimed. Rather, Peerun was described as being a worker who was robbed. Claims that the house was owned by "another man," removed the question of whether a native woman could live independently under her own protection and relied on a vision of justice in which the integrity of Peerun's personal possessions under the bodily protection of another man had been breached. The prosecution's case, supported by the testimony of Peerun's family, appealed to the logic that criminal injury had been committed against the man who reputedly protected Peerun in his home, and that the court should step in to punish the infringement committed against this anonymous man.

In the end, the prosecution's strategy of presenting Peerun as a hard-working woman failed and the jury were seemingly more sympathetic to Pyne's claims of being wrongly accused by a native woman and her family. Without hearing closing summaries, the jury decided that Henry Pyne was not guilty and released him.[40]

In spite of Pyne's acquittal, several months later, an East India Company judiciary official urged an investigation into Pyne's "character," suggesting that the Company should decide where his "general conduct and behaviour towards the natives that he is a proper person to be allowed to reside in the mofussil." Pyne's local magistrate noted that he could not recommend Pyne, but that he was uncertain whether "such disputes and irregularities . . . are sufficient grounds for depriving him of the indulgence of residing" in India. Ultimately, officials revoked Pyne's license to remain in India and ordered him back to England. Officials noted that Henry Pyne was well-known in Chittagong as an oppressive landlord and employer to local natives and they wrote, ". . . we have thought from his general bad character and mode of behavior . . . that he should not be indulged with permission to remain in this country." Pyne protested this order, arguing that he had a family to support in India, but officials were resolute and Pyne returned to England in the fall of 1790, a year after his acquittal.[41] Although Pyne was acquitted of robbing his bibi, his frequent appearance in court on various charges brought about his repatriation to Britain. Like William Orby Hunter at a roughly contemporaneous moment, although it was generally agreed by judges and judicial officials that European men had certain rights to physically discipline or sleep with the members of their households, these men also had a certain masculine code of conduct to uphold. As part of the colonial determination to project authority through appropriate behavior, men were charged with being moderate, fair in their punishments of household infractions. Where men failed to carry out this particular responsibility of the colonial mission, judges and officials stepped in to discipline errant European men.

The sense that a native woman "belonged" to a particular man and was subject to his punishments formed one of the crucial ways in which early colonial judicial decisions rationalized household crimes of intimate violence. Several decades later, Rex v. Michael Chestnut ended in an acquittal based on a similar logic. Chestnut was a private in H.M.'s 24th Regiment of Light Dragoons stationed in Kanpur and was accused by Doordana, a native woman, of robbing her jewels of a silver chain and four bangles. In the interrogations following the crime, Chestnut replied, "As the things were my own, I thought I could go and

---

[40] O.I.O.C., O/5/2, pp. 249–73.
[41] O.I.O.C., P/3/54, Bengal Public Consultations, 15 September 1790, no. 19.

take them away." When the prosecution countered that Doordana claimed that the jewels had been made by her in Meerut and Cawnpore, Chestnut remained resolute in his understanding that the jewelry was his and said, "I did not give her the chain and rings but I gave her the money with which she got them made up." Although the magistrate was reluctant to see how Michael Chestnut could lay claim to own something that was bought by his money, when the case was sent to the court in Calcutta, before the case was sent to a jury, the judges decided that since Chestnut had given the money that paid for the jewels in the first place, no crime had been committed.[42]

These cases of assault addressed the degree to which a man committed a crime against a person and home that could be considered as "his," given the history of his relationship with the victim. By demonstrating a pre-existing relationship between a European male defendant and a native female victim, defense attorneys could claim that no violence against the woman had occurred since the perpetrator could be understood to have had access to the body of the woman, even after the relationship had ended.

Among the piles of cases involving domestic violence, perpetrators were occasionally convicted, but very rarely. In two cases that appeared within several years of each other, European men were convicted of manslaughter of their female conjugal partners, but the court recognized that these homicides had occurred under extenuating circumstances in which the defendant had been within his legal rights to exercise "moderate correction," against the bad behavior of his "wife," but had exceeded this right when his physical punishment had resulted in her death. In drawing on the English common-law notion of "moderate correction," the judges went by Blackstone's eighteenth-century legal standard that a man had the right to "correct" the behavior of his wife by using the "rule of thumb," which stipulated he could use a stick no thicker than his thumb to physically chastise her.[43] It was when men went beyond this legal right to physical violence against their "wives," that the courts stepped in.

In Rex v. Dupont, William Dupont, a bootmaker who lived on Boitakhana Road in Calcutta, was convicted of beating to death his companion of five years when he found her drunk in the middle of

---

[42] O.I.O.C., O/5/16 (1815), pp. 549–65; O/5/25 (1815); P/131/60 Bengal Criminal Judicial Proceedings 16 May 1815, nos. 67–70.

[43] Amussen, "Being stirred," p. 71; Phillips, *Putting Asunder*, pp. 323–4. This legal right remained unchanged until the middle of the nineteenth century in England.

the afternoon. There were many witnesses to the crime, both native and European, who told the court that the woman was often drunk and prone to neglecting her household duties, which suggested to the court that she might have deserved a beating. The jury brought a conviction of murder against the defendant but the judges reduced it to manslaughter and gave him a sentence of six months because they argued, "the prisoner and the deceased lived on such terms as must have led him to regard her with the feelings of a husband and he had great cause for anger but not anything resulting in this type of violence."[44] Although this "wife"-murder resulted in a conviction, the judges presumed that sentiment that the man felt for killing his partner should be a mitigating factor in reducing his sentence.

Several years later, in Rex v. John Taylor (1817), Taylor was accused of kicking Jaunoo, a native woman with whom he had a child, to death.[45] Taylor, a private in H.M.'s 59th Regiment of Foot, had been washing the baby in another room when he heard a loud argument between Jaunoo and a Malay girl in the kitchen of the barracks. In pacifying Jaunoo, Taylor had struck her "with an open hand" to stop her from arguing. According to witnesses and the subsequent magistrate's report, Jaunoo fell down on the ground and Taylor kicked her, resulting in her spleen bursting which caused her to die several hours later.

As the magistrate reported to court officials in the Supreme Court in Calcutta when they agreed to try the case, it was kicking Jaunoo when she was on the floor that exceeded Taylor's legal right to hit Jaunoo and transformed an encounter of physical punishment into criminal violence. The magistrate wrote, emphasizing the gendered aspect of Taylor's transgression, "This [the kicking] was certainly an unmanly, and if done with violence, a brutal and dangerous act." Taylor was convicted and sentenced to six months' imprisonment and the opinion recorded by court officials shows that the real crime was his "unmanliness" in allowing his right to physical violence get out of control and killing the woman that the court understood as his "wife."

In contrast to earlier judicial questioning in the 1790s about whether cohabitive relationships between native women and European men should be cast as marital contracts in a legal sense, judicial practices by the 1810s demonstrated a widespread understanding among magistrates, judges, and juries, that cohabitation gave European men certain legal rights to the bodies of "their" native women. The sense that

[44] O.I.O.C., O/5/25 (1814).
[45] O.I.O.C., O/5/18 (1817), pp. 395–408.

European men enjoyed the legal benefits of a marital contract, even when such a contract did not exist, showed the ways in which colonial courts secured and legally rationalized sexual access to the bodies of native women on behalf of lower-ranking European men.

IV

Although seemingly unrelated, cases of rape were drawn into similar logics that were applied to household and domestic violence cases, particularly when the victims were young women or girls who were in the proximity of a native female known to consort with Europeans. The status of the parties and their acquaintance with one another were often central terms on which rape trials were based, particularly over the status of the victim. The judges asked how old was the victim? Was she a virgin? Had she started menstruating? While these questions about the victim are often standard in trials about rape, an issue that was specific to the British Indian context was the degree to which the victim's presence in a certain type of household made her sexually available to European men. As Radhika Singha has noted, "The notion that the Oriental woman ripened very early could sometime overqualify her as an offender, as for instances in cases of homicide, and underqualify as a victim, as in case of rape."[46] In at least a half dozen cases between the years of 1770 and 1840, the courts scrutinized cases of sexual assault committed by European men against young native females and decided against conviction. These acquittals were based largely on the understanding that native women who lived among Europeans and their acquaintances were assumed to be potential conjugal companions to European men and sexually available, thereby mitigating any accusation of rape. In arriving at these verdicts, courts consistently secured and legitimated the right of European men to experience sexual activity with girls and young women around military cantonments and colonial settlements, particularly if it could be shown that the victim had been somehow suspect.

Guilt by association was a prominent feature of Rex v. Pierre Bouton, which occurred in 1793.[47] It was a trial in which a Frenchman working as a merchant for the East India Company was accused of attempted rape on a girl named Mary Serraum. The main witness was a woman,

---

[46] Singha, *Despotism of Law,* p. 139; see also Singha, "Making the domestic more domestic."
[47] Hyde Papers, reel 5, 12 Dec. 1793.

Kitty Rozario, who was presumed to be a woman who provided sexual services to European men. The victim, Mary, was a converted Catholic girl who had been living in the home of John Drake, a local native watchmaker of Portuguese descent. John Drake had purchased Mary when she was five years old, but had had her baptized, thereby releasing her from her status as a slave. He testified that she was still a virgin, and was no more than ten years old. He also testified that she was a child, not a woman, indicating that he believed she had not started menstruating. John Drake told the court that because of her assault, he could not take her home as it would tarnish his family's reputation.

The prosecution's main testimony came from Kitty Rozario, a native Catholic woman who lived in the same compound as the defendant. She testified that she knew the defendant since they had dined at someone's home several months earlier. Kitty also clearly stated that she was not being kept by a European man, nor had she received any money from the men who were her neighbors. On the evening of the attack, she was sitting on her porch having tea when the girl Mary approached her and asked for some water. She gave it to her and Mary started to leave when the defendant, who was on a nearby porch with several other gentlemen asked her if she wanted to come and live with him and she said yes. He also asked if she was a maid to which she said no. He then led her inside by the hand. Kitty understood the request to come live with him as an offer of employment, not a sexual relationship. In her testimony, Kitty noted that she thought that the girl seemed too young to know what a maid was. Kitty saw Mary the next day and testified that Mary looked sick. She also heard from the chowkeydar that the defendant had bragged about deflowering her.

Gruesome testimony followed in which the local midwife who worked at the police station, Saidoo Dai, testified that she knew Mary and knew her to be between nine and a half and eleven years old and based on a medical examination, Saidoo Dai said that Mary had the private parts of a girl. Saidoo Dai stated that Mary had not yet started menstruating and that when she had examined Mary following the assault there were various sores and bruises. Mary had bled profusely for ten days following the attack.

The final testimony came from the police superintendent who had taken Pierre Bouton's testimony. According to Bouton, Kitty had offered the girl to him and had told him that Mary was not a virgin. He claimed that he had not done anything by force, that he had "had connection with her, but not by force, that she had made no noise, and that she was willing..." Based on this testimony, the trial resulted in an acquittal.

Another trial several years later, Rex v. William Tripp, was reminiscent of this earlier narrative. William Tripp was a sergeant in the East India Company army, stationed at Fort William, who was accused of raping a young Hindu girl named Clara.[48] Clara was a servant in the home of Noonoo Benson, the native widow of Sergeant Benson, who had been in the Company army and a friend of William Tripp. Clara professed to be a Hindu and so her testimony was sworn to truth on a glass of Ganges water, although she told the court she had lost caste as a result of the rape. As in the previous case involving Mary, the converted Catholic, rape brought dishonor to the victim, her family, and community. Interracial and intercaste sexual assault resulted in the victim becoming a social outcast, a fact that was noted in the testimony of trials of sexual assault.

Clara testified that the defendant had come to her mistress's house to sell some cloth that was being shown at the artillery barracks. Her mistress sent Clara with William Tripp to get some more fabric samples; on the way, he led her the wrong way behind some barracks, threw her on the ground, covered her face, and spread her legs. Although she resisted, she testified, "I was a virgin at the time, and he forcibly lay with me.... He put his private part into my body, and a great quantity of blood came from me. I suffered much pain." She testified that she thought she might be fifteen years old, but was definitely not twenty. After the attack, Sergeant Tripp ran away and Clara ran into the barracks where she saw Sergeant Marshall, Sergeant Lyon, Sergeant Dick, and Sergeant Major Fitzgerald and they noted that her petticoat was stained with blood. Clara then told her mistress, Noonoo Benson, who, accompanied by Sergeant Major Fitzgerald, took her to the commander of the troops to inform him of the crime. Two or three days later, the crime was reported to the magistrate who had her examined by a doctor.

Noonoo Benson confirmed Clara's account and added that she was certain that the blood was not Clara's period as she had not yet started to menstruate. The other soldiers testified to having seen Clara after the attack and that she was disheveled and her petticoat had blood on it. Sergeant Marshall went even further and testified that he had seen blood on the defendant's pants and that he had appeared agitated at roll call later that day.

Although the case seemed fairly straightforward, the surgeon, Thomas Lyon testified last and noted that he could find no blood, bruises,

---

[48] Ibid., reel 17, vol. 51, 10 Dec. 1796.

wounds, or lacerations. Moreover, Clara was "sexually mature," indicating that she had started menstruating and had lost her virginity much earlier. Based on the surgeon's opinion, the jury returned a verdict of not guilty and William Tripp was released.

While these outcomes might seem to fit with our notions of late eighteenth-century justice in British India, the surprising element is how frequently trials involving sexual assault came up in the East India Company's archives.[49] These two cases came up within five years of one another and were argued in front of the same group of judges. In both cases, the victims were acquainted, albeit tangentially, with the men who were accused of attacking them. In both cases, the primary witnesses for the prosecution were native women who cohabited with European men, and the line of questioning in court and the claims made by the defense implied that these witnesses lacked credibility and were even implicated in the crime. Although the spectacle of a trial brought considerable attention to incidents of sexual violence, native female witnesses and victims who were seen to be in the vicinity were considered sexually and morally suspect and their accounts counted for little in the final deliberations.

In Rex v. Bouton, the defendant asserted that Kitty, known for sleeping with European men, had pimped the young Mary. Whether this narrative reflected what happened is unclear; what is clear, however, is that certain types of narratives made sense to judges and juries and defendants made use of these sorts of stories to secure acquittals. The idea that a native woman who had been sexually compromised by a relationship with a European man might then sell the services of female children seemed entirely plausible became a staple in claims that defendants made for their innocence.

A case that occurred almost forty years later made use of the same sort of defense narrative, which suggests that the narrative of a rape victim being offered to the defendant by someone of ill repute was a durable idea. The King v. John Chilton Lambton Carter (1836), was found in a bundle of uncatalogued material at the Calcutta High Court.[50] Carter was accused of raping a nine-year-old girl named Peerun in the barracks at Fort William. In the depositions that were filed, various witnesses who

---

[49] Cornelia Dayton, *Women Before the Bar: Gender, Law and Society in Connecticut, 1639–1789* (Chapel Hill: University of North Carolina Press, 1995), p. 61, notes that the "reluctance to convict in rape cases were reflective of broad trends in eighteenth-century England and the colonies." See also Dayton, ch. 5.

[50] Although the accounts of crimes committed by Europeans were purportedly sent back to London, this case occurred after the O/5 series ended in 1829.

resided in Fort William testified to the relationship between the concubine of an officer and the victim. As in the other cases, the larger context of domestic arrangements and family and service relationships within the setting of the military cantonment informed the question of how local women became involved in relationships with European soldiers.

A range of witnesses testified, including the victim, the victim's mother, the victim's aunts, and finally domestic servants who worked in the fort. As the story unfolded, it became clear that the victim, Peerun, was a regular visitor to her aunt, Bibi Amsworth, who cohabited with Captain Amsworth in the fort. The Bibi's family, including her mother, her sister, her brother's widow, and *her* sister all resided within walking distance of the fort, showing that these cohabitive relationships linked the families of the native women to the cantonment.

Peerun's testimony began, "I live with my mother whose name I do not recollect, our house is at Koriat in the 24-Purgannahs." She then explained that she had met an old woman in the playground not far from the fort who had led her to the fort on the promise of giving her some food. After she had been at the old woman's house for "about a guntah [an hour]," a stout gentleman who was drunk came in and "had connexion" with her. Peerun then testified that she had no sisters, she had never been to the fort, and she did not know exactly how old she was.

Peerun's mother, Ameerun, testified next and said, "I am a widow and live with my mother-in-law Mohur Beebee [in Khidderpore]." She guessed that Peerun was nine and a half years old, based on the nine knots in a necklace that marked each Muharram that the child had celebrated, but the mother could not be sure. She also testified that Peerun had gone to the fort with a servant called Bengalee. When Cullo, Peerun's aunt testified, she stated that she was the sister of Peerun's mother and that they had married two brothers. It was in this capacity that they came to live with their mother-in-law. After the death of these two brothers, they had both become attached to a European regiment in Gazeepore and had subsequently followed them to Calcutta.

Peerun's grandmother's testimony followed and she confirmed what her daughter-in-law said and added, "I have a daughter named Motee Khunum who lives with Captain Amsworth in Fort William." Peerun went to the fort with Bengalee, their servant who took dinner up to Bibi Amsworth every evening.

Bengalee, the servant, testified, "I am in the service of Captain Amsworth . . . I know the girl Peerun . . . . I took her into the Fort four or five days ago, and left her at Captain Amsworth's quarters in the Royal Barracks."

Next the witnesses at the fort began their testimony. First, Lallun, Bibi Amsworth's ayah testified, "I am an ayah in the service of Bibi Amsworth [who was also known as Motee Khunum] who resides in Fort William, Calcutta, in quarter no. 101 on the second floor of the royal barracks." Lallun said that on the evening of the crime, she had seen Peerun come in with the servant at about 6 o'clock with the bibi's dinner. After Lallun put the bibi's infant to sleep, she went downstairs to the servants' quarters to eat. She was in the process of preparing her after-dinner *pan* when she heard screaming from the third floor. She ran upstairs and Lallun then testified that she saw Peerun bleeding profusely in Carter's room. Carter's valet and bearer instructed Lallun to "take away your Chotie [the young one]." Lallun insisted that she see Carter's room, which she did and saw the bloody bed and a trail of blood from the bed to where Peerun was sitting outside. Lallun took Peerun into her arms and was carrying her downstairs to the servants' quarters when Peerun went into convulsions; after that the fort surgeon took over the care of Peerun.

In this group of depositions, what is most remarkable is that a nine-year-old girl, her mother, her grandmother, and two servants came forth to give accounts of Anglo-Indian life in Fort William, the primary military cantonment in the Bengal Presidency. In spite of the oft-quoted image that cantonments cordoned off European soldiers from the local population, the permeability of the cantonment's boundaries are especially noteworthy here: the servant, the bibi, and the bibi's relations were all linked to a captain in His Majesty's forces and circulated through his quarters. The frequent visits of the servant and of Peerun, the young girl, to the fort suggest that the traffic of people through the royal barracks was not limited to military personnel. Another important, but confusing, revelation in these depositions is the extent to which family relationships brought these women to the cantonment. Peerun's mother, Ameerun, and Peerun's aunt, Cullo, were women who became attached to a European regiment when they were widowed and they then followed the regiment to Calcutta. Their mother-in-law, Mohur Beebee, testified that since the death of her sons, all three women had traveled together (presumably following the European regiment they were attached to in Gazeepore) and had come to Calcutta with the woman who was called both Bibi Amsworth and Motee Khanum.

In the accounts made by the defendants' witnesses, various servants and friends of Carter testified that Peerun was a prostitute and her aunt, Bibi Amsworth, had arranged to have Carter pay for having sex with her.

The ayah's involvement had been to extract payment from Carter on behalf of the Bibi. In the scenario offered by the defense, allies of Carter claimed no crime was committed since Peerun was offered to a group of soldiers, including Carter. They reasoned that since Peerun had willingly gone into Carter's rooms, and they argued that she said she had been with a man before, the case was not about the rape of a child but about prostitution. Although all the deponents testified that Peerun was young "about ten or twelve," and she was small enough to be carried from one room to the next, there was a presumption that she could be a prostitute based on her association with her frequent visits to her aunt, a companion to a soldier in the cantonment. Refuting the medical evidence of two surgeons who testified to Peerun's wounds and her profuse bleeding, all of Carter's colleagues who were in nearby rooms claimed that they had not heard any screams or protest from the girl.

Carter defended himself by saying, "I believed her [Peerun] to be a Prostitute and did not in any way use the least violence towards her. I consider the whole of this got up by the relatives of the girl with a view to extort money from me."

The case never went to trial because the clerk argued that "there was not sufficient evidence to warrant me in sending the case to jury."

On first reading, that rape crimes against girls were investigated at all is noteworthy. The vivid details and the medical testimony are unlike anything else that appear in court documents; indeed, these testimonies make graphic the ways that native female bodies were laid bare for the court's deliberations. The detail and length of the depositions suggests, as Lauren Benton and others have argued, that judicial processes offered restitution and justice to even the most marginal and disenfranchised members of society who sought it out.[51]

The recurring themes in the various testimonies about the ages of the victims – were they over the age of ten? – was a way of measuring the level of judicial protection that could be offered. The English common law widely recognized that for victims of sexual assault (assumed to be girls), ten was the age of sexual maturity and one in which sexual consent might be secured. The centrality of this age in defense and prosecutorial accounts suggests that various parties in trials were aware of the stakes in proving the victim's age and concomitant ability to claim whether any sexual violation had occurred. The widely used narrative

---

[51] Benton, *Law and Colonial Cultures*, 26, 256; Dayton, *Women Before the Bar*, Introduction.

that sex was being offered for sale was so often successful because females, even children, in the vicinity of local women who were known to have had conjugal relationships with Englishmen on the cantonment were seen to be less worthy of the courts' protection. Moreover, the judgments of these cases concluded that there had been no crime committed because of the implication that these girls were sexually active and publicly available. While the pursuit of justice brought these plaintiffs to the courts, the final verdicts consolidated the right of sexual access to native female bodies by European men.

Conclusion

Civil and criminal cases involving interracial households and families show the ways in which the Crown-appointed courts in the Bengal Presidency attempted to balance the legal subjectivity of individual persons against what were constituted as the rights and responsibilities that European men had over the bodies of native women and children. Judicial decisions elaborated and consolidated racial and gender distinctions between the different subjects in their jurisdiction, showing the rule of law to be an important component in the state's disciplinary regime, particularly in regulating the mixed-race households and families of European men.

In a precedent-setting civil case involving the families of Bibee Hay and James Robinson, court deliberations focused on the legal status, as it was defined in religious and quasi-national terms, of a mixed-race son who stood to lose the estate of his native mother. In affirming the right of the son to claim his father's British legal status, a case about inheritance allowed the court to martial legal arguments to make a material claim against Bibee Hay's estate on Robinson's behalf. In doing so, the state protected paternal right (assumed in the conjugal unit that had brought about the birth of James Robinson on the body of Bibee Hay) and overrode Bibee Hay's legal position and right to leave her estate to her adopted native granddaughter.

In the many criminal cases discussed here, in which native women were victims as well as perpetrators, the courts' lengthy deliberations, classifying the legal subjects involved, who stood for trial, and whose bodily safety was at stake, show how crucial was the judicial process for constructing and maintaining the political legitimacy of the early Company state. That witnesses included both natives and Europeans suggests that the open-ended process that judicial trials represented produced a widespread sense that some sort of state-sponsored justice was available and that the state's institutions protected every subject's rights, even if verdicts spoke against such an assumption. The reproduction of particular types of narratives that were likely to result in favorable verdicts shows that deponents and defendants, natives and non-natives, were knowledgeable about what would appeal to colonial judges and juries.

While judicial processes were invested in creating the image of a fair and just political order, verdicts dismissing European men of guilt in sexual crimes resulted in securing a racialized and gendered order in which European men's sexual access to native girls and women who associated with *bibis* was legitimized. As the courts' deliberations over the accountability of native women showed, judges drew on the idea that the men who were these women's "protectors" were ultimately to blame for household disorder. Rather than deprive men for their household transgressions, these verdicts reinstated the legal authority men had over their households.

Perhaps most important, judicial processes drew native women into institutional networks of the Company and granted them some agency by allowing women to make claims against their European attackers. Nonetheless, these same judicial processes understood native women as legal subjects who were constitutive of European-headed households. Judicial verdicts authorized ways to contain and limit female agency from exceeding the structures of the model patriarchal household. In early colonial practice of the law, British judges intervened in and enforced appropriate definitions of household hierarchies, thereby merging concerns of domestic and familial peace with the priorities of the early colonial state.

6   Servicing military families: family labor, pensions, and orphans

Hasan Shah's novel, *Nashtar*, written in Persian in 1790, describes a romance between a munshi and a native dancing girl.[1] The story begins when a troupe of dancing girls and the European military regiment to which they are attached arrives in Kanpur. The novel's heroine is a seemingly virtuous dancing girl, Khanum Jan, who refuses the attentions of an English officer, Ming-sahib, instead favoring his Persian-speaking munshi, Hasan Shah. The dancing troupe's interactions with the British military cantonment at Kanpur shows the ways in which military activities produced a complex contact zone, bringing local women and their associates into servicing the needs of British soldiers, offering entertainment, sex, companionship, and other personal services in exchange for a livelihood. As spaces in which different populations mixed, military camps and cantonments became central sites through which the East India Company established its political authority and continued to define who its subjects were. By regulating who would receive financial allowances from the military department and its charities and by categorizing these camp populations using racial markers, the military's bureaucracies were at the forefront of establishing the priorities of the emergent colonial government and its efforts to socially engineer productive populations from the families that became attached to military regiments.

In the novel, *Nashtar*, when the dancing troupe finds itself without a paying sponsor, the manager invites Hasan Shah to attend some entertainment in the tents of the troupe in the hope that he can find another wealthy European to support the troupe. The troupe had been earning about Rs. 700 every month, including an allowance for Gulbadan, the star dancer and sexual companion to the sponsor.

---

[1] There have been several editions of the novel, translated into English as *The Nautch Girl* or *The Dancing Girl*. Originally translated from Persian into Urdu in 1893 by Sajjad Hussain Kasmandavi, it was later translated into English by the Urdu writer, Qurratulain Hyder (New Delhi: Sterling Publishers, 1992).

When Gulbadan runs off, depriving the troupe of its main attraction, the troupe are left desperate for financial support. With the disappearance of Gulbadan, Khanum Jan, a young woman who was adopted by the troupe, was promoted as the replacement breadwinner. The various members of the troupe hoped that with her good looks and pleasing demeanor, she would be able to attract a European officer who might consent to pay for the entire company. The manager of the troupe approached Hasan Shah to convince his employer, Ming Sahib, to employ the troupe and to take Khanum Jan in as his concubine. Although Ming Sahib consented to pay an allowance to Khanum Jan sufficient to support the troupe, she refused to become his concubine and instead secretly formed a relationship with Ming Sahib's munshi, Hasan Shah.

As the transactions and negotiations between Ming Sahib, his munshi, and the dancing troupe demonstrate, by the late eighteenth-century, local communities in northern India were increasingly dependent on the financial resources of the British military. These communities provided a range of services and goods to traveling military regiments, including the sexual and domestic services of local women who formed conjugal relationships with European men. Individual women cohabited with European soldiers and their families became attached to military regiments as they moved from cantonment to cantonment.

By the standards of north India, a cadre of camp followers was not unusual, something that was noted by numerous observers.[2] This colonial practice followed a pre-colonial pattern; Mughal troops were well-known for traveling with large entourages of camp followers, often taking days to move several miles.[3] Officers in Mughal and British armies traveled with several personal servants, while rank-and-file soldiers were accompanied by local women who provided housekeeping labor as well as sexual labor. By some estimates, there were often twice as many non-military men and women on the march as there were soldiers.[4]

This type of military and civilian cooperation was commonplace for eighteenth century armies, particularly among the British. In Europe

---

[2] Martha Mary Sherwood, *The Life and Times of Mrs. Sherwood* (London, 1854), pp. 485–6, cited in K. K. Dyson, *A Various Universe* (Delhi: Oxford University Press, 1978, second edition 2002), pp. 89–90.

[3] H. S. Bhatia, *Military History of India, 1607–1947* (New Delhi: Deep & Deep Publications, 1977), pp. 64–5.

[4] Bhatia, *Military History*, pp. 104–5; Barton C. Hacker, "Women and Military Institutions in Early Modern Europe," *Signs* 6, 4 (1981): 647–8; Roger Beaumont, *Sword of the Raj: the British Army in India, 1747–1947* (Indianapolis and New York: Bobbs Merrill, 1977), pp. 56–9.

and abroad, particularly in the Americas, British armies relied very heavily on the labor of local women to sustain the military enterprise.[5] As Myna Trustram has shown, the pre-Victorian army lived among civilians, relying on housing from local establishments and provisions from local merchants. Women camp followers "were an integral part of the military train and moved freely between these roles [as wives, traders, cooks, laundresses, seamstresses] and others according to circumstance."[6] Although the army became more professionalized from the middle of the nineteenth century onward, managing labor resources provided by wives and female companions became a crucial part of harnessing local resources to support traveling military regiments. Some soldiers were allowed to marry with the understanding that their wives would supply necessary domestic labor, such as cleaning, washing, sewing, nursing, and teaching to the regiment. Thus, soldiers' families were made into "service families," allowing the regiment to rely on the informal labor of its collective wives.[7] Wives were given a small allowance for these services, but among military officials, it was widely assumed that women's labor was not meant to be a significant source of the family's income.[8] Few British soldiers in India were allowed to marry, although many cohabited with native women, paying for sexual and domestic services that they required.

British military movements had a significant impact on local economies, creating demands for services and goods that local inhabitants could provide. According to Douglas Peers, the military in north India was supplied by local merchants in ad hoc bazaars that sprung up around military cantonments: "In effect, these bazaars came to resemble compact and mobile cities, capable of providing the troops with a vast range of products and services."[9] He estimates that up to 70 percent of each soldier's salary was spent locally, so that towns or villages in which troops stopped became reliant on soldiers' spending habits. Military spending changed these local economies by creating

---

[5] Hacker, "Women and Military Institutions"; Walter Hart Blumenthal, *Women Camp Followers of the American Revolution* (Philadelphia: Ayer Company, 1988).

[6] Myna Trustram, *Women of the Regiment: Marriage and the Victorian Army* (Cambridge: Cambridge University Press, 1984), p. 11.

[7] "Service family" is a term most recently used by Christopher Hawes, *Poor Relations: The Making of an Eurasian Community, 1773–1833* (London: Curzon Books, 1996).

[8] Trustram, *Women of the Regiment*, ch. 6.

[9] Douglas Peers, *Between Mars and Mammon: Colonial Armies and the Garrison State in India, 1819–1835* (London: Aldershot, 1995), p. 131; see also Indrani Chatterjee, "Colouring Subalternity: slaves, concubines and social orphans in early colonial India," *Subaltern Studies X* (New Delhi: Oxford University Press, 1999), pp. 64–5.

consumption demands that were specific to the needs of European troops.[10]

Cities that were primarily European cantonment towns grew dramatically in this period. Kanpur, for instance, the city in which *Nashtar* was set, grew from a city of five thousand people in 1798 to over thirty thousand in 1830. Originally a base from which to fight the Marathas, Kanpur went from a temporary military base camp to a market town which was known for selling European goods.[11] Larger cities such as Calcutta experienced a huge influx of British soldiers and sailors and the concomitant growth of problems such as public drunkenness, vagrancy, domestic violence, petty theft, and prostitution. As the previous chapter showed, disciplining lower-class men and their violent behaviors toward those who were vulnerable became a crucial concern of Crown-appointed officials such as judges and magistrates. Military camps were especially vulnerable to scrutiny as high-ranking officials felt that the rank-and-file needed to be carefully managed in order to be productive.

As the East India Company's and Royal troops became more reliant on local men and women for provisions and services, indigenous men and women became increasingly dependent on the financial resources of the British military forces and became entangled with the Company's bureaucracies and institutions. The changing nature of the colonial economy in many of the subcontinent's rural and semi-rural areas led to a restructuring of labor patterns so that as more men left farms and became migrant laborers, women had to become self-sufficient. As Sugata Bose has suggested, the territorial and military expansion of the English East India Company created new demands on local economies.[12] As economic and social interdependence developed between the British military and local populations and produced a series of intimate encounters, regulating familial relations became a central concern for the East India Company's military administration.

The British military became similarly reliant on local populations. Ballhatchet's account of military prostitution and its regulation in the early nineteenth century shows that military officials were keenly aware that providing heterosexual sex and ensuring its safety was a necessary

[10] Peers, *Between Mars and Mammon*, p. 113; see also C. A. Bayly, *Rulers, Townsmen and Bazaars: North Indian Society in the Age of British Expansion, 1770–1870* (Cambridge: Cambridge University Press, 1983), pp. 54, 215.

[11] Zoe Yalland, *Traders and Nabobs: the British in Cawnpore, 1765–1857* (Wilton: M. Russell, 1987), ch. 1.

[12] Sugata Bose, *Peasant Labor and Colonial Capital: Rural Bengal Since 1770* (Cambridge: Cambridge University Press, 1993).

part of provisioning the troops.[13] And yet, sexual labor was only a part of the work that native women offered in the colonial economy. As Luise White has shown for colonial Nairobi, prostitution was not limited to the sale of sexual services. Rather, sex work involved the sale or transaction of domestic services that were meant to be a comfort for men who were far from home. Women entertained men by selling them conversation, a meal, clean clothes, bath water, and other forms of domestic sociality.[14] Moreover, as is clear from cases in India, many native women received some sort of payment or remuneration for their services and some formed long-term attachments with the men who became their "protectors" or "keepers." Wills left by rank-and-file soldiers demonstrate both the level of intimacy that some European men developed with native women and the financial provisions men made for their native companions. These ties could be very strong as almost three-quarters of all royal troops, upon being posted back to England, volunteered for the Company army as a way of remaining with their indigenous families.[15]

As Thomas Williamson noted in his manual for those traveling to India, "Whether married, or not, each soldier is generally provided with a companion, who takes care of his linen, aids in cleaning his accoutrements, dresses his hair, and sometimes proves no bad hand at a beard! ... on the whole, [these women] may be considered highly serviceable; especially during illness, at which time their attendance is invaluable."[16]

In spite of the emotional attachments created by these liaisons, various financial expectations structured and sustained companionate relationships between European men and native women. As the narrative of *Nashtar* demonstrates, income that native women earned through the sale of sexual services often supported their relatives and communities. But it was not only native women who assumed a financial basis for these domestic relationships. Military officials assumed that they had a kind of paternal responsibility to the families of European

---

[13] Kenneth Ballhatchet, *Race, Sex and Class Under the Raj: Imperial Attitudes and Policies, 1793–1905* (New York: St. Martin's Press, 1980), chs. 2 and 3; Philippa Levine, "Venereal disease, prostitution and the politics of empire: the case of British India," *Journal of the History of Sexuality* 4 (1994): 579–602 and "Rereading the 1890s: venereal disease as 'constitutional crisis' in Britain and British India," *Journal of Asian Studies* 55 (1996): 585–612. In England, see Judith Walkowitz, *Prostitution in Victorian Society* (Cambridge: Cambridge University Press, 1980).

[14] Luise White, *The Comforts of Home: Prostitution in Colonial Nairobi* (Chicago: University of Chicago Press, 1990).

[15] Peers, *Between Mars and Mammon*, pp. 81–2.

[16] Thomas Williamson, *The East India Vade Mecum* (London, 1810), vol. I, p. 458.

soldiers, although who would pay and for what type of families was always a disputed matter. Through charitable organizations, such as the Military Orphan Society and Lord Clive's Pension Fund, officers and high-ranking civil servants of the Company committed themselves to providing financial benefits for the families of European soldiers, drawing from a pattern of middle-class philanthropy that was common in England.[17]

A shared understanding between native women and the troops they followed about the transactional and economic nature of these relationships structured the provisions that the Company made for soldiers' families and what those families came to expect and claim. By creating an infrastructure to financially support European soldiers' families, the military and the Company state committed to upholding the paternal responsibilities of soldiers for their female companions and mixed-race offspring. These provisions compelled the Company to consider which widows to support and how to educate the mixed-race children of European soldiers in order to make them loyal and productive members of colonial society. Moreover, the provisions made by these charities gave monetary incentives to native women to remain attached to European soldiers within the regiment even when their consorts left. This growing bureaucracy allowed native women to make claims for payments or provisions they felt they were due, making themselves subjects of the growing Company state. In making themselves into particular types of subjects – spousal, maternal, widowed – native women petitioned the Company for allowances, pensions, and other forms of financial support, pleading that they belonged to the "service family" of the Company and deserved the Company's protection. By reacting to these requests, the military showed that it was part of a responsive and expanding colonial state that was taking responsibility for a growing number of women and children. While local administrative responses showed that this nascent colonial government was keen to claim paternal and political authority for a larger number of subjects by providing financial benefits, Company officials in London set up a series of exclusions that limited its financial responsibilities. By clarifying who could not be counted as members of the service family, the early Company bureaucracies were able to promote the making of colonial hierarchies along race and gender lines.

---

[17] Paul Langford, *A Polite and Commercial People: England, 1727–1783* (Oxford: Oxford University Press, 1989), pp. 128–45.

I

Two charities, Lord Clive's Pension Fund and the Bengal Military Orphan Society, were central to the military department's efforts to make financial provisions for its European soldiers and their families. Lord Clive's Pension Fund was founded in order to provide pensions to disabled European soldiers and officers of the Company army and after their deaths, to their widows. The Bengal Military Orphan Society was established as an educational institution that provided schooling to the orphans of European soldiers. Although there were many other voluntary charities and institutions that brought Calcutta's British elite together to provide relief to widows and orphans during this period, these two were the only institutions directly supported by the East India Company and its Court of Directors.[18] Founded initially as charitable organizations supported by contributions from its members, the pension fund and orphan society were eventually backed by Company funds. The growing financial relationship between these charitable organizations and the Company tied the pension fund and the orphanage more closely to the bureaucratic establishment in Bengal and brought them under parliamentary surveillance.

As the military expanded during the years from 1760 to 1833, military expenditures grew, in spite of the Company's efforts to be thrifty. Until the 1750s, there were several hundred British soldiers in India, mostly those who served the East India Company. By 1790, there were over 18,000 soldiers in the three presidencies, counting both the Company and Royal Armies.[19] In Bengal Presidency alone, there were about 6,000 European troops. By 1830, there were over 36,000 European troops on the subcontinent, including over 15,000 in Bengal.[20] Although the charities made provisions for the Company's troops, widows and orphans of the royal regiments posted to India occasionally made claims to the Company.

By creating a link between the Company state and its soldiers' families, the pension fund and the orphan society carried out the

[18] See Charles Lushington, *The History, Design and Present State of the Religious, Benevolent and Charitable Institutions Founded by the British in Calcutta and Its Vicinity* (Calcutta, 1824).

[19] O.I.O.C., H/85, p. 123, "General Abstract of the Last Return of His Majesty's and the Company's European Forces in India," Feb. 1790. During the period from 1760 to 1830, there were also varying numbers of royal troops in India. In 1803, there were 18 King's regiments and 6 Company regiments; by 1823, there were roughly equal numbers. Peers, *Between Mars and Mammon*, pp. 74–8, 81–2.

[20] See S. L. Menezes, *Fidelity & Honour: the Indian Army from the Seventeenth to the Twenty-first Century* (New Delhi: Viking Penguin, 1993), p. 13; Bhatia, *Military History*, p. 36.

practical and ideological work of socially engineering colonial settlements by educating Anglicized subjects and families and preventing them from falling into vagrancy. Because soldiers' families frequently included native wives and mixed-race children, the policy of supporting an Anglicized but mixed-race population funded by the Company became more complicated. In the process of defining who could receive benefits of these funds, these charities' reluctance to support native wives while educating mixed-race children marked an important moment in the emergence of discourses among governmental institutions in late eighteenth-century British India that understood its subjects by racial categories. Much like officials of the judiciary, military officials began to define what constituted an appropriate family for the purposes of colonial governance and eventually privileged children as objects of the Company's judicial and charitable protection while disenfranchizing their native mothers.

In spite of the well-known reluctance to accept mixed-race families within the Company's operations, there was no clear-cut progression or coherence in the Company's strategies toward its mixed-race subjects. In fact, as will become clear, over a period of seventy years, the Company state vacillated between providing native women and mixed-race children with financial benefits and cutting them off from charitable support. Mixed-race orphans and native wives were seen simultaneously as subversive elements within the colonial establishment and also as potential recruits to aid the Company's enterprises. As Indrani Chatterjee has noted, "... colonial practice as well as colonial law endowed the slave-born [mixed-race] with permanent jural marginality, while insisting on their cultural incorporation within religious and educational boundaries."[21]

Surrounding the founding of these charitable institutions was a discourse about the civic and public responsibilities of men to protect those less able. Paralleling the rise of charitable activity and associational culture in Britain in the eighteenth-century, middle-class men with aspirations to political virtue and sentimental affect were asked to take responsibility for the families of poor soldiers.[22] For military men, soldiers were members of a fraternal collective that had responsibilities toward *their* women and children. The notion that women and children belonged to a particular regiment, or way of life, suggests how deeply held was both the notion of women as possessions, but this sense

---

[21] Chatterjee, "Colouring Subalternity," p. 73.
[22] Markman Ellis, *The Politics of Sensibility: Race, Gender and Commerce in the Sentimental Novel* (Cambridge: Cambridge University Press, 1996), pp. 14–15, ch. 5.

of belonging also required paternal and fraternal responsibility for the upkeep of one's own female partner and an obligation to support the conjugal partner of one's brother in arms.

Both the pension fund and the orphan society provided benefits on the basis of proving a family relationship with a European soldier in the service of the East India Company.[23] Women had access to these benefits because they were the wives of soldiers, children were eligible because they were the offspring of soldiers, thus reaffirming the patriarchal contract that these social responsibilities were based on.

Initially founded on paternal ties and fraternal obligations, eligibility requirements were not about racial distinctions or blood relations. Indeed, Company soldiers had long been informally supporting their colleagues' children and concubines. When the East India Company became involved in the 1770s, the recipients of charity were more closely scrutinized by officials in India and in London. Because the widows in this case were Indian or half-Indian, and the children were mixed-race, the racial status of widows and orphans became a central subject for debate.

As in the judicial debates over crimes involving native women, military officials questioned who should be treated as a British subject. Although the founding of these institutions were not explicitly based on race and national identity but rather on familial ties, once these institutions came to deal with a growing mixed-race population, the criteria of who could be considered part of a soldier's "family" came under closer scrutiny. By making policies about the treatment of widows and orphans, determining who could and could not receive benefits and what kinds of benefits would be given to whom, military officials created and validated hierarchies based on class, gender, and race.

Although military expenses were the largest portion of the Company's budget, the Directors in London resisted spending money on programs such as these because they cut into the Company's profits. Nonetheless, as the number of Company troops grew, officials in Calcutta persisted in asking for increasingly more funds for the widows and orphans of its soldiers as a humanitarian gesture. In particular, administrators in India represented the charitable impulse of the Company as being as important to good rulership in India. The image of a beneficent and

---

[23] The King's army provided similar benefits in Britain for soldiers who fought in the Napoleonic Wars and their families. See Patricia Y. C. E. Lin, *Extending Her Arms: Military Families and the Transformation of the British State, 1793–1815*. Unpublished Ph.D. dissertation, University of California-Berkeley, 1997. As Myna Trustram suggests, the army often went to extra lengths to keep soldiers and their families comfortable when abroad. Trustram, *Women of the Regiment*, p. 69.

benevolent Company was frequently invoked in arguments that various military officials used to gain the Company's support for these institutions. As Seema Alavi has argued about the invalid Thanah, which was a program put into place by the Military Department for pensioning its native soldiers, "[it] demonstrated the benevolent character of the invincible Company 'Bahadur' thereby contributing to the Company's attempts to add legitimacy to its rule in India."[24]

Indeed, the historical portrait painted by Edward Penny of the Nawab of Bengal handing Lord Clive his bounty, which was commissioned by the East India Company to commemorate Clive's pension fund, captured the vision of a benevolent Company that took care of its widows and orphaned children in the aftermath of victorious battle (see figure 6.1).[25] The painting, set on the frontlines, shows the uniformed red-coated British officer (presumably representing Lord Clive) standing on the ground of victorious battle, handing a check to a mother sitting on a rock, cradling an infant. Neatly capturing several genres (historical painting, madonna-child, and European exploration on foreign land), the painting epitomized the type of paternal benevolence that the Company wanted to publicly display about its support for Clive's Pension Fund.

In spite of the various ways in which the Company tried to limit its obligations to native women, some native women who were married to or had cohabited with European soldiers behaved as if the state had promised them certain rights and financial benefits and attempted to gain the state's provisions. These institutions provided opportunities for native women to make requests, press for financial provisions and claim the benefits that British subjects were entitled to based on their familial relationship with a European man. Their awareness of their status under the provisions of the pension fund and the orphan society suggests that native women were keenly aware of what they were entitled to and they initiated their claims based on what they believed about their own status as subjects of the Company state. Writing in English, Persian, Hindustani, and Bengali, often with the help of professional letter-writers, native women produced letters on their own behalf. Their activities speak to the ways in which native women situated

---

[24] Seema Alavi, *The Sepoys and the Company: Tradition and Transition in Northern India, 1770–1830* (Delhi: Oxford University Press, 1995), p. 114.

[25] C. A. Bayly, ed., *The Raj: India and the British* (London, 1990), pp. 101–2, plate 111. This historical painting, commissioned by the East India Company in 1772, is displayed on the walls of the Oriental and India Office Collections at the new British Library in London.

Figure 6.1. Lord Clive receiving from Najm-ud-daula, nawab of Murshidabad, a legacy for the East India Company's Military Fund, London 1772 (oil on canvas), by Edward Penny, Oriental and India Office Collection, British Library.

themselves as subjects of the colonial state, particularly when there were financial concerns at stake.

While there is no doubt that the Company frequently relied on the unpaid domestic and sexual labor of native women as wives and conjugal companions of European soldiers, the native women who made these appeals saw the pension fund and the orphan society as providing some sort of compensation for their domestic and sexual work. In making these appeals, native women pushed the military to be more specific about its policies, resulting in the military making decisions to be explicitly racist in articulating its many exclusions.

II

Lord Clive's Pension Fund was established by the East India Company in 1770 using prize monies Lord Clive received for his services in the battle of Plassey and his victory over Siraj-ud-daulah. Under the terms of the agreement, the money was put into trust in East India Company bonds with the idea that it would produce an annual interest of 8 percent and that amount would be sufficient to cover the cost of pensions to European soldiers who had been in the Company's troops.[26]

The original agreement stated that pensions were granted to soldiers who were possessed of property under a certain amount and to "such objects of charity belonging to the United Company's Military Service or the widows or familys [sic] of *such objects as the said Court of Directors shall in their discretions think fit* [emphasis added]."[27] By linking charity with Company service, the terms of Clive's agreement was clear in its intent; however, by leaving open the question of who was a fit subject, the agreement was vague when it was applied to claims by widows. Through the period between 1770 and 1830, various officials debated the intent of Clive's agreement and in particular, whether Indian and mixed-race wives should be included as beneficiaries of Clive's fund.

As women made applications to the military department for pensions that were due to widows, it became increasingly clear that policy makers in London and in Calcutta disagreed about the intentions and provisions of Clive's Fund. In theory, women were supposed to apply to the Military Department at Fort William in Calcutta and local officials then recommended these requests to the Directors in London; while officials in Calcutta were acutely aware that many widows were not fully

[26] O.I.O.C., L/AG/23/2/1, "Agreement between the East India Company and Lord Clive respecting the Military Fund dated 6 April 1770." The main part of the text reads: "And whereas the said Robert Lord Clive, being zealous for the property of the said Company, the Security of their Territories, and territorial Revenues in India, belonging to them, and their Trade and Commerce, which greatly depend on the Bravery and Conduct of the said Company's Troops ... hath proposed to the Court of Directors to the said United Company, to appropriate the Interest of the said five lacks [sic] of Rupees, for the Support of a certain number of Officers, non-commissioned officers and private men, in the Service of the said Company, who from Wounds, Length of Service, or Diseases contracted during their Service, were unable or unfit to serve any longer, and whose Fortunes might be too scanty to afford the Officers a decent, and the Private Men a comfortable subsistence, in their native Country, and also to make them some provision for the widows of such Officers and private Men, as should have been entitled to the said Bounty ..." Although Clive received the money in 1757, the fund was not established until 1770; Peter Marshall and Huw Bowen, both historians of the British empire eighteenth century, have suggested that Clive initially accepted the money on behalf of the Company and kept a large portion of it for himself. Once he came under a Parliamentary inquiry for being corrupt, he established the fund as a way of cleansing the specter of financial impropriety. Personal communications.

[27] *Ibid.* The property limits were determined based on the rank of the soldier; so a Colonel was limited to £4,000, Lieutenant Col. (£3,000), Major (£2,500), Captain (£2,000), Lieutenant (£1,000), Ensign or Cornet (£750) and the same limits applied to their widows.

European, officials in London were much less sensitive to this reality. The widows of commissioned officers would be paid twice a year through the Company's offices in London, which revealed a foundational assumption that widows of officers would be sent home to live in London, or more specifically, the widows of officers were assumed to be of European birth.[28]

Because the rules for determining whether soldiers' wives were eligible to receive pensions were unclear, pensions were unevenly granted. In the early phase of distributing pensions, officials in the military department at Fort William in Bengal freely granted pensions to women whose connections with the military appeared legitimate. However, after about 1800 when the Company was attempting to reign in its military spending, officials began to deny the pensions to women who were not of European descent based on the argument that these pensions had never been intended for the Indian wives of European soldiers. A requirement was instituted that an affidavit be filed attesting to European parentage on both sides. By 1825, this policy had been reversed by the military department, in consultation with the Board of Control in London, and all women who could prove that they had been married to European soldiers in the Company's employ were eligible to receive a pension whether they were Indian or European. By 1860, all payments to native or mixed-race widows ended because the Board argued it could no longer afford to support local women.

Shifts in policy and the idiosyncratic application of grants for pensions indicate that military officials were rarely in agreement as to who was a deserving recipient of a pension. Indian and Eurasian women took advantage of this uncertainty and applied for the pension in the hopes of being granted financial relief even if they were not European. These applications, that spoke from the fuzzy margins of eligibility, often pushed policy makers to articulate more clearly what the policy for receiving a pension was. When these claims were denied, these women put pressure on other officials, such as chaplains, to argue the case on their behalf.

In the 1780s and 1790s, when the military was expanding due to battles on several fronts, requests were routinely granted based on the letters that the military board received from destitute widows. For example, when Mrs. Ann Baker wrote in 1792 requesting to be admitted to the pension fund as the widow of a lieutenant, the military

---

[28] The widows of non-commissioned officers and privates were ordered to prove their marriages to the satisfaction of the Court of Directors in order to receive a pension. Because these widows were assumed to be completely destitute, officials of the military department assumed they would be unable to afford the passage back to England and were thus likely to receive their pensions in India until they remarried.

department immediately approved her request and recommended her case to the Court of Directors.[29] Likewise, several years later, Mrs. Mariam Showers wrote to Governor-General John Shore that as a result of her husband's departure to England, she was left destitute. She requested enough money to travel up country with her son, Hastings, in order that she could seek the protection of friends who were willing to keep her until Col. Showers returned. The Governor-General approved a generous stipend of Rs. 250 per month until the military department received news of Col. Showers's whereabouts.[30] Typically, a provisional pension was granted until the Court of Directors approved the application; a pension request was rarely, if ever, denied by the Court once it was approved by the Military Department.

The cases of Mrs. Baker and Mrs. Showers illustrate how straightforward it was until about 1800 to receive benefits if one was married to a soldier or officer in the East India Company's army. By 1800, receiving the pension had become slightly more difficult and women were asked to provide additional evidence of their circumstances; occasionally, the matter was referred to the commander of the regiment for further investigation. In addition to proving that the estate did not exceed a certain amount, military widows were also asked to provide duplicate copies of a marriage certificate.[31]

Several women encountered increasingly stringent standards in order to receive benefits from the Company's military establishment. In 1804, Rosalinda Fitzgerald wrote asking for a pension from the Company because her husband, Mr. Henry Fitzgerald, Deputy Commissary at Bencoolen (modern-day Sumatra), had died leaving her destitute. Until her husband's death, she and her son had been receiving an allowance of Rs. 70 per month, which was considered part of her husband's salary. Upon his death, the executor to the estate sold all of Mr. Fitzgerald's belongings and refused to deliver the proceeds to Mrs. Fitzgerald. The Governor-General ordered that the matter be investigated but in contrast to the case of Mrs. Showers, no allowance or stipend was granted while the matter was being resolved.[32]

The same year, in 1804, Mrs. Maria Tavender wrote to the government that her husband, who had died a Private in the Company's army, had left a very modest estate of S. Rs. 5 and 13 annas that was being held in the Company's treasury. She enclosed a marriage certificate

[29] N.A.I., Military Department Proceedings, 29 Feb. 1792, no. 9.
[30] N.A.I., 7 March 1794, no. 80.
[31] See, for example, N.A.I., Military Department Proceedings, 4 August 1803, nos. 63–5; 25 August 1803, nos. 56–8.
[32] N.A.I., Military Department Proceedings, 22 March 1804, no. 96.

and authorized that the money be paid to a friend of hers in Calcutta as she was too old and infirm to travel from Berhampore to collect the money herself. This matter was referred to the commander at Berhampore for confirmation that this woman was who she claimed to be and that she was legitimately entitled to the estate.[33]

The cases of Mrs. Fitzgerald and Mrs. Tavender suggest that military officials were becoming increasingly more restrictive to whom they granted financial relief, often ignoring the circumstances that were stated in the correspondence; in the case of Mrs. Tavender, confirmation was sought for her status even though the amount at stake was only S. Rs. 5. In the case of Mrs. Fitzgerald, even though her husband had died two years before, the military department did not see fit to grant her some sort of allowance until the matter was sorted out.

When native women were unsuccessful at making their claims, they turned to other figures within the colonial establishment, such as the church. In 1805, the Company's chaplain at St. Mary's, which was located at Fort St. George, wrote to the military department in 1805 on behalf of "several native women, the widows of European soldiers who died in the service of the Honourable Company" and asked why the pension, which had been previously granted to Indian women, had been refused to these women on the grounds that Lord Clive's Fund had been intended only for European wives. As a result of the Company's denial, the chaplain wrote that many women were put in "a state of beggary" and had become dependent on the church for support. He noted that there had been a long-standing practice to grant the pension to women "of whatever denomination" and he encouraged the Governor (of Madras) to revert to the former practice and grant pensions to native women.[34] He further noted that since there was a very small number of European women who were married to officers and soldiers, the practice of limiting it to them would seem to negate the need for such a fund. In any case, the amounts disbursed were small: in Bengal between May 1800 through August 1803, between four and ten women received the pension every month. The amounts ranged from Sicca Rs. 58 to a high of Sicca Rs. 1,107 with the average disbursement being somewhere around Sicca Rs. 300. On a yearly basis, about Sicca Rs. 6,000 was remitted in total.[35]

[33] N.A.I., 10 May 1804, nos. 75–6.
[34] O.I.O.C., F/4/211, no. 4716, "Claims of Native Women married to European Soldiers to the Benefit of Lord Clive's Fund." See Extract Fort St. George from the Clerk of the Vestry, 22 April 1805.
[35] O.I.O.C., F/4/713, no. 3073, "List of Sums Paid on Account Lord Clive's Donation 1800 to 1803," Extract Bengal Military Letter, 11 August 1803, para. 279.

The chaplain's letter was forwarded to the government in Madras with a cover letter from the military department stating that an inquiry had shown that the pension benefit had been discontinued to native widows of European soldiers under the previous commander-in-chief because he argued that the fund had never been intended for native women. The current commander-in-chief, Lieutenant General Cradock, however, disagreed and argued that while he did not fully understand the agreement Clive had made with the Company, he believed that native women should receive the pension "especially if I learn that the native widow is charged with the maintenance of the offspring of the deceased European," thereby reminding the military department of its commitment to the offspring of its soldiers.[36] The military department concurred with the chaplain and new commander-in-chief but referred the matter to the Court of Directors for the final decision.

This chain of correspondence, from the chaplain and the commander-in-chief at Fort St. George to the government in Madras and the Directors in London, illustrates that many officials in India agreed that Indian widows were deserving of the benefits of the pension fund. As the commander-in-chief noted, "I am also [in favor of having] this justifiable policy which should lead to the adoption of a liberal government in the view of the native inhabitants."[37] Yet the military department was cautious of supporting a plan that would cost money and would commit the Company to providing more support than the Court of Directors in London would approve. Although as the figures suggest, the amount of money disbursed was never very large, the idea of fiscal restraint loomed large in the minds of colonial officials at various levels.

There was no response to this 1805 inquiry so the matter remained unresolved for a few years. In both the Madras and Bengal presidencies, however, the military department continued to grant pensions to native women once the women could produce a marriage certificate and a property affidavit attesting that they had no property. In practice, if not in policy, indigenous women continued to receive pensions from Lord Clive's fund.

Several years later, in 1810, relying on the example of several women who applied for the pension and were refused by the Court of Directors, the Madras Military Department inquired again what the policy for granting these pensions was. As in 1805, there was a lengthy chain

---

[36] O.I.O.C., F/4/211, no. 4716, "Claims of Native Women married to European Soldiers to the Benefit of Lord Clive's Fund." See Extract Mad. Mil. Cons, 29 April 1805.
[37] *Ibid.*

of correspondence from the women to the commander of the regiment to the military department and back inquiring why the pension had been refused.[38]

The correspondence was forwarded to the auditor-general who then summarized the Directors' decision on the matter and reminded the military department that the Company had rescinded extending benefits to native women "although they were properly married." By making this decision, the Directors effectively deferred any further claims that native widows could make on the Company. In rhetoric that appealed both to the vision of a benevolent, liberal and fair government and to the image of the Company as fiscally conservative, the Directors stated that on principle "... we should have, from the general reason for forming such an Establishment, answered in the affirmative ..." Yet, they argued that Clive's fund had always only been intended for those residing in Ireland or Britain; "The Company are therefore not warranted to admit any persons resident in India as pensioners on that fund."[39] Although the Directors were not ruling out aiding the local families of European soldiers in special cases, they were unprepared to uniformly grant pensions to "residents of India," because of the strain that such a plan would put on the Company's finances.[40] Thereafter, women were required to produce a marriage certificate, a property affidavit, and a certificate attesting that both their parents were European on both sides in order to receive the pension.

Seventeen years later in 1825, the widow of Conductor Abraham Ross came before the military board requesting financial assistance. She wrote that as a "country-born" (or mixed-race), she had no claims to Clive's pension fund but based on her husband's forty years of service to the Company, she hoped that a donation could be made for her family's subsistence. She also enclosed a marriage affidavit that she was married in 1786.[41] When the matter was resolved, it appeared that the Court of Directors had already ruled the previous year to pension widows who were legally married and not of European descent on both sides.[42] There is no evidence in the archives of when and why this occurred.

---

[38] N.A.I., Military Department Proceedings, 27 June, 4 August, 26 September, 1809.

[39] O.I.O.C., F/4/360, no. 8774, "Native Women not Allowed the Benefit of Lord Clive's Fund." Extract Mad. Mil. Cons., 7 Sept. 1808.

[40] *Ibid.* See also O.I.O.C., F/4/452.

[41] O.I.O.C., F/4/1115, no. 29907, "Country-born Widows of Soldiers now Admitted to Clive's Fund; Half Castes to be called Indo-Britons." Extract Mad. Mil. Cons., 24 August 1825.

[42] *Ibid.* Extract General Letter from the Court of Directors to Supreme Government, 15 September 1824, paragraphs 37, 64, 115.

This reversal was an important turn of events showing that through the determined applications of native and half-cast women, the decision to grant pensions exclusively to widows of purely European descent was abandoned. Between 1808 and 1825, some half-cast women, knowing that they were barred from receiving any benefits from Clive's fund, appealed to the military department for some support. In isolated cases, some were granted a half-pension because there had been no uniform policy.[43] Through this period, when the military department and the Directors vacillated on providing widows' pensions, native and Eurasian women who wrote to the military department kept bringing this matter to the Court of Directors' attention. In the letters that women wrote, they relied on the notion that there was reciprocity between service to the Company and the pensions the Company provided. They stated their husbands' rank and emphasized the years of faithful service their husbands had provided. They detailed how many children they had and how destitute they had become from having a lack of property. Finally, they called upon the humanity and honor of the Company to provide for its most faithful servants. By focusing on the destitution of their family and linking it with service to the Company, women invoked the terms on which Clive's Fund had been founded. Although none of the women's petitions directly addressed the inconsistency of granting pensions exclusively to European widows, by referring to the benevolence of the Company, they evoked the image from Edward Penny's portrait of Clive receiving the nawab's bounty: the vision of the unprotected widow and her child. In the narratives that they used to petition the Company, this was not simply charity for the poor; it was compensation for service and loyalty. Through these requests, native women articulated their claims based on what they believed their rights were as subjects of the Company state. By making these appeals indigenous women demonstrated that they understood very well the terms on which the founding of Clive's fund was based. This is not a story about a colonial institution and how it was resisted; rather, it is a narrative about the ways in which native women negotiated with a colonial institution to get what they needed, which was financial support. Women did not often achieve this aim.

---

[43] *Ibid.* Extract General Letter from the Court of Directors to the Military Department, 3 November 1815. Re: admission of Widow Maude to pension fund. "... the widow of the late Sergeant Maude although a Christian is a native Indian ... we authorize you to allow her a pension of half of the sum to which she would have had a claim had she been born of European parents ... [but] half pensions to native or country-born widows should not be considered a general regulation but granted in special cases only."

The benefits for native wives ended in 1860, two years after the East India Company transferred its power to the British crown and all European troops in India became members of the royal regiments. In its place, other charitable funds took over supporting European widows; for native women, however, charity was deemed too costly.

III

While Lord Clive's Pension Fund dealt with widows of Company soldiers, the Bengal Military Orphan Society addressed the needs of the offspring of European soldiers. The evolution of the orphan society's policies speak to the changing assumptions and distinctions made by school and Company officials in deciding how orphans of different social ranks, races, and gender were educated. As in the case of Lord Clive's Pension Fund, the arguments used for determining who was eligible to receive the benefits of the orphan society assumed that some orphans were more deserving than others of the schooling that the orphan society provided. Unlike the Pension Fund, however, the illegitimacy of orphans born out of wedlock rarely negated their right to receive Company benefits. Rather, the status of mixed-race children of European fathers secured their place as recipients of financial provisions of the Company. The question open to debate was how to best discipline and educate them into productive members of colonial society and how to differentiate between children born to officers and those born to the rank-and-file.

One primary goal of the military orphan society was to remove children from their lower-class European fathers in military cantonments in order to educate the children more appropriately and make them useful to the East India Company.[44] As Ann Stoler has noted, the education of children in the colonies was part of a larger project to produce civilized, bourgeois, and putatively "white" adults out of children whose sexuality was seen to require domestication.[45] Another goal of the orphan society was that the children were removed from their native mothers. Indeed, in the definition of orphan that the orphan society relied on, "orphan" was defined broadly as a child whose father

---

[44] N.A.I., Home Public Proceedings, 30 June 1783, pp. 2326–8. See also David Arnold, "European orphans and vagrants in India in the nineteenth century," *Journal of Imperial and Commonwealth History* 7 (1978): pp. 109–14. Educating army children in Britain was motivated by similar anxieties about the effects of cantonment life on impressionable youth. Trustram, *Women of the Regiment*, pp. 98, 103.

[45] Ann Stoler, *Race and the Education of Desire* (Durham: Duke University Press, 1995), ch. 5.

had died, whose father was living but unable to care for him, or whose father had been sent back to Europe.[46]

As in the case of the pension fund, arrangements for orphans prior to the establishment of the orphan society were most often temporary and ad hoc; pay and batta was given to each child in the regiment equal to that of a private's salary. Until 1779, just a few years before the founding of the orphan society, the army granted a separate allowance to the children of its European soldiers in regiments of Native Infantry.[47] In addition, commonly when a soldier died, his companions took up a collection to provide for the support of his female companion and children; indeed, often the woman moved in with another soldier in the regiment thereby maintaining her financial support from the regiment.

As matters of colonial policy, the question of how to deal with soldiers' families was rarely addressed until the 1780s when the rapid growth of the army and the Company establishment in Bengal necessitated the founding of the orphan society as a part of the Company's establishment in Bengal. In 1793, there were over five thousand European troops in Bengal, increasing to fifteen thousand just twenty years later in 1813.[48] This dramatic increase resulted in a sizable population of orphans and children who, as poor whites, threatened the authority of colonial rule.[49] The presence of these eighteenth-century Kims on the colonial landscape led to the founding of the orphan society and the infrastructure for economic and social support became more extensive as the numbers of orphans reached upwards of six hundred in the 1810s.[50]

Founded in 1782 by Lt. Col. William Kirkpatrick of the East India Company army, himself the father of several mixed-race children, and twelve other officers,[51] the Military Orphan Society solicited contributions from the salaries of its members in order to support the mixed-race orphans of European officers left behind by their fathers in India.

---

[46] Although Chatterjee implies that this definition of "orphan" was a matter specific to British India, p. 73, this definition was commonly used in England during this period and well into the nineteenth century. As Lydia Murdoch argues, lower-class or working-class parents of "orphans" in England often used orphanages as a time to regain their economic footing in order to later reclaim their children.

[47] Once it was brought to the attention of the Military Auditor, he discontinued the practice. "The Bengal Military Orphan Society," *Calcutta Review* 44: 87 (1867): 151–82, see p. 164.

[48] Menezes, *Fidelity and Honor*, p. 13; Bhatia, *Military History*, pp. 36–9.

[49] Arnold, "European Vagrants."

[50] N.A.I., Military Department, 6 March 1819, nos. 132–3. "Accounts of the Military Orphan Society, 1814–1817."

[51] William Kirkpatrick was himself born out of wedlock and fathered several illegitimate children with native women in Bengal.

The Society formalized a practice then prevalent in Bengal in which each regiment took up a collection when a child was orphaned and took over his or her care when the father died or was invalided back to Europe.

In June 1783, the managers of the Bengal Military Orphan Society in Calcutta wrote a letter to the Directors in London pleading for financial assistance in order to start a school for the orphans of non-commissioned officers and privates and to extend the benefits of the society to men who were not of the officer classes. The managers argued that with the benevolence of the Directors, the managers would be able to house, feed, clothe, and school about 200 orphans who had been born in military cantonments throughout the Bengal Presidency. As they eloquently stated,

> It can hardly be requisite to observe that hitherto little or no pains have been taken to render the numerous offspring of this Establishment ... useful to the community; it being a fact but too well known that not only the cultivation of their natural talents has been totally neglected; but that, owing to the habits unavoidably contracted in an European regiment, their morals also have been corrupted, and their constitutions destroyed ... It is sufficient to remark that the greater part of these wretched children are, at present, *no less idle, profligate and intemperate than the class of men with whom it is their misfortune to be brought up* ... [emphasis added].[52]

Their plan entailed taking the orphans out of the cantonments and placing them in a school in Calcutta, where under the careful surveillance and supervision of the orphan society, the orphans would be trained in appropriate vocations and therefore become "very valuable members of Society and by being through motives of gratitude, particularly attached and devoted to government."[53] The plan was accepted by the Court of Directors and starting in 1784, the charitable organization was supported by a contribution from the East India Company.

The managers initially asked for an allowance that would enable them to take in the children of non-commissioned officers and privates.[54] They asked for Rs. 5 per month per orphan and the Directors approved Rs. 3 per month. The managers responded that the smaller amount was equivalent to what a native coolee might receive emphasizing that

---

[52] O.I.O.C., P/2/61, Ben. Pub. Proc., 30 June 1783, pp. 588–606.
[53] *Ibid.*
[54] The monthly disbursements were paid for schooling or apprenticeships in Calcutta. Since there were no schools until about 1780, most children were educated by private tutors. By the time they were six or eight, many upper-class children, even mixed-race ones, were then sent to England to complete their education.

children of soldiers ought to have a higher social and economic status. They argued somewhat forcefully, "We might further observe that as the children of Europeans, all of whom have died, and many bled, in the service of the Company, they appear somewhat better entitled to the attention of Government than any class of natives ..."[55] Nonetheless, the managers agreed to this reduced allowance but wrote that they hoped that once the Directors saw how beneficial the school was for all concerned, they would provide additional funding. In the absence of adequate funding from the Company, the officers would provide for those less fortunate than they: "we assured ourselves that the *Gentlemen of the Army* would in the meantime, chearfully [sic] agree to our applying part of the surplus of the Fund established for the Orphans of Officers, towards the relief of the destitute offspring of the non-commissioned and private [emphasis added]."[56]

The managers felt the advantages of bringing the orphans to Calcutta were obvious: "they would be immediately under the eye of the management," anticipating a Benthamite image of modern surveillance for disciplining mixed-race children's bodies.[57] Under their "immediate inspection" in Calcutta, the orphans would be housed and instructed in trades and vocations that would enable them to find future employment and livelihood. The girls would find more opportunities for marriage within the European community while the boys would have increased access to jobs with the Company. These goals thus became the corner-stone of the educational policies of the orphan society: finding jobs and marriage partners. By upholding gendered conceptions of appropriate employment for orphan boys and girls, the managers hoped to channel the orphans in their charge into productive labor for the Company.[58]

A primary purpose was teaching the children English because often they came to the orphan society only speaking Hindustani, the local language. In the arguments to keep children until they were 15, rather than 12, the managers of the orphan society argued that it was impossible to "properly instill the precepts of morality into their minds" if the children didn't successfully learn English first.[59] The schedule also

---

[55] "The Bengal Military Orphan Society," *Calcutta Review* 44: 87 (1867): 151–82, see p. 165; see also O.I.O.C., P/2/61, pp. 598–9.

[56] O.I.O.C., P/2/61, Ben. Pub. Proc., 30 June 1783, pp. 588–606.

[57] *Ibid.*; Michel Foucault, *Discipline and Punish: The Birth of the Prison* (London: Penguin, 1977), pp. 175–84.

[58] N.A.I., Public Dept. Proceedings, 30 June 1783, pp. 2326–8.

[59] N.A.I., Public Dept. Proceedings, 9 June 1785. On the importance of teaching Indians English and inculcating Christian morality, see Gauri Viswanathan, *Masks of Conquest: Literary Study and British Rule in India* (New York: Columbia University Press, 1989).

included daily prayer and religious instruction three days a week.[60] The orphan society thus had a dual mission in the Bengal establishment: it re-educated mixed-race children into British subjects while providing an appropriate home environment for children removed from their natal homes.

Indeed, in the initial proposal to the Military Department, the officers' fund's managers hoped that "all orphans, legitimate and illegitimate" would eventually be relocated to England and boarded and lodged with "proper persons."[61] In this way, orphan children, whether mixed-race and/or illegitimate, would be reabsorbed into the British fold. An objection was raised by the Military Department to this point in the proposal: it was feared that no one in England would consent to take such an orphan. A further objection was raised – more to the point of what was at heart of this issue – whether it was appropriate to send illegitimate children of European soldiers to England. Should these children be treated as British subjects because of their fathers and in spite of their native mothers?

In the arguments against allowing illegitimate children to go to England, there was a concern about bringing mixed-race children to England as well as an anxiety about treating children of rank-and-file soldiers (usually born out of wedlock) and children of officers (occasionally legitimate) in comparable ways. By keeping mixed-race orphans in India, the Military Orphan Society was able to regulate the socialization of children born to different ranks. Thus, the status accorded to the child of an officer and a gentleman was affirmed both by keeping him or her separate from the children of non-commissioned officers and soldiers and also separate from the children of other ethnicities.

In the end, it was agreed by the managers of the orphan society and the military department that the society would provide benefits to all children of all soldiers but would only arrange for passage to Britain for those children who were considered "legitimate" in that their parents were both European and married. With this modification the plan was sent to the Court of Directors in London and was approved. Thus, in 1783, with the Court's approval, the managers of the orphan society were granted Rs. 3 per month per orphan and Rs. 40,000 to build an

---

[60] N.A.I., Military Dept. Proceedings, 10 July 1806, nos. 71–4.
[61] "The Bengal Military Orphan Society," *Calcutta Review* 44: 87 (1867): 151–82, see pp. 155–7.

orphanage for 300 children.[62] Pay stoppages were authorized from every soldier under the Company's command.[63]

A house was purchased in Dakhineswar and it was renovated as a school for the orphans of non-commissioned officers. The first group of orphans included 54 girls and 42 boys under the care of two sergeants and their wives. By 1785, the school had moved across the river to Howrah; the children of officers occupied the upper floors of the building at Howrah while the children of lower ranks moved into the ground floor and the terms Upper and Lower School came into common parlance. By then, there were 96 students in the Upper School and 160 in the Lower School.

In 1790, the schools moved yet again; this time the Upper School moved across the river to Kidderpore House, located in Alipore, which was south of Calcutta in the district known as 24 Parganahs. The buildings were grand buildings, made of white marble that showcased the Company's civic and architectural contributions to the city.[64] This move marked the separation of the two schools, the Upper and Lower, and effectively established the separation between the children of the officers and the children of the non-commissioned and privates in the army. The Governor-General noted the separation and supported the advantages that the officers' children would gain but noted that he hoped this new arrangement would not adversely affect the care given to the children of the Lower Orphan School.[65] By 1790, there were over 300 children in the Lower School; just four years later in 1803, there were over 500.[66]

Since the Upper School was maintained as a private institution run under the supervision of the Officers' Fund, there are few extant records of its activities in the India Office Records or in the records housed at the National Archives in Delhi.[67] The separation between officers' children and non-officers' children was built on the assumption that the orphans of the Upper School were more likely to be legitimate and by extension of this logic, of pure European extraction. In fact this was

---

[62] N.A.I., Bengal Military Cons. 5 January 1804, no. 54 Enclosure.

[63] The contributions were as follows (listed in sicca rupee amounts per month): Majors (9); Captains and Surgeons (6); Subalterns and Assistant Surgeons (3). The non-commissioned and privates never paid into the system but were subsidized by the money from the company. Officers above the rank of Major were asked to give voluntarily.

[64] See *Twelve Views of Calcutta*, by W. Baillie, 1794 (printed by an Act of Parliament), plate nos. 5 and 11 are of the Upper School and the Lower School.

[65] O.I.O.C., F/4/187, no. 4015. See Extract from Ben. Mil. Cons., June 20, 1790.

[66] O.I.O.C., F/4/187, no. 4015.

[67] N.A.I., Military Dept. Proceedings, 11 Feb. 1788, no. 14.

not so: more likely than not, the children of the Upper School were officers' children but mixed race. Beginning in 1788, children of officers whose fathers were living were also accepted into the Upper Orphan School if their fathers agreed to pay a monthly fee of Sicca Rs. 32 for girls and Sicca Rs. 30 for boys. Most often, these were mixed-race officers' children whose parents lacked the means to send them to Britain for their educations.

In contrast, the Lower School was funded in part by the Company, and because it became increasingly reliant on the Company for financial support, measures proposed by the managers of the orphan institutions filtered through various levels of colonial officials, who actively voiced the ways in which schooling mixed-race orphans of British soldiers intersected with the interests of the Company state.

The redistribution of money was a basic but fundamental facet of the orphan society's activities. The growth of the number of orphan committees, from none in 1784 to four in 1798 and then to eight in 1827, shows that with the increase in armed forces, there was a resulting increase in the network of charity extended to orphans.[68] The 25 percent increase in the amount of the orphan society's budget between 1804 and 1817, suggests as well that the orphan society was collecting, managing, and redistributing more money on behalf of its constituents and also on behalf of the Company.[69] By 1830, the orphan institution was a crucial source of financial, moral, and employment support for orphans of European soldiers in Bengal.

Financed through a number of different sources, the orphan society was a charitable organization, funded by the contributions of officers, fundraisers and private donations from other sources. The orphan society received a portion of its operating costs from the Company and funds gained from military successes, such as the Rohilla Donation and the spoils of the Maratha wars.[70] These links are important ways in which the orphan society became inextricably

---

[68] *Bengal Kalendar and Register (1801)*, p. 81; O.I.O.C., L/AG/23/7/5, "Rules and Regulations of the Bengal Military Orphan Society, applicable to the society's affairs in England," p. 8.

[69] N.A.I., Military Dept. Proceedings, 5 January 1804, nos. 49–50: the orphan society's total expenditure was Sicca Rs. 96,411; N.A.I., Military Dept. Proceedings, 6 March 1819, nos. 132–3: in 1817, the expenditures amounted to Sicca Rs. 145,236. By 1823, the fund was handling over Sicca Rs. 180,000 (Lushington, *Religious, Benevolent and Charitable Institutions*, p. xlvii.). By 1829, the fund's budget was at Rs. 211,267 a year (Hawes, *Poor Relations*, p. 34).

[70] The Rohilla Donation was a lump sum given to the heirs of officers who died during the Rohilla campaigns in October 1794. See N.A.I., Military Dept. Proceedings, 5 June 1795, no. 2. and no. 25.

connected with the military operations and financial practices of the Company. The managers of the orphan society thus had multiple roles: in addition to their Company employment as civil servants and military / officers, they were trustees, investors, social workers, and educators who were responsible for the redistribution of money to deserving orphans and their guardians.

In addition to the activities at the schools themselves, the orphan society provided a monthly allowance for all children which was given to their guardians until the children were four years old and could enter the school. Children under four years of age were to be left in the care of a close relative. More often than not, because of the absence of an appropriate close relative, the allowance went to another soldier in the regiment, who served as the guardian of the child.[71] For children of mothers who had died, the orphan fund also provided a wet nurse until the child was a year old. The guardian of the child would receive S. Rs. 3 per month that was due to the orphan under the agreement the orphan society had with the government. After the age of 4, however, it was compulsory that the child be admitted to the orphan school.[72] Further, the society also provided passage money to Britain for those who were born of European parents on both sides.

These allowances were disbursed through the local orphan committees at each cantonment, as long as the children had been registered from their birth as orphans belonging to a soldier of that regiment.[73] Because the payment of an allowance was provided if a child had been registered with a particular regiment, the child had to remain under the protection of another member of the regiment. The allowances were not paid to native women or their relatives, so native mothers attached themselves to other soldiers in the regiment in order to remain with their child until he or she was enrolled in the orphan institution. Through these policies, the idea that Indian women were not appropriate guardians was further consolidated and children were

[71] N.A.I., Military Dept. Proceedings, 3 February 1818, nos. 154–5. Fourteen orphans from H.M.'s 66th and 78th Regiments had been placed, along with their mothers with soldiers of H.M.'s 59th Regiment who were stationed at Fort William. The children were all Eurasians; thus, their mothers were assumed to be Indian or half-cast.

[72] In 1804, the goal of removing children from the cantonment lost its primacy and if it could be demonstrated that a child would be equally well treated at the home of a friend as at the orphan schools, the allowance would be given to the family who would keep him or her. By 1818, the monthly allowance for those who boarded outside the orphan school had risen to Sicca Rs. 20 per month for children under 5; Sicca Rs. 16 for those over 5; and Sicca Rs. 35 per month for young women over the age of 16. N.A.I., Military Orphan Society Letters, 3 June 1818.

[73] See N.A.I., Military Orphan Society Proceedings, 2 April 1818, pp. 141–3; 28 April 1818, pp. 143–4.

commonly removed from them unless the women could find another European guardian. By making and enforcing these policies about when and to whom money was disbursed, the orphan society effectively made clear that its efforts were focused toward sustaining putatively English notions of home, morality, and education in which native mothers were made marginal.

As a result of the policies of the Military Orphan Society, many women entered into a series of monogamous relationships with soldiers in one regiment in order to avail themselves of the orphan benefits their children received as long as the children remained in the care of the regiment in which they were born.[74] Rosters of children about to enter the orphan society recorded the name and the age of the child, the name, rank and corps of the father, race (recorded as "cast"), and where the mother resided, which was often with another soldier in the same regiment.[75] Concubinage in this context was supported by an extended network within the regiment: when a soldier died, his peers took in his children and his female companion. The regiment's commander then often took charge of securing an allowance for them through the local orphan committee. The presence of a multi-leveled bureaucracy to cope with the problem of destitute orphans of British soldiers speaks to the ways in which the lives of orphans' mothers remained tied to this bureaucracy, so that they circulated through the households of soldiers in a regiment in order to maintain their livelihoods and their ties to their children.[76]

---

[74] Serial monogamy was a standard feature of cantonment life; it was common for a woman to have children by other men and reside with a third man. As one army official noted in his correspondence to the orphan society, "No. 2 is a roll of two children born of a native woman by different fathers ... The mother was lately living with a Matross in the Pocket Troop, in which it appears the allowances for the children were paid ..." N.A.I., Military Orphan Society Proceedings, 23 June 1818, p. 210.

[75] See for instance, N.A.I., Military Orphan Society Proceedings, 23 June 1818, pp. 201–4.

[76] European mothers used a similar strategy when in India. As Trustram notes, *Women of the Regiment*, p. 92, "Many women, especially those widowed abroad, quickly married another soldier as the only means of survival." See Derek J. Oddy, "Gone for a Soldier: the anatomy of a nineteenth-century army family," *Journal of Family History* 25 (January 2000), p. 44, for the case of Jean McCulloch who was widowed in India in November, 1840, and left with three small children; she subsequently married again in February, 1841, and after being widowed for a second time in June, 1847, remarried three months later in September, 1847. See also Elizabeth Fenton, *A Narrative of her Life in India, the Isle of France and Tasmania during the years 1826–1830* (London: Edward Arnold, 1901). Mrs. Fenton traveled to India as the wife of Captain Neil Campbell in 1826; after he died, she married Captain Michael Fenton in 1828.

Comparable to the methods that women used to claim pensions under Clive's Fund, native women were again often aware of what they and their children were financially entitled to under the Company's provisions. Mrs. Mary Manuel, a native woman who had a child with an officer who had died wrote to the Military Department, ". . . I had a female child by the late Capt. John Peters of the Madras Establishment and that on Capt. Peters being killed [in a battle against Dowlut Rao Scindia] . . . my child was reduced to want and distress and I humbly solicit that some relief may be extended towards her maintenance in the event of the Honourable Governor General in Council deeming her *a fit subject* [emphasis added] . . ." She signed her name and wrote that she was currently under the protection of John Leonard, Private, H.M.'s 53rd Regiment stationed in Berhampore.[77] The matter was referred back to the commander at Berhampore who was asked to provide proof that the child was in fact Peters's daughter.

The commander, Major General William Palmer, perhaps sympathetic because of his own long-time relationship with a native woman, confirmed Mary Manuel's account. He also provided the results of his own investigation into the matter: Mary Manuel had cohabited with Capt. Peters for over 30 years and had five children with him, of which this was the only survivor. After his death, she had cohabited with Sergeant Moore who was in Peters's regiment. Moore had been transferred to Berhampore as a pensioner and had married a European woman on his arrival there at which point he discharged Mary Manuel and she went to live with John Leonard, a private in the regiment stationed at Berhampore.[78]

Mary Manuel's case illustrates how dependent women were made on their children, the army, the men they cohabited with, and indeed the regiment's commander for financial support. Even though the Company did not always provide pensions or allowances for the native domestic and sexual companions of its European soldiers, it did make financial provisions for soldiers' children. Thus, it was often by championing the cause of their children that native women received an allowance. In the end, the matter of Mary Manuel was referred to the Madras Military Department, because the father was of the Madras establishment and the child was entitled to benefits there. We hear no more of what transpired after that.

---

[77] N.A.I., Military Dept. Proceedings, 26 Feb. 1807, no. 99. Berhampore was a large military cantonment outside Calcutta.

[78] N.A.I., Military Dept. Proceedings, 26 March 1807, nos. 79–80.

In addition to providing financial support for orphans, the Military Orphan Society educated and apprenticed orphans in ways that affirmed the class and race positions of the children. In 1796, the Military Orphan Press was founded to train the boys in the printing trades. It was hoped that the profits of the press could be used to provide the girl orphans with marriage portions when they were betrothed. Although the press printed much of the government's materials, it rarely made a profit until it was taken over by the colonial government in 1863.[79] Aside from working at the press, male orphans were placed in apprenticeships and positions that correlated to the status of their fathers. Boys of the upper school often became cadets in the army or were sent as writers to further eastern Company outposts such as Bencoolen or Batavia. In spite of the 1791 prohibition to accept Eurasians into the Company's covenanted service, this did not preclude sending them further eastward. Mixed-race boys were assigned to stations outside of India, indicating that half-cast writers in India were seen as undermining the face of British rule in India but not in Indonesia and Malaysia.[80] Boys of the lower school were considered well suited to be drummers and fifers to sepoy regiments.[81] They were often sent off when they reached the age of 13 or 14; and then they were given a nominal allowance for their work.[82] Other boys were apprenticed to merchants and tradesmen at an early age with a goal toward finding suitable work and the orphan society paid these apprenticeship fees.

These experiments, however, were not uniformly productive and on several occasions proved harmful to the boys involved. In one instance in 1788, during the early days of the orphan schools, the management sent three boys from the Lower Orphan School on board various pilot vessels in order that they might learn to become seamen on the

---

[79] "The Bengal Military Orphan Society, part 2," *Calcutta Review* 48, 90 (1867): 296–316.

[80] N.A.I., Military Dept. Proceedings, 1 May 1806, nos. 60–1; 10 July 1806, nos. 71–4. Six boys were sent to Bencoolen to serve the company's interests. They were between 17 and 20 years old and were indentured to the company for five years. See also a letter from the management of the orphan society, offering boys who were old enough and sufficiently qualified to join the company's service. Military Dept. Proceedings, 15 Sept. 1807, no. 126.

[81] O.I.O.C., X/557, "A Code of the Pay Regulations of Various Military Establishments under the Presidency of Fort William," revised by Maj. William Sheppey Greene, Military Auditor General (Calcutta: Military Orphan Press, 1810), p. 210: cites a General Order dated 14 June 1798 that all fifers and drummers for sepoy regiments were to come from the Orphan Schools and they could not join until they were 13. I thank Peter Marshall for this reference. See also Chatterjee, "Colouring Subalternity," p. 89.

[82] N.A.I., Military Dept. Proceedings, 7 November 1808, no. 95.

Company's ships and become "faithful and grateful" servants to the Company. The school management hoped that the pilot service would become a "beneficial disposal for many of the objects of our trust." On this occasion, three boys who were sent on board Company vessels escaped because of the cruel treatment they received from the seamen on board. Two boys ran away and were never tracked down while the third returned to the orphan society. When he reappeared, he was almost naked, having had all of his clothes taken from him and was "in a starving condition." The boys' guardians had pocketed the monthly allowance that the orphan society gave to the pilot vessel on behalf of each boy.[83] These kinds of problems pervaded apprenticeships as well; from the records of the orphan society, it seems that the monthly allowance of S. Rs. 6 was often a magnet to unscrupulous employers and the boys were often left defenseless once they left the confines of the orphan school.[84]

After the 1791 general order excluding Eurasians from covenanted service in the Company establishment, the question of having boys from the Lower Orphan School serve on Company ships rarely came up.[85] Instead, most often, boys were sent to native regiments to serve as fifers and drummers and eventually became bandsmen. Between 1782 and 1820, 80 percent of the boys who were employed from the Lower Orphan School were sent to be fifers and drummers making the band become the most common form of employment for lower orphan school boys.[86] Although boys could be sent to be fifers and drummers when they were 13 or older, there were times when they were sent earlier as in the early 1800s when there was not enough housing at the Lower Orphan School; then they were sent at the age of nine. Fifers and drummers received a small stipend from the band. Most frequently, this sum was deposited with the orphan society or with the child's guardians for safekeeping. Occasionally, the money was used to support the boys' family, especially his mother, often native.

[83] N.A.I., Military Dept. Proceedings, 16 May 1788, no. 14.
[84] N.A.I., Military Dept. Proceedings, 17 November 1790: a case about twelve boys sent to Batavia to work for an English trader/shipper. The boys were detained by the Dutch authorities in Batavia because the goods that the boys were sent to sell were apparently stolen. In this case, the trader abandoned the boys, taking their money and left them in Batavia. Although an investigation was undertaken to discover what had transpired, the pilot service never became the outlet that the managers hoped.
[85] See Hawes, *Poor Relations*, pp. 61–4. This prohibition was a part of the Cornwallis Reforms which attempted to make the Company's activities in India more professional, less corrupt, and inured to outside influences, such as Eurasians who were kept from occupying positions of power or responsibility within the company structure.
[86] Lushington, *Religious, Benevolent and Charitable Institutions*, Appendix II, p. xlvii.

A case in point is contained in the series of letters exchanged between Hannah Mitchell, mother of James, a boy in the Lower Orphan School, and the orphan society. In April 1818, she wrote to the headmaster asking if her son, also the son of Quartermaster Sgt. Mitchell, deceased, could be sent to be a drummer to the Corps of Artillery at Dum Dum. She wrote that this would be "the means of alleviating my present unhappy situation as a widow as it will be in his [the boy's] to afford assistance to me in my declining years." In support of this request followed a letter from the commander of this corps asking that the boy be released for service.[87] A letter from the headmaster informed Mrs. Mitchell and the commander that the orphan society did not send boys until they were thirteen years old, and according to their records, this boy was only nine and a half. Mrs. Mitchell replied that the orphan society was mistaken: she provided notarized letters from the boy's godfather attesting that the boy had been born in 1806, thereby making him thirteen years old. By then, Mrs. Mitchell had married Lieutenant-General Rawston and the orphan society agreed to send the boy to Lieutenant-General Rawston's regiment as a fifer so that mother and son could reside within the same regiment. Although Mrs. Rawston had remarried and found a way out of her "unhappy situation," she was reunited with her son with some help from the regiment's commander and the military orphan society.

Girls from the school were trained primarily in domestic skills, such as sewing, embroidery, and knitting. In the initial plan for the lower orphan school, the managers proposed that girls could be trained to work in some of the Company's textile factories, such as at Pultah.[88] The plan was never adopted wholesale but the girls did make all the clothing, hats, and stockings for the children at all the orphan schools.[89] In this way, using the labor of some of the older female orphans, the orphan society procured clothing cheaply. The services of the orphan school females were also offered to the larger European public of Calcutta. As an advertisement placed in the *Calcutta Gazette* informed readers that female children, well trained in "Chicundoze" work, were available for work and that the profits would benefit the young women.[90]

Most important, however, the orphan society focused its efforts toward marrying the women off to European Company servants and soldiers. By providing men with skilled housewives, the Company did not have to import Englishwomen for the domestic comforts of its

[87] N.A.I., Military Orphan Society Proceedings, 3 April 1818, pp. 221 ff.
[88] N.A.I., Public Dept. Proceedings, 30 June 1783.
[89] N.A.I., Military Orphan Society Proceedings, 16 April 1818, p. 203.
[90] *Selections from the Calcutta Gazettes*, vol. VII, p. 429.

employees. For the female orphans of the Upper School, the school hosted balls where soldiers could meet the girls; in order that the girls carried themselves appropriately, a ballroom dancer was hired. The monthly balls provided an opportunity for soldiers to meet young women of marriageable age and an opportunity for the girls to meet men who were of an appropriate class and station. As one circular issued by the management of the orphan society stated, only gentlemen and "persons of respectability" would be admitted to the ball if they had an invitation or had received permission from the headmaster.[91]

The girls of the Lower Orphan School were the Cinderellas of the establishment. They did not attend balls but were contracted in marriage by the headmaster or headmistress. Once it was determined that a man was of good character and able to support a wife, the headmaster would allow him to come meet a female inmate of the orphan school. As Emma Roberts noted, "should the non-commissioned officers or privates of European regiments desire to take a wife out of this asylum, they are, if men of character, permitted to do so, but they must choose by the eye alone at a single interview."[92] The orphan society provided the Lower Orphan School girls with weddings and a sum of Rs. 500, known as marriage portions, when they married. Thus the scheme of arranging marriages ensured the financial support of female orphans after the orphan society's responsibilities were over. In support of this scheme, one commander noted, it was better for soldiers to be married rather than prone to the temptations of common prostitutes.[93]

An account of how many girls married from the orphan institution showed that the majority of girls from the Lower Orphan Schools had married men in the Company's service; the remainder married soldiers from the royal troops. The girls from the Upper Orphan School most often married officers, local merchants, or returned to England to marry there.[94] Through these marriages with soldiers, the girls of the orphan school stayed within the service family of the military and provided the

---

[91] *Ibid.*, pp. 440–1.

[92] Emma Roberts, *Scenes and Characters of Hindostan: with Sketches of Anglo-Indian Society*. London: Wm. H. Allen and Co., 1835, vol. I, pp. 108–9.

[93] N.A.I., Military Dept. Proceedings, 19 January 1819, no. 8, enclosure 2.

[94] N.A.I., Military Dept. Proceedings, 30 January 1819, nos. 283–7; O.I.O.C., P/28/48, nos. 283–7. Between 1800 and 1818, 274 girls were married to soldiers in the Company army, 65 were married to men of H.M.'s army and 41 were married to men of neither category. A sudden increase in the number of women married indicated that a number of women from the Orphan School were married *en masse* to soldiers in one regiment. This occurred, for instance, in 1810 and 1815, when 22 and 18 marriages respectively took place between H.M.'s Regiments stationed at Fort William.

domestic labor that was needed within military households. While the scheme had some advantages, it also had significant drawbacks.

By the 1830s, arranging marriages between European men and women of mixed-race was seen by the orphan society's directors to encourage the expansion of a mixed-race population and the practice of hosting balls was discontinued. Although there had been earlier criticisms of the practice, most notably from Lady Maria Nugent, the orphan society kept finding husbands for orphan girls.[95] From 1783 through the 1810s, marrying off half-caste orphan girls with European soldiers was seemingly uncomplicated by anxieties about promoting miscegenation. Instead, it was seen by military authorities as a way to maintain appropriate male guardianship over female orphans: arranging marriages were seen to provide a home for the women, and to secure domestic peace and order for its rank-and-file soldiers. But as British attitudes toward mixed-race persons became increasingly negative, the scheme of arranging marriages became less appealing to the military authorities.[96] By marrying off half-cast women to European soldiers, the orphan society was complicit in actively promoting interracial marriages, miscegenation, and the growth of a mixed-race or creole population that diluted the racial purity of the British community in India.[97] Officials voiced their concerns that supporting Eurasian wives, even if they had been raised in the orphan schools, had never been part of the expressed purpose of the military's activities in India.

The military orphan society's promotion of marriage for its female inmates were intended to reduce the Company's financial responsibilities to female orphans by finding husbands to support them. But the scheme unwittingly increased the financial demands put on the Company. In forwarding a petition submitted by the non-commissioned officers and privates of the Bengal Artillery who were married to Eurasian women, the orphan society and the military department supported the premise that Eurasian wives should receive the same

[95] See Lady Nugent, *A Journal from the year 1811 till the year 1815: a voyage to and residence in India, with a tour to the northwestern parts of the British possessions in that country under the Bengal government* (London, 1839), vol. I, p. 119; vol. II, pp. 264–5, 277.

[96] See Roberts, *Scenes and Characters*, vol. I, p. 43: "The prejudices against 'dark beauties' ... are daily gaining ground." See also Lady Nugent, *Journal*, vol. I, p. 122; Valentia, p. 241; The career of James Skinner, a Eurasian who commanded an irregular cavalry regiment in northern India, follow a similar trajectory. See Seema Alavi, "The Eurasian 'Other' in the British Empire: the case of James Skinner (1802–1840)" unpublished ms. This transition has also been marked by Ballhatchet and Hawes.

[97] Roberts, *Scenes and Characters*, vol. I, p. 42.

allowance as European wives. Although a certain amount of pay and allowance was given to each married soldier, additional income was guaranteed to men who were married to women born of European parents on both sides. From 1781 onwards, European wives were granted an allowance of Rs. 8 per month; children, whether legitimate or not, were granted an allowance of Rs. 3 per month.[98] In a resolution dated March, 1810, the council had decided against continuing any allowance to women who were not descended from Europeans on both sides.[99]

In spite of the prohibition against giving the allowance to women who were not of European parentage, in 1814, "free Black" wives of H.M.'s troops from the West Indies were granted an allowance, with the reasoning that the government ought to look after subjects who, although not European, were "British subjects" nonetheless, rewarding them for marrying within their own racial and ethnic group. In appealing to the Military Department on behalf of these women, the commanding officer of the regiment made up of black soldiers from the West Indies referred to the dangers of Anglo-Indian sex and miscegenation and noted "the [original] order in its spirit probably was meant to prevent an encouragement to Europeans for marrying women, natives of the East Indies, but his lordship does not think it could have intended to affect in its operation the few West Indian blacks attached to His Majesty's Regiments ..."[100] At the center of this commanding officer's appeal was a reminder that avoiding conjugal liaisons between soldiers and native women of India was justified, but providing for "black" soldiers who had married black women was part of H.M.'s responsibility.

At issue in the 1819 petition from soldiers with mixed-race wives, was the provision that European wives of soldiers were given an allowance while Eurasian wives were not. This petition spoke on behalf of all Eurasian female orphans and argued that the allowance be extended to all Eurasian wives because these women had been born and raised under the Company's protection. In the process of summarizing the soldiers'

[98] O.I.O.C., X/557. Initially ordered by Minutes to the Court of Directors in 1783 and 1784, these allowances were later confirmed by General Orders in 1795 and 1799.
[99] O.I.O.C., F/4/485, no. 11644; Extract Military Letter from Bengal, dated 23 Dec. 1814; Cons. 19 Nov., nos. 19 and 20; Cons. 23 Dec., nos. 71 and 72.
[100] O.I.O.C., F/4/485, no. 11644.

case, the commander-in-chief argued that

> They [the girls] have for the greater part, it may be fairly said, been born in the service, supported in infancy, educated in adolescence and are now in puberty, married by the instructions of Government to Persons in the service of His Majesty ... hence that Government which has deemed the service rendered to the state by the father, sufficient to entitle his daughter to its support in early life is in a certain degree morally bound not to withdraw its assistance and leave her to penury or vice at a mature age.[101]

Furthermore, the commander reasoned that since the girls were "induced to accept an offer of marriage, the disadvantages of which, she could not calculate, and to which, indeed her consent was scarcely desired ..." the government was obliged to provide a stipend for them.[102] This commander's petition appealed to the responsibilities that government had to these young women, who had been raised under the watchful eyes of the orphan society.

In the process of providing reasons for these claims, the commander maintained that the wives chosen from the orphan schools were a steadying influence on wayward soldiers and as such ought to be rewarded. He argued that any commanding officer would "prefer these connections to a system of concubinage, or still more to a promiscuous and hazardous intercourse with the profligate women of the bazar ..."[103] The letter concluded by appealing to the liberal ideas of the government in providing a "respectable" subsistence for soldiers and wives under its employ.[104]

Several years later an allowance was approved for Eurasian wives of Company and of royal troops. In a general order that applied to the Bengal, Bombay, and Madras presidencies, the military department agreed to pay an allowance of Rs. 4 per month to Eurasian wives compared to Rs. 5 per month that was already paid to European wives.[105] The indexing of allowances to racial status suggests that not all wives were equal. One local official resorted to a somatic explanation and noted that half-caste wives were often more reliable and helpful to soldiers than were European women because their bodies were acclimatized to the weather and living conditions of India.[106]

---

[101] N.A.I., Military Dept. Proceedings, 19 January 1819, no. 7.
[102] *Ibid.*
[103] *Ibid.*
[104] *Ibid.*
[105] O.I.O.C., F/4/787, no. 21363; F/4/1240, no. 40737. Extract Ben. Military Letter dated 31 March 1825, nos. 54–5.
[106] O.I.O.C., F/4/1454, no. 57236, see copy of a Minute by H. S. Grome, dated 10 November 1824.

Although there were concerns that such a policy would increase the mixed-race population and further add to the burdens of the Company, most officials made a priority of their paternal responsibilities toward the female orphans married into the Company's army and agreed that allowing soldiers' families to be destitute was a far greater threat to British authority.[107] Amid a period in which mixed-race subjects, known at the time as East Indians or Eurasians were refused recognition from Parliament as British subjects, this allowance for Eurasian wives appears contradictory. Yet granting allowances and pensions to the mixed-race wives of European soldiers confirmed the Company's financial obligations to women who were identified as members of the families of British men and subjects of the British empire.[108]

These policy decisions by officials in London privileged the paternal responsibilities that the Company and its servants held so dear over racial identities of the women and children involved. In this one way, familial identities seemed to override questions of race, although this was never consistently the case.

IV

Maintaining familial ties, particularly the obligations and rights men had over their families, was a central tenet of military decisions at the local level, particularly in cases of destitution or poverty that arose in the course of military activities. The complicated issue of women camp followers came up in several decisions over soldiers' families in which the rights of native women fell into a web of political choices about fiscal restraint, appropriate rulership and defining English-ness. In a dispute involving military authorities in India and officials in England, royal troops and their families became a financial liability for the resources of the East India Company when a regiment was posted back to Europe and was required to leave behind the native women and children who were their families. As this dispute unfolded, it became clear that commanding officers often made ad hoc arrangements for native women and children left behind that challenged the interests of the Crown and the Company.

The case of H.M.'s 66th and 78th foot regiments shows the challenges presented by the familial bonds that tied European soldiers, native women, and their children. H.M.'s 66th and 78th were

---

[107] O.I.O.C., F/4/787, no. 21363, Minute by T. Munro, dated November 1824.
[108] See O.I.O.C. F/4/1564, no. 64132, and F/4/1551, no. 62218 for a similar result involving the military funds of Bombay and Madras presidencies.

stationed in Ceylon; while there, the soldiers in these regiments took up with local women and had children. When the regiments were posted to Bengal, the commanders allowed the women and children to accompany them to Fort William in Calcutta. H.M.'s 66th traveled with 55 unmarried women and 51 children, including 2 orphans. The 78th had slightly fewer with 38 women and 43 children. When these two regiments were sent back to England, the women and children were left with no means of support.

Most of the women and their children were sent back to their homes in Ceylon, while others formed attachments with soldiers from regiments that were posted locally. Sixteen "half-cast" children and their [nine] native mothers moved in with soldiers of H.M.'s 59th regiment, which was then stationed at Fort William. For the women involved, being exchanged to a new regiment was presumably a way to continue their support for their children.[109] According to a list made in November, 1817, four of the children's fathers were dead while the remaining had been transferred to St. Helena or to Europe. The 59th regiment wrote to the Military Orphan Society asking to enroll three of its own orphans (whose mothers and fathers were both dead) in the Lower Orphan School as well as the sixteen children they had temporarily adopted from H.M.'s 66th and 78th regiments.[110] Because the Military Orphan Society had a policy of admitting children over the age of four, nine of the nineteen orphans were kept with the 59th until they became old enough to start school.[111] Guardians of children under the age of four were eligible to receive a stipend of Rs. 3 per month for their care but these stipends were only disbursed through regiments to soldiers, so nine native women formed domestic attachments to soldiers within the 59th in order to continue receiving support for their infant children while being allowed to stay with them.

Although these were the families of royal troops and thus not a responsibility of the Company, the East India Company's military authorities made arrangements for these families and then applied to the crown for reimbursement. In the Company's correspondence on the matter, one official hoped that the crown could outline what

---

[109] O.I.O.C., L/MIL/5/376/7, Extract Bengal Military Cons., 3 February 1818, nos. 154–5, 24 Nov. 1817. The oldest child was nine years old, while the youngest was eighteen months.

[110] O.I.O.C., P/28/25, Bengal Military Cons., 3 February, 1818, Cons. 154–6; P/28/28, Bengal Military Cons., 31 March, 1818, Cons. 87; NAI, Military Orphan Society Proceedings, April to Dec. 1818 (incomplete), s. 50, vol. 62, pp. 201–4.

[111] N.A.I., Military Dept. Proceedings, 31 March 1818, nos. 87–9.

ought to be done in future cases in which women and children were left behind when European troops returned to Europe.

> I have the honor to request that you will submit ... [an] opinion as to the mode in which [you] would wish the Orphan European children now maintained & educated by the Government of Bengal to be disposed of and also on the general subject regarding the provision to be made for the maintenance of the orphans of European Soldiers of H.M.'s Regiments by European or native mothers who on the death of their parents or the return of the Regiments to Europe may be left in India destitute of every source of comfort.[112]

The crown's response, while appreciative of the Company's efforts, was to argue that they should not be held accountable for the cost. The crown's official wrote, "the local government appear to have acted with extreme humanity in making arrangements for their return to their relations and connections in Ceylon, rather than they should be left to starve or obtain a livelihood in vice in Bengal."[113] However, the crown argued that this was an expense that benefited the local police in Calcutta because it prevented vagrancy and it should be paid from the Company's purse. Moreover, because the practice of cohabitation and miscegenation was borne of local customs, the crown ought not to have to pay for the outcome. The words they used were:

> it appears to His Royal Highness that the embarrassment attending the provision and maintenance of Orphans of Soldiers by Native Women or other Children of the same description left in India upon the departure of a Regiment for Europe grow out of the local habits incidental to the Country and the expense could not in any case be recognized, or provided for, under the disbursements of His Majesty's Army.

They reiterated their position that only children born of European parents on both sides would be allowed to return to England to be educated at the Military Asylum in Chelsea, thereby containing the threat of miscegenation by ensuring that mixed-race children never came to England, but remained in India. Although neither set of officials were keen to financially support the families of European troops, the crown's officials treated the matter as an exceptional case. From their perspective, native women, because they were native and not married, had no standing to receive financial benefits from the Crown. In contrast, the Company's officials, equally reluctant to support native women and their mixed-race children, acknowledged that it was such

---

[112] O.I.O.C., L/MIL/5/376/7, Joseph Dart to Thomas Courtenay, 26 August 1819; this sentiment was echoed by the Managers of the Orphan Society, see N.A.I., Military Dept. Proceedings, 17 February 1818, no. 115.

[113] *Ibid.*, Sir Henry Torrens to Joseph Dart, 18 September 1820.

a common problem that a policy was needed to deal with the abandoned families of royal troops. A year later, without fanfare, three of the children in H.M.'s 59th Regiment were enrolled in the Bengal Military Orphan Society; the three boys were aged 5, 7 and 8; two of their mothers resided with soldiers in the regiment while one mother had died.[114]

Conclusion

Disagreement between the crown and the Company was a constant feature of debates about who would pay for the families of soldiers, but at the root of these debates remained the question of who could be counted as "family" in a context in which cohabitation and out-of-wedlock birth was a common practice. In the process of deciding who belonged to the family and who did not, officials in Britain and in India expressed their anxieties about financially supporting mixed-race families who were seen to mar the image of a racially pure and white society that was at the center of colonial authority. Yet, as some officials made clear, without the means of supporting their putative families, Company soldiers and officials would be unable to claim and maintain their paternal privileges as heads of households. In the absence of external financial support, the soldier's authority over his family was eroded. More important, some Company and military officials felt that this loss of paternal authority might damage the political authority of the Company. Maintaining the collective ability of men within the military and the Company's bureaucracies to sustain the livelihood of military families was at some moments judged to be more critical than the question of racial exclusion.

The practices and policies of Lord Clive's Pension Fund and the Bengal Military Orphan Society created an infrastructure tied to the East India Company for providing financial benefits and material protection to family members of soldiers who were in the Company's army. While officials in India knew that families of Company soldiers were often of mixed race, they were hard pressed to argue why Company officials in Britain should approve financial support for families who were considered less British than those of European lineage on both sides. Although both parties were in agreement that the Company had a social and paternal obligation to the families of soldiers, disagreement about what a "family" constituted pitted the father's patriarchal responsibilities against racial anxieties about interracial sex

---

[114] N.A.I., Bengal Military Dept. Proc., 6 March 1819, nos. 135–6.

and miscegenation. Native and mixed-race women capitalized on this tension. By challenging unofficial conceptions of who should receive benefits from Lord Clive's Pension Fund and by taking advantage of the official policy requirements for eligibility, native women brought about policy changes that resulted in their temporarily gaining pensions, allowances, and benefits for their children. By attaching themselves to successive soldiers within the regiment in which their children were born, native women were able to continue to live with their children, thus temporarily subverting the military's aims of removing orphans from their mothers. For the native women who applied for various types of benefits, they relied on their rights as members of military families and unintentionally consolidated the paternal structures from which these institutions had been founded.

The idea that interracial conjugal relationships were structured by various financial considerations was well acknowledged both by native women who supplied domestic and sexual labor and by rank-and-file soldiers to whom they became attached. From the perspective of military officials who knew how reliant they were on the local services provided by native women and their families and on constructing and maintaining an image of British benevolence and charity toward those sired by British men, fulfilling the financial obligations of family was central to how they understood the terms on which familial relationships of service were based. But exclusions based on race were rarely clearly articulated and native women were able to exploit some of the vagueness in the Company's policies to gain provisions. Unwittingly, native women's requests pushed the Company into making its racial exclusions more plain. In doing so, the East India Company's strategies for making loyal subjects and productive families were laid bare.

Conclusion

The most famous story of interracial intimacy on the Indian sub-continent between a European man and a local woman was that of Job Charnock, founder of Calcutta and his unnamed female companion. Job Charnock was reputed to have rescued a *sati* from the funeral pyre, brought her home and lived with her as his wife. In the years before his death in 1693, they reportedly lived very happily and produced three children. His eldest daughter married Charles Eyre, who became Charnock's successor as the Governor of Bengal and head agent of the English East India Company and its commercial affairs in Bengal.

Alexander Hamilton, a free-trader of the early eighteenth century, described how Charnock came to the rescue:

[he] went one Time ... to see a young widow act that tragical catastrophe, but he was so smitten with the widow's beauty, that he sent his Guards to take her by force from the Executioners, and conducted her to his own lodgings. They lived lovingly many years, and had several children, at length she died, after he had settled in Calcutta, but instead of converting her to Christianity, she made him a Proselyte to Paganism, and the only Part of Christianity that was remarkable in him, was burying her decently, and he built a Tomb over her, where all his Life after her Death, he kept the anniversary Day of her Death by sacrificing a Cock on her Tomb, after the Pagan manner ..."[1]

As the origin narrative of the founding of Calcutta, the Job Charnock story suggests that British overseas commerce and territorial expansion was linked with the rescue of local women and interracial intimacy.[2]

---

[1] Alexander Hamilton, *A New Account of the East Indies*, 2 vols. (Edinburgh, 1727), ii, pp. 8–9, cited in Kate Teltscher, *India Inscribed: European and British Writing on India, 1600–1800* (Delhi: Oxford University Press, 1995), p. 67.

[2] The Charnock tomb, which is in the burial yard of St. John's Church, stands as a reminder of Calcutta's hybrid origins. See N. R. Ray, *The City of Job Charnock* (Calcutta: Victoria Memorial Library, 1979), pp. 3–8; "Exhibition on the occasion of Calcutta's Tercentenary," Victoria Memorial; J. P. Losty, *Calcutta: City of Palaces, a Survey of the City in the Days of the East India Company, 1690–1858* (London: British Library, 1990).

The narrative foreshadowed a nineteenth-century historical narrative which constructed colonial officials as heroes, rescuing Indian women from committing sati, forced marriages, and other distasteful local customs.[3] This narrative pitted a British, humanitarian, benevolent masculinity against a barbaric, despotic one. Although Charnock could have persuaded his companion to convert to Christianity, Charnock was converted to "Paganism," losing himself to the charms of his companion and her heathenism. Hamilton's narrative explained very plainly the dangers of "going native" while in the service of the imperial nation.

Similar origin narratives about other colonial contexts suggest that interracial sexual intimacy between colonizers and colonized has been a standard trope in creating historical narratives and constructing national identities. In a range of historical and literary work, interracial relationships have stood for the contests and negotiations between different cultures.[4] In the Americas, Pocahontas and her relationship with John Rolfe has received much attention, including a Disney animated film.[5] Similarly, the romance between Cortes and La Malinche, his Aztec native informant/lover has become constitutive of Mexican and, to some extent Chicano, identity.[6] The ongoing controversy over Thomas Jefferson and his relationship with his slave, Sally Hemings, has provoked questions about who has been considered rightfully descendant of a Founding Father of America.[7] As Gary Nash has persuasively argued, the erasure of hybrid origins has been central to

---

[3] Lata Mani, *Contentious Traditions: The Debate on Sati in Colonial India* (Berkeley: University of California Press, 1998); Gayatri Spivak, "Can the subaltern speak?" in Cary Nelson and Lawrence Grossberg, eds., *Marxism and the Interpretation of Culture* (Urbana: University of Illinois Press, 1988); Jyotsna Singh, *Colonial Narratives/Cultural Dialogues: Discoveries of India in the Language of Colonialism* (London: Routledge, 1996), ch. 3.

[4] See Werner Sollors, *Neither Black nor White Yet Both: Thematic Explorations of Interracial Literature* (New York: Oxford University Press, 1997); Peter Hulme, *Colonial Encounters: Europe and the Native Caribbean, 1492–1797* (London: Routledge, 1986), see especially chs. 4 and 6; Mary Louise Pratt, *Imperial Eyes*, pp. 78–85.

[5] Robert S. Tilton, *Pocahontas: The Evolution of an American Narrative* (Cambridge: Cambridge University Press, 1994); J. A. Leo Lemay, *Did Pocahontas Save Captain John Smith?* (Athens, GA: University of Georgia Press, 1992).

[6] Doris Sommer, *Foundational Fictions: the National Romances of Latin America* (Berkeley: University of California Press, 1991); Jean Franco, *Plotting Women: Gender and Representation in Mexico* (New York: Columbia University Press, 1989); Mary Louise Pratt, "'Yo soy la Malinche': Chicana writers and the poetics of ethnonationalism," *Callaloo* 16 (Fall 1993): 859–74; Sandra Messenger Cypess, *La Malinche in Mexican Literature: from History to Myth* (Austin: University of Texas Press, 1992).

[7] Jan E. Lewis and Peter Onuf, eds., *Sally Hemings and Thomas Jefferson: History, Memory and Civic Culture* (Charlottesville, VA: University of Virginia Press, 1999).

supporting the notion that Americans are descended from the pilgrims who came on the *Mayflower*.[8] Historical narratives of colonial contact in various colonies have produced distinct legacies for national identities in the colonial and post-colonial eras. These narratives and the questions they raise about hybridity – broadly defined by race, ethnicity, and lineage – amplify the multiple complications in locating racially diverse, multicultural communities within post-colonial national identities.

Colonial interracial conjugality and the ways in which it fits abstractly and specifically in the histories of colonial contact is a subject that is understudied in historical studies, given how central these relationships were to producing anxieties about hybridity and challenging notions of a "pure" racial and cultural national identity. In the historiography of British India, scholarly studies have ignored colonial companions because they are not easily situated either as a part of British imperial history nor as part of Indian history. Marginal to the territorial and commercial interests of the East India Company and the nascent colonial state, native women were often considered outside what some scholars have called the "limited Raj," characterizing the Company's superficial and largely ineffective governance of the Indian subcontinent, particularly before 1858.[9] Neither British nor Indian, colonial companions were often subjects in discourses and debates that enabled British political intervention in domestic and household affairs, particularly as the East India Company turned from a commercial body into a bureaucratic one charged with ruling ever larger parts of the India subcontinent. Although colonial social reform of native women focused on spectacular incidents, such as committing sati, or abduction into slavery or child marriage, this book has shown the ways in which the everyday lives of native women became the grounds on which political and historical debates were worked out, particularly within colonial discourses of establishing racial, cultural, and gender superiority.

In British imperial historiographies, native women were the sexual partners of Englishmen who preceded the more respectable middle-class Englishwomen. Serving as the "subaltern shadow" of the Englishwoman, households with native women were rarely respectable enough to pass muster among colonial communities.[10] Upwardly

---

[8] Gary B. Nash, "The hidden history of Mestizo America," *Journal of American History* 82 (Dec. 1995): 941–64.

[9] Anand Yang, *The Limited Raj: Agrarian Relations in Colonial India, Saran District, 1793–1920* (Berkeley: University of California Press, 1989).

[10] The term "subaltern shadow" is paraphrased from Jenny Sharpe, *Allegories of Empire* (Minneapolis: University of Minnesota, 1994), p. 12.

mobile, socially conscious European men tried to mitigate the circumstances of their conjugal relationships by sending their children abroad to improve upon their mixed-race status. Empire was, thus, constantly in the process of being "made respectable." While colonial bureaucracies instituted various policies that resulted in gender hierarchies and racial exclusions, within their households and families, British men governed themselves in ways that converged with the aims of colonial governance. From as early as the 1770s, the managers of the Military Orphan Society agreed that removing mixed-race children from the homes of their native mothers and maintaining British cultural practices was necessary toward resocializing children and erasing the putatively negative effects of an indigenous upbringing. Even when the numbers of men acknowledging interracial relationships and illegitimate children declined in the early 1800s, the number of mixed-race children born grew every year paralleling an increase in colonial companions leaving wills, suggesting that interracial sex did not fade away, but that it was recorded with less frequency in colonial archives.

While cohabiting with a local woman and Anglicizing mixed-race children was sometimes seen as beneficial to the nascent colonial state of the East India Company, these practices met with little resistance from native elites, probably because these relationships involved women of the lower social and caste orders. In South Asian history, the absence of colonial companions has sustained the image of a pure indigenous culture uncorrupted by miscegenation or interracial sex. As I mentioned at the outset, vernacular sources for this period are scarce; indeed, many of the recent feminist histories produced of this period have relied almost exclusively on British sources and have read the documents critically and carefully in order to extract histories of women and gender that would be otherwise obscured.[11] Nonetheless, while there are many studies that address the ways in which British colonial rule destroyed indigenous state forms and local economies, and disrupted local social relations, there has been no comparable work examining how colonial households affected the economy of indigenous families attached in intimate ways to Europeans.

Although the period under consideration preceded the growth of a fully-fledged nationalist movement in India by several generations,

---

[11] Indrani Chatterjee, "Testing the local against the colonial archive," *History Workshop Journal* 44 (1997): 215; Mani (1998), see esp. pp. 60, 66 and fn. 44–6; Indrani Chatterjee, *Gender, Slavery and the Law in Colonial India* (Delhi: Oxford University Press, 1999); Radhika Singha, *A Despotism of Law* (Delhi: Oxford University Press, 1996).

by overlooking the place of colonial companions and interracial sex between local women and Englishmen, Indian nationalists have unwittingly accomplished what Benedict Anderson (following Ernest Renan) argues is crucial to imagining a nation: selectively remembering and forgetting a collective past.[12] Nationalism in India, forged in the context of anti-colonial resistance, required a hermetically sealed domestic "spiritual" space from which colonizers were kept out.[13] As Uma Chakravarti has noted, "Vast sections of women did not exist for the nineteenth century nationalists ... Recognizing her [the Vedic dasi's] existence would have been an embarrassment to the nationalists. The twentieth century has continued to reproduce, in all essentials, the same kind of womanhood that the nineteenth century has so carefully, and so successfully, constructed as an enduring legacy for us."[14]

Even the advent of the Subaltern Studies collective and its efforts toward recuperating histories of non-elite and marginal historical actors has not fully explored the historical subjectivity of lower-status indigenous women.[15] Indeed, by some account, by forgetting the interracial component of the colonial past, the domestic space of the nationalist imagination is left undisturbed by colonialism and the specter of interracial sexual activity.[16] To follow Ann Stoler's argument, "If this [the family] was one of the principal discursive sites where

---

[12] Benedict Anderson, *Imagined Communities* (London: Verso, 1983), ch. 11.

[13] Partha Chatterjee, *The Nation and Its Fragments* (Princeton: Princeton University Press, 1993).

[14] Uma Chakravarti, "What happened to the Vedi *Dasi*? Orientalism, nationalism and a script for the past," in Kumkum Sangari and Sudesh Vaid, eds., *Recasting Women: Essays in Indian Colonial History* (Delhi: Kali for women, 1988), p. 28.

[15] The Subaltern Studies Collective has been criticized several times for its tendency to ignore the question of women. See Gayatri Spivak, "Deconstructing historiography," in Ranajit Guha and Spivak, eds., *Selected Subaltern Studies* (Delhi: Oxford University Press, 1988); Kamala Visweswaran, "Small Speeches, Subaltern Gender: nationalist ideology and its historiography," *Subaltern Studies IX* (Delhi: Oxford University Press, 1996); Julie Stephens, "Feminist Fictions: a critique of the category 'non-western woman' in feminist writings on India," *Subaltern Studies VI* (Delhi: Oxford University Press, 1989). Recent volumes have shown that this is changing: see Indrani Chatterjee, "Colouring Subalternity: slaves, concubines and social orphans in early colonial India," *Subaltern Studies X* (Delhi: Oxford University Press, 1999); and *Subaltern Studies XI*, edited by Partha Chatterjee and Pradeep Jeganathan, which is subtitled, "Community, gender, and violence" (New York: Columbia University Press, 2000).

[16] See Dipesh Chakrabarty, "The Difference-Deferral of a Colonial Modernity: public debates on domesticity in British India," *Subaltern Studies VIII* (Delhi: Oxford University Press, 1994). For an example of how a feminist scholar views British practices of domestic household slavery during this period, see Chatterjee, "Colouring subalternity."

bourgeois culture defined and defended its interests, in colonial perspective it was also one of the key sites in which racial transgressions were evident and national identities formed."[17] Colonial British and subsequent imaginings of Indian domestic spaces, marginalizing the female transgressor, figured in the body of the indigenous mother, sustained colonialist and nationalist fictions that the family, central to national identity, remained unsullied under colonial contact.

This book, with its close attention to the dynamics and nuances of interracial conjugal intimacy in the early colonial period, complicates the development of the fiction of "respectable" domesticity so central to British colonial authority and later, in a different way, to the Indian nationalist imagination. By bringing indigenous women back into the story, this study has argued that the "problem" of interracial sex was a constant source of anxiety and focus of social and racial regulation, largely because its existence seemed to be ever present.

By gaining a fuller grasp on the experiences that constituted the subjectivities of local women who became the conjugal partners of European men, this book has argued that the existence of a marginal group of native female subalterns contributed to the formation of early colonial institutions of governance. For many native women, having an interracial relationship had severe social consequences. Many experienced social death by having their names changed and were cast out of their religious and caste communities, as witnesses in trials about sexual violence testified. Becoming itinerant sex workers, many women followed military regiments and men across the Indian subcontinent, hoping to find a way to support themselves and their families, becoming tied to the Company's bureaucracies in various ways.

Native women were often the silent, unnamed other that enabled the elaboration of various types of hierarchies and social anxieties, based on race, class, and gender. By bringing native women into the political authority of courts, pension funds, schools and other colonial institutions, the emerging colonial state was able to show its power by acting to protect female subjects on the margins of colonial society while defending the paternal rights of European men to have sexual and legal authority over these women. In the process, the agency and subjectivity of native women was overridden, but only partially so. As the examples of Begum Samru, Helen Bennett, and other elite women show, women's subjectivity was not completely foreclosed, giving rise to a range of

---

[17] Ann Stoler, *Race and the Education of Desire* (Durham: Duke University Press, 1995), p. 137.

multiple forms of identification and familial and social affiliations. While Begum Samru was able to negotiate modes of self-fashioning and self-representation in multiple ways to political advantage, Helen Bennett had relatively fewer options, particularly when it came to her children. Judicial scrutiny of Peggy's crime, the murder of a slave by scalding her with hot oil, is very suggestive for demonstrating how female subjectivity and agency was viewed by the early colonial courts: the judges held a pregnant Peggy accountable for the crime and attempted to facilitate a fair and just sentence by finding a jury of her peers. The existence of these women in colonial archives demonstrates the ways in which they were made into and made themselves into subjects of the early colonial state.

The question of historical agency, variously construed, although seemingly out of reach of many colonial companions, was also not completely absent in this period. As we saw from the various women and groups of native women who claimed pensions from Clive's Pension Fund, the conjugal partners of European men often had a keen awareness of the financial benefits of being partnered with a European and developed expectations of the nascent colonial state. Punna Purree Pearse, companion to Thomas Deane Pearse, knew to write to her consort's old friend, Warren Hastings when her stipend was stopped by the executor to Pearse's estate. Eurasian women who had entered into marriages arranged by the Military Orphan Society were successfully able to assert their claims for an allowance using the guidelines of the Company's regulations. These strategic and tactical moments of agency suggest that local women – in spite of their absence from traditional histories – had a sense of their position, the claims they could make, and to whom they should direct their appeal.

As I have noted throughout, we need to be more critical in our dealings with historical documents that deny that local women existed; we also need to expand our range of methodologies in reading texts and representations that deal with historical subjects who were unnamed, partially named, and renamed. Although the large majority of colonial companions were nameless and/or renamed, careful reading allows us to elaborate methodologies for the subaltern to be heard and understood.

By examining how naming coded the identities of women, this study has exposed the ways in which a standard form of reading historical documents – reading for names – is a problematic strategy in finding colonial companions. In the absence of sources with women's names, this book has pieced together fragments to make a fuller account of this early period of Anglo-Indian colonial contact, particularly in locating indigenous women within this historiography. Nonetheless, we should acknowledge that this is still a partial story: native women's voices are still very difficult to decipher in the archives of this period. While this study has relied on many moments in the lives of women as they struggled for pensions, appealed for financial restitution, appeared in court, or, in the case of Begum Samru, negotiated for imperial protection, there are few complete life stories that give a sense of how these women might have seen themselves before and after they entered the surveillance of colonial archives.[18]

One of the most important instruments of colonial political authority was the archive. By reading archival documents along and against the grain, we can learn much about the social priorities of the emerging colonial state, particularly in how it hierarchized the diverse populations it ruled by gender, race, and class. And yet, we need to pay attention to the ways in which the archive serviced the imperatives of the government by erasing or excluding various subjects. That so many men had native mistresses, out-of-wedlock children, and multiple families out of the public eye of the archive suggests the ways in which the archives are both incomplete and inadequate as sources for reconstructing a history of the family. As we know, European men and Indian women carried on producing mixed-race children until well into the twentieth century, well after the Cornwallis codes of the 1790s explicitly prohibited these liaisons and yet the archival evidence of these relationships declined. This suggests not that the number of interracial relationships declined, but that men and women were careful to suppress any archival traces of these relationships in their letters, wills, diaries, and other written accounts as time went on.

By bringing British imperial history and South Asian history into the same analytical field, I have tried to unsettle the distinctions between colonizer/colonized, British/Indian, and metropole/colony that are often reaffirmed by treating these historiographies as separate. This strategy has enabled several conclusions, particularly in specifying the continuities and fractures between the development of modern families and colonial families and its concomitant relationship to the emergence of the colonial state.

The empire was, in many ways, the family writ large: made up of multiple racial and religious identities, colonial households were highly gendered, mapping the racial and sexual politics of the nascent imperial state. The families discussed in the study demonstrate the wide range

---

[18] See Carolyn Steedman, *Dust: The Archive and Cultural History* (New Brunswick, NJ: Rutgers University Press, 2002), ch. 7.

of positions that one family could occupy; indeed, several examples suggest that members of the family situated themselves in distinct but overlapping cultural milieus. Within the politics of late eighteenth-century India, sentimental patriarchs such as James Kirkpatrick and William Palmer, both political agents of the East India Company, benefited by cohabiting with local noblewomen who were well-connected in the local princely courts. These eighteenth-century men of sentiment were different from their nineteenth-century successors in empire in that they were not aware of scientific racism, or arguments about the benefits of upholding racial purity. Nonetheless, the anxiety they both expressed for the fate of their mixed-race children suggests that "going native" was not nearly as straightforward a cultural conversion as it might have seemed. Their personal and private dilemmas reveal the ways in which anxieties about race, comportment, and social status structured their decisions to send their children to England to be re-educated, resocialized, and Anglicized. In these cases, empire allowed men to send their children abroad was a way of "fixing" the problem of miscegenation and undoing the effects of living in an indigenous household. In the process of re-education, the mothers of these children, Khair-un-nissa and Bibi Faiz Baksh, respectively, were dispossessed and separated from their children while living predominantly native lives, continuing to pray as they had before.

By bringing together the ways in which overlapping discourses about family, politics, race, religion, and sexuality buttressed British moral and political authority in India, this book provides a partial explanation for how bourgeois bodies and modern selves, both Indian and European, were fashioned in the late eighteenth and nineteenth centuries. In writing their wills, British men relied on similar strategies to keep women from inheriting the family estate in Britain and in India, upholding a gender order that worked across national lines as a sign of the modern family. Rather than view discourses of modernity emanating entirely from Europe, several scholars have urged us to rethink how "Europe" and the "third-world" are constitutive parts of each other.[19] The domestic space and the family was a crucial terrain in which bodily discipline was elaborated, and this process was felt in British and in Indian households. As recent scholars have shown, middle-class Bengali households often had concerns similar

---

[19] Dipesh Chakrabarty, *Provincializing Europe* (Princeton: Princeton University Press, 2000).

to the British in terms of cleanliness, household order, and bodily regulation.[20]

Finally, the question of the family was intricately connected with the question of the nation-state in terms of establishing rights and citizenship. There has been much scholarship on the question of racial identity and national citizenship, particularly in terms of how modern European nation-states negotiated these questions when they involved colonial families with metis children born in the colonies.[21] Within the context of British India in the late eighteenth century, the question of who belonged to which family and by extension, to which nation, was at the heart of debates of who could be counted as British. Judicial disputes about jurisdiction and the discussions over financial provisions for native widows and mixed-race orphans emphasize the political and material stakes involved for natives as well as for the colonizing populations; moreover, these questions engage directly with which men – Indian or British – were best positioned to speak for and protect the legal subjectivities of native women. The way in which the Eurasian community in India campaigned actively to be considered British subjects in the 1830s, but were denied this right, suggests how crucial the question of family lineages was to establishing national identity and rights attending to that identity.[22] These eighteenth-century debates raised important questions about the nature of rights and who would defend them within colonial states, questions that were further expanded in the nineteenth century.

For the British, the increasing awareness that interracial sexual relationships were problematic worked in tandem with anxieties that these relationships reflected poorly on imperial authority and by extension on the national image. For middle-class Indians, the creation of a modern family – with an educated and spiritually minded mother

---

[20] Chakrabarty, "The difference-deferral of modernity"; Chatterjee, *The Nation and its Fragments*; Kaviraj, *The Unhappy Unconscious*.

[21] See Ann Stoler, "Sexual Affronts and Racial Frontiers: European identities and the cultural politics of exclusion in colonial southeast Asia," and Lora Wildenthal, "Race, gender and citizenship in the German colonial empire," in Ann Stoler and Frederick Cooper, eds., *Tensions of Empire: Colonial Cultures in a Bourgeois World* (Berkeley: University of California Press, 1997); Jean Elisabeth Pedersen, "'Special Customs': paternity suits and citizenship in France and the colonies, 1870–1912," and Alice Conklin, "Redefining 'Frenchness': citizenship, race regeneration, and imperial motherhood in France and West Africa, 1914–1940," in Julia Clancy-Smith and Frances Gouda, eds., *Domesticating the Empire: Race, Gender, and Family Life in French and Dutch Colonialism* (Charlottesville: University of Virginia Press, 1995).

[22] Christopher Hawes, *Poor Relations: The Making of a Eurasian Community in British India, 1773–1833* (London: Curzon Books, 1996), chs. 4, 5, and 7, 8.

who protected the spiritual realm of the family and sustained traditions untouched by colonialism – was a necessary part of an emergent Indian nationalism.[23] Because the majority of colonial companions were neither middle-class nor politically desirable within the imperialist or nationalist project, their role in historical narratives of this period has been erased.

In early colonial India, local women were slaves, concubines, housekeepers, wives, and companions to a range of European officials, merchants, traders, soldiers, and officers. The range of relationships as well as the different positions that local women occupied suggest that there are no easy ways to understand their subjectivity or to categorize their agency. In immediate and intimate ways, indigenous women brought local knowledges, sexual labor, domestic expertise, and linguistic abilities into their relationships with European traders, explorers, and colonial officials. In less obvious ways, they also crossed various boundaries – cultural, ethnic, religious, racial – when they entered into these domestic arrangements. Although they were set on the margins of historical and literary narratives, local women proved to be critical to the colonial enterprise in the contact zone between Britons and the peoples they encountered on the Indian subcontinent.

---

[23] Partha Chatterjee, "The nationalist resolution of the women question," in Kumkum Sangari and Sudesh Vaid, eds., *Recasting Women* (New Brunswick, NJ: Rutgers University Press, 1989).

Bibliography

ARCHIVES AND ABBREVIATIONS USED

IN INDIA

National Archives of India, New Delhi (N.A.I.)
National Library, Rare Books Room, Calcutta
West Bengal State Archives, Calcutta (W.B.S.A.)
Victoria Memorial Records Room, Calcutta
High Court, Original Side, Calcutta (H.C.O.S.)
St. John's Church, Calcutta
Serampore Baptist Collection, Serampore

IN BRITAIN

Oriental and India Office Collections, London, Great Britain (O.I.O.C.)

PRINTED PRIMARY SOURCES

A Complete History of the War in India from 1749 to 1761 between the English and the French ... With an accurate detail of Colonel Clive's military transactions, etc., London, 1761.

Bacon, Thomas, *First Impression and Studies from Nature in Hindostan*, London, Wm. H. Allen, 1837.

Cambridge, R. O., *An Account of the War in India, between the English and French, on the Coast of Coromandel, from the year 1750 to the year 1760*, London, 1761.

Carlyle, T., *Reminiscences*, London, 1823.

Compton, Herbert, *A Particular Account of the European Military Adventurers of Hindustan, from 1784 to 1803*, Karachi: Oxford University Press, 1976 reprint, 1892 original.

Costumes and Customs of Modern India, from a collection of drawings by Charles D'oyley, Esq., Preface and copious descriptions by Captain Thomas Williamson, Calcutta, 1810.

d'Osmond, Adele, Comtesse de Boigne, *Memoirs of the Comtesse de Boigne*, New York: Scribners, 1907.

Dow, Alexander, *The History of Hindostan*, London, 1768.

The European in India, from a collection of drawings by Charles D'oyley, Esq., Preface and copious descriptions by Captain Thomas Williamson, London, 1813.

Fenton, Elizabeth, *A Narrative of her Life in India, the Isle of France and Tasmania during the years 1826–1830*, London: Edward Arnold, 1901.

Ghulam Hussain, trans. by Nota Manus, *Seir-Mutaqherin*, 4 vols., Calcutta, 1783.

Greene, William Sheppey, *A code of the pay regulations of the various military establishments under the Presidency of Fort William to which is added a staff table*, Kidderpore: Military Orphan Press, 1810.

Guyon, Claude Marie, *A New History of the East-Indies, Ancient and Modern*, London, 1757.

Hartly House, Pluto, 1989.

Hodson, Maj. V. C. P., *List of the Officers of the Bengal Army, 1758–1834*, London: Constable & Co., 1927.

Holwell, J. Z., *Interesting Historical Events, Relative to the Province of Bengal the Empire of Indostan*, London, 1761.

Hyder, Qurratulain, translator, *The Nautch Girl or The Dancing Girl*. Translated from Persian into Urdu in 1893 by Sajjad Hussain Kasmandavi; English translation, New Delhi: Sterling Publishers, 1992.

Lushington, Charles, *The History, Design and Present State of the Religious, Benevolent and Charitable Institutions founded by the British in Calcutta and Its Vicinity*, Calcutta, 1824.

Meadows, Taylor, *The Story of My Life*, London, 1878.

Memoirs of William Hickey, Alfred Spencer, ed., London: Hurst & Blackett, Ltd, 1839.

Military Memoirs of Lt. Col. James Skinner, J. Baillie Fraser, ed., London, 1851.

Morley's Digest, 181: Sir Edward Hyde East's Notes.

Muhammad Faiz Baksh, trans. William A. Hoey, *Memoirs of Delhi and Faizabad*, 2 vols., Allahabad, 1888.

Nugent, Lady Maria, *A Journal from the year 1811 till the year 1815: a voyage to and residence in India, with a tour to the northwestern parts of the British possessions in that country under the Bengal government*, London, 1839.

Oriental Field Sports, from a collection of drawings by Charles D'oyley, Esq., Preface and copious descriptions by Captain Thomas Williamson, London, 1807.

Original Letters of Eliza Fay, E. M. Forster, ed., New York: Harcourt Brace, 1925.

Orme, Robert, *A History of the Military Transactions of the British Nation in Indostan*, 2 vols., London, 1763.

Roberdeau, Henry, "A young civilian in Bengal," *Bengal Past and Present*, vol. XXIX, pt. II (April–June 1925).

Roberts, Emma, *Scenes and Characters of Hindostan: with Sketches of Anglo-Indian Society*, London: Wm. H. Allen and Co., 1835.

Sketches of India; or observations descriptive of the Scenery etc. in Bengal, written in the years 1811, 1812, 1813, 1814, London: Black, Parbury and Allen, 1816.

Sleeman, William, *Rambles and Recollections of an Indian Official*, Westminster, 1893.

Steel, Flora Annie, *On the Face of Waters*, London, 1896.

The Baboo and Other Tales Descriptive of Society in India, 2 vols., London: Smith and Elder, 1834.

The East-India Sketch Book, comprising an Account of the Present State of Society in Calcutta, 2 vols., London: Richard Bentley, 1832.
Twelve Views of Calcutta, by W. Baillie, Calcutta, 1794.
Williamson, Thomas, *East India Vade Mecum or complete guide to gentlemen intended for the civil, military, or naval service of the Honourable East India Company*, London: Black, Parry and Kingsbury, 1810.

SECONDARY SOURCES

Adams, Julia, "Principals and agents, colonialists and company men," *American Sociological Review* **61** (1996): 12–28.
Alam, Muzaffar, *The Crisis of Empire in Mughal North India: Awadh and the Punjab, 1707–1748*, Delhi: Oxford University Press, 1986.
Alam, Muzaffar and Seema Alavi, *A European experience of the Mughal Orient: the I'jaz-i Arsalani (Persian letters 1773–1779) of Antoine-Louis Henri Polier*, New Delhi: Oxford University Press, 2001.
Alavi, Seema, *The Sepoys and the Company: Tradition and Transition in Northern India, 1770–1830*, Delhi: Oxford University Press, 1995.
Alexander, Adele Logan, *Ambiguous Lives: Free Women of Color in Rural Georgia*, Fayetteville: University of Arkansas Press, 1991.
Alice L. Conklin, "Redefining 'Frenchness': citizenship, race regeneration, and imperial motherhood in France and West Africa, 1914–40," in Julia Clancy-Smith and Frances Gouda, eds., *Domesticating the Empire: Race, Gender and Family Life in French and Dutch Colonialism*, Charlottesville: University of Virginia Press, 1998, pp. 65–83.
Alloula, Malek, *The Colonial Harem*, Minneapolis: University of Minnesota Press, 1986.
Althusser Louis, "Ideology and ideological state apparatuses," in *Lenin and Philosophy and Other Essays*, trans. Ben Brewster, New York: Monthly Review Press, 1971.
Amussen, Susan Dwyer, " 'Being Stirred to Much Unquietness': violence and domestic violence in early modern England," *Journal of Women's History* 6 (1994): 70–89.
An Ordered Society: Gender and Class in Early Modern England, Oxford: Blackwell, 1988.
Andaya, Barbara Watson, "From Temporary Wife to Prostitute: sexuality and economic change in early modern southeast Asia," *Journal of Women's History* 9 (1994): 11–34.
Anderson, Benedict, *Imagined Communities*, London: Verso, 1983.
Archer, Mildred, "Artists and Patrons in Residency Delhi, 1803–1858," in R. E. Frykenberg, ed., *Delhi Through the Ages*, Delhi: Oxford University Press, 1986.
Early Views of India: the picturesque journeys of Thomas and William Daniell, 1786–1794, New York: Thames and Hudson, 1980.
India Revealed: The Art and Adventures of James and William Fraser, 1801–1835, London: Cassell, 1989.

Indian and British Portraiture, 1770–1825, London: Sotheby Parke Benet, 1979.

Archer, Mildred and Toby Falk, *India Revealed: The Art and Adventures of Janes and William Fraser, 1801–1835,* London: Cassell, 1989.

Arnold, David, "European orphans and vagrants in India in the nineteenth century," *Journal of Imperial and Commonwealth History* 7 (1978): 104–27.

Ballhatchet, Kenneth, *Race, Sex and Class Under the Raj: Imperial Attitudes and Policies, 1793–1905,* New York: St. Martin's Press, 1980.

Banerji, Brajendranath, *Begam Samru,* Calcutta: M. C. Sarkar and Sons, 1925.

Bannerjee, Sumanta, *Under the Raj: Prostitution in Colonial Bengal,* New York: Monthly Review Press, 1998.

Barnett, Richard, *North India Between Two Empires,* Berkeley: University of California Press, 1980.

Baxi, Upendra, " 'The State's Emissary': the place of law in Subaltern Studies," *Subaltern Studies* VII, Delhi: Oxford University Press, 1992, pp. 247–64.

Bayly, C. A., *Rulers, Townsmen and Bazaars: North Indian Society in the Age of British Expansion, 1770–1870,* Cambridge: Cambridge University Press, 1983.

Indian Society and the Making of the British Empire, Cambridge: Cambridge University Press, 1988.

Imperial Meridian: the British Empire and the World, 1780–1830, New York: Longman, 1989.

ed., *The Raj: India and the British* (London: National Portrait Gallery, 1990).

Empire and Information: Intelligence Gathering and Social Communication in India, 1780–1870, Cambridge: Cambridge University Press, 1996.

"The British and Indigenous Peoples, 1760–1860: power, perception and identity," in Martin Daunton, and Rick Halpern, eds., *Europe and Its Others: British Encounters with Indigenous Peoples, 1600–1850,* Philadelphia: University of Pennsylvania Press, 1999, pp. 19–41.

Bayly, Susan, *Saints, Goddesses and Kings: Muslims and Christians in South Indian Society, 1700–1900,* Cambridge: Cambridge University Press, 1989.

Bearce, George, *British Attitudes Toward India, 1784–1858,* London: Oxford University Press, 1963.

Beaumont, Roger, *Sword of the Raj: the British Army in India, 1747–1947,* Indianapolis and New York: Bobbs Merrill, 1977.

Beckles, Hilary, *Centering Woman: Gender Discourses in Caribbean Slave Society,* Kingston, 1999.

Benton, Lauren, "Colonial Law and Cultural Difference: jurisdictional politics and the formation of the colonial state," *Comparative Studies in Society and History* 41 (1999): 563–88.

Law and Colonial Cultures: Legal Regimes in World History, 1400–1900, Cambridge: Cambridge University Press, 2002.

Berger, Mark, "Imperialism and Sexual Exploitation: a response to Ronald Hyam's 'Empire and sexual opportunity'", *Journal of Imperial and Commonwealth History* 17 (1988): 83–9.

Bhabha, Homi, *The Location of Culture,* London: Routledge, 1992.

Bhatia, H. S., *Military History of India, 1607–1947*, New Delhi: Deep & Deep Publications, 1977.

Bhattacharya, Nandini, *Reading the Splendid Body: Gender and Consumerism in Eighteenth-Century British Writing on India*, London: Associated University Presses, 1998.

Blaikie, Andrew, *Illegitimacy, Sex, and Society: Northeast Scotland, 1750–1900*, Oxford: Clarendon Press, 1993.

Blumenthal, Walter Hart, *Women Camp Followers of the American Revolution*.

Blusse, Leonard, *Strange Company: Chinese Settlers, Mestizo Women and the Dutch in VOC Batavia*, Dordrecht, Holland: Foris Publications, 1986.

Borthwick, Meredith, *The Changing Role of Women in Bengal*, Princeton: Princeton University Press, 1984.

Bose, Sugata, *Peasant Labor and Colonial Capital: Rural Bengal Since 1770*, Cambridge: Cambridge University Press, 1993.

Bowen, Huw, "British India, 1765–1813: the metropolitan context," *Oxford History of the British Empire*, vol. II, Oxford: Oxford University Press, 1998.

Revenue and Reform: The Indian Problem in British Politics, 1757–1773, Cambridge: Cambridge University Press, 1991.

Boxer, C. R., *Race Relations in the Portuguese Colonial Empire, 1415–1825*, Oxford: Clarendon, 1963.

Brantlinger, Patrick, *Rule of Darkness: British Literature and Imperialism, 1830–1914*, Ithaca: Cornell University Press, 1988.

Brathwaite, Kamau, *The Development of Creole Society in Jamaica, 1770–1820*, Oxford: Clarendon Press, 1971.

Brown, Jennifer S. H., *Strangers in Blood: Fur Trade Company Families in Indian Country*, Vancouver: University of British Columbia, 1980.

Brown, Kathleen M., "The Anglo-Algonquin gender frontier," in Nancy Shoemaker, ed., *Negotiators of Change: Historical Perspectives on Native American Women*, New York: Routledge, 1995.

Good Wives, Nasty Wenches, and Anxious Patriarchs: Gender, Race and Power in Colonial Virginia, Chapel Hill, NC: University of North Carolina Press, 1996.

Buckland, C. E., *Dictionary of Indian Biography* (London: Swan, Sonnenschein and Co., 1906).

Burnard, Trevor, "Inheritance and Independence: women's status in early colonial Jamaica," *William and Mary Quarterly*, 3rd series, 48 (1991): 93–114.

"Family continuity and female independence in Jamaica, 1665–1734," *Continuity and Change* 7 (1992): 181–98.

Bush, Barbara, *Slave Women in Caribbean Society, 1650–1838*, Bloomington, IN: Indiana University Press, 1990.

Butler, Judith, *Gender Trouble: Feminism and the Subversion of Identity*, New York: Routledge, 1990.

Carr, Lois Green and Lorena Walsh, "The Planter's Wife: the experience of white women in seventeenth-century Maryland," *William and Mary Quarterly*, 3rd series, 34 (1977): 542–71.

Chakrabarti, H., *European Artists and India, 1700–1900*, Calcutta: Victoria Memorial, 1987.

Chakrabarty, Dipesh, "The Difference-Deferral of a Colonial Modernity: public debates on domesticity in British India," *Subaltern Studies VIII*, Delhi: Oxford University Press, 1994, pp. 50–88.

Provincializing Europe, Princeton: Princeton University Press, 2000.

Chakravarti, Uma, "What Happened to the Vedi *Dasi?* Orientalism, nationalism and a script for the past," in Kumkum Sangari and Sudesh Vaid, eds., *Recasting Women: Essays in Indian Colonial History*, Delhi: Kali for women, 1988, pp. 27–87.

Chambers, Sarah, *From Subjects to Citizens: Honor, Gender, and Politics in Arequipa, Peru, 1780–1854*, State Park, PA: Pennsylvania State Press, 1999.

Chander, Sunil, *From a Pre-colonial Order to a Princely State: Hyderabad in Transition, c. 1748–1865*, Ph.D. Dissertation, Cambridge University, 1987.

Chaplin, Joyce, "Race," in David Armitage and Michael Braddick, eds., *The British Atlantic World, 1500–1800*, New York: Palgrave/Macmillan, 2002, pp. 154–72.

Chatterjee, Indrani, "Testing the local against the colonial archive," *History Workshop Journal* 44 (1997): 215–24.

"Colouring Subalternity: slaves, concubines and social orphans in early colonial India," *Subaltern Studies X*, Delhi: Oxford University Press, 1999, pp. 49–97.

Gender, Slavery and Law in Colonial India. Delhi: Oxford University Press, 1999.

Chatterjee, Partha, "The nationalist resolution of the women question," in Kumkum Sangari and Sudesh Vaid, eds., *Recasting Women*, New Brunswick, NJ: Rutgers University Press, 1989, pp. 233–53.

The Nation and Its Fragments, Princeton: Princeton University Press, 1993.

Chattopadhyay, Swati, *Representing Calcutta: Modernity, Nationalism, and the Colonial Uncanny*, London: Routledge, 2005.

Clancy-Smith, Julia and Frances Gouda, eds., *Domesticating the Empire: Race, Gender and Family Life in French and Dutch Colonialism*, Charlottesville: University of Virginia Press, 1998.

eds., *Domesticating the Empire*, Charlottesville: University of Virginia Press, 1998.

Cohn, Bernard S., "Representing authority in Victorian India," in Eric Hobsbawm and Terence Ranger, eds., *The Invention of Tradition*, Cambridge: Cambridge University Press, 1983, pp. 168–74, 165–209.

"The command of language and the language of command," *Subaltern Studies IV*. Delhi: Oxford University Press, 1985, pp. 281–95.

An Anthropologist Among the Historians, Delhi: Oxford University Press, 1987.

Colonialism and Its Forms of Knowledge, Delhi: Oxford University Press, 1996.

Colley, Linda, *Britons: Forging the Nation, 1707–1837*, New Haven: Yale University Press, 1992.

Collingham, Elizabeth M., *Imperial Bodies: the Physical Experience of the Raj, c. 1800–1947*, London: Polity Press, 2001.

Cooper, Frederick and Ann Stoler, eds., *Tensions of Empire: Colonial Cultures in a Bourgeois World*, Berkeley: University of California Press, 1997.

Craton, Michael, "Reluctant Creoles: the planters world in the British West Indies," in Bernard Bailyn and Philip D. Morgan, eds., *Strangers within the Realm: Cultural Margins of the First British Empire*, Chapel Hill: University of North Carolina Press, 1991, pp. 314–52.

Cypess, Sandra Messenger, *La Malinche in Mexican Literature: from History to Myth*, Austin: University of Texas Press, 1992.

Dabydeen David, *Hogarth's Blacks: Images of Blacks in Eighteenth Century English Art*, Athens: University of Georgia Press, 1987.

Dalrymple, William, *White Mughals: Love and Betrayal in Eighteenth-century India*, London: HarperCollins, 2002.

Daniels, Christine, "Intimate violence, now and then," in Daniels and Michael V. Kennedy, eds., *Over the Threshold: Intimate Violence in Early America*, New York: Routledge, 1999, pp. 1–22.

Davies, Philip, *Splendours of the Raj*, London: John Murray, 1985.

Davis, Natalie Zemon, *Fiction in the Archives: Pardon Tales and Their Tellers in Sixteenth Century France*, Stanford: Stanford University Press, 1987.

Dayton, Cornelia, *Women Before the Bar: Gender, Law and Society in Connecticut, 1639–1789*, Chapel Hill, NC: University of North Carolina Press, 1995.

Derrett, J. D. M., *Religion, Law and State in India*, London: Faber and Faber, 1968.

Dirks, Nicholas, *Castes of Mind: Colonialism and the Making of Modern India*, Princeton: Princeton University Press, 2001.

Dubow, Saul, *Scientific Racism in Modern South Africa*, Cambridge: Cambridge University Press, 1995.

Dyson, K. K., *A Various Universe*, Delhi: Oxford University Press, 1978, second edition 2002.

Eaton, Richard M., *The Rise of Islam and the Bengal Frontier, 1204–1760*, Berkeley: University of California Press, 1993.

Edwardes, Michael, *The Nabobs at Home*, London: Constable, 1991.

Edwards-Stuart, Ivor, *The Calcutta of Begum Johnson*, London: BACSA, 1990.

Ellis, Markman, *The Politics of Sensibility: Race, Gender and Commerce in the Sentimental Novel*, Cambridge: Cambridge University Press, 1996.

Erickson, Amy Louise, *Women and Property in Early Modern England*, London: Routledge, 1993.

Fisch, J., *Cheap Lives and Dear Limbs: The British Transformation of the Bengal Criminal Law, 1769–1817*, Wiesbaden: Steiner, 1983.

Fisher, Michael, *A Clash of Cultures: Awadh, the British and the Mughals*, Delhi: Manohar, 1987.
Indirect Rule in India: Residents and the Residency System, 1764–1858, Delhi: Oxford University Press, 1991.

Flint, Michael, "The Family Piece: Oliver Goldsmith and the politics of everyday in eighteenth-century domestic portraiture," *Eighteenth-Century Studies* 29 (1995–1996): 127–52.

Forbes, Geraldine, *Women in Modern India*, Cambridge: Cambridge University Press, 1996.

Foucault, Michel, *Discipline and Punish: The Birth of the Prison*, London: Penguin, 1977.
The History of Sexuality, 2 vols., New York: Pantheon, 1978.

Essential Works of Foucault, 1954–1984, vol. 3, edited by James D. Faubion, New York: The New Press, 2000.

Ferguson, Niall, *Empire*, New York: Basic Books, 2003.

Franco, Jean, *Plotting Women: Gender and Representation in Mexico*, New York: Columbia University Press, 1989.

Gagnier, Regenia, *Subjectivities: A History of Self-Representation in Britain, 1832–1920*, Oxford University Press, 1991.

Garber, Marjorie, *Vested Interests: Cross-dressing and Cultural Anxiety*, New York: Routledge, 1992.

George, Rosemary Marangoly, *The Politics of Home: Postcolonial Relocations and Twentieth-century Fiction*, Cambridge: Cambridge University Press, 1996.

Ghosh, Durba, "Decoding the Nameless: gender, subjectivity, and historical methodologies in reading the archives of colonial India," in Kathleen Wilson, ed., *A New Imerial History: Culture, Identity, Modernity, 1660–1840*, Cambridge: Cambridge University Press, 2004, pp. 297–316.

Gillis, John, "Servants, sexual relations, and the risks of illegitimacy in London, 1801–1900," *Feminist Studies* 5 (1979): 142–73.

For Better, For Worse: British Marriages, 1600 to the Present, New York: Oxford University Press, 1985.

Gilman, Sander, "Black Bodies, White Bodies: toward an iconography of female sexuality in late nineteenth-century art, medicine and literature," in Henry Louis Gates, Jr., ed., *"Race," Writing and Difference*, Chicago: University of Chicago Press, 1985.

Godbeer, Richard, "Eroticizing the Middle Ground: Anglo-Indian sexual relations along the eighteenth-century frontier," in Martha Hodes, ed., *Sex, Love, Race: Crossing Boundaries in North American History*, New York: New York University Press, 1999, pp. 91–111.

Goldschmidt, Janice Bailey and Martin Kalfatovic, "Sex, Lies and European Hegemony: travel literature and ideology," *Journal of Popular Culture* 26 (1993): 141–53.

Gordon, Stewart, *The Marathas, 1600–1818*, Cambridge: Cambridge University Press, 1993.

Gouda, Frances, *Dutch Culture Overseas: Colonial Practices in the Netherlands Indies*. Amsterdam: Amsterdam Book Depot, 1995.

Greenblatt, Stephen, *Renaissance Self-Fashioning: From More to Shakespeare*, Chicago: University of Chicago Press, 1980.

ed., *New World Encounters*, Berkeley: University of California Press, 1993.

Grewal, Inderpal, *Home and Harem*, Durham, NC: Duke University Press, 1996.

Guha, Ranajit, "Chandra's death," *Subaltern Studies* V, Delhi: Oxford University Press, 1987, pp. 135–65.

Gutierrez, Ramon A., *When Jesus Came, the Corn Mothers Went Away: Marriage, Sexuality, and Power in New Mexico, 1500–1846*, Berkeley: University of California Press, 1991.

Hacker, Barton C., "Women and military institutions in early modern Europe," *Signs* 6, 4 (1981): 643–71.

Hall, Catherine, *White, Male and Middle-class: Explorations in Feminism and History*, New York: Routledge, 1992.

Hall, Catherine and Leonore Davidoff, *Family Fortunes: Men and Women of the English Middle Class, 1780–1850*, London: Hutchinson, 1987.

Hall, Kim F., *Things of Darkness: Economies of Race and Gender in Early Modern England*, Ithaca: Cornell University Press, 1995.

Hartley, Shirley, "Illegitimacy in Jamaica," in Peter Laslett, Karla Oosterveen and Richard M. Smith, eds., *Bastardy and Its Comparative History*, Cambridge: Harvard University Press, 1980.

Hawes, C. J., *Poor Relations: the Making of a Eurasian Community in British India, 1773–1833*, London: Curzon, 1996.

Hulme, Peter, *Colonial Encounters: Europe and the Native Caribbean, 1492–1797*, London: Routledge, 1986.

Hunt, Margaret, "Wife beating, domesticity, and women's independence in eighteenth-century London," *Gender & History* 4 (1992): 10–33.

  The Middling Sort: Commerce, Gender, and the Family in England, 1680–1780, Berkeley: University of California Press, 1996.

Hussain, Nasser, *The Jurisprudence of Emergency: Sovereignty and the Rule of Law in British India*, Ann Arbor: University of Michigan, 2003.

Hyam, Ronald, *Empire and Sexuality: The British Experience*, Manchester: Manchester University Press, 1991.

Irschick, Eugene, *Dialogue and History*, Berkeley: University of California Press, 1994.

Jain, M. P., *Outlines of Indian Legal History*, Fifth edition, Bombay: N. M. Tripathi, Ltd., 1990.

Jasanoff, Maya, "Collectors of Empire: objects, conquests and imperial self-fashioning," *Past and Present* 184 (2004): 109–35.

Joseph, Betty, *Reading the East India Company, 1720–1840: Colonial Currencies of Gender*, Chicago: University of Chicago, 2004.

Juneja, Renu, "The Native and the Nabob: representations of the Indian experience in eighteenth-century English literature," *Journal of Commonwealth Literature* 27 (1992): 183–98.

Kabbani, Rana, *Europe's Myths of the Orient*, Bloomington: Indiana University Press, 1986.

Kale, Madhavi, *Fragments of Empire: Capital, Slavery and Indentured Labor Migration in the British Caribbean*, Philadelphia: University of Pennsylvania Press, 1998.

Karlekar, Malavika, *Voices from Within*. Delhi: Oxford University Press, 1991.

Kincaid, Dennis, *British Social Life in India, 1608–1937*, London: Routledge and Kegan Paul, 1938.

Kirk, Sylvia, *Many Tender Ties: Women in Fur Trade Society, 1670–1870*, Norman: University of Oklahoma Press, 1980.

Kondo, Dorinne, *Crafting Selves: Power, Gender and Discourses of Identity in a Japanese Workplace*, Chicago: University of Chicago Press, 1990.

Krishnamurty, J., ed., *Women in Colonial India: Essays on Survival, Work and the State*, Delhi: Oxford University Press, 1989.

Kuznesof, Elizabeth, "Sexual politics, race and bastard-bearing in nineteenth-century Brazil," *Journal of Family History* 16 (1991): 241–60.

Lall, John, *Begum Samru: Fading Portrait in a Gilded Frame*, New Delhi: Roli Books, 1997.

Langford, Paul, *A Polite and Commercial People: England, 1727–1783*, Oxford: Oxford University Press, 1989.

Laslett, Peter, "The bastardy prone sub-society," in Peter Laslett, Karla Oosterveen and Richard M. Smith, eds., *Bastardy and Its Comparative History*, Cambridge: Harvard University Press, 1980.

Lawson, Philip and Jim Philips, "'Our Execrable Banditti': perceptions of nabobs in mid eighteenth-century Britain," Albion XVI (1984): 225–41.

Lemay, J. A. Leo, *Did Pocahontas Save Captain John Smith?*, Athens, GA: University of Georgia Press, 1992.

Lemmings, David, "Marriage and the Law in the Eighteenth Century: Hardwicke's Marriage Act of 1753," *Historical Journal* 39 (1996): 339–60.

Leonard, Karen, "Banking firms in nineteenth-century Hyderabad politics," *Modern Asian Studies* 15 (1981): 177–201.

Leppert, Richard, "Music, Domestic Life and Cultural Chauvinism: images of British subjects at home in India," in Leppert and Susan McClary, eds., *Music and Society: The Politics of Composition, Performance and Reception*, Cambridge: Cambridge University Press, 1987.

Levine, Philippa, "Venereal Disease, Prostitution and the Politics of Empire: the case of British India," *Journal of the History of Sexuality* 4 (1994): 579–602.

"Rereading the 1890s: venereal disease as 'constitutional crisis' in Britain and British India," *Journal of Asian Studies* 55 (1996): 585–612.

Lewis, Jan E. and Peter Onuf, eds., *Sally Hemings and Thomas Jefferson: History, Memory and Civic Culture*, Charlottesville, VA: University of Virginia Press, 1999.

Lin, Patricia Y. C. E., *Extending Her Arms: Military Families and the Transformation of the British State, 1793–1815*, Unpublished Ph.D. dissertation, University of California-Berkeley, 1997.

Llewellyn-Jones, Rosie, *A Very Ingenious Man: Claude Martin in Early Colonial India*, Delhi: Oxford University Press, 1992.

Losty, J. P., *Calcutta: City of Palaces, a Survey of the City in the Days of the East India Company, 1690–1858*, London: British Library, 1990.

Lowe, Lisa, *Critical Terrains*, Ithaca: Cornell University Press, 1991.

Ludden, David, "Orientalist Empiricism: transformations of colonial knowledge," in Carol A. Breckenridge and Peter van der Veer, eds., *Orientalism and the Post-colonial Predicament*, Philadelphia: University of Pennsylvania Press, 1993.

Majeed, Javed, *Ungoverned Imaginings: James Mill's* The History of India *and Orientalism*, Oxford: Clarendon Press, 1992.

Mani, Lata, "Contentious Traditions: debates about sati in colonial India," in *Recasting Women: Essays in Colonial Indian History*, New Brunswick, NJ: Rutgers University Press, 1989, pp. 88–126.

Contentious Traditions: the Debate on Sati in Colonial India, Berkeley: University of California Press, 1998.

Marshall, P. J., *The Impeachment of Warren Hastings*, Oxford: Clarendon Press, 1965.

The Launching of the Hastings Impeachment 1786–1788: The Writings and Speeches of Edmund Burke, Oxford: Oxford University Press, 1991.

"British Society in India under the East India Company," *Modern Asian Studies* 31 (February 1997): 89–108.

Bengal: The British Bridgehead, Eastern India 1740–1828, Cambridge: Cambridge University Press, 1987.

Martinez-Alier, Verena, *Marriage, Class and Colour in Nineteenth-century Cuba*, Cambridge: Cambridge University Press, 1974.

McCaa, Robert, "*Calidad, Clase* and Marriage in Colonial Mexico: the case of Parral, 1788–1790," *Hispanic American Historical Review* 64 (1984): 477–501.

McClintock, Anne, *Imperial Leather: Race, Gender and Sexuality in the Colonial Contest*, New York: Routledge, 1995.

McKendrick, Neil, John Brewer, and J. H. Plumb, *The Birth of a Consumer Society*, Bloomington: Indiana University Press, 1982.

Melman, Billie, *Women's Orients: English Women and the Middle East, 1718–1918*, Ann Arbor: University of Michigan Press, 1992.

Menezes, S. L., *Fidelity & Honour: the Indian Army from the Seventeenth to the Twenty-first Century*, New Delhi: Viking Penguin, 1993.

Menon, Ritu and Kamla Bhasin, *Borders and Boundaries*, New Delhi: Kali for Women, 1999.

Merry, Sally Engle, "Legal pluralisms," *Law & Society Review* 22 (1988): 869–96.

"Law and colonialism," *Law & Society Review* 25 (1991): 889–922.

Metcalf, Thomas R., *Ideologies of the Raj*, Cambridge: Cambridge University Press, 1994.

Meteyard, Belinda, "Illegitimacy and marriage in eighteenth-century England," *Journal of Interdisciplinary History* 10 (1980): 479–89.

Misra, B. B., *The Judicial Administration of the East India Company, 1765–1781*, Patna, 1953.

Mohanty, Chandra Talpade, *Feminism without Borders: Decolonizing Theory, Practicing Solidarity*, Durham, NC: Duke University Press, 2003.

Mohapatra, Prabhu, " 'Restoring the Family': wife murders and the making of a sexual contract in Indian Caribbean colonies," *Studies in History* 11, 2 (1995): 227–60.

Morgan, Philip, *Slave Counterpoint: Black Culture in the Eighteenth-century Chesapeake and Low Country*, Chapel Hill: University of North Carolina Press, 1998.

Mullan, John, *Sentiment and Sociability*, New York: Oxford, 1988.

Nair, Janaki, "On the question of agency in Indian feminist historiography," *Gender & History* 6 (1994): 82–100.

Nash, Gary B., "The hidden history of Mestizo America," *Journal of American History* 82 (1995): 941–64.

Nazzari, Muriel, "Concubinage in Colonial Brazil: the inequalities of race, class, and gender," *Journal of Family History* 21 (1996): 107–24.

Nevile, Pran, "Early European portrayal of Indian women," *India Perspectives* (September 1998): 41–4.

Nussbaum, Felicity, *Torrid Zones: Maternity, Sexuality and Empire in Eighteenth-Century English Narratives*, Baltimore: Johns Hopkins Press, 1995.

Oddy, Derek J., "Gone for a Soldier: the anatomy of a nineteenth-century army family," *Journal of Family History* 25 (January 2000): 39–62.

O'Hanlon, R., "Recovering the Subject: *Subaltern Studies* and histories of resistance in colonial south Asia," *Modern Asian Studies* 22 (1988): 189–224.

Okin, Susan Moller, "Patriarchy and Married Women's Property in England: questions on some current views," *Eighteenth-century Studies* 17 (1983–1984): 121–38.

Ong, Aihwa, "Cultural Citizenship as Subject-Making: immigrants negotiate racial and cultural boundaries in the United States," *Current Anthropology* 37 (1996): 737–62.

  Flexible Citizenship: the cultural logics of transnationality, Durham, NC: Duke University Press, 1999.

Pagden, Anthony, *Lords of All the World: Ideologies of Empire in Spain, Britain and France, c. 1500–c. 1800*. New Haven: Yale University Press, 1995.

Pal, Pratapaditya and Vidya Dehejia, *From Merchants to Emperors: British Artists and India, 1757–1930*, Ithaca: Cornell University Press, 1986.

Pateman, Carole, *The Sexual Contract*, Stanford: Stanford University Press, 1988.

Paxton, Nancy, "Mobilizing Chivalry: rape in British novels about the Indian uprising of 1857," *Victorian Studies* 36 (Fall 1992): 5–30.

  Writing under the Raj: Gender, Race and Rape in the British Colonial Imagination, 1830–1947, New Brunswick, NJ: Rutgers University Press, 1999.

Pearsall, Sarah, "Gender," in David Armitage and Michael Braddick, eds., *The British Atlantic World, 1500–1800*, New York: Palgrave/Macmillan, 2002, pp. 113–32.

Pedersen, Jean Elisabeth, "'Special Customs': paternity suits and citizenship in France and the colonies, 1870–1912," in Julia Clancy-Smith and Frances Gouda, eds., *Domesticating the Empire: Race, Gender and Family Life in French and Dutch Colonialism*, Charlottesville: University of Virginia Press, 1998, pp. 43–64.

Peers, Douglas, *Between Mars and Mammon: Colonial Armies and the Garrison State in India, 1819–1835*, London: Aldershot, 1995.

Peirce, Leslie, *The Imperial Harem*, New York: Oxford University Press, 1993.

Phillips, Roderick, *Putting Asunder: a History of Divorce in Western Society*, Cambridge: Cambridge University Press, 1988.

Plane, Ann Marie, *Colonial Intimacies: Indian Marriage in Early New England*, Ithaca: Cornell University Press, 2000.

Pleck, Elizabeth, "Wife beating in nineteenth-century America," *Victimology* 4 (1979): 60–74.

Pointon, Marcia, *Hanging of the Head: Portraiture and Social Formation in Eighteenth-century England*, New Haven: Yale University Press, 1994.

Prakash, Om, *European Commercial Enterprise in Pre-colonial India*, Cambridge: Cambridge University Press, 1998.

Pratt, Mary Louise, *Imperial Eyes: Travel Writing and Transculturation*, London: Routledge, 1992.

  "'Yo soy la Malinche': Chicana writers and the poetics of ethnonationalism," *Callaloo* 16 (Fall 1993): 859–74.

Ray, Bharati, ed., *From the Seams of History: Essays on Indian Women*. Delhi: Oxford University Press, 1995.

Ray, N. R., *The City of Job Charnock*, Calcutta: Victoria Memorial Library, 1979.

Regani, Sarojini, *Nizam-British Relations, 1724–1857*, Hyderabad, 1963.

Rice, James D., "Laying Claim to Elizabeth Shoemaker: family violence on Baltimore's waterfront, 1808–1812," in Christine Daniels and Michael V. Kennedy, *Over the Threshold*, pp. 192–3.

Rich, Paul, *Race and Empire in British Politics*, Cambridge: Cambridge University Press, 1986.

Richards, John, "Norms of comportment among imperial Mughal officers" in Barbara D. Metcalf, ed., *Moral Conduct and Authority: the Place of Adab in South Asian Islam*, Berkeley: University of California Press, 1984, pp. 255–89.

Robb, Peter, *The Concept of Race in South Asia*, Oxford: Oxford University Press, 1992.

"Clash of Cultures?: An Englishman in Calcutta in the 1790s," School of Oriental and African Studies, University of London, Inaugural Lecture, March 12, 1998.

Rocher, Rosanne, "British Orientalism in the Eighteenth Century: the dialectics of knowledge and government," in Carol A. Breckinridge and Peter van der Veer, eds., *Orientalism and the Postcolonial Predicament*, Philadelphia: University of Pennsylvania Press, 1993

Rubin, Gayle, "The Traffic in Women: notes on the political economy of sex," in Rayna R. Reiter, ed., *Towards an Anthropology of Women*, New York: Monthly Review Press, 1975.

Rudolph, Lloyd and Susanne Hoeber, *The Modernity of Tradition*, Chicago: University of Chicago Press, 1967.

Sainsbury, Alison, "Married to the Empire: the Anglo-Indian domestic novel," in Bart Moore-Gilbert, ed., *Writing India, 1757–1990: the Literature of British India*, Manchester: Manchester University Press, 1996.

Scott, James C., John Tehranian and Jeremy Mathias, "The Production of Legal Identities Proper to States: the case of the permanent family surname," *Comparative Studies in Society and History* 44 (2002): 4–44.

Scott, Joan W., "The evidence of 'Experience,'" *Critical Inquiry* 17 (1991): 773–97.

Scully, Pamela, "Race and ethnicity in women's and gender history in global perspective," in Bonnie Smith, ed., *Women's History in Global Perspective*, vol. 1, Urbana, IL: University of Illinois Press, 2004.

Seed, Patricia, *To Love, Honor and Obey in Colonial Mexico: Conflicts over Marriage Choice, 1574–1821*, Stanford: Stanford University Press, 1988.

Sen, Samita, "Offences against Marriage: negotiating custom in colonial Bengal," in Janaki Nair and Mary E. John, eds., *A Question of Silence: the Sexual Economies of Modern India*, New Delhi: Kali for women, 1998.

Women and Labour in Late Colonial India: the Bengal Jute Industry, Cambridge: Cambridge University Press, 1999.

Sen, Sudipta, *Distant Sovereignty: National Imperialism and the Origins of British India*, New York: Routledge, 2002.

Sharma, M. N., *The Life and Times of Begam Samru of Sardhana*, Sahibabad, 1985.

Sharpe, Jenny, *Allegories of Empire*, Minneapolis: University of Minneapolis Press, 1993.

Ghosts of Slavery: a Literary Archeology of Black Women's Lives, Minneapolis: University of Minnesota Press, 2003.

Shorter, Edward, *The Making of the Modern Family*, New York: 1975.

Singh, Jyotsna, *Colonial Narratives/Cultural Dialogues: Discoveries of India in the Language of Colonialism*, London: Routledge, 1996.

Singh, S. B., *European Agency Houses in Bengal (1783–1833)*, Calcutta: Firma K. L. Mukhopadhyay, 1966.

Singha, Radhika, "Making the domestic more domestic: criminal law and the 'head of the household,' 1772–1843," *Indian Economic and Social History Review* 33 (July–Sept. 1996): 309–44.

A Despotism of Law: Crime and Justice in Early Colonial India, Delhi: Oxford University Press, 1998.

Sinha, Pradip, *Calcutta in Urban History*, Calcutta: Firma, 1978.

Smith, Raymond, "Hierarchy and the dual marriage system in West Indian society," in Jane F. Collier and Sylvia Yanagisako, eds., *Gender and Kinship: Essays Toward a Unified Analysis*, Stanford: Stanford University Press, 1987, pp. 163–96.

Solkin, David, *Painting For Money*, New Haven: Yale University Press, 1993.

Sollors, Werner, *Neither Black nor White Yet Both: Thematic Explorations of Interracial Literature*, New York: Oxford University Press, 1997.

Sommer, Doris, *Foundational Fictions: the National Romances of Latin America*, Berkeley: University of California Press, 1991.

Spear, T. C. P., *The Nabobs: English Social Life in 18th Century India*, New York: Penguin, 1963.

Spivak, Gayatri C., "The Rani of Sirmur: an essay in reading the archives," *History and Theory* 24 (1985): 247–72.

"Can the subaltern speak?" in Cary Nelson and Lawrence Grossberg, eds., *Marxism and the Interpretation of Culture*, Urbana: University of Illinois Press, 1988.

"Deconstructing historiography," in Ranajit Guha and Gayatri Chakravorty Spivak, eds., *Selected Subaltern Studies*, Delhi: Oxford University Press, 1988.

A Critique of Postcolonial Reason: Toward a History of the Vanishing Present, Cambridge: Harvard University Press, 1999.

Staves, Susan, *Married Women's Separate Property in England, 1660–1833*, Cambridge: Harvard University Press, 1990.

Steedman, Carolyn, *Dust: The Archive and Cultural History*, New Brunswick, NJ: Rutgers University Press, 2002.

Stepan, Nancy, *The Idea of Race in Science: Great Britain, 1800–1960*, Hamden, CT: Archon Books, 1982.

Stephens, Julie, "Feminist Fictions: a critique of the category 'non-Western woman' in feminist writings on India." *Subaltern Studies VI*, Delhi: Oxford University Press, 1989, pp. 92–125.

Stocking, George, *Colonial Situations: Essays on the Contextualization of Ethnographic Knowledge*, Madison: University of Wisconsin Press, 1991.

Stoler, Ann, "Making Empire Respectable: the politics of race and sexual morality in 20th-century colonial cultures," *American Ethnologist* 16 (1989): 634–60.

Race and the Education of Desire, Durham: Duke University Press, 1995.

"A Sentimental Education: native servants and the cultivation of European children in the Netherlands Indies," in Laurie J. Sears, ed., *Fantasizing the Feminine in Indonesia*, Durham, NC: Duke University Press, 1996.

"Sexual Affronts and Racial Frontiers: European identities and the cultural politics of exclusion in colonial southeast Asia," in Ann Stoler and Frederick Cooper, eds., *Tensions of Empire: Colonial Cultures in a Bourgeois World*, Berkeley: University of California Press, 1997.

"Colonial Archives and the Arts of Governance: on the content in the form," in Carolyn Hamilton, *et al.*, eds., *Refiguring the Archive*, Cape Town: David Philip, 2002.

Carnal Knowledge and Imperial Power: Race and the Intimate in Colonial Rule, Berkeley: University of California Press, 2002.

Stone, Lawrence, *The Family, Sex and Marriage in England, 1500–1800*, London: Harper and Row, 1977.

Broken Lives: Separation and Divorce in England, 1660–1857, New York: Oxford University Press, 1993.

Suleri, Sara, *The Rhetoric of English India*, Chicago: University of Chicago Press, 1992.

Tadmor, Naomi, "The Concept of the household-family in eighteenth-century England," *Past & Present* 151 (May 1996): 111–30.

Taylor, Jean Gelman, *The Social World of Batavia: European and Eurasian in Dutch Asia*, Madison, WI: University of Wisconsin Press, 1983.

Teltscher, Kate, *India Inscribed: European and British Writing on India, 1600–1800*. Delhi: Oxford University Press, 1995.

Thomas, Ardel Marie, *Victorian Monstrosities: Sexuality, Race and the Construction of the Imperial Self, 1811–1924*, Ph.D. dissertation, Stanford University, 1998.

Thompson, Elizabeth, *Colonial Citizens: Republican Rights, Paternal Privilege and Gender in French Syria and Lebanon*, New York: Columbia University Press, 2000.

Tilton, Robert S., *Pocahontas: The Evolution of an American Narrative*, Cambridge: Cambridge University Press, 1994.

Tirmizi, S. A. I., *Edicts from the Mughal Harem*, Delhi, 1979.

Tobin, Beth Fowkes, *Picturing Imperial Power: Colonial Subjects in Eighteenth-century British Painting*, Durham: Duke University Press, 1999.

Trautmann, Thomas, *Aryans and British India*, Berkeley: University of California Press, 1997.

Trumbach, Randolph, *The Rise of the Egalitarian Family*, New York: Academic Press, 1978.

Trustram, Myna, *Women of the Regiment: Marriage and the Victorian Army*, Cambridge: Cambridge University Press, 1984.

Twinam, Ann, *Public Lives, Private Secrets: Gender, Honor, Sexuality, and Illegitimacy in Colonial Spanish America*, Stanford: Stanford University Press, 1999.

Viswanathan, Gauri, *Masks of Conquest: Literary Study and British Rule in India*, New York: Columbia University Press, 1989.

Outside the Fold, Conversion, Modernity, and Belief, Princeton: Princeton University Press, 1998.

Visweswaran, Kamala, "Betrayal: an analysis in three acts," in Inderpal Grewal and Caren Kaplan, eds., *Scattered Hegemonies: Postmodernity and Transnational Feminist Practices*, Minnesota: University of Minnesota Press, 1994, pp. 90–109.

"Small Speeches, Subaltern Gender: nationalist ideology and its historiography," *Subaltern Studies* IX, Delhi: Oxford University Press, 1996, pp. 83–125.

Wagoner, Philip, "Sultans Among Hindu Kings: dress, titles and the Islamicization of Hindu culture at Vijayanagara," *Journal of Asian Studies* 55 (1996): 851–80.

Walkowitz, Judith, *Prostitution in Victorian Society*, Cambridge: Cambridge University Press, 1980.

Washbrook, David, "Law, state and agrarian society in colonial India," *Modern Asian Studies* 15 (1981): 649–721.

We Were Making History!, New Delhi: Kali for Women, 1988.

Wheeler, Roxann, "The Complexion of Desire: racial ideology and mid-eighteenth-century British novels," *Eighteenth Century Studies* 32 (1999): 309–32.

The Complexion of Race: Categories of Difference in Eighteenth-century British Culture, Philadelphia: University of Pennsylvania Press, 2000.

White, Luise, *The Comforts of Home: Prostitution in Colonial Nairobi*, Chicago: University of Chicago Press, 1990.

White, Richard, *The Middle Ground: Indians, Empires, and Republics in the Great Lakes Region, 1650–1815*, Cambridge: Cambridge University Press, 1991.

Wildenthal, Lora, "Race, gender and citizenship in the German colonial empire," in Ann Stoler and Frederick Cooper, eds., *Tensions of Empire: Colonial Cultures in a Bourgeois World*, Berkeley: University of California Press, 1997.

"Race, gender and citizenship in the German empire," in Frederick Cooper and Ann L. Stoler, eds., *Tensions of Empire: Colonial Cultures in a Bourgeois World*, Berkeley: University of California Press, 1997, pp. 263–83.

Wilson, Kathleen, *The Island Race: Englishness, Empire and Gender in the Eighteenth Century*, New York: Routledge, 2003.

Wink, Andre, *Land and Sovereignty in India: Agrarian Society and Politics Under the Eighteenth-century Maratha Svarajya*, Cambridge: Cambridge University Press, 1986.

Wood, Peter, *A Vassal State in the Shadow of Empire: William Palmer's Bank in Hyderabad, 1810–1824*, Ph.D. Dissertation, University of Wisconsin, 1981.

Yalland, Zoe, *Traders and Nabobs: the British in Cawnpore, 1765–1857*, Wilton: M. Russell, 1987.

Yang, Anand, *The Limited Raj: Agrarian Relations in Colonial India, Saran District, 1793–1920*, Berkeley: University of California Press, 1989.

Young, Desmond, *Fountain of the Elephants*, New York: Harper & Brothers, 1959.

Young, Robert, *Colonial Desires: Hybridity in Theory, Culture and Race*, London: Routledge, 1995.

Index

Printed in the United States
98816LV00002B/14/A

9 780521 673792